THE CURIOUS TRAJECTORY OF CASTE IN WEST BENGAL POLITICS

Studies in Critical Social Sciences Book Series

Haymarket Books is proud to be working with Brill Academic Publishers (www.brill.nl) to republish the *Studies in Critical Social Sciences* book series in paperback editions. This peer-reviewed book series offers insights into our current reality by exploring the content and consequences of power relationships under capitalism, and by considering the spaces of opposition and resistance to these changes that have been defining our new age. Our full catalog of *SCSS* volumes can be viewed at https://www.haymarketbooks .org/series_collections/4-studies-in-critical-social-sciences.

THE CURIOUS TRAJECTORY OF CASTE IN WEST BENGAL POLITICS

Chronicling Continuity and Change

AYAN GUHA

Haymarket Books
Chicago, IL

Published in paperback in 2023 by
Haymarket Books
P.O. Box 180165
Chicago, IL 60618
773-583-7884
www.haymarketbooks.org

ISBN: 979-8-88890-012-3

Distributed to the trade in the US through Consortium Book Sales and
Distribution (www.cbsd.com) and internationally through Ingram Publisher
Services International (www.ingramcontent.com).

This book was published with the generous support of Lannan Foundation,
Wallace Action Fund, and the Marguerite Casey Foundation.

Special discounts are available for bulk purchases by organizations and
institutions. Please call 773-583-7884 or email info@haymarketbooks.org for more
information.

Cover design by Jamie Kerry and Ragina Johnson.

Printed in the United States.

Library of Congress Cataloging-in-Publication data is available.

Contents

Acknowledgements

Writing this book was an immensely enriching and intellectually stimulating endeavour for me and several individuals were responsible for making this endeavour so satisfying. So, in the course of writing this book I have accumulated considerable academic and personal debts. The theme of the book relates to the topic of my doctoral thesis submitted to the Centre for the Study of Social Exclusion and Inclusive Policy, Jamia Millia Islamia, New Delhi. In terms of content the resemblance between my doctoral thesis and this book is not very substantial. Only a few portions of three chapters of the book (Chapters 4, 6 and 7) bear some amount resemblance with my doctoral thesis primarily due to the evolving nature of the topic and rapidly fluctuating socio-political scenario of West Bengal in recent times. Thus, this book is largely based upon my post-PhD research. But throughout my research on this topic, I have greatly benefitted from the guidance, encouragement and inputs I have received from my doctoral supervisor Arvind Kumar, (Jamia Millia Islamia, India)

I am particularly thankful to David Fasenfest (Wayne State University, US) whose valuable feedback and advice have played an instrumental role in organising my scattered research output into the form of a book. I am also grateful to several scholars who despite their multiple engagements obliged me by going through different chapters of the manuscript. Debi Chatterjee (Jadavpur University, India) Dwaipayan Bhattacharyya (Jawaharlal Nehru University, India), Hugo Gorringe (University of Edinburgh, UK), Jagpal Singh (Indira Gandhi National Open University, India), Padmanabh Samarendra (Jamia Millia Islamia, India), Ross Mallick (Author, Canada), Sanober Umar (York University, Canada), Sekhar Bandyopadhyay (Victoria University of Wellington, New Zealand), Shibashis Chatterjee (Shiv Nadar University, India) and Timothy David Amos (National University of Singapore, Singapore) were generous enough to provide me with their valuable comments on the manuscript as it took shape. Their comments and suggestions have proved immensely helpful in plugging many of the loopholes of the initial drafts. My long discussion with Hugo Gorringe over email on theoretical aspects of identity politics and a number readings suggested by him have helped me in conceptualizing some of the theoretical dimensions of caste politics explored in the book. I am immensely indebted to all those people who provided me access into their lives during my field research. I sincerely appreciate the valuable assistance I have received from two young and dynamic research scholars, Mithun Majumder (Jadavpur University) and Satnik Pal (National University of Singapore) in connection with field study and access to ground level contacts.

On the personal front, I must acknowledge the immense contribution of my parents, who have always supported me and also ensured that my taste buds remain sufficiently satisfied . The priceless companionship of Neha and her unmatched capacity to lift my spirts during periods of gloom were instrumental in keeping me in a right frame of mind, that made writing this book possible. Last but not the least, I take this opportunity to fondly remember my late grandfather, Nikhil Krishna Guha who had introduced me to the fascinating world of reading and writing and made all efforts to equip me with a spirit of critical reasoning and inquisitiveness.

I sign off my saying that despite the assistance I have received from a host of individuals, I alone stand responsible for any inadvertent error that might have crept into this book.

Tables

CHAPTER 1

Introduction

Setting the Agenda of Analysis

The idea behind this book is a product of a specific political context. The political transition in West Bengal in 2011 from the Left Front to the Trinamool Congress (TMC) after thirty-four long years of Communist rule was in many ways a momentous and possibly a watershed event. The electoral decline of the Left has inspired renewed debates in recent scholarship about many of the taken-for-granted assumptions about the nature of state-society interface in West Bengal. One major debate relates to the role of caste in West Bengal politics. There has been a growing interest in the politics of caste in West Bengal in recent years and this interest has grown proportionally with the steady electoral decline of the Left Front since 2009.

Caste has always been a theme of obsessive preoccupation in the scholarship on Indian politics and society. As Nicholas Dirks points out in the opening lines of his seminal work *Castes of Mind* "when thinking of India, it is hard not to think of caste. In comparative sociology and in common parlance alike, caste has become a central symbol for India, indexing it as fundamentally different from other places as well as expressing its essence".[1] The over-emphasis on caste dynamics has often produced reductionist and essentialized portrayal of socio-political reality of India. However, the analytical preoccupation with caste is not without some basis, given the ubiquitousness of caste dynamics in Indian social life and their quotidian tendency to spill over to other spheres of life including politics. Even after seventy years of independence and a significant dose of modernization, the political landscape of India continues to be dominated by caste. In large parts of India caste figures prominently as an immensely influential political factor in electoral calculus. This holds true for both southern parts of India, which have experienced remarkable anti-Brahman movement and northern parts of India, most notably, states like Uttar Pradesh and Bihar, which have witnessed significant political mobilization of the *dalits* (ex-untouchable communities)[2] and backward castes.

---

1   Nicholas B. Dirks, *Castes of Mind: Colonialism and the Making of Modern India* (Princeton, N.J.: Princeton University Press, 2001), 3.

2   The term '*dalit*' was popularized by the Dalit Panther movement in Maharashtra in the 1970s. Earlier it had been used by Jyotirao Phule and also by B. R Ambedkar in his Marathi

However, West Bengal, which had come under British colonial influence or colonial modernity much earlier than other parts of India and thus became exposed to a more prolonged and intense process of westernization, undergoing a remarkable cultural awakening, known as '19th century Bengal Renaissance', stands remarkably apart from the above-mentioned political pattern. Post-colonial West Bengal has travelled through a distinctive political trajectory, shaped to a considerable extent, by the ideological and political influence of the Communist parties and a strong Left movement. After independence the Communist parties while failing to make their presence felt in other states found a fertile ground for their political growth in West Bengal along with Kerala. In West Bengal they played a leading role in Food Movement, Refugee Rehabilitation Movement and a number of other agitations which ultimately enabled them to develop a mass base. Under the impact of Left politics, trade unionism in Calcutta became powerful and militant and in rural areas, Communist led peasant bodies like the Kisan Sabha developed strong base among the farmers. Electoral success followed soon. The Communist parties became major constituents of two coalition Governments in the late 1960s. Finally, the Left Front, a coalition of Left parties led by the CPI(M) [Communist Party of India (Marxist)] acquired political power after comprehensively win-ning the 1977 Assembly elections. The CPI(M) uninterruptedly ruled West Bengal for a record duration of thirty-four years from 1977 to 2011, becoming the world's longest serving democratically elected Communist party.

Caste has remained a marginal factor in electoral politics of West Bengal and this marginality is generally attributed to the prevalence of progressive Left politics. Therefore, with the electoral decline of the Left the role of caste in West Bengal politics has become a point of contention. As the Left regime enabled the dominant paradigm of class to silence all community affiliations including caste, the steady decline of Left politics is now being seen by many as a necessary impetus to the upsurge of 'a new politics of caste'. The hypothesis regarding the enhanced role of caste in electoral politics has also gained plau-sibility due to hitherto unseen political mobilization of the *Matua-Namasudra* community in recent times. It is in this backdrop that this book aims to assess

---

writings and speeches. Literally, *'dalit'* means 'oppressed', 'broken' or 'crushed'. Therefore, it is an inclusive and broad identity which can be claimed by any marginalised group. In other words, *dalit* is a condition not necessarily a caste. But since the 1970s, several lower caste/ex-untouchable groups defined as Scheduled Castes by the Constitution have adopted this term for the purpose of self-description and self-identification. As a result, *dalit* identity and lower caste identity have become synonymous today. Hence, the term *dalit* today stands for lower castes/ ex-untouchables/ Scheduled Castes.

the role of caste in West Bengal politics and to find out the future possibilities of caste-based identity politics in the state.

1 Posing the Problem: West Bengal's Exceptionalism

Most of the scholars today are of the opinion that the traditional caste system is on a steady decline. However, at the same time they also point out that the decline of the caste system rather than being accompanied by the demise of caste identity has opened up spaces (such as electoral politics) for caste identity to operate, resulting in a paradoxical scenario of 'castes without the caste system'. Dipankar Gupta, for instance, has argued that caste identity has trumped the caste system.[3] Despite his much-criticized obsession with the ritual structure of the caste system, Louis Dumont has also acknowledged the possibility of castes existing independently of the caste system. He has drawn a distinction between structuralist model and substantialist model of the caste system. The structuralist model which Dumont endorses sees caste as a system of relations not of elements, suggesting that individual caste groups exist due to the persistence of the caste system. But while exploring the possibility of transformation of caste, Dumont has advanced his secondary thesis of 'substantialisation of caste'. 'Substantialisation of caste' implies a transition from interdependence between castes to competition between them and also a transformation of hierarchically and vertically ranked caste groups into horizontally disconnected groups.[4] While 'substantialisation of caste' is only a secondary thesis for Dumont, other scholars have taken a cue from it to argue that castes today persist as cultural communities independent of a caste system (understood as a relational system with economically interdependent castes) and vigorously compete with each other as political entities. Chris Fuller has interpreted the process of substantialisation in terms of a transformation of caste groups into horizontally disconnected ethnic groups with their distinctive cultures and ways of life.[5] Adrian Mayer has also pointed out that caste distinctions have today turned into cultural distinctions giving way to horizontal separation in place of hierarchical interdependence. Caste practices such

---

3 Dipankar Gupta, "Caste and Politics: Identity over System," *Annual Review of Anthropology* 34 (2005): 409–427.
4 Louis Dumont, *Homo Hierarchicus: The Caste System and Its Implications* (London: Weidenfeld and Nicolson, 1970), 226–228.
5 C.J Fuller, "Introduction," in *Caste Today*, ed. C.J Fuller (Delhi: Oxford University Press, 1996), 1–31.

as endogamy are now-a-days justified through the claim that *khan-pin* (food and drink) and *rahan-sahan* (way of life) of different castes are different.[6] The breakdown of interdependence has paved the way for caste groups to compete in the arena of politics by articulating their demands through the idiom of caste. Caste associations and caste federations have made it possible for caste groups to operate in the political realm without the traditional caste system being actively operative in socio-economic life.[7]

Though West Bengal like other states has experienced the retreat of the traditional caste system as a relational system constituted by interdependent units, surprisingly such retreat has not facilitated political competition between caste groups and their emergence as culturally distinct political interest groups. During the long Left rule, West Bengal remained immune from large scale political mobilization along the lines of caste. There is a consensus in the existing scholarship on West Bengal politics that, being true to their ideology, the Left parties set in motion the legacy to view politics through the prism of class rather than any primordial identity. This enabled political parties to take over the role of the caste and other social institutions, making it difficult for caste forces to carve out an independent space for themselves in electoral politics. As a result, caste and other identity related concerns have not made any remarkable impact on mainstream electoral politics of the state. Though West Bengal consists of second largest population of Scheduled Castes, politics of the state since independence has seen a virtual absence of identity politics based on caste. The state has also not witnessed any large-scale caste oriented social movement. The undivided Bengal province in the colonial era had experienced strong social and political assertion by the *Namasudra* community. But the *Namsaudra* movement petered out after independence and the Partition of the province in 1947. Moreover, it is also pointed out quite often that compared to other states of India, in West Bengal the incidence of caste violence and caste discrimination has been quite negligible. Academic literature has articulated this apparent invisibility of caste in different spheres of life as 'West Bengal's exceptionalism', in most part attributing it directly or

---

6   Adrian Mayer, "Caste in an Indian Village: Change and Continuity 1954–1992," in *Caste Today,* ed. C.J Fuller (Delhi: Oxford University Press, 1996), 32–64.

7   See, Robert Hardgrave, *The Nadars of Tamilnad: The Political Culture of a Community in Change* (Berkeley: University of California Press, 1969); Lloyd I. Rudolph and Susanne Hoeber Rudolph, *Modernity of Tradition* (Chicago: University of Chicago Press, 1967); Rajni Kothari and Rushikesh Maru, "Federating of Political Interests: the Kshatriyas of Gujarat," in *Caste in Indian Politics,* ed. Rajni Kothari (New Delhi: Orient Longman, 1970), 70–101.

indirectly to the dominance of Left politics.[8] For a long time the caste question in West Bengal had predominantly been understood through the prism of this notion of exceptionalism. One of the popular discourses professed by the middle-class Bengalis of predominantly higher caste background is that West Bengal is 'casteless' and 'exceptional' compared to other states. This sense of uniqueness from the rest of India forms one of the key dimensions of the modern Bengali identity.[9]

In this context, it is important to engage with the fundamental assumptions underlying the thesis of 'West Bengal's exceptionalism'. The view that exceptionalism of West Bengal vis-à-vis other states is reflected in relatively marginal role of caste in its politics is supported by several noteworthy facts. First, there are no caste based political parties which are dependent upon caste-centric political loyalties in West Bengal. While in other parts of India caste based regional parties have come up and increasingly made their presence felt in electoral politics since the late 1970s, no such political parties have emerged in West Bengal. The TMC emerged as a strong regional party in the late 1990s and ultimately became successful in achieving political power in 2011. However, unlike regional parties in other parts of India such as BSP (Bahujan Samaj Party), SP (Samajwadi Party), RJD (Rashtriya Janata Dal), JD(U) [Janata Dal (United)], TDP (Telegu Desam Party), INLD (Indian National Lok Dal), neither the CPI(M) nor the TMC has any identifiable caste base. Second, while caste was a major political factor behind the ascendancy of many regional political parties, the rise of the CPI(M) nor the TMC had anything to do with caste. Unlike most other regional parties neither the CPI(M) nor the TMC has any identifiable caste agenda. No party representing any dominant OBC (Other Backward Classes) interests has also emerged as a political force in the post-*Mandal* era in West Bengal. Third, while the national parties in various states have made attempts to develop vote bank based on caste loyalties, no such manifest attempts have so far been made in West Bengal. In Uttar Pradesh (UP) the Congress had once forged a coalition of extremes consisting of the upper castes and the *dalits*.[10] At various times it had cultivated the support of *Vokkaligas*

---

8   The term 'West Bengal's exceptionalism' has been used to imply many things. It generally refers to the absence of identity politics based on caste and religion in West Bengal in contrast to other states. It has also been used to convey that West Bengal's political discourse is more modern, civilized and progressive. I have used this term in a limited sense here, implying by it the absence of caste-based identity politics only.

9   Sandip Mondal, "Demystifying Caste in Bengal," *Economic and Political Weekly* 56, no. 3 (2021): 21.

10   Paul Brass, "The Politicization of the Peasantry in a North Indian State – part II," *Journal of Peasant Studies* 8, no. 1 (1980): 3–36.

and *Lingayats* in Karnataka, *Jats* in Rajasthan, *Kshatriyas* in Gujarat and *Reddys* in Andhra Pradesh. But in West Bengal Congress or any other party has rarely adopted any caste based political mobilization strategy in formal institutional politics. Similarly, no significant efforts to manufacture a broader *bahujan* political identity based on a conglomerate of castes and communities have also been made. Thus, in the realm of politics, West Bengal's exceptionalism has found manifestation most remarkably in the practice of non-communal mode of political mobilization, that has determinedly shied away from caste and other identity concerns, while other states of the country have increasingly come under the grip of caste-based identity politics.

2   Contemporary Critiques of West Bengal's Exceptionalism

With steady electoral decline of the Left Front since 2009, the so-called exceptionalism thesis has come under a great deal of skepticism. This skepticism has received further credence due to some recent attempts by mainstream political parties to mobilize and consolidate support of some communities, particularly the *Matuas*. In this context, a case has been made for re-examination of the so-called exceptionalism thesis. Currently, academic debate is raging on the apparent hyper invisibilisation of caste in West Bengal. The ongoing debate has so far spawned some serious critiques of the long-held notion of 'West Bengal's exceptionalism'. It is important here to identify the major strands of this critique of the notion of 'West Bengal's exceptionalism'. In my view three strands of this critique can readily be identified for analytical purposes though they are somewhat interconnected and overlapping. I would like to label them as dispositional, conspiratorial, and ethnographic.

The dispositional critique is concerned with social outlook or disposition towards caste as an identity. According to the dispositional critique the thesis of exceptionalism is based upon the mistaken belief that thirty-four years of Left Front rule in West Bengal somehow abolished caste prejudices or caste-based discrimination. It attempts to demonstrate that caste loyalties have not disappeared from popular consciousness; caste is still a part of social perception and cultural attitudes in West Bengal just like in other parts of the country. This critique has mostly emanated from the attempts by the marginalized individuals and *dalit* writers to document their lived experiences and from several reports about disturbing instances of caste discrimination. Arguably, the best specimen of this critique is represented by famous Bengali *dalit* writer Manoranjan Byapari's startling autobiography *Itibritte Chandal Jibon* (translated in English

with the title *Interrogating My Chandal Life – An Autobiography of a Dalit*).[11]
It describes with uncompromising honesty appalling caste discrimination
and caste prejudices faced by the author, challenging the general perception
about non-existence of caste bias in Bengali society. In this connection, it must
be mentioned that though caste discrimination is not a major public issue in
West Bengal, incidents of brazen caste discrimination are not uncommon. In
1992 Chuni Kotal, the first woman to graduate from Lodha tribe, which the
British had once branded as a criminal tribe, committed suicide while she was
a post-graduate student of Anthropology in Vidyasagar University, Midnapur.
She had allegedly been subjected to repeated casteist humiliation at the hands
of one of her professors. The suicide of Chuni, committed almost thirty years
ago has an uncanny resemblance to that of Rohith Vemula, a doctoral student
at Hyderabad University, which created a nationwide outrage a few years ago
and is still fresh in public memory. Chuni complained that she was constantly
taunted for being a member of a 'criminal tribe' not worthy of obtaining education, unfairly debarred from appearing for examinations and deliberately
awarded low marks, which caused her loss of two academic years. Chuni
submitted her complaint in writing to the Vidyasagar University authorities,
but her repeated complaints failed to bring any redress.[12] After her suicide
the West Bengal Government constituted a one-man inquiry committee by
a retired judge of the Calcutta High Court, which ultimately acquitted the
accused teacher.[13] But Chuni's death exposed the prevalence of casteism in

11 Manoranjan Byapari, *Itibritte Chandal Jibon* (Kolkata: Kolkata Prakashan, 2012).

12 Mahasveta Devi, "The Story of Chuni Kotal," *Economic and Political Weekly* 17, no. 35
(1992): 1836–1837; Abhijit Guha, "How the Lodhas Became Criminal or Meeting of the
Past and the Present," *The Eastern Anthropologist* 69, no. 1 (2016): 79, 85.

13 The Ganguly Commission of Enquiry appointed by the Governor of West Bengal, 1995
concluded: "On a consideration of all the materials on record we are constrained to
hold, therefore, that the allegations brought against Falguni Chakraborty (the accused
teacher) by Chuni Kotal were not sustainable and further that Falguni Chakraborty never
practised nor had he any reason to discriminate against Chuni simply because she was a
Lodha. It may be that on occasions Falguni Chakraborty took Chuni to task for her late
or non-attendance or for some such reason". It further stated- "These were mere trivialities which occur as a matter of course between the teacher and the taught without
any personal involvement from either side. These trivialities were blown big beyond all
proportions to transform them into the items of petition of complaint. On the findings
arrived by us, we conclude that the behaviour meted out by Falguni Chakraborty to Chuni
was not as to cause intense mental pain to Chuni so as to break her heart and lead her
ultimately to commit suicide". The clean chit given to the accused teacher raised many
eyebrows giving rise to further questions. Well-known journalist Suman Chattopadhyay
in an article published in Bengali newspaper *Anandabazar Patrika* asked whether it
was a case of a helpless tribal girl being victimized by some powerful and politically

Bengali society and particularly in university campuses. It also paved the way for public debates on casteism, bringing into question the cherished liberal credentials of the Bengali society. Jnanpith and Magsaysay award winning writer and activist Mahasweta Devi, who had worked for tribal people all her life made a lot of efforts to arouse public conscience over this unfortunate incident.

In 2001 a survey on primary education carried out by Pratichi Trust in three districts of West Bengal – Midnapur, Birbhum and Purulia reported that in some schools Scheduled Caste students were still forced to sit separately.[14] In 2004 it was widely reported in Calcutta newspapers that, in a number of districts, higher caste parents objected to their children eating cooked meals in schools prepared by volunteers from the Scheduled Castes.[15] Such discriminatory practices, many of which are carried out silently outside the scrutiny of public eye without much resistance from the victims, inflict what Pierre Bourdieu calls 'symbolic violence'. Operating through cultural mechanisms, it facilitates internalization by the victims of a sense of inferiority and normalization of the social domination faced by them.[16] Interestingly Bourdieu and Passeron also highlight that the educational system is the major institution through which symbolic violence is practiced.[17] Various incidences of everyday casteism in West Bengal seem to confirm this. A.K Biswas in an article published in *Mainstream Weekly* has documented several instances of casteism in Bengal's educational institutions.[18]

Even as recently as in 2019, there was a great outcry over alleged casteist slurs hurled at a *dalit* professor by students at Kolkata's Rabindra Bharati University.[19] This incident was followed by the publication of an article in a widely circulated Bengali newspaper by Dr. Maroona Murmu, who teaches at Kolkata's esteemed Jadavpur University.[20] In this article, which created a

---

connected people for their vested interests. See, Suman Chattopadhyay, "Chuni Kotaler Attahatta: Bishwyabidyaloie Rajnitir Fal," *Anandabazar*, June 6, 1995.

14   Anjan Ghosh, "Cast(e) out in Bengal," *Seminar*, May 2001, no. 508.

15   *Anandabazar Patrika*, September 24, 2004, December 28, 29, 30, 2004.

16   Pierre Bourdieu and L.J. D. Wacquant, "The Purpose of Reflexive Sociology (The Chicago Workshop)," in *An Invitation to Reflexive Sociology*, eds. Pierre Bourdieu and L.J. D. Wacquant (Chicago: University of Chicago Press, 1992), 61–215.

17   Pierre Bourdieu and Jean-Claude Passeron, *Reproduction in Education, Society and Culture* (London: Sage, 1970).

18   A.K Biswas, "Saraswati Karketta," *Mainstream Weekly* 57, no. 34 (2019).

19   *Anandabazar Patrika*, June 18, 2019.

20   Murmu Maroona, "Ei Bonge Naki Jati Bhittik Bibhed bole Kichu Nei?,"*Anandabazar Patrika*, June 29, 2019.

lot of uproar and debate, Murmu busted the myth that caste discrimination does not exist in West Bengal by describing several experiences of everyday casteism faced by her even in so-called progressive social circles. Very recently in another incident which again created a great amount of furor, Murmu was subjected to casteist abuse by a student of Kolkata's Bethune College on social media. Murmu was called 'incompetent' and 'worthless', implicitly suggesting that she had enjoyed undue advantage of affirmative action because of her identity. The student also followed up her comment with another post on her own Facebook wall, bragging that how she, 'in polite language', had put a certain 'Santhali Murmu' in place. This set off a chain of reactions, with people defending as well as ridiculing Dr. Murmu on social media. [21] All these incidents suggest that just like in other parts of India the symbolic violence of casteism is present in West Bengal too.

Furthermore, contrary to common perception, West Bengal has also not shown itself fully immune from caste violence. Recent research has uncovered the unimaginable scale and intensity of police brutality committed on a group of *dalit* refugees during the Marichjhapi massacre of 1979, which unfortunately remains a largely forgotten chapter of history.[22] Marichjhapi incident initially had not attracted the kind of attention that a brutality of such scale should have generated. It was later taken up by a few scholars with notable accounts by Ross Mallick.[23] Marichjhapi massacre also provides the backdrop of Amitabha Ghosh's famous novel, *The Hungry Tide.*[24] The most notable recent addition to this list is Deep Halder's book *Blood Island* which has meticulously

---

21   Bishwanath Ghosh, "Jadavpur University Professor Trolled Over Tribal Status," *Hindu*, September 5, 2020, https://www.thehindu.com/news/national/other-states/jadavpur-uni versity-professor-trolled-over-tribal-status/article32529928.ece.

22   After Partition in 1947 while the upper caste Hindu migrants were allowed to settle in Calcutta and its thriving suburbs, the *Namasudra* refugees were mostly sent outside the state of West Bengal, mainly to the rocky plateau of Dandakaranya where economic opportunities were limited and living conditions were harsh. As the Communists had earlier promised settlement of all Bengali refugees in West Bengal only, a large scale migration of lower caste Bengali refugees from Dandakaranya to West Bengal began immediately after the Left Front government had been elected in 1977. They chose to settle in the Sundarbans. Going back on its earlier promise the Left Front government forcibly sent back most of the refugees but around 10,000 *Namasudra* refugee families managed to settle in Marichjhapi, an island in the Sunderbans. The Left Front government first launched an economic blockade of the island and then unleashed a massive and brutal police crackdown reportedly killing several hundreds of men, women and children.

23   Ross Mallick, "Refugee Resettlement in Forest Reserves: West Bengal Policy Reversal and the Marichjhapi Massacre," *The Journal of Asian Studies* 58, no. 1 (1999): 104–125.

24   Amitav Ghosh, *The Hungry Tide* (London: Harper Collins, 2004).

documented first hand accounts of several survivors of Marichjhapi massacre, presenting an eye-opening revelation of the sheer monstrosity of the cruelty faced by the Marichjhapi victims.[25]

On the other hand, the conspiratorial critique of the notion of West Bengal's exceptionalism delves into the political agenda and social motives of the upper caste dominated power structure. It puts forwards the argument that contrary to the general perception, in West Bengal too, as in other states, the upper castes have suppressed the *dalits* and deliberately ensured their social subordination. In other words, the absence of political assertion by lower castes in West Bengal and unchallenged higher caste domination of all walks of public life are results of a carefully crafted upper caste conspiracy, involving discreet deployment of multifarious means and clandestine contrivances. According to this perspective, what hides the upper caste agency is the nature of upper caste domination. The social and cultural domination of the upper castes, while being quite pervasive and potent in West Bengal, is much more subtle and overtly less coercive. This has made possible dilution of *dalit* diffidence to upper caste supremacy. Several recent studies have uncovered efforts which have been undertaken to establish upper caste supremacy. For instance, Dwaipayyan Sen has critically engaged with the vexed question of upper caste agency by focusing upon the policy of reservation. His study has attempted to show that the upper castes in West Bengal consciously used their political power to ensure sustained non-implementation of constitutional provisions concerning reservation. This has led him to seriously consider the possibility that the upper-caste Hindus of West Bengal actively sought their domination and undertook deliberate steps to marginalize the lower castes in social and political spheres. Similarly, the refugee rehabilitation policy planned by the upper caste political leadership of the state also raises suspicion about an organized conspiracy to prevent political regrouping of the lower caste *Namasudras*. While the upper caste Hindu migrants were allowed to settle in Calcutta and its thriving suburbs, the *Namasudra* refugees were mostly sent outside the state of West Bengal, mainly to the rocky plateau of Dandakaranya where economic opportunities were limited and living conditions were harsh.[26] Uditi Sen has also explored the contentious issue of caste bias in refugee rehabilitation policy. She has documented how lower caste refugees, mostly *Namasudras* were subjected to social

---

25   Deep Halder, *Blood Island: An Oral History of Marichjhapi Massacre* (New Delhi: Harper Collins, 2019).

26   Dwaipayan Sen, "An Absent-minded Casteism?," *Seminar*, May 2013, no. 645; Dwaipayan Sen, "An Absent-minded Casteism?," in *The Politics of Caste in West Bengal*, eds. Uday Chandra, Geir Heierstad and Kenneth Bo Nielsen (New Delhi: Routledge, 2016), 103–124.

segregation. The upper caste refugees were not only allowed to illegally occupy land and settle in squatters' colonies in Calcutta, but special care was also taken to reserve squatters' colonies only for respectable higher caste people by not accommodating there refugees deemed to be *chotolok* (of low status). Though such illegal occupation was justified on the ground of dehumanizing condition in refugee camps and pavement shelters, upper castes refugees had rarely encountered the experience of living in refugee camps, railway stations or pavement shelters. They had taken shelter either in rented accommodation or in their relatives' houses and later moved to squatters' colonies to lay claim to their own plots of land. One of the reasons for them to avoid refugee camps was the desire to maintain social distance from the lower caste refugees.[27] Thus, Uditi Sen's scholarly investigation of refugee rehabilitation in Kolkata's Bijoygarh colony also somehow hints that the making of upper caste supremacy in West Bengal was a conscious process. Dwaipayan Sen in his recent work on Bengali *dalit* leader Jogendranath Mandal has analysed Mandal's failed efforts to build autonomous Ambedkarite *dalit* politics in West Bengal in the 1950s and 1960s through conspiratorial lens. He has chronicled how the upper-caste leaders of Bengal, whether of the Congress, the Hindu Mahasabha, or the Left, sought to foil Jogendranath Mandal's political project of enabling the articulation of an independent *dalit* voice in West Bengal and used their political organizations to that effect at different critical junctures, ultimately ensuring Jogendranath Mandal's failure in electoral politics. According to Sen "Bengal's acclaimed castelessness was not the consequence of any intrinsic nationalistic unfolding, nor merely contingent circumstance alone, but the result of concerted efforts by upper-caste elites to contain autonomous *dalit* political organization".[28] Thus, a perusal of the conspiratorial critique of the notion of 'West Bengal's exceptionalism' helps us to unpack the critical question of upper caste agency more closely. This critique tries to bring forth the point that the rejection of caste as an illogical and irrelevant analytical category by political and academic discourses flows from their inability to uncover the real nature of upper caste agency in West Bengal. From this point of view, the absence of open political articulation of caste interests does not make West Bengal any different from other states, since this is only a result of an upper caste agency working towards a process of veiled suppression of *dalits*. Hence, the absence

---

27   Uditi Sen, "The Myths Refugees Live By: Memory and History in the Making of Bengali Refugee Identity," *Modern Asian* Studies 48, no. 1 (2014): 37–76.

28   Dwaipayan Sen, *The Decline of the Caste Question: Jogendranath Mandal and the Defeat of Dalit Politics in Bengal* (Cambridge: Cambridge University Press, 2018), 12.

of caste in organized electoral politics itself is a subtle expression of caste politics of a different kind.

Lastly, many anthropologists employing ethnographic approach have also drawn the conclusion that caste does shape local relations of power and influence in West Bengal. On this basis they are inclined to argue that caste does have a political role in West Bengal just like in other states. For them, West Bengal is not so different from other states where political parties have coalesced diverse communities along caste lines, and where the impact of caste on organized politics is more noticeable. They tend to suggest that caste has always been an important factor, but it was not evident because of lack of ethnographic research. According to Partha Chatterjee in the "apparently un-institutionalised world of what may be called 'politics among the people' caste categories have continued to provide many of the basic signifying terms through which collective identities and social relations are still perceived."[29] Several field studies have confirmed this observation. Dayabati Roy's field research has divulged how the undercurrents of caste feelings influence local power relations. She has highlighted that it is due to the existence of caste bias that the lower caste *Panchayat* functionaries are rendered powerless and are made dependent upon the upper caste party leaders for political and administrative guidance.[30] Similarly, Mukulika Banerjee's field research on the modality of the CPI(M)'s leadership in two villages in Birbhum district, has shown how a local party leader belonging to the dominant *Syed* caste commands the loyalty of lower-caste Muslims, such as *Sheikhs and Pathans*.[31] Furthermore, political role and functions in the domain of micro politics are often dictated by factors relating to caste. Kenneth Bo Nielsen's study on caste question in Singur movement has described how caste stereotypes determine political role of individuals in popular politics. The image of the *Bauris* as indisciplined, idle, habituated to drinking, insensible and irresponsible relegated them to the position of foot soldiers and leadership positions within the SKJRC (Singur Krishi Jami Raksha Committee) came to be monopolized by the locally dominant

---

29   Partha Chatterjee, *The Present History of West Bengal* (New Delhi: Oxford University Press, 1997), 84.

30   Dayabati Roy, "Caste and Power: An Ethnography in West Bengal, India," *Modern Asian Studies* 46, no. 4 (2012): 947–74.

31   Mukulika Banerjee, "Leadership and Political Work," in *Power and Influence in India: Bosses, Lords and Captains*, eds. Pamela Price and A. E Ruud (New Delhi: Oxford University Press, 2010), 20–43.

and ritually pure *Mahishya* community.[32] In local politics, localized mobilization of caste groups by political parties is also not uncommon. At local level political parties often strike local alliances with particular caste groups. A.E Ruud has demonstrated how in two villages in Bardhaman district the CPI-M maintained a mutually beneficial alliance with the *Bagdi* caste. The rowdy image of the *Bagdis* made them useful to the local party for terrorising its political opponents and this in turn helped the *Bagdis* to extract economic patronage and benefits from the CPM Raj.[33] Glyn Williams' study on the dynamics of micro politics in three Birbhum villages has also found out that the centre stage of local politics is often occupied by informal networks of *dols* (groups) formed on the basis of caste and kinship affiliations. The voting preference of a person is often dictated by the leaders of such *dols*.[34]

These critiques of the notion of West Bengal's exceptionalism have raised valuable points. But, while it is necessary to highlight the presence of casteism in Bengali society and critically engage with the same, it is also important not to lose sense of proportion. It is true that casteism is not absent in Bengali society and in all probability, is deeply entrenched too. Therefore, some of the critiques of Bengal's exceptionalism have rightfully challenged the mistaken notion of 'casteless Bengal', a myth created and nourished by the long rule of the Left. But it is also necessary to keep in mind that the extent of overt caste violence and blatant caste discrimination in West Bengal still appears to be much less compared to other parts of the country. There are no accepted scales, criteria or metrics to compare the prevalence of caste prejudices across spatial realms. However, if the existing data concerning caste violence and caste discrimination as well as frequency of cases of caste prejudices as reported in the media are considered, then it clearly emerges that, at least in magnitude casteism in West Bengal does not compare with that in other parts of the country. As per the Annual Reports on Crime in India published by the NCRB (National Crime Records Bureau) the rate of crime in West Bengal against the Scheduled Castes has consistently remained much lower compared to the

---

32   Kenneth Bo Nielsen, "The Politics of Caste and Class in Singur's Anti-land Acquisition Struggle," in *Politics of Caste in West Bengal,* eds. Uday Chandra, Geir Heierstad and Kenneth Bo Nielsen (New Delhi: Routledge, 2016), 125–146.

33   Ruud, A. E, "From Untouchable to Communist: Wealth and Status among Supporters of the Communist Party (Marxist) in Rural West Bengal," in *Sonar Bangla? Agricultural Growth and Agrarian Change in West Bengal and Bangladesh,* eds. Ben Rogaly, Barbara Hariss-White and Sugata Bose (New Delhi: Sage, 1999), 253–78.

34   Glyn Williams, "Panchayati Raj and the Changing Micro Politics of West Bengal," in *Sonar Bangla? Agricultural Growth and Agrarian Change in West Bengal and Bangladesh,* eds. Ben Rogaly, Barbara Hariss-White and Sugata Bose (New Delhi: Sage, 1999), 229–252.

rates of crime against the Scheduled Castes in other states with substantial Scheduled Caste population (See Table 1). Hence, even if we can't find a difference of kind, there is certainly a difference of degree.

Further, historical research has also established that historically caste system had been less rigorous in Bengal. All standard historical accounts of the ancient society of Bengal have emphasized its late Brahmanization . According to R.C Majumdar, the Aryanization process in Bengal did not start till "a comparatively late period represented by Epics and *Manusmriti*".[35] This delayed the adoption of Brahmanical values. As a result, caste system did not emerge as a rigorous order unlike in North India.[36] According to Kunal Chakrabarti the influence of Buddhism started to decline, and Brahmanism started to gain momentum in Bengal since the eighth century. But Brahmanical culture had to accommodate ingredients of indigenous culture, resulting in cultural fusion. This process of cultural fusion, which he calls 'Puranic process', ultimately produced a 'syncretic socio-religious system'. In his words, "the Brahmanization of Bengal, if it may be so described, has been a continuous creative process, which in its ever increasing sweep, seems to have engulfed most of the indigenous local cultures by the time the last reductions to the Puranas were made, and succeeded in forging common religious cultural tradition, flexible enough to accommodate sub-regional variations and indifference to the emerging consensus on the dominant cultural mode among some social groups, and strong enough to take dissent in its stride".[37] Moreover, in the medieval times caste rules and norms underwent a process of dilution as a result of the influence of *Vaishnavism* and various heterodox religious sects which posed a considerable challenge to Brahmanism.[38] Drawing upon evidences from the Mangalkavya, Sekhar Bandyopadhyay has argued that "medieval Bengali society was segmented and hierarchised but not strictly segregated". Highlighting the example of the untouchable *Chandals* portrayed as city-dwellers in *Chandimangala*, he has pointed out that the standard *Manusmriti* regulation debarring the untouchable castes to live within the territory of the villages and cities was not strictly followed in Bengal. According to Bandyopadhyay the "pre-colonial Bengali society was never so rigidly

---

35   R. C Majumdar, *History of Ancient Bengal* (Calcutta: G. Bharadwaj, 1971), 413.

36   See, Niharranjan Ray, *Banglalir Itihas: Adi Parva, Volume I* (Calcutta: Paschimbanga Nirakharata Durikaran Samiti, 1980), 267–319.

37   Kunal Chakrabarti, *Religious Processes: The Puranas and the Making of a Regional Tradition* (New Delhi: Oxford University Press, 2001), 16, 32, 52, 319, 320.

38   See, Ramakanta Chakravarti, *Vaishnavism in Bengal* (Calcutta: Sanskrit Pustak Bhandar, 1985), 71–90, 320–45.

TABLE 1   Crime/atrocities against scheduled castes (SCs) by non-SCs and non-scheduled
           tribes (2017–2019)

State/UT	2017	2018	2019	Percentage state share to all-India (2019)	Population of SCs (in lakhs)	Rate of total crime against SCs (2019)
Andhra Pradesh	1969	1836	2071	4.5	84.5	24.5
Arunachal Pradesh	2	0	0	0.0	0.0	-
Assam	10	8	21	0.0	22.3	0.9
Bihar	6747	7061	6544	14.2	165.7	39.5
Chhattisgarh	283	264	341	0.7	32.7	10.4
Goa	10	5	3	0.0	0.3	11.8
Gujarat	1477	1426	1416	3.1	40.7	34.8
Haryana	762	961	1086	2.4	51.1	21.2
Himachal Pradesh	109	130	189	0.4	17.3	10.9
Jammu and Kashmir	0	1	2	0.0	9.2	0.2
Jharkhand	541	537	651	1.4	39.9	16.3
Karnataka	1878	1325	1504	3.3	104.7	14.4
Kerala	916	887	858	1.9	30.4	28.2
Madhya Pradesh	5892	4753	5300	11.5	113.4	46.7
Maharashtra	1689	1974	2150	4.7	132.8	16.2
Manipur	0	0	0	0.0	1.0	0.0
Meghalaya	0	0	0	0.0	0.2	0.0
Mizoram	0	0	0	0.0	0.0	0.0
Nagaland	0	0	0	0.0	0.0	-
Odisha	1969	1778	1886	4.1	71.9	26.2
Punjab	118	168	166	0.4	88.6	1.9
Rajasthan	4238	4607	6794	14.8	122.2	55.6
Sikkim	5	5	4	0.0	0.3	14.1
Tamil Nadu	1362	1413	1144	2.5	144.4	7.9
Telangana	1466	1507	1690	3.7	54.3	31.1

TABLE 1   Crime/atrocities against scheduled castes (SCS) (*cont.*)

State/UT	2017	2018	2019	Percentage state share to all-India (2019)	Population of SCs (in lakhs)	Rate of total crime against SCs (2019)
Tripura	1	1	0	0.0	6.5	0.0
Uttar Pradesh	11444	11924	11829	25.8	413.6	28.6
Uttarakhand	96	58	84	0.2	18.9	4.4
ªWest Bengal	138	119	119	0.3	214.6	0.6
Total State(s)	43122	42748	45852	99.8	1981.6	23.1

a   Due to non-receipt of data from West Bengal in time for 2019, data furnished for 2018 has been used

SOURCE: CRIME IN INDIA, 2019, STATISTICS, VOLUME II, NATIONAL CRIME RECORDS BUREAU, MINISTRY OF HOME AFFAIRS, GOVERNMENT OF INDIA, NEW DELHI, P. 509

structured or hopelessly immobile".[39] Untouchability was not rigidly practiced in strict ritual sense but was used only as a means by the upper castes to assert social authority and power. Furthermore, untouchability in Bengali society generally meant untouchability of the water touched by the *antyaja* (lower) castes rather than avoidance of all physical contacts with them.[40] Caste also did not act an insurmountable barrier to social mobility. Hiteshranjan Sanyal's study on caste mobility in Bengali society has illustrated several cases of social mobility of caste groups such as *Teli, Sadgope* and *Bhumij-Kshatriya*.[41]

---

39   Sekhar Bandyopadhyay, *Caste, Culture and Hegemony: Social Dominance in Colonial Bengal* (New Delhi: Sage, 2004), 20.
40   Sekhar Bandyopadhyay, *Caste, Protest and Identity in Colonial India: The Namasudras of Bengal, 1872–1947* (New Delhi: Oxford University Press, 2011), 15–18.
41   See, Hiteshranjan Sanyal, *Social Mobility in Bengal* (Calcutta: Papyrus, 1981), 33–64; Hiteshranjan Sanyal, "Continuities of Social Mobility in Traditional and Modern Society in India: Two Case Studies of Caste Mobility in Bengal," *Asian Survey* 30, no. 2 (1971), 315–39.

However, the more relevant point about the contemporary critiques of the notion of 'West Bengal's exceptionalism' is that they have only been partially successful in negating this widely held viewpoint. Though caste sentiments and prejudices exist in West Bengal and caste also matters in social and political relations just like in other states, still there is no way in which we can deny the fact that the domain of institutional or mainstream electoral politics of West Bengal unlike in other states has remained largely free from any caste based political agenda and large-scale caste based political mobilization. Therefore, as far as the mainstream macro politics is concerned there remains a key difference between West Bengal and other states. The contemporary critiques of the notion of 'West Bengal's exceptionalism' in their eagerness to dismiss the idea of exceptionalism, exhibit a tendency to brush aside the unique absence of political articulation and aggregation of caste interests in formal macro politics of West Bengal by focusing their attention solely on micro-politics and everyday social experiences. For instance, the dispositional critique mounts a credible challenge to West Bengal's social exceptionalism, but political exceptionalism clearly escapes its analytical reach. While its attempt to unveil hidden caste prejudices through anecdotal evidences does uncover the presence of caste in social relations, this does not explain how such caste dynamics interact with mainstream electoral politics, which clearly appears to be non-accomodative of large-scale caste based mobilization. On the other hand, the conspiratorial critique aims to demonstrate that West Bengal is not unique from other states since, its power structure also guided by an upper caste agenda serves the interests of the upper castes to the detriment of the *dalits*. But this begs the question as to whether the absence of *dalit* political mobilization in West Bengal as a reaction to higher caste domination should not be regarded as a unique phenomenon, given the fact that higher caste supremacy has often provided an impetus to large scale lower caste mobilization in other states. In other words, the absence of *dalit* politics in West Bengal despite higher caste supremacy confirms rather than shatters the notion of 'West Bengal's exceptionalism'. Lastly, the ethnographic critique only deals with the role of caste in micro-politics, pointing out significance of caste dynamics in local power relations. But it is necessary to make a distinction between various levels of politics in order to make a holistic sense of the phenomenon of 'West Bengal's exceptionalism'. Whether caste plays a role in politics or not depends on how we define politics. If politics is seen as a localized phenomenon of exercise of power and influence, (which without any doubt is an important facet of politics) then it is difficult to ignore the role of caste dynamics in shaping political processes. However, politics comprises of not only micro dynamics of power and but is also constitutive of the large and possibly more significant field of mainstream electoral politics. If mainstream electoral politics of West Bengal is considered, then the absence of caste based political agenda and of articulation of caste interests is quite evident. In this regard, it is necessary for analytical purposes to make a clear distinction between two levels of politics, macro and micro and avoid conflation between them. In other words, it is imperative to be sensitive to and cognizant of differentiation between various levels of polity in order to develop a nuanced understanding of the notion of 'West Bengal's exceptionalism'. While there are evidences which point towards the role of caste in shaping local micro level power relations, surprisingly such micro dynamics of caste have failed to produce adequate ramifications for organized politics at the macro level. It is this inability of the effects of micro-dynamics of caste to spill over into organized macro politics that makes the role of caste in West Bengal politics extremely intriguing and worthy of academic investigation.

3   Research Rationale

Despite being confronted with serious scholarly critiques, the thesis of West Bengal's exceptionalism can't be fully ruled out as mistaken. It can't be denied that the mainstream organized party politics of West Bengal unlike in other states has consistently denied space to any caste based political agenda. The tendency to dismiss West Bengal's exceptionalism as a complete myth has emanated from insufficient exploration of the structural factors which have a bearing on the interplay between caste dynamics and macro level political processes. It is in this backdrop that this study finds a rationale to diagnose the reasons for absence of caste politics in West Bengal through an exhaustive study of micro and macro levels of politics as well as all other relevant domains of life connected to politics, i.e., society, economy, culture and demography.

The starting point of this endeavour should be a careful reformulation of the thesis of West Bengal's exceptionalism. The preceding discussion has already highlighted the inaccuracy of the common assertion that caste is an entirely insignificant factor in West Bengal. As already pointed out, several studies have imploded this myth by demonstrating the existence of caste prejudices in social psyche and the prevalence of caste dynamics in grassroot politics. Therefore, 'West Bengal's exceptionalism' does not consist in the fact that unlike in other states of India, political and social landscape of West Bengal has completely ousted caste. This is indeed not the case. But also at the same time, it needs to be acknowledged that, to a significant extent, West Bengal does fall outside the all India pattern in the sense that caste has largely failed to infiltrate the domain of formal electoral politics. But since politics is not

purely a formal process and caste is present in informal politics (as the ethnographic accounts convincingly tell us) the ontological claim of West Bengal
politics being 'casteless' appears to be not only a sweeping generalization
but also an unpersuasive assertion. In this context, it would be apt to argue
that West Bengal's exceptionalism consists in persistence of two contrasting
trends: presence of caste in informal politics and social relations on one hand
and absence of caste in formal politics on the other. In other words, the dis-
juncture between micro and macro levels of politics and also the disconnec-
tion between everyday social relations and formal institutional politics with
regard to the operation of caste dynamics clearly imbue West Bengal politics
with some amount of uniqueness.

Therefore, the academic agenda of this book is not to refute the role of caste
in social relations and everyday politics at the local level. As highlighted, several
studies have demonstrated quite convincingly that in non-institutionalized
micro politics at the grassroots caste still survives. In other words, non-assertion
of caste identity in formal electoral politics has not resulted into a scenario
where caste is completely ruled out of all socio-political considerations at
the grassroots. Caste factor often figures in local politics. Caste linkages often
prove useful to various political parties at the local level and political parties
do make efforts to mobilize different caste groups in local politics. However,
such association has remained localized and has not extended to other areas
preventing the en bloc alignment of a caste group with a particular political
party throughout the state and identification of a political party with a particular caste or a group of castes. Hence, an acknowledgment of the continuing relevance of caste in micro politics makes it incumbent on an observer to
provide an explanation as to why caste dynamics, while remaining relevant
at the grassroots have failed to make any significant impact upon the organized domain of formal politics. What has blocked its natural transportation
from informal to formal, from micro to macro? This is an important research
question which this book intends to grapple with. The considerable amount
of literature produced in recent times to refute West Bengal's exceptionalism,
while successfully demonstrating hidden caste dynamics in socio-political
relations has not bothered to answer this fundamental question. One reason
for the inability to answer this critical question is excessive focus on micro-
politics and ethnographic analysis combined with an analytical neglect of various structural factors having a bearing on formal party politics. Therefore, a
satisfactory response to this critical question necessitates an extensive analysis of mainstream electoral politics along with other prominent structural factors falling within the domains of society, economy, culture and demography.
This requires going beyond ethnographic approach, while not abandoning

it altogether. The analytical strategy followed by this study has attempted to combine an exploration of structural factors with ethnographic interpretation.

From a theoretical standpoint, this analytical strategy sees insignificance of caste in mainstream macro politics largely as an outcome of the constraining influence of macro structures on collective political action. 'Structure' in scholarly literature is generally understood as relatively enduring though not immutable circumstances and institutions within which actors operate. Anthony Giddens defines structure as those properties which facilitate similar social practices to exist across varying spans of time and space, lending them a systemic form. Structures, for him, are sustained by 'recurrent social practices' or repeated actions. The repetition of similar acts by individual agents reproduces a structure. In other words, structures find their manifestation in reproduced practices.[42] Based on this perspective, it can be argued that political processes and practices which have become quite entrenched and long-standing due to their regular reproduction are likely to assume structural forms. For quite some time the mainstream political currents of West Bengal while remaining amenable to class based political aspirations and interests have exhibited remarkable reluctance to facilitate the operation of caste as a political idiom of marginalization. Therefore, based on Giddens' theoretical insights, it is possible to argue that the long-standing practice of privileging class over caste as an organizing principle of politics has developed a structural form in West Bengal.

Now, from an analytical point of view, the pertinent issue is how we should understand the role of a structure. Emile Durkheim tells us that structures can be understood through other structures, or to be more specific, by discovering the constraining role of the latter. Macro level structures such as cultural values, economic system and political norms and institutions often have a bearing on collective mentality and social action. According to Durkheim social structures (such as system of law, the economy, church and many aspects of religion, the state and educational institutions) and cultural norms and values, which he calls 'social facts' constrain actors.[43] Unlike Durkheim, Giddens sees structure both as constraining and enabling, suggesting that structural constraints are often exaggerated. But Giddens also does not deny the fact that structure can impose constraints on action. According to him structures depending on the

---

42   Anthony Giddens, *The Constitution of Society: Outline of the Theory of Structuration* (Berkeley: University of California Press, 1984).

43   Emile Durkheim, *The Rules of Sociological Method* (New York: Free Press, 1895).

circumstances and the actors in question, can constrain actors as well as facilitate their preferred actions.[44]

An application of these theoretical perspectives to the context of West Bengal can give us valuable insights. If caste politics is absent in West Bengal, then it is quite likely that large scale caste mobilization has been prevented by constraints generated by existing social structures. In other words, there is a promising possibility to find an explanation about the absence of large-scale caste based collective political action in the constraining influence exercised by various structural factors. According to Durkheim a social fact is explainable only through other social facts, which can be material or observable (such as mode of economy, forms of technology, and legal codes) as well as non-material or non-observable (norms, values, morality and culture). They can't be reduced to the individual level. Even non-material social facts are shaped by social interactions. In his seminal work on suicide Durkheim has shown how suicide rate in a society is influenced by social facts such as divorce rate, religion of a country, and pace of economic and social change.[45] Thus, explanation for social phenomena can be found in social facts and social interactions.[46] In other words, structural factors are important. Therefore, a long-lasting political norm like non-identitarian politics or non-politicisation of caste identity in West Bengal can't simply be understood by exploring micro level individual agency but by investigating other social facts or structures relating to economy, culture, society etc. Pierre Bourdieu has also emphasized the structuring role of structures, highlighting the crucial role of the habitus, which he defines as an internalized mental or cognitive structure. Habitus stands for socialized norms or tendencies that guide behaviour and thinking. Habitus in the words of Bourdieu is "the way society becomes deposited in persons in the form of lasting dispositions, or trained capacities and structured propensities to think, feel and act in determinant ways".[47] This happens when a person internalizes the rules, roles, relationships, and expectations associated with a particular field in which he operates. Bourdieu understands the social world as being divided up into a variety of distinct arenas or 'fields' of practice like art, education, religion, law, etc., each with their own unique set of rules. Bourdieu is concerned with the dialectical relationship between the habitus and the field. The field conditions the habitus; on the other hand, the habitus constitutes the field as something

---

44   Giddens, *The Constitution of Society.*
45   Emile Durkheim, *Suicide* (New York: Free Press, 1951).
46   Durkheim, *The Rules of Sociological Method.*
47   Pierre Bourdieu, *Distinction: A Social Critique of the Judgment of Taste* (Cambridge: Harvard University Press, 1984), 468.

that is meaningful. Bourdieu's analysis thus, highlights how the internal and external worlds are interdependent as external structures become internalized in habitus. Therefore, habitus for him is the "dialectic of the internalization of externality and the externalization of internality". On one hand, habitus is a 'structured structure'; i.e., a structure that is structured by the social world. It stands for a consciousness which is an internal representation of external social structure. But at the same time, it is also a 'structuring structure' in the sense that it also structures the social world.[48] Thus, habitus is a socially constituted system of dispositions that orient thinking and actions. In other words, habitus is an internalized social structure that also constrains thought and choice of action. Therefore, if we apply the theoretical approach of Bourdieu to our discussion about the trajectory of the politics of caste in West Bengal, two interrelated questions become extremely pertinent which deserve thorough analytical exploration: whether and how the mentality shaped by the social environment. i.e., socialized norms constrains the deployment of caste as a tool of political mobilization and as an idiom for interest articulation, and how such norms and mentality generated through socialization are structured by the wider social environment.

While three strands of the critique against the notion of 'West Bengal's exceptionalism', discussed so far have failed to establish non-exceptionalism of the state's formal and mainstream electoral politics, another interesting counter has been presented by what I would like to call the 'rise of caste thesis'.[49] The 'rise of caste thesis' is fundamentally different from the three other critiques which are non-epochal in character. They contend that West Bengal politics has never been exceptional. But the 'rise of caste thesis' argues that until recently West Bengal politics, in comparison to politics of other states had truly been exceptional, since in West Bengal unlike in other states, caste had never been a relevant political category. But now with the electoral decline of the Left this exceptionalism is on retreat and the caste factor is now well poised to dominate party politics. In this connection, recent attempt by mainstream political parties to mobilize the *Matua* community has mainly been used as evidence to argue that the long period exceptionalism of West Bengal's mainstream electoral politics is finally over. Thus, the 'rise of caste thesis' is an epochal response to the thesis of West Bengal's exceptionalism,

---

48   Pierre Bourdieu, *Outline of a Theory of Practice* (London: Cambridge University Press, 1977), 72.

49   See, Praskanva Sinharay, "A New Politics of Caste," *Economic and Political Weekly* 47, no. 34 (2012): 26–27; Praskanva Sinharay, "The West Bengal's Election Story: The Caste Question in Lok Sabha Elections," *Economic and Political Weekly* 49, no. 16 (2014): 10–12.

as it draws a distinction between the epoch of exceptionalism and the epoch of non-exceptionalism. This thesis apparently looks more promising as it concedes exceptionalism of West Bengal's formal mainstream politics until the inauguration of the process of the Left Front's electoral decline. Implicit in its argumentation is endorsement of the general assumption that under the impact of an exceptionally long Left regime, the field of political contestation was structured and configured in a manner that the dominant paradigm of class pushed all community affiliations including caste to the margins. This assumption logically leads to the speculation that the electoral decline of the Left is likely to aid the upsurge of caste politics. Thus, the 'rise of caste thesis' gives us two more related research questions to ponder over: whether caste politics is on the rise due to the decline of the organized Left wing in West Bengal and whether caste factor will play a dominant role in post-Left electoral politics. These questions have sparked off a great deal of debate since the electoral defeat of the Left. This ongoing debate makes a good case for a critical, comprehensive, and systematic inspection of the role of caste in West Bengal politics.

In this backdrop, this book aims to analyse the role of caste in post-colonial West Bengal politics, and also to discover the future possibilities of caste-based identity politics in the state. In pursuit of this broad objective an elaborate assessment of the intellectual speculation about the rise of caste politics in post-Left West Bengal has been made. This assessment involves identification and analysis of all kinds of factors: social, political, economic, cultural and demographic, responsible for marginalization of caste identity in mainstream party politics of the state. In this regard, efforts have also been made to find out whether factors traditionally unfavourable to politicisation of caste identity are undergoing any significant metamorphosis that can facilitate the rise of caste on the big stage of electoral politics.

4   Thematic Outline and Approach

Though this study is concerned with the political role of caste, it is grounded in the crucial understanding that caste is a multidimensional social organization. It entails a mix of social, political, economic and cultural experiences and therefore, the political processes and events generated by it could not be seen in isolation. The political aspects of caste are often influenced by the structural dynamics which emanate from the larger socio-economic and cultural backdrop. Hence, it is important to discover those social, economic, and cultural processes and experiences which inform the political trajectory of caste. In other words, a satisfactory scholarly treatment of the political role of caste demands investigation of political, social, economic, demographic, and cultural settings. Therefore, this study has brought under its scrutiny an entire gamut of factors to understand whether and how these factors independently or in combination with one another have contributed to the inconsequentiality of caste in mainstream party politics of West Bengal. To be more precise, the reasons for the absence of caste politics have been identified through an exhaustive study of micro and macro levels of politics as well as all kinds of relevant factors connected to politics: social, economic, cultural, and demographic.

This book is divided into eight chapters, each of which (barring introduction and conclusion) deals with one particular factor. It separately engages in a systematic manner with political, social, economic, demographic, and cultural milieu with regard to the question of caste. Chapter 2 and Chapter 3 respectively deal with political mobilization and political representation, two relevant political aspects, which are believed to manifest signs indicative of politicisation of caste identity. An analysis of the nature of recent political mobilization of the *Matua-Namasudra* community in Chapter 2 has led to the finding that there has been a gradual shift from sporadic caste based mobilization of the *Matuas* to *Hinduization* of *dalit Matua* identity. In Chapter 3, it has been demonstrated that the declining electoral strength of the Left parties has not led to any enhancement in political representation of the lower castes. This suggests that the political outlook towards political empowerment of the *dalits* and caste based political representation still remains unfavourable. Thus, the nature of recent political mobilization and trends of political representation do not indicate rising importance of caste as a political category. Chapter 4 furnishes an updated analysis of caste demography of West Bengal. In the ongoing debate about the role of caste in West Bengal politics, the demographic scenario of the state has not been subjected to sufficient analytical scrutiny. The findings of an essay by Partha Chatterjee which came out more than two decades ago are still widely referred to.[50] Therefore, an analysis of latest data from Socio-Economic Caste Census (SECC) of 2011 has been made and the same has been correlated with data from the last caste census of 1931 and with comparable data relating to caste demography of other states. This has resulted in the identification of a number of demographic handicaps which are unfavouable to caste based political mobilization. Chapter 5 deals with various aspects of political economy having a bearing on politicisation of caste

---

50   See, the chapter "Caste and Politics in West Bengal" in Partha Chatterjee, *The Present History of West Bengal* (New Delhi: Oxford University Press, 1997), 69–86.

identity, in order to bring out the material basis of collective political inaction on the part of the *dalits* in West Bengal. In this connection, a number of factors relating to political economy, which are unfavourable to political articulation of caste as an idiom of marginalization and political aggregation of interests and demands along the lines of caste, have been identified. This chapter has mainly come up with three broad findings. First, the lack of homogeneity in the caste identities of the landholding class in West Bengal has prevented their conversion into a cohesive political bloc, which is potentially capable of being mobilized in favour of any political party unlike in other states. Second, low level of relative economic deprivation faced by the Scheduled Castes in West Bengal vis-à-vis other states does not augur well for emergence of caste as an idiom of socio-economic marginalization. Third, in West Bengal there is limited scope for political aggregation of the interests of the lower castes due to their uneven economic development. Chapter 6 deals with the working of social, economic and cultural dynamics of caste in micro-politics. Ground level evidences gathered through field study divulge that caste silently performs the key function of shaping political and economic power relations between groups and communities in rural society. But deep penetration of *bhadralok* values into lower caste consciousness has led to an absence of sustained social dialogue on caste practices and experiences, preventing the emergence of a counterculture in the form of a *dalit* public sphere as a necessary catalyst to the process of emergence of caste as an effective political category. Chapter 7 deals with the cultural roots of West Bengal politics in order to understand the relationship between caste and political culture in West Bengal. By exploring the recent political history of West Bengal, it has shown that, social and cultural imagination produced by a marriage between *bhadralok* values and Left politics has become an integral part of the commonsensical conception of politics in modern West Bengal. As a result, the electoral decline of the Left has failed to engender any fundamental change in general political discourse and to provide an impetus to the emergence of a different kind of politics, which is more accommodative of a political agenda of social justice.

Thus, this book aims to produce a systematic, organized, comprehensive and thematic treatment of caste question in West Bengal politics. Each chapter deals with the relationship between politics and one realm of life connected to politics such as economy, demography, society and culture. It deals with two purely political aspects, political mobilization and political representation in Chapter 2 and Chapter 3 respectively, relationship between politics and demography in Chapter 4, nexus between politics and economy in Chapter 5, interrelationships between political, social, economic and cultural factors in rural micro-politics in Chapter 6 and the interplay between macro level organized party politics and political culture in Chapter 7. In this way this study has attempted to consider all relevant settings, i.e., micro and macro politics, economy, demography, society and culture and seen them not as isolated but interconnected domains in making sense of caste as a political category in West Bengal. This analytical approach has led to the identification of several intermingling and interwoven factors spanning across multiple domains. Though it is difficult to assess the extent of impact of each of these factors on shaping the political trajectory of caste, it is quite evident that these factors complement and reinforce each other. It is unveiling of this process that constitutes the core agenda of this book.

CHAPTER 2

Politics of Memory

Caste and Nature of Political Mobilization

While caste based political mobilization started to gain momentum in various parts of the country in the late 1970s, West Bengal under the Left rule remained largely immune from caste politics. The Communist Party of India (Marxist) [CPI(M)] stood for a non-identitarian model of politics which was not accommodative of politicisation of caste identity. In CPI(M)'s political discourse, class is a more relevant, progressive, and legitimate category, whereas the question of caste is perceived as a mere part of the superstructure and a legacy of feudalism. This prevented the use caste as a basis for political mobilization and as a political idiom for interest articulation.[1] The discourse of class overpowered that of caste. The electoral decline of the Left Front since 2009 has provided a vantage point for a re-examination of the relationship between politics and community in West Bengal. To many political observers the erosion of the Left seems promising for creation and consolidation of independent *dalit* political platforms. The hypothesis suggesting an enhanced role of caste in institutional politics of the state has derived some amount of vindication from the increasing political correspondence between mainstream political parties and Matua Mahasangha, which is a religious association of the *Matuas* as well as their political mouthpiece. The *Matuas* are a heterodox sect mostly belonging to the lower caste *Namasudra* community, the second largest Scheduled Caste community of West Bengal. The *Namasudras* account for 17.41 percent of total Scheduled Caste (SC) population of the state and 3.84 percent of total population of the state.

Apart from the emergence of Matua Mahasangha as an important political factor, the formation of an organization called Social Justice Forum (SJF) by Abdur Rezzak Mollah, a former Left Front Minister was another noteworthy development that coincided with the electoral decline of the Left Front. The SJF was established with the goal to fight for the combined interests of the *dalit*s and Muslims.[2] Although these developments were at a rudimentary stage,

---

1 The ideological approach of the Left Front towards the question of caste politics has been discussed in detail in Chapter 3.

2 This political experiment did not ultimately succeed. The Forum was supposed to contest the 2016 assembly elections appealing to the *dalit* and Muslim votes. Abdur Rezzak Mollah urged

it was envisaged that they would unleash some long-term tendencies in favour of consolidation of caste-based forces in electoral politics of the state. In other words, these developments lent increasing plausibility to the hypothesis about rising relevance of caste in mainstream politics of the state. The main advocate of the view that with electoral decline of the Left Front caste politics has finally arrived in West Bengal is Praskanva Sinharay, who quite unequivocally argued that "the organized politics of the *Matuas* – a minor sect of the *Namasudras* – under the banner of their community organisation Matua Mahasangha had introduced 'a new politics of caste' in the state".[3] According to him caste which until recently was not a determinant category in the electoral politics of post-colonial West Bengal due to class based political mobilization has finally made its appearance as an important political factor with rising political assertion of the *Matua-Namasudra* community. Thus, the possibility of a fundamental structural metamorphosis of the nature of the state-society interface in West Bengal has been suggested based on the political assertion of the *Matua-Namasudra* community. In this context, this chapter grapples with the question whether the demise of the long Left rule has caused any fundamental break from the past regarding the role of caste in institutional politics of West Bengal, by bringing under close scholarly scrutiny the nature of emerging patterns of political mobilization in the state. To be specific, the purpose here is to find out whether and to what extent caste has become an organizing principle of political mobilization in West Bengal. In this context, I shall specifically analyse of mobilization of the *Matua-Namasudra* community. The reason for focusing upon the *Matua-Namasudra* community is two-fold. First, it is the political assertion of the *Matua-Namasudra* community which forms the basis of the argument that suggests the rise of caste as a significant political factor in the organized politics of the state. In other words, the view that caste factor

---

the *dalit*s and Muslims to desist from political schism and to fight against the *bhadralok* domination of mainstream political parties. The outspoken leader claimed that his purpose was to see a *dalit* as West Bengal's Chief Minister with a Muslim as his deputy. Thus, he envisaged some kind of a 'Mulayam–Mayawati model' to make a dent into upper caste hegemony. But the Forum remained an unknown quantity all through and failed to mobilize the *dalit*s and the Muslims. Instead of fighting the elections as a leader of the Social Justice Forum Abdur Rezzak Mollah joined the TMC before the 2016 Assembly elections. He successfully fought the elections as a TMC candidate and got inducted into the newly formed Ministry. As the Social Justice Forum was virtually synonymous with Abdur Rezzak Mollah the organisation also petered out.

3 Praskanva Sinharay, "The West Bengal's Election Story: The Caste Question in Lok Sabha Elections," *Economic and Political Weekly* 49, no. 16 (2014): 10. Also see, Praskanva Sinharay, "A New Politics of Caste," *Economic and Political Weekly* 47, no. 34 (2012): 26–27.

is now poised to play a significant role in mainstream electoral politics of West Bengal has acquired growing credence with the political mobilization of the *Matuas*. Second, only the *Namasudras* as a caste have so far demonstrated sufficient political activism and organization to merit an independent analysis in the context of a scholarly investigation of caste mobilization in West Bengal. Other lower caste groups in the state are yet to exhibit any comparable level of collective social and political activity.

The *Namasudras* were the second largest Hindu caste group in undivided Bengal province of colonial India and the largest in the eastern part of the province, which became East Pakistan after the Partition of India in 1947 and later Bangladesh after 1971. The *Namasudra* movement began in 1872 as a response to social discrimination and economic exploitation faced by the members of the community at the hands of the higher castes. The movement came to be built around an anti-Brahmanical and egalitarian *sahajiya Vaishnava* religious sect, known as the *Matua* which emerged in the 1870s among the *Namasudras*. The leaders of the *Namasudra* movement promoted the *Matua* identity to generate community consciousness and solidarity among the *Namasudras* and to mobilize them against socio-economic domination of the higher castes. This led to the induction of a large number of *Namasudras* of eastern Bengal into the *Matua* sect.[4] *Matua* identity is an inclusive one with anyone accepting the social and spiritual philosophy of the sect can become a *Matua*. But the members of the sect mostly belong to the *Namasudra* caste. Similarly, the *Namasudras* are mostly the followers of the *Matua* sect. Therefore, by and large the caste and sect identities of the members of the *Namasudra-Matua* community coincide. Hence, *Matua* identity and *Namasudra* identity need not be treated as two separate analytical categories. In this chapter two terms '*Matua*' and '*Namasudra*' have been used interchangeably.

Matua sect had been founded by Harichand Thakur (1812–1878) at Orakhandi in Faridpur district of present-day Bangladesh to fight against Brahmanism. After the death of Harichand Thakur leadership of the community passed on to his son Guruchand Thakur (1846–1937), who further organized the community by uniting its members on the basis of a blueprint for socio-economic development and collective political action.[5] The *Namasudra* leaders established Sri Sri Harichand Mission at Orakandi, Faridpur in 1915.

---

4 Sekhar Bandyopadhyay, *Caste, Protest and Identity in Colonial India: The Namasudras of Bengal, 1872–1947* (New Delhi: Oxford University Press, 2011), 53–54.

5 For a historical account of the *Matua* movement see, Sekhar Bandyopadhyay, *Caste, Protest and Identity in Colonial India: The Namasudras of Bengal, 1872–1947* (New Delhi: Oxford University Press, 2011).

In 1932 the organization was renamed as Matua Mahasangha under Pramatha Ranjan Thakur, grandson of Guruchand Thakur. After independence Pramatha Ranjan Thakur established the sect's headquarters at Thakurnagar in North 24 Parganas district of West Bengal. Thereafter, Thankurnagar became a pilgrimage centre for the *Matuas*. The *Matuas* worship Harichand Thakur and Guruchand Thakur as divine personalities.[6] Thakurnagar also houses *Thakur Bari*, the home of the descendants of Harichand and Guruchand. It is *Thakur Bari* which by and large controls the Mahasangha.

As a community the *Namasudras* have experienced displacement and struggle due to the Partition of Bengal in 1947. The Partition is regarded as one of the principal reasons for the decline of the *Namasudra* movement which had presented a powerful challenge to the higher caste hegemony in colonial Bengal. As a result of the Partition the *Namasudras* lost their traditional habitat as the *Namasudra* dominated districts went to East Pakistan. Pramatha Ranjan Thakur arrived in India in 1947, and a year later he along with his wife, Binapani Devi (Boroma), founded the Thakurnagar town in North 24 Parganas district. Slowly and steadily thousands of refugees, mainly belonging to the *Namasudra* community settled in Thakurnagar and nearby areas in the districts of North 24 Parganas and Nadia. The first wave of migration in the immediate aftermath of the Partition mostly consisted of relatively better off higher caste families capable of coping with economic effects of dislocation. They mostly belonged to the class of gentry and the educated middle classes with jobs, who were in a position to sell or arrange exchange of properties. Few belonging to *Namasudra* and other lower caste groups could migrate at this stage because of livelihood concerns. In December, 1949 communal violence broke out in Khulna and it quickly spread to other parts of East Pakistan. With rise in communal tension after the riots in Khulna the *Namasudras* began to migrate to India.[7] Many of the higher caste families took shelter in squatters' colonies in and around Calcutta and the government after initial reluctance turned a blind eye to the mushrooming of such colonies. But when the impoverished *Namasudras* arrived in West Bengal, they were dispatched to refugee camps in various districts. Afterwards, these camps were closed and the refugees were transported to Dandakaranya (situated mainly in Chattisgarh and Orissa) and Andaman islands. The Congress government of West Bengal refused to rehabilitate them

---

6   For details regarding the ritual practices and religious narratives of the *Matuas* see, Carola Erika Lorea, "Contesting Multiple Borders: Bricolage Thinking and Matua Narratives on the Andaman Islands," *Southeast Asian Studies* 9, no (2020): 231–276.

7   Nilanjana Chatterjee, "The East Bengal Refugees: A lesson in Survival," in *Calcutta: The Living City, Vol. II*, ed. Sukanta Chaudhuri (Calcutta: Oxford University Press, 1990), 72–73.

in the state on the ground of scarcity of land and resources. The refugees under the banner of organizations like the United Central Refugee Council (UCRC) organized mass protest against the refugee rehabilitation policy of the government demanding resettlement in West Bengal. Realising the potential of East Bengali refugees as a political support base, the Communist party of India (CPI) actively took up their cause. By raising livelihood issues and decrying class based inequalities the Communists managed to strike a chord with the refugees. By 1951 the UCAR, the most significant umbrella organization coordinating refugee agitation came to be dominated by the leaders of the CPI (Communist Party of India).[8]

Interestingly, the spiritual leader of the *Matuas*, Pramatha Ranjan Thakur who had joined Congress provided full backing to the official rehabilitation policy. He was urging the *Namasudra* refugees to take shelter wherever the government was making arrangement for their resettlement.[9] But down the line he also lost faith in the Congress government. In 1964 he resigned from the Assembly accusing the government of failing to protect the Hindus of East Pakistan and to provide promised rehabilitation to lower caste refugees. However, by that time the *Namasudra*s had already lost their geographical cohesiveness. Due to the official rehabilitation policy they had become dispersed across the country leading to the decline of the once powerful *Namasudra* movement. This made Pramatha Ranjan Thakur to devote his efforts towards inventing a spiritual space in the form of Matua Mahasangha where the dispersed *Namasudra* community could eventually unite and reinvent their collective self. In 1986 he formally registered Matua Mahasangha as a socio-religious organisation to preach the messages of Harichand Thakur and Guruchand Thakur. The idea behind the reinvented Matua Mahasangha was to offer the *Namasudras* a new imagined space for rediscovering a sense of common identity and community based solidarity.[10]

But for most part of the Left rule the Matua Mahasangha remained at the periphery of state politics. Ideologically, the class based political strategy of the Left did not offer much space to the community as an unit of mobilization

8   Sekhar Bandyopadhyay, "Partition and the Ruptures in Dalit Identity Politics in Bengal," *Asian Studies Review* 33, no. 4 (2009): 462.

9   He was elected on a Congress ticket to the West Bengal Legislative Assembly in 1957 from Haringhata and also in 1962 from Hanskhali. He briefly became a Minister in B.C Roy's Cabinet in 1962, only to be removed in 1963.

10   Sekhar Bandyopadhyay and Anasua Basu Ray Chaudhury, "In Search of Space: The Scheduled Caste Movement in West Bengal after Partition," *Policies and Practices* 59 (2014): 12–17.

and also to the articulation of identity related concerns in mainstream politics. Electorally, the CPI(M) and other Left parties were also in a position to follow their ideological line of steering clear of identity politics, since they virtually monopolized the entire political space with opposition parties never really in position to challenge, let alone, dislodge the Left Front from power. Therefore, for most part of the Left regime the option to closely engage with non-Left opposition parties, which were more amenable to identity politics did not seem very prudent to communities like the *Namasudras*.

Staying away from mainstream politics, the reinvented Matua Mahasangha through its spiritual and social activities silently worked in the direction of building a sense of community feeling among the members of the *Namasudra* community, which had also been steadily gaining numerical strength owing to continued influx of *Namasudra* refugees from Bangladesh. Working independently of institutional politics, the Matua Mahasangha recruited members, held gatherings of *Matua* devotees and propagated *Matua* philosophy by regularly publishing books, pamphlets and magazines. The spill over effects of the work of spiritual unification undertaken by the Matua Mahasangha among the *Namasudras* on state politics began to become apparent when the Matua Mahasangha started to mobilize the *Namasudras* against the Citizenship Amendment Act, 2003 which had created a great deal of uncertainty over the citizenship status of the *Namasudra* refugees. Incidentally, after the re-election of the Left Front in 2006 Assembly elections the politics of the state started to become more competitive with the TMC appearing to finally emerge as a formidable political force capable of unseating the Left from political power. Under such situation neither the Left nor the TMC could afford to ignore the concerns of the *Namasudra* community. In order to woo the community the Left Front government conferred Harichand- Guruchand Thakur Award on Kapil Krishna Thakur, the eldest son of Boroma Binapani Devi, who was at that time the spiritual head of the Matua sect, laid foundation stone of a government college (Sri Sri Harichand – Guruchand Thakur Government College) in Gaighata to be named after Harichand Thakur and Guruchand Thakur and also provided an assurance that *Matua*s crossing over from Bangladesh would not be pushed back. The TMC chief Mamata Banerjee, who was then central Minister of Railways promised renovation of Thakurnagar Railway station and establishment of a railway stadium in Bongaon.[11] Most importantly, Matua Mahasangha started to openly engage with mainstream political parties

---

11   Trijita Gonsalves, "Where are the Women?: A Study of Electoral Promises in the West Bengal Assembly Elections," *The Indian Journal of Political Science* 72, no. 4 (2011): 986.

seeking their support on the principal demand of the *Matuas* concerning citizenship.

The most important issue facing the *Matua* community today is citizenship. The Citizenship Amendment Act, 2003 categorized those people who had migrated to India without valid documents as illegal migrants or infiltrators. The 2003 Amendment to the Citizenship Act defines an 'illegal migrant' as a "foreigner who has entered into India without a valid passport or other travel documents". Since most of the *Namasudras* arrived in West Bengal to escape from communal persecution, they could not bring with them valid documents like passport and visa. After the enactment of the 2003 Amendment to the Citizenship Act they became illegal immigrants in legal terms. Further, 2003 Amendment also contributed towards the process, which has been interpreted as a gradual shift from a more inclusive birth-based principle of *Jus Soli* to a less inclusive descent-based principle of *Jus Sanguinis*.[12] The 2003 Amendment provides that, those born after December 3, 2004 will only be deemed as citizens of India by birth if one of their parents is an Indian and the other is not an illegal immigrant. This means that if one of the parents of a child born after December 3, 2004 is an illegal immigrant, the child has to acquire Indian citizenship through other means, not simply by birth. As a result, after the enactment of the 2003 amendment to the Citizenship Act, it also became impossible for children born in *Namasudra* refugee families after the cut off date of December 3, 2004, to become Indian citizens by birth, if either of their parents is legally an 'illegal migrant'. Previously, for obtaining citizenship it was sufficient if either of the parents of a person was an Indian citizen at the time of his or her birth.[13] Since the enactment of the 2003 amendment, *Matua* refugees have been regularly suspected of being 'Bangladeshis' or illegal infiltrators during registration for the electoral rolls and issuance of documents like passport and caste certificate. Therefore, understandably the main demand of the Matua Mahasangha is repeal of the Citizenship Amendment Act, 2003.

This chapter presents a critical analysis of how the *Matua* community has become politically active since the decline of the organized Left in West Bengal politics. Early political mobilization of the community was mainly anchored by the TMC which welcomed the arrival of Matua Mahasangha on the political

---

12   For details see, Nirja Gopal Jayal, *Citizenship and Its Discontents: An Indian History* (Ranikhet: Permanent Black, 2013).

13   Aditi Mukherjee, "Public Discourses on Citizenship in West Bengal: Insights from the Propaganda of Dalit Refugee Organisations," in Interrogating Citizenship: Perspectives from India's East and North East, *Policies and Practices* 109 (December 2019): 23–26.

scene. TMC's mobilization of the *Matuas* happened mainly on the lines of caste with its outreach efforts directed towards an appeal to the *Matua/Namasudra* identity. But due to TMC's inability as a regional party to address the complexities involved in the core demand of the community relating to citizenship, its efforts to mobilize the *Matuas* could not be consistent, with periods of intense political outreach frequently punctuated by periods of lull. Therefore, the TMC's *Matua* mobilization was at best scattered, limited and confined to a few geographical pockets with substantial *Matua* population. However, with the political rise of the Bharatiya Janata Party (BJP) in West Bengal since 2018–2019, the *Matua* mobilization has intensified, and the community has acquired unprecedented political visibility. It is quite evident from the recent electoral success of the BJP in regions with high concentration of the *Matua* population, that it has built a strong support base among the *Matuas*. Interestingly, instead of appealing to the caste identity of the *Matua-Namasudra* Community, it is playing the 'Hindu card' among the *Matuas* who have migrated from East Pakistan and later Bangladesh in large numbers due to religious persecution and communal tension. The BJP government at the centre has enacted the Citizenship Amendment Act, 2019 to satisfy the demand for citizenship of the Hindu refugees including the *Matuas*. BJP's strategy seems to be to mobilize the *Matuas* by treating them as Hindu refugees. This has brought the issue of religious persecution of the *Matuas* into mainstream public discourse, reopening the repressed wounds of Partition and reawakening their muffled memory of religious victimization. My analysis will demonstrate how this process has set in motion a 'politics of memory' that is facilitating incorporation of the lower-caste groups into the *Hindutva* fold by obscuring caste divisions and by supplanting caste consciousness with Hindu belongingness. In other words, the rise of the BJP seems to be facilitating a shift in nature of *Matua* mobilization from a caste conscious activity to a process directed towards *Hinduization* of *dalit*s. This chapter closely engages with this shift pointing out that the current pattern of mobilization of the *Matuas* does not fit into the traditional template of conventional caste politics and exhibits greater affinity to the politics of *Hindutva*.

My analysis of 'politics of memory' in this chapter is concerned with the contemporary political project of mobilizing collective historical memory in the service of present political purposes. A dissection of the historical authenticity of the collective memory that is presently invoked for political purposes is not an analytical objective that this chapter intends to accomplish. In other words, a discovery of the extent of real or imagined nature of the collective memory in question through a historical analysis is beyond the scope of this study. It is limited to the interpretation of how the present political discourse is being derived from the invocation of a collective historical memory and also how this political discourse is driving the ongoing political mobilization of the *Namasudra-Matua* community. To fulfil this limited objective three main analytical strategies have been employed in this chapter: (1) a critical contextualization of contemporary *Matua* politics in the light of emerging political developments (2) a discursive interpretation of the political narrative of *Hindutva* politics through relevant documents and (3) an exploration of ground level political narrative through interviews with *Namasudra* political workers and activists connected to the *Matua* movement.

1   Rise of the *Matua* Factor

The *Matuas* appeared as a vote bank on the political horizon sometime around national elections in 2009. Matua Mahasangha dramatically burst onto the political scene demanding repeal of the Citizenship Amendment Act, 2003. It emerged as an important political player before the 2009 Lok Sabha elections by organizing large rallies and meetings demanding citizenship for the *Matua* refugees. Till then the institutional politics of West Bengal had rarely experienced any significant caste-based mobilization. The collective strength of the *Matuas* started to become more apparent in the run up to the crucial state Assembly elections in 2011. People of West Bengal witnessed the hitherto alien phenomenon of open political articulation of caste identity when on 28th December, 2010 Matua Mahasangha organized a massive public rally at Esplanade at the heart of Kolkata, demanding repeal of the Citizenship Amendment Act, 2003. Thousands of *Matuas* beating drums and waving crimson flags hit the streets of Kolkata on that day in an unprecedented show of strength. Most importantly, prominent leaders of different political parties were also present at the rally.[14] The public spectacle of the event created an impression that the politics of the state had finally become ready to embrace large scale political mobilization along the lines of caste. It was in this backdrop that it was forcefully argued that political assertion of the *Matuas* marked the beginning of a 'new politics of caste' in West Bengal.

Matua Mahasangha had elicited attention from political parties across ideological spectrum before the 2011 Assembly elections. But because of its ideological baggage and its long neglect of the concerns of the *Matuas*, the Left Front was at a disadvantageous position vis-à-vis the TMC when it came to politically

---

14   *New Indian Express,* "CPM, TMC Leaders Share Dais at *Matua* Meeting," December 29, 2010, https://www.newindianexpress.com/nation/2010/dec/29/cpm-tc-leaders-share -dais-at-matua-meeting-214851.html.

mobilizing the community. TMC's lack of inhibition towards identity politics enabled it to openly mobilize the *Matua* community along caste lines. It reached out to Matua Mahasangha hoping that the Mahasangha could ensure en bloc support of the entire *Namasudra* community in its favour. Mamata Banerjee, a Brahman by birth publicly declared her wish to embrace the *Matua* faith. This gesture greatly appealed to the *Matuas*. At a ceremony on 5th December, 2009 she was inducted as a member of the Matua Mahasangha. In March, 2010 she was appointed as the Chief Patron of the Matua Mahasangha. In this way, by becoming an insider she was able secure the support of the *Matuas* for the 2011 Assembly elections.[15] In 2011 Assembly elections the Matua Mahasangha backed the TMC.[16] After winning the 2011 Assembly elections, Mamata Banerjee, reciprocated by appointing Manjul Krishna Thakur, the Saha-Sanghadhipati (Vice President) of the Matua Mahasangha, as the Minister of State for Refugee Rehabilitation and Relief.

In this way, the Matua Mahasangha attained considerable political prominence and spotlight by demonstrating its potential to mobilize the support of the entire *Namasudra* community in favour of a single political party. The *Matuas* are generally expected to vote according to the wishes of the spiritual leader of the sect if he/she decides to hold before them a clear-cut political choice. Before the 2011 Assembly elections Boroma Binapani Devi, the then spiritual leader of the sect had put her weight behind TMC chief Mamata Banerjee, who was able to garner substantial support of the *Matua* community. Out of the 50 seats of Nadia and North 24 Parganas, where there is high concentration of the *Matua* population, the TMC and Congress alliance won 43 seats with the TMC alone winning in 41 of those constituencies. This further cemented the perception that the Matua Mahasangha could guarantee the support of the entire *Matua* community. But this perception began to gradually erode after the 2011 Assembly elections due to increasing divisions within the ranks of the Matua Mahasangha. Manjul Krishna Thakur, son of Boroma, and Subrata Thakur, son of Manjul Krishna Thakur, joined the BJP just before the 2014 Lok Sabha polls. Subrata Thakur contested elections on a BJP ticket from Bongaon constituency against his aunt and TMC candidate, Mamatabala Devi, the wife of late Kapil Krishna Thakur, Boroma's elder son. After the defeat of Subrata Thakur, his father Manjul Krishna Thakur passed into political oblivion, losing his ministerial position and political

15   Bandyopadhyay, *Caste, Protest and Identity*, 271.
16   Monobina Gupta, "Understanding Bengal's Namasudras, Who Are Divided between TMC and BJP," *Wire*, February 28, 2019, https://thewire.in/caste/understanding-the-history-of -bengals-namasudras-who-are-divided-between-tmc-and-bjp.

prominence. Most importantly, the entire episode sent the wrong political signals. It divulged the inability of the Matua Mahasangha to mobilize the support of the entire *Matua* community in favour of a single political party. In the 2016 assembly elections too, the internal feud prevented the emergence of a clear-cut political choice equipped with the backing of all sections of the Thakur family.[17]

Factionalism within the Matua Mahasangha created skepticism about the capacity of the organization to mobilize en-bloc support of the *Matuas*. Being a divided house, Matua Mahasangha appeared to steadily lose its political relevance, becoming increasingly isolated from mainstream politics. Accordingly, the whole community became afflicted with debilitating political fragmentation. As a result, political parties also appeared to be losing interest in the Matua Mahasangha and turned non-committal on the citizenship demand of the *Matuas*. Consequently, political visibility of Matua Mahasangha diminished drastically. The media also turned its attention away from the *Matua* factor and the rallies organized and demands made by the community started to go unnoticed. For instance, the pre-election rally organized by *Matua Mahasangha* in Kolkata before the 2016 Assembly elections did not generate any headlines in the mainstream print and electronic media, unlike its previous pre-election rally before the 2011 Assembly elections, which had brought on the same dais high-profile political leaders cutting across political divide, like CPI(M)'s Gautam Deb and TMC's Mukul Roy.[18]

After remaining politically dormant for some time, the *Matuas* again started to make political headlines when the issue of National Register of Citizens (NRC) in Assam created a great deal of controversy.[19] More than 40 lakh of the 3.29 crore applicants in BJP-ruled Assam were left out of the draft NRC published on 31st July, 2018. The excluded 40 lakh people largely comprised of the Muslims, but large number of Bengali Hindus were also excluded from

---

17   Ayan Guha, "Caste Factor in West Bengal Elections," *Mainstream Weekly* 56, no. 33 (2016): 24.

18   Ayan Guha, "Is There A Second Wave of Dalit Upsurge in West Bengal?" *Economic and Political Weekly* 54, no. 2 (2019).

19   The National Register of Citizens (NRC) is a register containing names of all genuine Indian citizens. The register was first prepared after the 1951 Census of India and since then it has not been updated. At present, only Assam has such a register. The process to update NRC in Assam began following a Supreme Court order in 2013. The idea behind the NRC is to identify infiltrators who have been living in India illegally, detain them and deport them. As per the Assam Accord of 1985 foreigners who came to the state till March 24, 1971 will only be regularised as Indian citizens by the NRC.

the draft list. A vast majority of them were *Namasudras*.[20] According to Matua Mahasangha, nearly six lakh persons among the excluded belonged to the *Matua* sect.[21] After the publication of the NRC in Assam, BJP's stance on the NRC became a cause of concern for the *Namasudra* community in West Bengal. The BJP had demanded NRC like exercise in West Bengal too. The *Namasudras* found BJP's insistence on NRC in West Bengal quite perturbing. As many belonging to the *Namasudra* community had migrated to India after 1971 without official documents, they became afraid that their names might not appear in the NRC, in case of a similar exercise in West Bengal. In the context of the NRC issue the *Matuas* overcoming their political dissensions again started to regroup, regaining their collective power to some extent. Matua Mahasangha organised massive protests against the NRC in various parts of the state to prevent the possibility of a similar exercise in West Bengal.

The NRC issue opened up opportunities for the TMC to consolidate the support of the *Namasudras* and the party promptly seized this opportunity. The TMC government announced a number of measures for the community. In early November 2018, the West Bengal government declared its plan to set up development boards for the welfare of the *Namasudras* and the *Matuas*.[22] Most importantly, Mamata Banerjee paid a visit to the headquarters of Matua Mahasangha at Thakurnagar on 15th November, 2018 to attend an event held for the commencement of year-long celebrations of Boroma Binapani Devi's birth centenary. This visit came after a long gap of almost five years. Mamata Banerjee had last visited Thakurnagar while she was campaigning for the 2014 Lok Sabha polls. This visit thus, gave the indication that the *Matua* factor was again back in political reckoning. At the event, Mamata Banerjee announced the conferring of Bengal's highest civilian award, *Banga Vibhushan* on Boroma.[23] She also promised to set up a new university to be named after Harichand Thakur and

20   *Business Standard*, "Exclusion of Hindu Bengalis from Assam NRC Changing Political," September 22, 2019, https://www.business-standard.com/article/pti-stories/exclusion-of -hindu-bengalis-from-assam-nrc-changing-political-119092200259_1.html.

21   *Hindu*, "West Bengal Witnesses Protests against NRC," August 1, 2018, https://www.thehi ndu.com/news/national/other-states/west-bengal-witnesses-protests-against-nrc/arti cle24574853.ece.

22   Statesman News Service, "West Bengal to set up Separate Boards for Namasudras, Matuas before LS Polls," *Statesman*, November 6, 2018, https://www.thestatesman.com/cities/ west-bengal-to-set-up-separate-boards-for-namasudras-matuas-before-ls-polls-1502705 316.html.

23   Special Correspondent, "Mamata Showers Sops on Matuas," *Hindu*, November 16, 2018, https://www.thehindu.com/news/national/other-states/mamata-showers-sops-on-mat uas/article25511259.ece.

Guruchand Thakur, the founding fathers of the *Matua* sect, at a place named Chandpara, just five kilometers away from Thakurnagar.[24] All theses attempts by the TMC to politically mobilize the *Matua-Namasudra* community largely through symbolic measures suggests that the party is not ideologically averse to caste based mobilization unlike the CPI(M). But the TMC's mobilization of the *Matuas* has remained quite ad-hoc and sporadic with occasional recourse to mostly symbolic initiatives directed towards pandering to the sentiments of the community. The absence of any systematic blueprint for a sustained and large-scale mobilization of the community is quite evident. In contrast, the BJP since its emergence as a significant political player in the state has been attempting to mobilize the *Matuas* in accordance with a *Hindutva* blueprint, which is proving to be potent and effective.

2   BJP's *Matua* Outreach: A New Relationship

Since the 2009 general elections the *Matuas* by and large had supported the TMC. But the results of the 2019 general elections clearly indicated that the political support of an overwhelmingly large section of the community had moved towards the BJP. The *Matuas* are mainly concentrated in three Lok Sabha constituencies – Ranaghat, Bangaon and Krishnanagar. BJP comprehensively won Ranaghat and Bangaon with high vote shares while losing to the TMC in Krishnanagar by a narrow margin.[25] In the recently concluded 2021 Assembly elections the party did not perform as well as it had expected in the state as a whole but in the *Matua* belt it did very well wining most of the *Matua* dominated seats. It is possible to form some idea about the extent of *Matua* support the party has been able to garner from the Hindu CSDS-Lokniti post-poll survey (See Table 2). From this survey it is quite clear that there has been consistent erosion in the support base of the TMC among the *Namasudras*, while the BJP's vote share among the *Namasudras* has been seeing a steep rise. A majority of the *Namasudras* now seem to support the BJP electorally. What

---

24   All India Trinamool Congress Website, "Bangla CM Gifts a University to Thakurnagar On Boro Ma's Birth Centenary," http://aitcofficial.org/aitc/bangla-cm-gifts-a-university-to -thakurnagar-on-boro-mas-birth-centenary/.

25   In Krishnanagar the percentage of Muslim population is close to 40 percent. Therefore, it is quite certain that the BJP received majority of the *Matua* votes. This is because the BJP was unlikely to obtain any sizeable section of Muslim support and the vote share of the TMC candidate was 45 percent. See, Biswabrata Goswami, "Trinamool Congress may Find the Going Tough in Jhargram," *Statesman*, May 12, 2019 https://www.thestatesman.com/ elections-2019/tmc-may-find-going-tough- jhargram-1502754411.html.

TABLE 2   Percentage of Namasudra vote share

Party	Assembly elections, 2016	Lok sabha elections, 2019	Assembly elections, 2021
TMC	43	38	31
BJP	10	54	58

SOURCE: THE HINDU CSDS-LOKNITI POST-POLL SURVEY 2021

is striking is that the BJP despite performing poorly in the state in the 2021 Assembly elections compared to the its stellar performance in the 2019 Lok Sabha elections has increased its vote share among the *Namasudras* by 4 per-cent.[26] Electoral outcomes in those constituencies where the *Matuas* have a large presence also confirm the rising support of the BJP among the members of the community. Of those Assembly constituencies in two districts of Nadia and North 24 parganas, where the *Matuas* play the deciding role, the TMC won only five seats- Tehatta, Nabadwip, Habra, Ashoknagar, and Sandeshkhali and the BJP won thirteen- Chakdah, Santipur, Ranaghat Northeast, Ranaghat Northwest, Ranaghat South, Santipur, Krishnaganj, Kalyani, Haringhata, Bagdah, Bongaon Uttar, Bongaon Dakshin, and Gaighata. In these two districts, the BJP won mostly those seats which have a significant *Matua* population.[27]

To understand this shift in political allegiance of the *Matuas*, the current political narrative relating to the interconnected issues of citizenship, illegal Bangladeshi infiltration and persecution of Hindus in Bangladesh need to be closely examined. These issues are politically contentious and potentially polarising. They tend to excite and activate ideological biases. My plan here is not to assess the claims and counterclaims generally made on these issues by both sides across the ideological divide. I only intend to discover the impact of

26   The BJP could only manage to win 77 Assembly seats in 2021. Though it was no doubt a phenomenal improvement from three seats which it had won in the previous Assembly elections held in 2016, the overall results were disappointing for the party, as it had expected to win a comfortable majority (more than 147 seats). Its performance was far worse than its performance in 2019 Lok Sabha elections, where it had won 18 seats, just trailing behind TMC's 22 seats. In terms of Assembly segments, its 18 seats in 2019 would have translated into 121 Assembly seats, which is much higher than the 77 seats won by the party in 2021.

27   Snigdhendu Bhattacharya, "BJP Wins Pro-CAA Matua Votes But CAA to Hit Mamata Hurdle," *Outlook*, May 3, 2021.

the political narrative that is gaining ground around these issues on the role of caste in political mobilization, without attempting any scrutiny of the factual basis of this narrative.

It is argued quite forcefully by many that illegal infiltration has changed the demography of West Bengal, particularly the demography of those districts which border Bangladesh. Those who make this argument mainly furnish two evidences. One evidence is drawn from the figures of Indian censuses, which show a consistent rise in the proportion of Muslim population in West Bengal, particularly in the border districts of the state and a corresponding decline in the proportion of Hindu population (see tables 3 and 4). The other evidence is derived from the census figures of Bangladesh, which suggest that the share of Hindu population of Bangladesh has decreased from 22 percent in 1951 to 9.5 percent in 2001.[28] Whether and how far the rise in Muslim population is caused by illegal infiltration from Bangladesh are questions which are beyond the scope of this study, which is only concerned with the political ramifications of the current political discourse with regard to the issues of citizenship and illegal migration. The limited point that needs to be underscored in this context is that these census figures are frequently used in political debates and public conversation to link demographic change with illegal infiltration of Bangladeshi Muslims. As a result, over the years a public perception has crystallised that illegal infiltration of Bangladeshi Muslims is contributing to the steady rise of Muslim population and a consequent decline of the demographic strength of the Hindus. In other words, in the prevailing public narrative the growth of Muslim population is widely attributed to the unabated illegal migration of Bangladeshi Muslims. It is also widely believed that the Left Front Government in West Bengal consistently overlooked this serious problem. Rather, for the sake of vote bank politics, it gave some sort of clandestine recognition to illegal migrants by providing them with ration cards and other government documents.[29] As a result, the issue of illegal migration created strong undercurrents of socio-economic

---

28   See, Chandan Nandy, "Illegal Immigration from Bangladesh to India: The Emerging Conflicts" (Slifka Program in Inter-Communal Coexistence, Brandeis University, 2005), 152–157; Bimal Pramanik, "Illegal Migration from Bangladesh: A Case Study of West Bengal," in *Illegal Migration from Bangladesh*, ed. B.B.Kumar (Delhi: Astha Bharati, 2006), 140; Pushpita Das, *Illegal Migration from Bangladesh: Deportation, Border Fences and Work Permits*, Monograph Series no. 56 (New Delhi: Institute for Defence Studies and Analyses, 2016), 23, 31.

29   Sandip Bandyopadhyay, "Who are the *Matuas*," *Frontier Weekly* 43, no. 37 (2011); Kanchan Gupta, *Beyond the Poll Rhetoric of BJP's Contentious Citizenship Amendment Bill*, Special Report no. 89 (New Delhi: Observer Research Foundation, 2019).

TABLE 3   Population percentage of Hindus and Muslim in West Bengal (1951–2011)

Religious community	1951	1961	1971	1981	1991	2001	2011
Hindus	78.45	78.80	78.11	76.96	74.72	72.47	70.54
Muslims	19.85	20.00	20.46	21.51	23.61	25.25	27.01

SOURCE: CENSUS OF INDIA (1951–2001) DATA HAS BEEN TAKEN FROM MOHIT RAY, "ILLE-GAL MIGRATION AND UNDECLARED REFUGEES – IDEA OF WEST BENGAL AT STAKE," *DIA-LOGUE* 11, NO. 2 (2009). CENSUS 2011 DATA HAS BEEN TAKEN FROM HTTPS://WWW.CENSUS2 011.CO.IN/DATA/RELIGION/STATE/19-WEST-BENGAL.HTML

insecurity. But such concerns failed to obtain a political outlet with no major political party of West Bengal making the issue of illegal migration a major part of its political agenda. It is in this backdrop that the growing support of the BJP among the *Namasudras* needs to be understood. The recent political success of the BJP in West Bengal has been partly abetted by long-standing concerns among sections of Bengali Hindu voters over illegal migration of Bangladeshi Muslims, whom the BJP brands as 'Muslim infiltrators', and also by the growing resentment among certain sections over Mamata Banerjee's so-called pro-Muslim politics. The BJP has been able to achieve a fair degree of success in politically organizing the lower caste *Namasudras* against what it perceives as demographic invasion by the Muslims. Further, it has connected the issue of illegal infiltration with minority appeasement in order to create a political narrative to attract the *Namasudras* who are living with the memory of religious persecution.

Cracks in the *Matua* vote bank of the TMC first emerged with one section of the Matua Mahasangha aligning with the BJP before the 2014 national elections. But at that time the BJP was yet to become a powerful political force in the state and the *Matuas* by and large had supported the TMC till 2018–19. The BJP also faced considerable backlash from the *Namasudra* community after the publication of draft NRC in Assam on 31st July, 2018 as it had excluded a large number of *Namasudras*. But things started to change dramatically when the BJP led central government in its attempt to counter backlash on the issue of exclusion of Hindus from the NRC proposed to amend the Citizenship Act to fast track the grant of citizenship to non-Muslim immigrants from the neighbouring Islamic countries. The BJP government at the centre had first introduced such an amendment in 2016 but it got stalled due to widespread

TABLE 4   Population percentage of Hindus and Muslims in major border districts in West
Bengal (1951–2011)

District	1951 (Hindu percentage)	2011 (Hindu percentage)	1951 (Muslim Percentage)	2011 (Muslim percentage)
Maldah	62.92	47.99	36.97	51.27
Dinajpur	69.30	North Dinajpur-49.31 South Dinajpur-73.55	29.94	North Dinajpur-49.92 South Dinajpur-24.63
Murshidabad	44.60	33.21	55.24	66.27
24 Parganas	73.90	North 24 Parganas-73.46 South 24 Parganas-63.17	25.35	North 24 Parganas-25.82 South 24 Parganas-35.57
Nadia	77.03	72.15	22.36	26.76
Cooch Behar	70.90	74.06	28.94	25.54
Jalpaiguri	84.18	81.51	9.74	11.51
Darjiling	81.71	74.00	1.14	5.69

SOURCE: CENSUS OF INDIA (1951) DATA HAS BEEN TAKEN FROM BIMAL PRAMANIK, "INFIL-
TRATION FROM BANGLADESH: A CRITICAL ANALYSIS," *DIALOGUE* 10, NO. 2 (2008). CEN-
SUS 2011 DATA HAS BEEN TAKEN FROM HTTPS://WWW.CENSUS2011.CO.IN/DATA/RELIGION/
STATE/19-WEST-BENGAL.HTML

protests in the north-eastern states of India.[30] In order to showcase its intent
the BJP government at the centre re-introduced the proposed amendment
and got it passed from the Lok Sabha on 8th January, 2019. However, this
amendment could not be passed by the Rajya Sabha before the general elections in April-May 2019. In its election campaign the BJP gave assurance to
the *Matuas* that it would revive the lapsed amendment citizenship bill if
re-elected. It further assured that even those Hindu migrants who had been
left out of the NRC would be recognised as citizens after the enactment of

30   Protests in the north-eastern states were motivated by the fear that the proposed amend-
      ment would encourage migration from Bangladesh, threatening the identity, culture and
      livelihood of the native people.

the proposed Citizenship Amendment Act (henceforth referred to as CAA). Prime Minister Narendra Modi chose Thakurnagar, the headquarters of Matua Mahasangha, to start BJP's poll campaign in West Bengal for 2019 national elections. While addressing a massive crowd he made a strong pitch in favour of the CAA. During his Thakurnagar visit he met *Matua* matriarch Boroma Binapani Devi and touched her feet. Undoubtedly, it was a hugely significant symbolic gesture directed towards earning the goodwill of the *Matua* community.[31] It is primarily due to the promise of the enactment of the CAA that the political allegiance of the *Matuas* shifted to the BJP in the 2019 general elections. TMC's vehement opposition to the CAA also contributed to this shift.

After the 2019 general elections BJP's *Matua* outreach intensified further. After getting re-elected the BJP government at the centre got the CAA passed by the Parliament on 10th December, 2019.[32] Prime Minister Modi during his Bangladesh visit in March, 2021 visited Orakandi, a sacred place for the *Matuas*, where Harichand Thakur had founded the *Matua* sect. Interestingly, his visit to Orakandi coincided with the first phase of voting for the Assembly elections in West Bengal. Prime Minister Modi interacted with a delegation of the *Matua* community after offering *puja* (worship) at Harichand-Gurichand Temple. He also declared that the Indian government would upgrade one girl's middle school and set up a primary school in Orakandi.[33]

3 'Politics of Memory' and Political Narrative

Apparently, recent attempts by mainstream political parties to mobilize the *Namasudras* seem to suggest that, caste has finally arrived on the big stage of organized electoral politics of West Bengal. But if we delve a bit deeper, we

---

31   Ayan Guha, "Caste Politics, Secular Idiom," *Indian Express*, May 3, 2019.

32   CAA contains provisions to fast track the conferment of Indian citizenship on migrants belonging to all major religious faiths of the Indian sub-continent (Hindus, Sikhs, Parsis, Jains, Buddhists and Christians) except the Muslims, if they had entered India by 31st December, 2014 from Pakistan, Afghanistan and Bangladesh. It has reduced duration of residency from existing eleven years to just five years for them. Most importantly, they will no longer be treated as illegal immigrants. The rationale that has been furnished to justify this move is that the non-Muslims are facing severe religious persecution in these three Islamic countries. As persecuted Hindu refugees from Bangladesh the *Matuas* are expected to be the direct beneficiaries of this legislative measure.

33   Scroll Staff, "PM Modi Visits Temple in Orakandi in Bangladesh in Reach Out to Matua Community," *Scroll,* Mar 27, 2021, https://scroll.in/latest/990735/pm-modi-visits-temple-in-orakandi-in-bangladesh-in-reach-out-to-matua-community.

shall be able to encounter a different reality. On the surface the BJP's outreach to the *Matua* community appears as caste mobilization. At one level, by satisfying the long-standing demand of the lower caste Hindu refugees through the CAA, the BJP is attempting to posture itself as a defender of *dalit* interests. A number of top BJP leaders have made statements justifying the CAA as a pro-*dalit* legislative measure on the basis of the claim that most of the Hindu refugees to be benefited by the CAA are *dalits*. In December, 2019, at a rally in Delhi Prime Minister Modi asked his critics, "*Dalits*, who came here from Pakistan, among beneficiaries of citizenship law; why you can't see their pain".[34] Home Minister Amit Shah went a step further. While addressing a meeting of Delhi BJP workers in February, 2020 he said that the CAA would largely benefit the *dalit*s and therefore people opposing it were anti-*dalit*.[35] J.P Nadda, the working President of the BJP also termed the opponents of the legislation as anti-*dalit* while addressing a programme organized by a *dalit* group in December, 2019.[36]

Thus, it looks that the BJP is attempting to cultivate the support of *dalit* groups not only in West Bengal but across the country by projecting the CAA as a pro-*dalit* legislative measure. But a closer analysis will make it evident that this pro-*dalit* narrative is closely linked to the party's larger agenda of *Hinduization* of *dalit*s. BJP's *dalit* outreach through the CAA is directed towards the larger political goal of bringing about Hindu consolidation. First and foremost, the CAA is projected as a measure to safeguard the interests of the Hindu community. The displaced *dalit*s who happen to constitute the bulk of the proposed beneficiaries of this legislation are being promised the grant of citizenship because of their Hindu identity. In January, 2020 the BJP released a booklet to clarify doubts concerning this legislation in both English and Hindi. The Bengali version of the booklet released by the state BJP unit was mostly a translation of the Hindi publication, except for the additional reference to

---

34   *Economic Times Online*, "Delhi Rally: Modi Lashes out at Rivals for Spreading Lies over Citizenship Law," December 22, 2019, https://economictimes.indiatimes.com/news/polit ics-and-nation/land-ownership-to-40-lakh-people-narendra-modi/articleshow/72923 629.cms.

35   Staff Reporter, "Amit Shah Accuses Rahul, Priyanka, Kejriwal of Instigating Riots by Misleading People over Citizenship Amendment Act," *Hindu*, February 5, 2020, https:// www.thehindu.com/news/national/amit-shah-accuses-rahul-priyanka-kejriwal-of -instigating-riots-by-misleading-people-over-citizenship-amendment-act/article30484 670.ece.

36   Press Trust of India, "Those Opposing Citizenship Law are 'Anti-*Dalits*', Says JP Nadda," NDTV, December 29, 2019, https://www.ndtv.com/india-news/caa-protests-those-oppos ing-citizenship-act-are-anti-*Dalits*-says-jp-nadda-2156008.

the NRC. The English and Hindi versions have no mention of the NRC. Bengali version however, carries a question: "Is NRC coming next? How necessary is this? Won't Hindus, too, have to land in jails in case of an NRC, just like in Assam?" The answer says, "Yes, NRC comes next. At least that's the intention of the Union government". It further goes on to say, "We must make it clear that no Hindu in Assam landed in detention centres because of NRC. The Hindus who are allegedly in detention camps had landed there much before due to the Foreigners Act. The Foreigners Act was created by Congress and the NRC was implemented under orders from and supervision of the Supreme Court. The Assam government, on the other hand, has decided to move to the apex court against that NRC. Those detained in camps would hopefully get released soon due to CAA". The booklet concludes by stating that "after the passage of the Citizenship Amendment Bill (CAB), no Hindu, Sikh, Jain, Buddhist, Christian or Parsi will find their name in the D-voter' (doubtful voters) list. The Hindus and Sikhs have their homelands secured".[37] Thus, the BJP's political narrative on the CAA conveys an assuring message to the *Matuas* and other Hindu refugees that even if they are not included in the NRC, by virtue of being Hindus they will come under the purview of the CAA and rather than facing detention they will be granted citizenship. Thus, the BJP's *Matua* outreach is part of its broader strategy of *Hinduization* of *dalit*s. This marks a significant departure from the patterns of *Matua* mobilization, which until recently had relied upon politicisation of caste consciousness.

The idea behind the CAA is based upon a conceptual distinction between 'refugee' and 'infiltrator'. This has paved the way for politicisation of religion. Prime Minister Modi, during an election rally in West Bengal in 2014, declared: "People who enter India are of two types – illegal immigrants and refugees. The refugees are part of our family. India has a duty to respectfully rehabilitate them". On another occasion he said that the people who worship *Maa Durga* could remain in this country while the others who had crossed over with ulterior designs would have to leave.[38] This refugee-infiltrator distinction appears to be embedded in an ethno-religious premise as it aims to communicate a contrast between hapless and displaced Hindus and oppressive and encroaching Muslims. In West Bengal it caters to the BJP's overall

---

37   Hindustan Times, "CAA Saves Hindus from NRC Screening, Says Bengal BJP Booklet; Sets
      Up Row," January 6, 2020, https://www.hindustantimes.com/india-news/caa-saves-hin
      dus-from-nrc-screening-says-bengal-bjp-booklet-sets-up-row/story-gAH3tBvi1MbD1nj
      Dm3GoKP.html.
38   Ayan Guha, "West Bengal at Crossroads: An Insight into the Emerging Political Dynamics,"
      Mainstream Weekly 53, no. 14 (2015): 13.

political strategy of embracing Hindu migrants, mostly lower caste *Namsudra*s by treating them as persecuted Hindu refugees, while projecting infiltrator as the conceptual category for Bangladeshi Muslim immigrants. Thus, a political narrative has been constructed to lend legitimacy to the status of Hindu immigrants from Bangladesh such as the *Matuas* as persecuted refugees while delegitimizing the cross-border migration of Muslims as infiltration. This has paved the way for politicisation of the memory of religious persecution faced by the *Namasudras* during the Partition in 1947 and afterwards. It is this process of politicisation of collective memory that needs to be seriously unpacked to understand the nature of the current patterns of *Matua* mobilization. Maurice Halbwachs, who is widely credited for producing the earliest systematic study on collective memory, argues that human memory can only function within a collective context. Memory for him is a fundamentally social phenomenon. Individual acts of recollection are dependent on social structures and institutions like family, religion, class, nation-state etc. Collective memory is socially constructed and its construction is influenced by the needs of the present times. Therefore, it is also selective based on selective remembrance of past occurrences directed towards producing a validation of a particular narrative in tune with present necessities. This also implies that memory is by nature plural. In other words, different groups select different memories to interpret and make sense of present issues and current concerns. That is why different groups of people possess different collective memories, which in turn result in different modes of behaviour.[39] Pierre Nora by expanding Halbwach's analysis emphasizes that collective memory is both an instrument and object of power. Collective memory according to Nora "remains in permanent evolution, open to the dialectic of remembering and forgetting, unconscious of its successive deformations, vulnerable to manipulation and appropriation, susceptible to being long dormant and periodically revived".[40] In line with this 'presentist' approach towards the conceptualisation of collective memory, it is possible to understand the political behaviour of the *Matuas* as an outcome of their collective memory shaped by present socio-political dynamics.

The BJP has traditionally seen the Hindu refugees as a potential support base and its campaign in Assam and Bengal has always revolved around the issue of consistent increase of the Muslim population in border districts due to illegal infiltration. While demographic change in border districts is considered

---

39   See, Maurice Halbwachs, *On Collective Memory*, trans. Lewis A. Coser (Chicago: University of Chicago Press, 1992).

40   Pierre Nora, "Between Memory and History: Les Lieux de Mémoire," *Representations* 26, no. 1 (1989): 8.

a reality by many, the BJP and the RSS (Rashtriya Swayamsevak Sangh) have gone a step further by equating demographic change with demographic invasion or an organized conspiracy to turn West Bengal into an Islamic land. RSS Weekly Organiser had warned as early as in 1991 of a conspiracy to "convert the border areas into Muslim-dominated areas, so that they (Muslims) can finally raise a plea for their annexation to Bangladesh or to increase the Muslim population in India so that in due course they will be demanding more and more rights for the Muslims in a planned and organised way".[41] Similarly, an article published in 2008 in the magazine *Dialogue*, a publication of Astha Bharati, an organization affiliated to the RSS talked about a similar kind of conspiracy:

> A long term plan of forcing out Hindus from the border region of West Bengal is evidently in operation ... . Islamic fundamentalists operating in Bangladesh as well as in India are encouraging Muslim infiltration to reduce pressure of population on Bangladesh, and to expand Islamic influence in the border region so that the Hindu population living in this area is forced to leave the region out of fear, particularly, all the Muslim dominated Subdivisions and Blocks of the entire Indo-Bangladesh border. Hindus are selling their hearth and home at a throw away prices to the Muslims. Over and above, the anti-social elements of this border region, hand in glove with Bangladeshi Muslims, are creating a fear psychosis among the Hindu community. Theft, robbery, rape and murder of the Hindus are routinely performed. The administrative machinery of the Left Front government is politically motivated and remains a silent spectator in this regard.[42]

In fact, the refugee-infiltrator distinction is not a new one. Infiltration has always remained an issue of concern in West Bengal. But the BJP has recently politicised this issue like never before by linking infiltration with minority appeasement in order to bring about electoral consolidation of the Hindus. Michael Gillian's analysis of BJP's discourse on Bangladeshi migration finds in the narrative of the BJP-RSS several references to this distinction, which suggests that its origin could very well go back to as far as early to mid 1980s.[43] Speaking to the *Frontline* magazine in 2007, the then state president of the

---

41   Michael Gillan, "Refugees or Infiltrators? The Bharatiya Janata Party and 'Illegal' Migration from Bangladesh," *Asian Studies Review* 26, no. 1 (2002):86.

42   Bimal Pramanik, "Infiltration from Bangladesh: A Critical Analysis," *Dialogue* 10, no. 2 (2008).

43   See, Gillan, "Refugees or Infiltrators?,"73–95.

BJP, Tathagata Roy had also made a clear distinction between Hindu and Muslim immigrants, calling the former asylum-seeking refugees and the latter illegal immigrants.[44] Hence, this discourse is not a recent innovation. But earlier it could not gain much acceptability due to the countervailing force of Bengaliness or a sense of common linguistic identity which was able to override religious divisions.[45] But now due to the rise of the BJP as the principal opposition party in the state and the enactment of the CAA, the refugee-infiltrator distinction has gained greater social and political currency particularly among the *Matuas*, who expect to derive benefits due to the enactment of the CAA.

In BJP's political discourse on the CAA the Partition of Bengal in 1947 is a key temporal reference point. The party links the rationale of the CAA with events connected to the Partition. In projecting the CAA as the ultimate solution to the unfinished business of the Partition, the memory of Partition is being repeatedly invoked. A document entitled *The Constitutionality of the Citizenship Amendment Act and Why it was Essential?* published by Dr. Syama Prasad Mookerjee Research Foundation (SPMRF), a think-tank affiliated to the BJP and tasked with social and intellectual outreach in West Bengal explains the rationale of the CAA in terms of the Nehru-Liaquat Pact, signed between India and Pakistan in 1950. The document argues that, unlike India, Pakistan has failed to honour the Nehru-Liaquat Pact, which rejecting exchange of population as a solution to the communal problem had committed both India and Pakistan to provide safety and security to their religious minorities. Attributing the rationale of the CAA to the abject failure of Pakistan to protect its minorities, it states that, "the intent was to give rights to the immigrant who were flowing in and who had settled as an unfinished task of the partition".[46] Thus, by raking up the Partition and the following events of atrocities on the Hindus, a conscious effort is being made to politicise collective memory of the displaced communities. The historical event of Partition as a result, has gained unprecedented currency in the current political discourse of the state, fuelling a process of politicisation of collective memory. The *Namasudras*, who account for the bulk of the displaced and persecuted Hindus, are the main target of this project of politicisation of historical memory. SPMRF has also

44   Suhrid Sankar Chattopadhyay, "Constant traffic," *Frontline*, June 15, 2007, https://frontline
      .thehindu.com/cover-story/article30191822.ece.

45   Rizwana Shamshad, "Bengaliness, Hindu Nationalism and Bangladeshi Migrants in West
      Bengal, India," *Asian Ethnicity* 18, no. 4 (2017): 433–451.

46   Ayush Anand and Shubhendu Anand, eds., *Constitutionality of the Citizenship Amendment
      Act, 2019 and Why it was Essential* (New Delhi: Dr. Syama Prasad Mookerjee Research
      Foundation, 2020), 38–39.

come up with an important white paper on the CAA. Describing the CAA as a landmark legislative measure directed towards resolving the citizenship woes of the *Matua* community, it states:

> The case of *Matua* Community which constitutes a large section of *Namasudras* in Bengal is really heart rending. A large section of this community migrated in West Bengal in 1960s to save their Hindu roots from the atrocities inflicted by Islamists in East Pakistan.[47]

The white paper goes on to say-

> One thing is for sure that her (Mamata Banerjee's) opposition of NRC or her concerns about Citizenship Bill are not moved by genuine concerns of Hindu Bengali refugees, but who she cares is the interests of Illegal Bangladeshi Muslim Infiltrators who want to overtake the entire Bengal and *repeat 1947* [emphasis added]. She opposed the bill with a single point agenda of appeasing the Islamists in Bengal who want to turn it into another Pakistan with every passing day.[48]

This narrative has the potential to produce long term implications by shaping the consciousness of religiously persecuted groups like the *Matuas* in a particular political direction. It imagines a historical continuum that connects an unpalatable past with a disagreeable present leading up to a dreadful future, and this continuum has been constructed through the invocation and politicisation of a collective historical memory. A few interconnected aspects of this narrative are noteworthy. First, there is a clear attempt to *hinduize* the *Matua* identity by highlighting its Hindu roots. Second, the opposition to the CAA is interpreted as Muslim appeasement and endorsement of illegal infiltration of Muslims from Bangladesh. Lastly, highlighting continuous infiltration of Bangladeshi Muslims, an apprehension is raised about an impending Muslim takeover of the entire state, resulting in a repetition of the events of the Partition in 1947. 'Repeat of 1947' clearly alludes to the persecution of the Hindus displaced after the Partition. This analogical remembrance of the past is a familiar form of 'politics of memory'. As Peter J. Verovšek points out, when politics is conducted through the remembrance of the past this kind of

---

47   Ayush Anand and Shubhendu Anand, eds., *White Paper on Citizenship Amendment Act* (New Delhi: Dr. Syama Prasad Mookerjee Research Foundation, 2020), 20.
48   Anand and Anand eds., *White Paper,* 21.

historical analogy is often used to frame and conceptualize important issues of the present times.[49]

The attempts to politicise collective historical memory also become quite evident in the way the violent anti-CAA protests that broke out in different parts of West Bengal from 13th December to 15th December, 2019 has been interpreted. A report authored by Dr. Mohit Ray (along with Sujit Sikdar), the convener of West Bengal BJP's refugee cell compared the anti-CAA violence of December, 2019 with the Direct Action Day (16th August, 1946), when violent anti-Hindu riots had been orchestrated in Calcutta by the Muslim League government of undivided Bengal. The report points out several similarities between the Direct Action Day and violent protests by the Muslims against the CAA between 13th December and 15th December, 2019. It highlights that both started on Friday or *Jummabar* and that in both cases the strategy was to frighten the Hindus. Further, according to this report deliberate police inaction marked both these unfortunate incidents. Finally, in terms of objective behind these incidents, the report also finds a pattern. It argues that while the riots of August, 1946 had been motivated by the desire to include the whole of undivided Bengal into Pakistan, the violent anti-CAA agitation in West Bengal was aimed at transforming West Bengal into an extension of Pakistan or 'West Bangladesh', a term frequently used by the BJP supporters and leaders. The report concludes with a question for readers to ponder over: "if infiltrators are not resisted now, the West Bengal of tomorrow will become West Bangladesh. Are you ready to become a refugee again?"[50] 'West Bangladesh' has become a widely used political idiom in BJP's campaign to raise the issue of demographic change or rapid increase of Muslim population and also the growing assertiveness of the Muslims resulting out of Muslim appeasement. A Bengali e-book uploaded on the West Bengal BJP's website entitled *Poschimbonger Astitva Rakhhai Natunbhabe Bhabtei Hobe* (We Must Think Afresh to Save the Existence of West Bengal) also states that now it is time to ask whether the very existence of West Bengal is in deep crisis:

> The entire Hindu society in West Bengal is in danger. When in Deganga, Kaliachak and Dhulagarh the homes of the Hindus were set ablaze no distinction was made between the supporters of the TMC, CPI(M) and BJP. All Hindus came under attack. But have you heard the TMC, CPI(M) or

---

49   Peter J. Verovšek, "Collective Memory, Politics, and the Influence of the Past: The Politics of Memory as a Research Paradigm," *Politics, Groups, and Identities* 4, no. 3 (2016): 529.

50   Mohit Ray and Sujit Sikdar, *Analysing the Anti CAA Violence in West Bengal*, trans. Ahana Chaudhuri (SPMRF and Refugee Cell, BJP West Bengal, 2020).

Congress to ever talk about this? In Nadia's Juranpur when five Scheduled Caste individuals were murdered by Muslim miscreants no Scheduled Caste organization or political party came forward to protest. All these events raise the question- whether West Bengal was created 70 years ago for this purpose? Lakhs of refugee families who have taken shelter in West Bengal to escape from Islamic Pakistan or Bangladesh would never have anticipated destruction of their homes and exploitation of their women at the hands of Muslim criminals in West Bengal too.[51]

This narrative has better scope of purchase among the religiously persecuted group of Bangladeshi immigrants, particularly the *Matuas,* possessing still fresh in their minds, a collective memory of forced displacement and victimization. They are more susceptible to the fear of an uncertain future expressed by *Hindutva* politics. This is also because the circumstances surrounding their migration were different from those which had led the higher caste Hindus to migrate from East Pakistan to West Bengal in the immediate aftermath of the Partition in 1947. In the popular and dominant narrative of Partition all East Bengali migrants are simplistically portrayed as Bengali Hindu refugees. The overarching 'Hindu' label conceals differences in the caste identities of the refugees. This has resulted in non-recognition of the diversity of experiences faced by Bengali Hindu migrants and of the role of caste identity in shaping such diversity of experiences.[52] Most of the upper caste families who had relatively more economic resources and cultural capital swiftly crossed over to West Bengal immediately after Partition. Of the 1.1 million Hindus who had migrated from East Pakistan to West Bengal by 1st June 1948, 350000 belonged to urban middle classes and 555000 belonged to the rural middle classes.[53] Only a few of them could manage to arrange sale or exchange of their properties in East Bengal but because of being equipped with social and cultural capital they were in a position to restart their professional career in West Bengal. Their exodus was mainly motivated by a fear of losing *dhon* (property) and *maan* (honour) rather than *pran* (life). On the other hand, many lower caste families largely dependent on manual labour were not in a position to immediately leave their traditional cultivable land due to livelihood concerns

---

51   Mohit Ray, *Poschimbonger Astitva Rakhhai Natunbhabe Bhabtei Hobe* (Kolkata: Bharatiya Samaskriti Trust, 2017), 2.

52   Carola Erika Lorea, "Religion, Caste, and Displacement: The Matua Community," *Oxford Research Encyclopedia of Asian History* (2020): 12.

53   Prafulla Kumar Chakrabarti, *The Marginal Men: The Refugees and the Left Political Syndrome in West Bengal* (Kalyani: Lumiere Books, 1990), 1.

and lack of family connections on the other side of the border. Many of them also stayed back as one of their tallest leaders Jogendranath Mandal reposed faith in *dalit*-Muslim alliance. Mandal who shared a great rapport with Jinnah and a close association with Muslim League, felt that *dalit* interests would be better protected in Pakistan. After the Partition, Mandal became a member of Pakistan's Constituent Assembly in 1947. He was later appointed as Pakistan's first Law and Labour Minister. But he could not prevent the religious persecution of the *dalit*s and ultimately becoming thoroughly disillusioned with the state of affairs in Pakistan resigned from his cabinet position and left Pakistan to settle in West Bengal. In the 1950s, the migration of lower caste refugees, belonging to *Namasudra*, *Mahishya* and *Sadgope* communities started, triggered by communal violence in December, 1949 in Khulna. They were mainly peasants and agricultural labourers who were initially hesitant to migrate to West Bengal. But constant threat to their *pran* (life) forced them to leave East Pakistan.[54]

The migration of lower caste refugees, mostly the *Namasudras* occurred in waves. In Punjab the refugee influx was mostly over by 1949. But in Bengal, Partition induced migration did not stop so quickly. Exodus of Hindu refugees, mostly comprising the *Namasudras* kept happening following major events of communal disturbances.[55] Ishita Dey finds out that the years when significant refugee influx happened were 1947, 1948, 1950, 1960, 1962, 1964 and 1970.[56] The largest exodus happened in 1970–71 during the Bangladesh liberation war

---

54 Anasua Basu Raychaudhury, *Life after Partition: A Study on the Reconstruction of Lives in West Bengal.* Panel 33: Ethnic Cleansing, Migration, and Resettlement: Partition and Post-Partition Experiences, Proceedings of the 18th European Association for South-Asian Studies, Sweden: Swedish South Asian Studies Network (2004): 1–15; Also see, Joya Chatterjee, *The Spoils of Partition: Bengal and India, 1947–1967* (New Delhi: Cambridge University Press, 2018), 107–119.

55 For an analysis of the reasons and impact of refugee influx into West Bengal see, Sekhar Bandyopadhyay and Anasua Basu Ray-Chaudhury, "In Search of Space: The Scheduled Caste Movement in West Bengal after Partition," *Policies and Practices* 59 (Kolkata: Mahanirban Calcutta Research Group, 2014); Willem van Schendel, *The Bengal Borderland: Beyond State and Nation in South Asia* (London: Anthem, 2005); Abhijit Dasgupta, "The Puzzling Numbers: The Policies of Counting 'Refugees' in West Bengal," *South Asian Refugee Watch* 2, no. 2 (2000): 64–73; Anindita Ghosal, "Acquisition of Rehabilitation Rights by East Bengal Refugees Post- 1947," *Proceedings of the Indian History Congress* 70 (2009–10): 1210–1219; Sarbani Banerjee, "Different Identity Formations in Bengal Partition Narratives by Dalit Refugees," *Interventions* 19, vol. 4 (2017): 550–565; Archit Basu Guha-Choudhury, "Engendered Freedom: Partition and East Bengali Migrant Women," *Economic and Political Weekly* 44, no. 49 (2009): 66–69.

56 Ishita Dey, "On the Margins of Citizenship: Principles of Care and Rights of the Residents of the Ranaghat Women's Home, Nadia District," *Refugee Watch* 33 (2009): 9.

in response to unprecedented violence unleashed upon the East Bengalis by Pakistan's military. A distinction is generally drawn between migration due to economic reason, which is a pull factor and migration due to religious reason, which is a push factor. Both Hindus and Muslims migrate in search of better economic opportunities. But it is generally believed that it is the Muslims who mostly migrate for economic reasons. Insecurity of life due to religious persecution acts as a major push factor behind migration of the Hindus.[57] A report of Indian Statistical Institute on undocumented Bangladeshi migrants has found that political instability, fear of riots and terrorism, inhuman attitude and activities of political leaders, absence of democratic rights, Muslim domination, religious instigation by political leaders, insecurity feeling of Hindus, are major push factors behind migration of the Hindus from Bangladesh. About 59 percent of the respondents interviewed by the author of the report expressed that religious fundamentalism/insecurity/discriminating law and order against Hindus caused their migration. According to this report these were the major factors behind mass exodus of the Hindu population from Bangladesh up to 1971. Afterwards economic factors also came into play, but the factors mentioned above continued to cause displacement of people, and from mid 2001 onwards they again became predominant causing more Hindu migration.[58] Another survey conducted among a total of 100 migrant households has also found that insecurity, riots and religious oppression worked together as the major push factors behind cross border migration. These factors caused 56 families out of a total sample of 100 families to migrate from Bangladesh to West Bengal, while only 11 families migrated due to economic hardships.[59] Furthermore, economic hardship is also not fully divorced from communal dynamics. Land grabbing of the Hindu peasantry with the help of Enemy (Vested) Property laws is widespread in Bangladesh.[60] These laws allow

---

57   See, Sharat G. Lin and Madan C. Paul, "Bangladeshi Migrants in Delhi: Social Insecurity, State Power, and Captive Vote Banks," *Bulletin of Concerned Asian Scholars* 27, vol. 1 (1995): 3–20.

58   Pranati Datta, *Push-Pull Factors of Undocumented Migration from Bangladesh to West Bengal: A Perception Study*, Qualitative Report, *Indian Statistical Institute*, vol. 9, no. 2 (2004): 335–358.

59   Jyoti Parimal Sarkar, *Bangladeshi Migration to West Bengal: A Cause of Concern* (New Delhi: Centre for the Study of Regional Development, Jawaharlal Nehru University, 2008).

60   It has been estimated that as a result of the Enemy Property Act/ Vested Property Act 1.2 million Hindu families accounting for about 43 percent of all Hindu households have become affected. The Hindus have lost around 2.01 million acres of land, which accounts for 5.5 percent of Bangladesh's total land and 45 percent of land owned by the Hindu community. See, Abul Barkat, et al, *Deprivation of Hindu Minority in Bangladesh: Living with Vested Property* (Dhaka: Pathak Shamabesh, 2008). Also see, Pranab Kumar Panday,

the government to confiscate land of those people identified as the enemies of the state. They are mostly applied to the Hindu families with one or more family members outside the country, causing continuing influx of Bengali Hindus from Bangladesh to West Bengal. It is mainly the Hindu peasantry of Bangladesh, mostly composed of the *Namasudras* who are systematically robbed of their land through the use of Enemy (Vested) Property laws. This leaves them with little option but to migrate to West Bengal. Land grabbing is one of the major reasons why the bulk of the Hindu migration from Bangladesh continues to be accounted for by the lower castes, mainly the *Namasudras* who are largely dependent on cultivation.[61] Thus, the lower castes migrated under much more challenging conditions and faced much greater degree of actual violence or threat of violence compared to the caste Hindus. Further, their displacement is much more recent than that of the caste Hindus, most of whom had left East Pakistan in the immediate aftermath of the Partition. Hence, the *Namasudras'* memory of displacement is more bitter and fresh compared to that of the caste Hindus. As a result, they are likely to be more receptive to the BJP's narrative. Being loaded with religious undercurrents the refugee-infiltrator distinction offers a perfect recipe for religious polarization in the *Matua* belt bordering Bangladesh. The refugee-infiltrator distinction as well as TMC's vociferous opposition to the CAA created a fertile ground for Hindu consolidation in favour of the BJP in *Matua*-dominated constituencies and constituencies close to the Indo-Bangladesh border in the 2019 general elections.[62] BJP was able to make significant inroads into the *Matua* belt of South Bengal. It registered comprehensively victories in *Matua* dominated Ranaghat and Bangaon constituencies with high vote share of 53 percent and 49 percent respectively. Clearly, it was BJP's promise of the enactment of the CAA during election campaigns which turned the tide in its favour in the *Matua* belt of South Bengal. As already pointed out, in the recently concluded 2021 Assembly elections too the BJP won most of those seats where *Matuas* have a high concentration.

"Politics of Land Grabbing: The Vested Property Act and the Exploitation of Hindu Communities in Bangladesh," *International Journal on Minority and Group Right* 23, no. 3 (2016): 382–401; Taslima Yasmin, "The Enemy Property Laws in Bangladesh: Grabbing Lands under the Guise of Legislation," *Oxford University Commonwealth Law Journal* 15, no. 1 (2015): 121–147.

61   Ranabir Samaddar, *The Marginal Nation* (Delhi: Sage, 1999), 91–92.

62   Ayan Guha, "Polarization Plus Anti-incumbency: A Full Scale View of BJP's Rise in Bengal," *Mainstream Weekly* 57, no. 34 (2019).

Consistent electoral success of the BJP in *Matua* dominated areas suggests that the BJP's 'politics of memory' has found substantial resonance among the *Matuas*. Under favourable circumstances historical memory despite being based on past occurrences has the potential to emerge as a powerful factor in contemporary politics. As Peter J. Verovšek quite instructively points out, "while the politics of memory is rooted in the past, its illocutionary content, that is, the desired communicative effect of these discourses, is motivated by contemporary political considerations. In many cases, memory has real perlocutionary consequences, changing the way that important actors think about and react to situations in the present".[63] To comprehend the actual working of the 'politics of memory' on the *Namasudra* minds and to assess the depth of Hindu consciousness among them I conducted interviews with several *Namasudra* individuals who are either ground level political workers or activists connected to the *Matua* movement. I also engaged in informal conversation with numerous people belonging to the *Matua* sect. Those I interviewed are mostly based in areas which fall within the *Matua* belt in Nadia's Ranaghat Lok Sabha constituency. I also came into contact with a group of *Matua* refugees who live in abject poverty in a refugee colony in Howrah's Uluberia. Through these conversations I have been able to discover that the increasing association of the leaders of the *Matua* community with the BJP has impacted the political language and worldview of the members of the community. But the process of *Hinduization* of the *Matua* movement has been a long and continuing process, which has now received a strong and fresh impetus due new and emerging political circumstances. To understand the receptivity of *Hindutva* politics among the members of the anti-Brahmanical *Matua* sect, it is imperative to first probe the evolving character of the *Matua* movement by placing it in the wider context of *dalit* and caste movements in India. Thereafter, we shall explore the ground level political narrative among the *Matuas*.

4   Contextualising *Dalit* mobilization in West Bengal

Gail Omvedt identifies two strands within the *dalit* movement: one integrationist or reformist and the other autonomous or radical. The former aims to reform Hinduism by removing caste hierarchy and untouchability and was represented by Gandhi's Harijan movement, Congress leader Jagjivan

---

63   Verovšek, "Collective Memory," 530.

Ram, *dalit* leaders associated with Hindu Mahasabha such as M.C Rajah and G.A Gavai and many other prominent leaders like Arigay Ramaswamy in Hyderabad, Kisan Faguji Bansode in Nagpur, V.R Shinde in Bombay Presidency and Murugesh Pillai in Mysore. The latter strand asserts radical autonomy from Hinduism claiming to adopt a non-Hindu identity and was represented by leaders like Bhagya Reddy Varma in Hyderabad, by much of the Adi-Andhra movement and most famously by Ambedkar.[64] Despite resorting to this radicalism versus reformism binary in her analysis and identifying a clear and well-developed reformist trend within the *dalit* movement, Omvedt surprisingly characterizes the entire *dalit* movement as an anti-systemic movement which seeks transformation of the basic structure of Indian society. Eva-Maria Hardtmann takes issue with this characterization, criticizing Omvedt's analytical strategy of placing reformers and anti-caste radicals within the same movement. According to Hardtmann, Omvedt has mistakenly downplayed the difference between two traditions of opposition again caste. These two traditions, one 'Hindu caste reform tradition' and the other 'autonomous anti-caste tradition' in Hardtmann's view are not only different but also conflicting to one another and therefore, they must be seen as separate movements. According to Hardtmann various caste associations and caste federations by and large functioned within the Hindu caste reform tradition as they were working for the upliftment of socio-economic status of lower castes through social and religious reforms. On the other hand, the *dalit* movement with its claim for an identity separate from the Hindus began in the 1920s with the *Adi* movement (Adi-Dharm movement in Punjab and Adi-Hindu movement in today's Uttar Pradesh). From the 1930s to 1950s an autonomous anti-caste strand crystallized under B.R Ambedkar as its main spokesperson. In the 1960s and 1970s it was carried forward by *Dalit Sahitya* (literature) and Dalit Panthers.[65]

Christophe Jaffrelot in his analysis of caste movements has re-casted this autonomy versus reformism binary by highlighting a contrast between two kinds of strategies followed by different caste movements- *ethnicization* and *sanskritization*. Rather than focusing his attention only on untouchable castes, he has studied all caste-based movements, i.e. movements led by untouchable castes as well as those led by other backward castes. Interestingly, Jaffrelot has also factored in the regional divide, by arguing that *sanskritization* characterized the caste movements of North India while the caste movements of

---

64   Gail, Omvedt, *Dalits and the Democratic Revolution: Dr. Ambedkar and the Dalit Movement in Colonial India* (New Delhi: Sage, 1994), 10, 132, 163.

65   Eva-Maria Hardtmann, *The Dalit Movement in India: Local Practices, Global Connections* (New Delhi: Oxford University Press, 2009), 45–86.

southern and western parts of India adopted a different strategy of *ethnicization*. *Sanskritization* refers to the tendency of the lower castes to improve their social position by emulating the behaviour and ways of life of the upper castes.[66] It leads to a positional change of the concerned caste groups within the caste system, not any structural change of the system itself. On the other hand, *ethnicization* for Jaffrelot implies the tendency of the lower castes to invent and acquire an alternative ethnic identity in order to reject their Hindu caste identity and to simultaneously adopt a culture that is distinct from that of the wider Hindu society. Through the examples of a number of prominent caste associations of North India, such as Ahir Yadav Kshatriya Mahasabha, All India Kurmi Kshatriya Mahasabha, Adi-Hindu movement of Swami Acchutanand, Jatav Conference and the Bundelkhand Prantia Kori Sabha, Jaffrelot shows that they all worked to elevate the ritual status of the castes they represented in the Hindu caste hierarchy in order to escape untouchability and degrading social status. Their goal was therefore to rise within the caste system not to annihilate it. On the other hand, led by non-Brahman and *Dravidian* movements the lower and backward castes in South India and also in western parts of India claimed themselves as the descendants of India's original inhabitants or *Dravidians* in opposition to the Brahmans, who were portrayed as the descendants of the foreign Aryan conquerors and were accused of imposing Hindu culture including its caste system on the indigenous society. Thus, through the use of the idiom of ethnicity several lower and backward castes in South India and West India attempted to articulate a common racial identity as an alternative to their Hindu caste identity, thereby causing a break with the Hindu culture and value system. The main ideological architects of *Dravidianism* were Jyotirao Phule and E.V Ramaswamy Naicker, alias Periyar. Influenced by their ideology, several non-Brahman South Indian associations adopted the name '*Dravida*' and the term '*Adi*'-meaning initial or primordial in their titles. In this way influential caste associations like Adi-Dravida Mahajan Sabha and Adi-Andhra Mahajan Sabha came into existence.[67]

Based on the insights derived from the above discussion, it can be underlined that with regard to the characterization of caste-based movements, a broad distinction has been drawn between Hindu reformist caste movement and an autonomous non-*Hinduized* caste movement. The key distinction

---

66   The concept of *sanskritization* was originally advocated by M.N Srinivas. See, M.N Srinivas, *Religion and Society among the Coorgs of South India* (Oxford: Oxford University Press, 1952).

67   Christophe Jaffrelot, "Sanskritization vs. Ethnicization in India: Changing Identities and Caste Politics before Mandal," *Asian Survey* 40, no. 5 (2000): 756–766.

between these two traditions concerns their attachment or non-attachment to Hinduism. The reformist caste movements derive their rationale for reform from the need to improve the state of the Hindu society, thus demonstrating some sense of inherent emotional attachment to the Hindu religion. This sense of emotional attachment is conspicuously absent in radical anti-caste tradition that by equating Brahmanism with Hinduism calls for complete abnegation of Hindu religion. However, this distinction between Hindu reformist caste movement and autonomous non-*Hinduized* caste movement can't be always applied in an unproblematic manner to all caste-based movements. This is mainly because some of the caste-based movements which had claimed to invent a separate identity vis-a-vis Hinduism, in practice demonstrated a great deal of ambivalence in respect of their relationship with Hinduism. For instance, though the activists of the Adi Dharm movement in Punjab in the 1920s claimed that they were not Hindus, they derived their inspiration from the *Bhakti* tradition and a sixteenth century *Bhakti* poet Ravidas, which are placed securely within the larger Hindu fold.[68] Thus, even in case of radical anti-caste movements the break with Hinduism was never complete. The same dilemma has also confronted the Ambedkarites or neo-Buddhists who in their fight against caste have given up their Hindu identity and converted to Buddhism undergoing what Eleanor Zelliot describes as *pali-ization* as opposed to *sanskritization*.[69] Anupama Rao has also argued that the conversion of the *dalits* into Buddhism was preceded by their political conversion into a non-Hindu minority as Ambedkar had positioned the *dalits* as a non-Hindu minority.[70] However, in reality the radical *dalits'* relationship with Hinduism has not undergone a full fledged divorce. Owen Lynch's study on the *Jatavs* of Agra in Uttar Pradesh brings out the complex relationship of the neo-Buddhists with Hinduism. Lynch has observed that though most of the converted *Jatavs* regard themselves as Buddhists, they continue to practice Hindu rituals and celebrate Hindu festivals. Lynch, therefore, argues that they are both Hindus and Buddhists at the same time. Buddhism for them is a system of belief or a social philosophy and interestingly, they identify Buddhism not with the teachings of Buddha but with Ambedkarism or teachings and deeds of Ambedkar. On the other hand, they practice Hinduism as a system of rites and rituals.[71] Neera Burra's fieldwork among 102 neo-Buddhist respondents

68   Hardtmann, *The Dalit Movement in India*, pp. 56–58.

69   Eleanor Zelliot, "Buddhism and Politics in Maharashtra," in *South Asian Politics and Religion*, ed. Donald E. Smith (Princeton: Princeton University Press, 1966), 205.

70   Anupama Rao, *The Caste Question: Dalits and the Politics of Modern India* (Ranikhet: Permanent Black, 2019), 118–160.

71   Owen M. Lynch, *The Politics of Untouchability* (Delhi: Gautam Book Centre, 2015), 159–163.

belonging to the *Mahar* caste also presents more or less similar findings. She has found the presence of the images of Hindu Gods and Goddesses along with pictures of Buddha and Ambedkar in *Mahar* households. She has also noticed the continuing practice by most of the respondents of Hindu ritual practices. While identifying a change in the self-perception of the converted *Mahars*, she notes that they describe themselves as Buddhists not to reject Hinduism but only to signal to the higher castes that they no longer remain untouchables. The religious aspects of Buddhism, its rituals and rites have not become integrated into their everyday life. Therefore, Burra argues that the despite conversion to Buddhism the inner core of the consciousness of the neo-Buddhist *Mahars* remains Hindu.[72] Nicolas Jaoul's fieldwork among the neo-Buddhist Dalit Panther activists in Kanpur has also yielded to a number of interesting findings further problematizing radical *dalits*' relationship with Hindu religion. Jaoul has found out that in the households of the activists of the Dalit Panther movement Hindu rituals are performed during marriage ceremonies along with neo-Buddhist rituals. Even the women of such households religiously perform Hindu rituals during Hindu festivals and visit Hindu temples defying the diktats of the male members.[73] Jaoul has also discovered a tendency even among staunch neo-Buddhists to retain popular figures of the Hindu mythology in their socio-political discourse though they claim to dissociate from Hinduism. Dalit Panthers in Kanpur celebrate *Bauddh Diksha* (Ambedkar's conversion to Buddhism) as *Ravan Mela* and claim that Ravana was a virtuous king and most importantly a Buddhist.[74] Thus, far from a complete discursive dissociation from Hindu religion and mythology, the autonomous anti-caste tradition's strategy of opposition to Hinduism is itself rooted in selective borrowing and inversion of ideas and symbols drawn from Hinduism. This strategy can be traced back to Jyotirao Phule, the earliest and most original proponent of non-Brahman and *Dravidian* politics. Phule while making a case for a new racial identity for the lower and backward castes resorted to selective inversion of stories and ideas drawn from Hindu mythology. He presented ten incarnations of God *Vishnu* as different stages of the struggle between the Aryans, the

---

72   Neera Burra, "Buddhism, Conversion and Identity: A Case Study of Village Mahars," in
       Caste: Its Twentieth Century Avatar, ed. M.N Srinivas (Gurgaon: Penguin, 1996), 152–173.

73   Nicolas Jaoul, "Citizenship in Religious Clothing? Navayana Buddhism and Dalit
       Emancipation in late 1990s Uttar Pradesh," *Focaal – Journal of Global and Historical
       Anthropology* 76 (2016): 57–60.

74   Nicolas Jaoul, "Dalit Processions: Street Politics and Democratization in India," in *Staging
       Politics: Power and Performance in Asia and Africa*, eds. J.C. Strauss & D.B. Cruise O'Brien
       (London: I. B. Tauris, 2007), 185.

ancestors of the Brahmans and the original inhabitants of India, the ancestors of the non-Brahman backward castes.[75] Thus, it seems that the tradition of autonomous non-*Hinduized* caste movements has been unable to completely free itself from the hegemonic influence of Hindu culture. Therefore, in practical terms, the difference between the tradition of autonomous non-*Hinduized* caste movements which today mainly survives in the form of neo-Buddhist Ambedkarite movement and that of Hindu reformist caste movements is not always very substantial.

Against this wider backdrop we can now try to contextualize the *Matua* movement teasing out the nuances of some of its complex dimensions. According to historian Sekhar Bandyopadhyay, who has produced the most authoritative account of the *Namasudra* movement, the founder of the *Matua* sect, Harichand Thakur, established it on the basic of a non-ritualistic doctrine of *Bhakti* by selectively borrowing ideas and symbols from traditional Hinduism as well as *Gaudiya Vaishnavism*. The philosophy of the sect as propounded by Harichand Thakur repudiated and negated Brahmanism (the ritual superiority and social dominance of the Brahmans in Hindu society), *Gurubaad* (the idea that one must be guided in his or her spiritual life by a guru, who invariably a Brahman, acts as an intermediary between God and ordinary mortals), *avatarbaad* (the idea that God takes birth among human beings in order to guide them towards the right path) and all rituals and deities of Vedic Hinduism except chanting the name of *Hari* or the supreme God and performance of *Kirtan* (group singing of devotional songs). In a way the philosophy of the sect presented a holistic critique of the classical Hinduism of the elite, i.e. Vedic Hinduism or *Advaita Vedantism*.[76] However, by the time Guruchand Thakur, son of Harichand Thakur assumed the leadership of the community, the *Matuas* had moved away from this holistic critique charted out by Harichand during his lifetime. It is possible to identify several dimensions of the evolving orientation and strategies of the movement, which reflect this transformation. Beginning with *Vaishnavite Kabial* (folk poet) Tarak Chandra Sarkar's writing of Harichand Thakur's hagiography *Sri Sri Harililamrita*, which had been commissioned and approved by Guruchand Thakur and other *Matua* leaders, aspects of Hinduism such as overt references to and worship of Hindu Gods and Goddesses started to find a place within the community. *Sri Sri Harililamrita* presents Harichand Thakur as an avatar of God *Vishnu*. The text clearly inspired by *Vaishnavism* is replete with references to avatars

75 Rosalind O'Hanlon, *Caste, Conflict and Ideology: Mahatma Jyotirao Phule and Low Caste Protest in Nineteenth Century Western India* (Ranikhet: Permanent Black, 2016), 143–146.

76 Bandyopadhyay, *Caste, Protest and Identity in Colonial India,* 37–39.

and Hindu pantheon of deities and is devoid of the spirit of vehement opposition against Vedic Hinduism present in Harichand Thakur's thinking. Similarly, in Guruchand Thakur's biography, author Mahananda Halder too portrays Guruchand as an avatar of God *Shiva*. Further, the signage and symbolism used by the *Matuas* today in their posters and banners clearly indicate their growing *Hinduization*. Matua Mahasangha today draws from the universalist anti-caste ideology of Harichand Thakur avoiding elements of his ideology which are exclusivist.[77] Further, the religious practices of the community have undergone substantial *Hinduization* over the years. A great deal of absorption of Hindu rituals by the *Matuas* has also taken place. Later editions of *Sri Sri Harililamrita* even claim that Harichand Thakur descended from a high-caste *Maithili* Brahman lineage.[78] Sekhar Bandyopadhyay points out that as the movement matured the *Matuas* started to increasingly adopt the social practices of the caste Hindus such as *Sradh* (funeral ceremony), dowry and even claimed a Brahman ancestry of their forefathers by starting to don scared thread. Bandyopadhyay notes that this behaviour can't be fully understood through the model of *sanskritization* as underlying this process of emulation of the behaviour of the higher castes existed strong undercurrents of protest. Those undercurrents were often directed towards negating the value of the symbols of social authority associated with the Brahmans through defiance of prohibition on appropriation of those symbols by the lower castes. Yet such emulative behaviour, as Bandyopadhyay points out, was not always culturally subversive and often reflected the impact of ideological hegemony of the Hindu social order on the *Matuas*.[79] This hegemony today finds its manifestation in the enthusiastic celebration of Hindu festivals by the *Matuas*. Though Harichand Thakur was against worshipping of different Gods and Goddesses, the *Matuas* today freely worship various Gods and Goddesses of classical Hinduism. Most of the members of the *Matua* community I have come across claim that they worship as eagerly as other Bengali Hindus, Goddess *Durga* and Goddess *Kali*, two most popular Goddesses of Bengal. Many of them also worship Goddess *Saraswati* and Goddess *Laxmi*. Some are also actively involved in several *puja* (worshipping) committees which organizes these *pujas*.[80]

---

77   Sipra Mukherjee, "In Opposition and Allegiance to Hinduism: Exploring the Bengali Matua Hagiography of Harichand Thakur," *South Asia: Journal of South Asian Studies* 41, no. 2 (2018): 435–451.

78   The mention of *Maithili* Brahman lineage first appeared in the 1940 edition of the book.

79   Bandyopadhyay, *Caste, Protest and Identity in Colonial India,* 49.

80   Manosanta Biswas, "Caste and Socio-cultural Mobility in West Bengal: A Hybrid Cultural Elocution of *Matua* Reforms Movement," *Contemporary Voice of Dalit* 10, no. 2 (2018): 241.

With the recent rise of the *Hindutva* politics in West Bengal their political and religious vocabulary as well as their social and political conduct are
conspicuously becoming even more *Hinduized. Hari Bol* which is a traditional
religious slogan of the *Matuas* is now routinely accompanied by the chant of
Jai Shri Ram in political rallies and other occasions. *Matua* leaders in their
political speeches and social media posts are now using these two slogans
together. Kalyani Thakur Charal, a *dalit* writer and editor of Neer, a *dalit* wom-
en's magazine points out that she has even found to her utter bewilderment
the tendency among some *Matuas* these days to omit the slogan *Hari Bol* altogether in favour of *Jai Shri Ram* even in *Matua* bastion of Thakurnagar.[81] In an
attempt to showcase their Hindu credentials, the *Matuas* led by the top leader
of the Matua Mahasangha and a direct descendant of Harichand-Guruchand,
Shantanu Thakur collected holy soil from the shrine of Harichand Thakur and
sent the same for the foundation stone laying ceremony of the Ram temple at
Ayodha when soil and water were being collected from all prominent Hindus
religious sites across India. The celebration of Hindu festivals by the *Matuas*
could be traced back even to the times of Guruchand Thakur. Pramatha Ranjan
Thakur, the grandson of Guruchand Thakur in his autobiography *Atmacharit
ba Purba Smriti* (Autobiography or Old memories) has described his grandfather as a devoted Hindu whose family celebrated *Vaishnava* festivals like
Doljatra, Rathjatra and *Raslila* as well as *Sakta* festivals like *Durga Puja* and
Kali Puja.[82] But what is interesting is that many *Matuas* worship Gods and
Goddesses of Vedic/classical Hinduism in a non-Vedic way by employing non-
Brahman *Matua gosains* (preachers) as priests and chanting hymns in Bengali,
not in Sanskrit. Priyanka Mondal, secretary of BJP's Nadia south district com-
mittee explains the rationale behind this:

> As per my limited knowledge the Bengali mantras that are chanted
> during *Durga puja* and *Kali puja* are basically the translated versions of
> the Sanskrit mantras. But since we had been discriminated in the past as
> a result of Vedic injunctions which were all in Sanskrit language, use of
> Bengali mantras and non- Brahman priests allow us to register our pro-
> test against our past discrimination while conveying our devotion to the
> deities at the same time. Harichand Thakur said, *Kukurer ucchistho pro-
> shad peleo khai, bedbidhi souchachar nahi mani tai* (I am even ready to eat

---

81   Moumita Chaudhuri, "They are Using *Dalit* Votes for Selfish Ends," *The Telegraph*,
      December 20, 2020, https://www.telegraphindia.com/culture/people/they-are-using
      -*Dalit*-votes-for-selfish-ends/cid/1801105.
82   Mukherjee, "In Opposition and Allegiance to Hinduism," 10.

the leftovers of the food consumed by a dog but I shall not comply with Vedic injunctions). Though it would not be correct to say that the majority of the *Matuas* practice this form of worship, a sizeable section of the *Matua* community at least in Nadia follow this.[83]

Mondal is here alluding to the intimate connection between Sanskrit language and Brahmanhood as acquisition of knowledge of Sanskrit was once considered a monopoly right of the Brahmans only. What is interesting is that there is not much difference according to Mondal between the Bengali mantras and the original Sanskrit ones in terms of content. This indicates that the idea behind the renouncement of Sanskrit mantras is not to advocate a radical departure from Hindu religion but only to register a powerful protest against Brahman domination. The rejection of Sanskrit communicates an awareness of the past discrimination as well as a continuing disapproval of Brahman domination and caste rules. Mondal also informs that the Bengali mantras are chanted from the booklets published by Matua Mahasangha containing hymns and ritual rules, which are meant to be followed also during other social ceremonies like marriage, *Sradh* and so on. Thus, the *Matuas* are still involved in a complex process of negotiation with the ideas and symbols of traditional Hinduism. But this process of negotiation clearly reflects their growing assimilation into the larger fold of Hinduism without much dilution in their social posture of opposition against Brahmanism. In other words, the *Matuas* tend to make a distinction between Hinduism and Brahmanism harbouring the belief that it is possible to struggle against caste hierarchy and Brahman domination while adhering to a reformist version of Hinduism. In this connection, it is also worth pointing out that administering the worship of Goddess *Durga* and Goddess *Kali* through non-Brahman priests in accordance with *Matua* rituals and Bengali hymns is possibly not a pan-Bengal phenomenon. This seems to be mainly prevalent in the *Matua* belt of Nadia and North 24 Parganas. The *Matuas* of Uluberia I talked to have stated quite unequivocally that they perform normal Hindu rituals and use Sanskrit mantras during *Durga puja* and *Kali puja* in the exact same manner as other Bengali Hindus do, adding that some *Matuas* in and around Thakurnagar may prefer to do it in a typical *Matua* style. It seems that with the growth of the *Matua* population a great deal of diversification in *Matua* ritual practices has taken place. Subir Mondal, former Deputy Chairman of Nadia's Betna Gobindapur *Panchayat* and a local TMC leader states:

---

83   Interview with Priyanka Mondal, Secretary of BJP's Nadia south district committee.

With increase in the population of the *Matuas* many self-proclaimed gurus or *gosains* who have little connection with *Thakurbari* have emerged and they have created their own groups of followers prescribing to their disciples rituals invented by them. As a result, these days you will find little commonalities in the rituals practices of the *Matuas*. Let me give you a concrete example. In religious occasions when *Ghot puja* (worshipping an urn symbolising the Goddess) is performed, many *Matuas* following the general practice place mango leaf above the *Ghot* (urn) and then place a *dub* (unripe coconut) over it. Others employ a rationalist logic and say that we should not waste a coconut and they therefore use *haritaki* (greenery). I ask – is greenery also not useful? Why should we waste greenery then?'[84]

While being asked by me whether these slightly deviant religious practices performed by the *Matuas* imply that they follow a religion which is different from Hinduism he shot back saying:

> We can't say that *Matua* faith is different from Hindu religion. We believe that Harichand Thakur is an eighth generation descendent of Sri Sri Chaitanya Mahaprabhu. The *Brahmanyavadis* (Brahman supremacists) in the past had used us as their *sevadas* (slaves for discharging various services). They believed that our touch was polluting. Do you know the origin of *Harir looth* [the practice of throwing *proshad* (food offered to the deities) among the devotees] that happens during *kirtans*? This practice emerged as we were not served *proshad* on our hands as our touch could pollute the *Brahmanyavadis*. It was the *Brahmanyavadis* who had spread misinformation that we were not Hindus. Nothing can be far from truth than this. I have not heard of any *Matua* declaring his religion as *Matua* while filling up various official forms. We all declare our religion as Hinduism in the official documents because we are Hindus.[85]

However, a radical anti-caste ideology has also been gaining ground among a small but relatively educated section of the *Matuas*. They have embraced an Ambedkarite political discourse and are playing an instrumental role in pioneering a radical *dalit* literary movement. I find them to be much more

---

84   Interview with Subir Mandal (name changed), former Deputy Chairman of Nadia's Betna Gobindapur *Panchayat* and a local leader of the TMC.

85   Interview with Subir Mandal.

skeptical about the intentions of the BJP and much less enthusiastic about the CAA-NRC. Most importantly, they tend to believe that *Matua* is a separate religion and therefore, the *Matuas* are not Hindus. They want to dissociate the *Matua* faith from its supposed Hindu roots and highlight the futility of making a distinction between Brahmanism and Hinduism.[86] This standpoint is not new but of late it has started to receive greater attention with the growing popularity of internet and social media platforms. The proponents of this standpoint today regularly write in their own websites, blogs, and social media platforms to popularise their radical anti-caste discourse. For providing a glimpse of the broad contours of the contemporary Ambedkarite discourse among the *Matuas*, I shall here briefly deal with the writings of Sudhir Ranjan Halder, a popular *Matua* activist.

Dealing with the question of the relationship between Hindu religion and *Matua* faith Halder dwells a great deal on *Sri Sri Harililamrita's Vaishnava* and Vedic moorings. Halder claims that Harichand Thakur did not authorize publication of his biography written by two of his disciplines during his lifetime because he found it to be infused with Vedic spirit. It was after his demise that *Sri Sri Harililamrita* was composed by Tarak Chandra Sarkar. He accuses Sarkar of introducing Vedic materials, references to Hindu Gods and Goddesses and *Vaishnava* devotional aspects in accordance with his own religious beliefs contravening the basic spirit of the *Matua* religion. It is because of Sarkar's flawed drafting, he believes, that *Matua* religion has become synonymous with *Vaishnavism* in the eyes of the common *Matuas*.[87] Harichand Thakur, according to Halder had deep antipathy to the *Vaishnavs*. Manoranjan Byapari, a well-known *dalit* author also points out Harichand's aversion for *Vaishnavism*. Both Byapari and Halder mention an incident when Harichand had defied his father's instruction to touch the feet of the *Vaishnavs*.[88] Halder while castigating Sarkar for his drafting also highlights that now it is not possible to access the original manuscript of *Sri Sri Harililamrita* as it was not returned by the press where it had been printed. Halder claims that the original manuscripts written by Sarkar underwent substantial revisions. He points out that at that

86   See, Debendralal Biswas Thakur, *Matuýāra Hindu Naý: Dalit Aikyer Sandhāne* (Kolkata: Harichand Mission Press, 1977); Debendralal Biswas Thakur, *Bauddha Dharma o Matuẏā Dharmer Samīkṣā* (Kolkata: Matua Literary Council, 1991); Jibankumar Sarkar, *Matuẏā: Manane o Sahitye* (Murshidabad, India: Shilpanagari Printers, 2015).

87   Sudhir Ranjan Halder, *Sri Sri Harililamrita Prasange*, http://generalbooksonmatuya.blogs pot.com/2016/03/blog-post_36.html.

88   Manoranjan Byapari, *Matua* Ek Mukti Sena, in *Hatebajare Patrika*, Utsab Sankhya 1420 (Bardhhaman: Pranab Kumar Chakrabarty, 2013), 24; Sudhir Ranjan Halder, *Harichand Thakur*, http://dalitliteratures.blogspot.com/2017/03/blog-post_19.html.

time the publishing industry was controlled by the conservative Brahmans who were reluctant to publish anti-Vedic content. Therefore, the original manuscript of *Sri Sri Harililamrita* had to be substantially revised to address the objections raised by the Brahmans. In addition, the clerk of the press also had to be bribed for publishing a manuscript like this. Moreover, Halder notes that, later editions of the biography have kept increasing in volume with addition of new content. The ninth edition of the book contains hundred more pages than its first edition.[89] All of these anomalies, according to Halder have created a situation, where it is no longer possible to identify the original content which had been drafted by Sarkar himself. Therefore, Halder argues that only the teachings and deeds of Harichand Thakur documented by Sarkar should be accepted, while other parts of *Sri Sri Harililamrita* should not be blindly accepted at face value.[90]

Many of these arguments are not backed by any credible historical evidence and they also seem conjectural and speculative . Nevertheless, they stand for a radical anti-caste vision premised on an alternative identity. For instance, echoing Ambedkar, Halder claims that the *Namasudras* were originally Buddhists, and that due to their refusal to accept the Vedic religion the curse of untouchability was imposed upon them.[91] These views have started to make some impact on the minds of some among the *Matua* community. Though not entirely receptive to all of these radical ideas, they are not entirely dismissive of them like others and on occasions tend to lean towards the radical Ambedkarite discourse. Krittibas Thakur, a *gosain* who has served in the central committee of Matua Mahasangha and is currently the president of Matua Mahasangha's gosain parishad (council) is sympathetic towards the position that *Matua* is a non-Hindu identity. He tends to suggest that *Matua* faith is a part of *Sanatan Dharma* which is wrongly equated with Hinduism by the general public. According to him *Matua Dharma* prescribes only the worship of Harichand and Guruchand and it is not permissible to worship other deities and chant *Jai Shri Ram*. "We the real *bhaktas* (devotees) of Harichand and Guruchand are emotionally hurt by other *Matuas* chanting *Jai Shri Ram* and worshiping different deities of Hinduism. Our only slogan is *Hari Bol*", he said. Explaining further he stated that even a Muslim could become a *Matua*, something which is not possible in case of other Hindu sects. Like Sudhir Ranjan

89   Sudhir Ranjan Halder, *Harichand Thakur o Matua Dharma*, http://generalbooksonmat uya.blogspot.com/2015/10/9433814298-7407103432_72.html.

90   Sudhir Ranjan Halder, *Dicharitai Matua Dharma*, http://dalitliteratures.blogspot.com/ 2017/02/dwicharitay-matuyadharma.html.

91   Halder, *Harichand Thakur o Matua Dharma*.

Halder, he is also skeptical of the Hindu leanings of *Sri Sri Harililamrita*. Castigating *Manuvaad* he asserted that *Sri Sri Harililamrita* had to incorporate many Hindu elements as a compromise in order to pass scrutiny by the Brahmans, who being very powerful at that time had wanted to prevent it from being published. While being asked about addition of content filled with Hindu ideas and symbols in the later editions of the book and reasons for the absence of any initiative to reverse its clear-cut Hindu *Vaishnava* orientation, he was candid enough to admit, "we are confused and still not sure about many aspects of the *Matua* belief system and so, we are still trying to understand and work out a lot of things". But at the same time, he narrated a number of recent incidents of caste discrimination, suggesting that the casteless *Matua* faith not the Brahman dominated Vedic Hindu religion with its innumerable Gods and Goddesses is the way forward. At the moment the radical anti-caste activists clearly constitute a fringe element within the *Matua* community. Despite being quite vocal, their views are yet to percolate down to the common *Matuas*. These radical anti-caste activists also seem to acknowledge the widespread tendency of the general *Matuas* to see themselves as followers of *Vaishnava* Hinduism. "It is a pity", Krittibas argued, "that almost all *Matuas* barring a few perform Hindu rituals and worship Hindu Gods and Goddesses". Therefore, the whole point of their activism, according to Krittibas is to convince the *Matua* masses of their religious misconceptions and flawed self-perception. But his imagination of a non-Hindu *Matua* identity is not fully free from the Hindu influences as he ends up drawing symbols from traditional Hinduism. This is evident in his rationale for rejection of the deities of Hinduism:

> Harichand is an incarnation of Lord *Narayan* and Guruchand is an incarnation of Lord *Mahakal*. Similarly, Harichand's wife is Goddess *Laxmi* and Guruchand's wife is Goddess *Kali*. Therefore, it is sufficient to worship Harichand and Guruchand and their wives. Worshipping any other deities is prohibited in *Matua* religion.'[92]

We here find the same dilemma that has confronted the radical anti-caste Amedkarite movement all along. As has already been discussed, radical anti-caste movement's strategy of opposition to Hinduism is often rooted in selective borrowing and inversion of ideas and symbols drawn from Hinduism itself due to deep-rooted hegemonic influence of the Hindu culture. As a result,

---

92   Interview with Krittibas Thakur, President of Matua Mahasangha's Gosain Parishad.

despite manifest attempts to give up Hindu identity, the discursive break with Hinduism often remains incomplete and contradictory.

My formal and informal conversations with the *Matuas* divulge that almost all of them across the political divide firmly place themselves within the religious and cultural fabric of Hinduism and treat their faith as a reformist and progressive offshoot of Hindu religion. Historical evidences also point towards the fact that over the years the *Matua* movement has evolved more and more into a Hindu caste reform movement. I find strong awareness about this evolution process among the *Matuas* who have an active spiritual life like Hriday Pal, a former cashier of Matua Mahasangha's Nadia district committee office at Bagula. 71-year-old Hriday is a self-taught person who has read Marx and Rousseau. But most importantly, he possesses a wealth of knowledge and information about *Matua* religious texts and practices and regularly takes part in discussions and conferences on *Matua* religion. He charted out to me the evolving relationship between Hinduism and *Matua* faith with impressive clarity:

> *Matua* faith is a '*Sukkhho Sanatan Dharma*' (fine version of *Sanatana Dharma*). There were many flaws in Vedic religion. Our Thakurs (Harichand and Guruchand) took an initiative to reform the Vedic religion and presented before us '*Sukkhho Sanatan Dharma*' which is free from the flaws of the Vedic religion. So *Matua* faith is non-Vedic version of the Hindu religion. That is why the *Matuas* consider themselves as Hindus. At the same time, it is also true that we have gradually incorporated various aspects of Vedic religion. For instance, we believe that Guruchand Thakur is an incarnation of Lord *Shiva*, who is a Vedic deity and so is Lord *Vishnu* who we believe had incarnated as Harichand Thakur.' [93]

Hriday's term '*Sukkhho Sanatan Dharma*' perfectly captures the reformist nature of the *Matua* faith as conceived by the common *Matuas* and also indicates an awareness among the *Matuas* of the growing intimacy of their faith with classical Hinduism. During my conversation with the people of the *Matua* sect their repeated references to Sri Sri Chaitanya Mahaprabhu and other figures of *Vaishnavism* as well as a range of *Vaishnavite* ideas, symbols and practices clearly convey to me that they see themselves belonging to the

---

93   Interview with Hriday Pal (name changed), former cashier of *Matua* Mahasangha Nadia district committee's office at Bagula.

Hindu *Vaishnava* religious tradition. The spiritual discourse professed by most of them does not seem to be inherently oppositional to Hindu religion though it communicates a powerful message of protest against caste discrimination and Brahman domination. Therefore, *Matua* movement can't be placed in the genre of radical autonomous anti-caste movement. It is true that during the days of Harichand Thakur, *Matua* movement demonstrated considerable radicalism spawning a vehement critique of not only the institution of caste but also various aspects of traditional Hinduism. But thereafter the movement became less radical and the *Matuas* gradually came to embrace deities, rituals, and festivals of traditional Hinduism, while retaining a spirit of determined opposition to the ritual order of caste hierarchy and the idea of social and ritual supremacy of the Brahmans. But even during its most radical phase the *Matua* movement despite being equipped with a critique of Vedic Hinduism did not perfectly fit into the mould of autonomous anti-caste tradition. The *Matua* identity was not explicitly conceptualized as a non-Hindu identity since the spirit of Hindu *Vaishnavism* acted as the main inspiration behind the movement. The *Matua* identity has always been much wider in scope than an innovative religious identity like neo-Buddhism or a fixed ethnic identity invented by the *Dravidian* movement. The idea behind the promotion of neo-Buddhist identity or *Dravidian* identity was to disassociate the marginalized communities from Hinduism with the goal of ensuring social dignity for them. On the contrary, conversion to the *Matua* sect is not tantamount to religious conversion. It is possible for any Hindu to become a *Matua* by taking the membership of the Matua Mahasangha and still remain a Hindu. Akshay Chakrabarty, a Brahman was one of the most prominent disciples of Harichand Thakur. West Bengal's current Chief Minister Mamata Banerjee, a Brahman became a member of the Matua Mahasangha in 2009 and still she is able to claim without any qualms that she is a practicing Hindu. It is quite interesting that there are even Muslim *gosains* like Tin kari Miyan, Panch Kari Miyan, Jalil gosain and Dilwar Hussein.[94]

The reformist nature of the *Matua* movement has generated important political implications for the community. Presently the absence of any oppositional religious discourse against Hinduism among the common *Matuas* and the steady *Hinduization* of the *Matua* movement over the years make the community a much easier target for *Hindutva* politics than caste groups which had in the past been endowed with a non-Hindu identity and an alternative non-Hindu value system by radical anti-caste movements. A brief perusal of

---

94   I have gathered this interesting piece of information from Krittibas Thakur.

the ways in which Hindu nationalists have historically approached questions of caste and untouchability will also suggest that *Hindutva* politics has always welcomed reformist caste movement to achieve its goal of bringing about Hindu unity. The overarching goal of *Hindutva* politics has always been to remove differences between all sections of the Hindus in order to transform them into a unified political force. As caste divisions and untouchability militate against the larger goal of Hindu unity and create possibilities for conversion of *dalits* into Islam and Christianity, elimination of caste divisions through reforms of Hindu social order has remained one of the core concerns of the *Hindutva* movement. Even before the RSS came into existence, B.S Moonje (who would later act as the President of the Hindu Mahasabha from 1927 to 1937), the mentor of the RSS founder Dr. Hedgewar in a report written by him on the Malabar riots of 1921–22 had expressed resentment about the fact that the Muslims were far more united than the Hindus owing to the existence of caste system among the Hindus. He recommended inter-caste marriage to put an end to caste divisions and thus unify the Hindus by preventing the conversion of lower castes into other faiths.[95] V.D Savarkar, the father of the *Hindutva* movement also considered caste system as the greatest impediment to Hindu *Rashtra*. He felt that caste system was responsible for injecting eternal conflict between the Hindus and weakening Hindu unity against external threat.[96] In present times too, full incorporation of the untouchables into the Hindu society constitutes one of core agendas of the Hindu nationalists. They do not take the Hindu identity of the untouchables for granted and therefore actively engage in reformist activities in order to build bridges with the untouchable communities.[97]

Most importantly, the *Hindutva* movement recognizes the need for reformist caste movements in order to facilitate integration of the untouchables into Hindu society. Hindu Mahasabha had strong links with the Depressed Classes Association (DCA) which was organized in 1915 in Nagpur by Kisan Faguji Bansode and G.A Gavai who were prominent leaders of the lower castes before the rise of Ambedkar. They were also active in Prarthana Samaj and V.R Shindhe's Depressed Classes Mission, which was the most prominent organization working for the lower castes in the 1920s in western India. These

---

95   Christophe Jaffrelot, *The Hindu Nationalist Movement and Indian Politics: 1925 to the 1990s* (New Delhi: Penguin, 1999), 20–21.

96   Savarkar Samaagra, vol. 7, pp. 76- 84, English translation taken from Vikram Sampath, *Savarkar: Echoes from a Forgotten Past (1883–1924)* (Gurgaon: Penguin Viking, 2019), 423.

97   Peter van der Veer, *Religious Nationalism: Hindus and Muslims in India* (Berkeley, CA: University of California Press, 1994), 28, 52.

organizations propagated *Bhakti* reformist Hinduism. G.A Gavai also became a formal member of the Hindu Mahasabha and harshly criticized Ambedkar's conversion call. The DCA with its deep links with the Hindu Mahasabha was in fact the earliest of the three All India *dalit* (*dalit* is here understood as lower castes) organizations that had emerged by the 1930s, the other two being the Depressed Classes League which formed by Jagjivan Ram in 1936 represented the Gandhian tradition and Depressed Classes Federation established by Ambedkar in 1930.[98] Condemning the tendency to blindly adhere to scriptural injunctions Savarkar observed that scriptures were relevant in a particular context and that they should be discarded if in a changed social scenario they lose their relevance and hamper progress towards modernity.[99] Calling for reforms to abolish caste discrimination he branded the critics of social reform as the biggest enemies of the *Sanatan Dharma* and Hindu *Rashtra* (state).[100] Savarkar during his internment at Maharashtra's Ratnagiri undertook a number of initiatives to dismantle caste divisions such as setting up a school for lower-caste children, encouraging collective celebration of Hindu festivals by all castes and facilitating entry of the lower castes in temples. He even established a temple where people from all castes could worship.[101] In line with Savarkar's reformist spirit the RSS has been encouraging inter-caste marriages and inter-caste dining as ways to dismantle social distance between different castes for the sake of Hindu consolidation.[102] To undermine the notions of purity/pollution and to foster a sense of fellow-feeling and unity, in the RSS camps all the participants are required to serve food to each other. Similarly, they are also required to clean latrines and perform sweeping and other so-called defiling activities on rotational basis.[103] The RSS has floated a number of social organizations and groups like the Samajik Samrastra Manch (a group which arranges interaction of *dalit*s and tribals with high caste Hindus), All India Vanavasi Kalyan Ashram (an affiliate that works for socio-economic empowerment of the tribals) and Seva Bharati (a confederation of social service groups which

---

98   Omvedt, *Dalits and Democratic Revolution*, 110–111, 181.

99   Savarkar Samaagra, vol. 7, pp. 76- 84, English translation taken from Vikram Sampath, *Savarkar: Echoes from a Forgotten Past (1883–1924)* (Gurgaon: Penguin Viking, 2019), 423.

100   Savarkar Samaagra, vol. 7, 33–46, English translation taken from Vikram Sampath, *Savarkar: Echoes from a Forgotten Past (1883–1924)* (Gurgaon: Penguin Viking, 2019), 428.

101   Vaibhav Purandare, *Savarkar: The True Story of the Father of Hindutva* (New Delhi: Juggernaut, 2019), 206–210.

102   Walter K Andersen and Shidhar D. Damle, *The RSS: A View to Inside* (Gurgaon: Penguin Viking, 2018), 170.

103   Walter K Andersen and Shidhar D. Damle, *The Brotherhood in Saffron: The Rashtriya Swayamsevak Sangh and Hindu Revivalism* (Gurgaon: Penguin, 2019), 99.

work among the poor and *dalits*) to quietly work towards the goal of Hindu consolidation by performing reformist activities among the lower castes and tribes.[104] According to Peter Van der Veer such social reformists efforts undertaken by the Hindu nationalists cater to their long term project of *Hinduization* of *dalits*.[105]

However, a great deal of skepticism has also been expressed by scholars about the ability and actual intention of the *Hindutva* forces to eliminate or mitigate caste divisions through such reformist initiatives. According to Balmurli Natrajan the *Hindutva* movement cannot undertake any fundamental redressal of casteism since its own practices are based on notions of Brahmanical supremacy. In his view *Hindutva* movement today rather than seeking to redress caste divisions only attempts to hide the realities of caste divisions by projecting caste as a system of benign difference, not a system of hierarchy. He also points that this ironically complements and resembles with a scholarly point of view known as the *ethnicization* of caste thesis, which argues that caste system is changing from a vertical hierarchy into a horizontal ethnic system with each caste emerging as a benign ethnic group, marked only by cultural differences rather than inequality in status, wealth, and power.[106] In this connection, the fundamental point that needs further emphasis is that the *Hindutva* movement is primarily concerned with the goal of Hindu unity. Therefore, for *Hindutva* politics caste divisions as well as other social divisions are unwelcome in so far as they adversely affect the goal of national unity and integration. This also by implication means, that the community feeling generated by caste identity may not a problem so long as it does not conflict with the unity of the Hindu nation. For the proponents of *Hindutva*, as Thomas Blom Hansen points out, "caste divisions are, like other divisions and hierarchies, undesirable insofar as they hamper national unity and integration, but acceptable insofar as they provide a community feeling compatible with that of the nation and that of the RSS".[107] Therefore, in the *Hindutva* discourse abolition of caste divisions is not seen as an end-in-itself but only as a means to the larger end of Hindu unity. This is where it differs from the radical Ambedkarite discourse. For Ambedkar, annihilation of caste is an end-in-itself, a goal important enough to be pursued for its own

---

104   Andersen and Damle, *The RSS*, 246.

105   Veer, *Religious Nationalism*, 52.

106   Balmurli Natrajan, "Racialization and Ethnicization: Hindutva Hegemony and Caste," *Ethnic and Racial Studies*, https://doi.org/10.1080/01419870.2021.1951318.

107   Thomas Blom Hansen, *The Saffron Wave: Democracy and Hindu Nationalism in Modern India* (Princeton: Princeton University Press, 1999), 122.

sake. But for the *Hindutva* movement, abolition of caste divisions is only a means to the larger end of Hindu unity. For instance, M.S Golwalkar, the second *Sarsanchalak* (chief) of the RSS envisaged that the Hindu society must ultimately transform itself into an organic whole in which all social differences like divisions on the basis of caste will lose their meaning.[108] In what is considered by many as one of the most important speeches in the history of the RSS, in 1974 Balasaheb Deoras, the then chief of the RSS publicly blamed the practice of untouchability for social divisions among the Hindus calling it a sin. Echoing Savarkar, Deoras argued that religious texts which appear to justify caste hierarchies must be evaluated with the goal of Hindu consolidation, a view also enshrined in Deendayal Upadhyay's *Intergral Humanism* which is considered by the RSS to be a central catechism of its ideology.[109] Thus, it is mainly out of the concern for Hindu unity that the proponents of the *Hindutva* politics have pursued the agenda of *Hinduization* of *dalit*s by attempting to bring about reforms to remove caste barriers and untouchability. In other words, in *Hindutva* ideology the agenda of *Hinduization* of *dalits* and the goal of Hindu unity are closely connected to the idea of caste reforms. This *Hindutva* drive for Hindu unity was on display when a *dalit* was made to lay the foundation stone of the proposed the Ram temple in Ayodhya in 1989.[110] We can easily draw a parallel here to the recent event of the *Matuas* dispatching holy soil from the temple of Harichand Thakur at Thakurnagar to Ayodha for foundation stone laying ceremony of Ram temple or to their frequent invocation of *Jai Shri Ram* in social and political ceremonies. In drawing the rationale for reform from the perceived need to improve the state of the Hindu society rather than completely overhauling it, the reformist caste movements in a way display an inherent sense of attachment to Hindu religion. Therefore, compared to the radical anti-caste movements based on the promotion of a non-Hindu identity, reformist caste movements are naturally more prone to embracing a brand of politics like that of *Hindutva,* which heavily draws from Hindu idioms. Hence, the reformist character of the *Matua* movement and its growing *Hinduization* have made it possible for the BJP to build bridges with the *Matuas* with relative ease and politicise their past memory of religious persecution more effectively.

---

108   Jaffrelot, Christophe. *The Hindu Nationalist Movement,* 59.
109   Andersen and Damle, *The RSS*, 6–7.
110   Ayan Guha. "RSS and the Reservation Riddle," *Statesman,* October 4, 2019.

5   Interplay of Memory and Politics at the Grassroots

We have already analysed in sufficient detail how the BJP has been encouraging increasing public conversation about religious persecution of the *Matuas*
to justify the CAA. It is imperative also to make sense of the impact which
this political campaign has generated on the political and social worldview
of the *Matuas*. The nationwide political debate and conversation around
the CAA issue have retrieved the buried saga of religious persecution of the
Namasudras from the fringes of public memory to the mainstream political
discourse. This seems to have rekindled the unhealed trauma of Partition in
the minds of the *Matuas*, creating a fertile ground for the interplay of 'politics
of memory.' Prasenjit Mondal, a youth in his twenties and born and brought up
in West Bengal exhibits his intimate embeddedness in a collective historical
memory and an earnest acceptance of an imagined relationship between past
and future when he says:

> We have come here because of our religion oppression. If the past is again
> repeated and we are again victimised at the hands of the same people,
> who are increasing in numbers, where will we go this time? We ask our-
> selves this question. Why are they (Muslims) coming in such huge num-
> bers from Bangladesh. They already have established an Islamic state
> there. They can't be persecuted on religious grounds there like us.[111]

Prasenjit is an active political worker of the BJP and currently the general
secretary of BJP's Yuva Morcha unit in a Mandal which falls within Uluberia
East Assembly constituency. He lives in a refugee colony consisting of several
Matua refugee families. This colony is unrecognized and has little civic ameni-
ties. The inhabitants are quite resentful of the fact that they have received little
assistance from the government. No inhabitant has been given *patta* (legal title
deed). Most of them have voter and ration cards. But they complain that, these
cards are often not accepted as proofs of citizenship and as a result they face
difficulties in securing passport, Scheduled Caste certificate, jobs and benefits
of various government schemes. For instance, Prasenjit's passport application
got rejected as he was asked to produce pre-1971 documents in his or his parents' name. These people entertain a general belief that the CAA will solve all
their problems and that the NRC will secure their future by halting Muslim

---

111   Interview with Prasenjit Mondal, General Secretary of BJP's Yuva Morcha unit in a Mandal
       within Uluberia East Assembly constituency.

infiltration from Bangladesh. Prasenjit told me that it was because of several bold steps taken by the BJP government like the NRC and the CAA that he had got attracted to the party and started to actively work for it. A general appreciation for the pro-Hindu measures undertaken by the BJP appears to be quite evident among many of the *Matua* refugees. More importantly, the BJP's larger objective of Hindu consolidation also seems to have struck a chord with many of them. For instance, explaining the need for Hindu unity Hriday Pal stated:

> Modi (Prime Minister) is doing the sacred task of uniting the Hindus. I have read Gopal Godse (one of the conspirators in the assassination of Mahatma Gandhi). I do not support his actions but he was right when he said that the Hindus never learn from history and past blunders while the Muslims always prioritise their religion over everything else. All other parties are opposing the NRC-CAA and other good moves by Modi because if he is able to unite the Hindus, all these parties will simply vanish.[112]

Thus, it appears that the BJP's political narrative has been able to create among the *Matuas* a renewed awareness about an unpalatable past. More importantly, it seems to have also generated an excessive obsession to see the future through the prism of anxieties inherited from the past. This clearly indicates that the political project of politicisation of collective memory associated with the CAA and NRC has been able to make a crucial intervention in the consciousness of the *Matuas* by making them perceive themselves primarily as Hindus before everything else, pitted against their projected other- the Muslims.[113] In this context, it is pertinent to note that collective memory is always intimately tied with identity. As LaPierre notes "collective identity relates to a collective memory through which the contemporary group recognizes itself through a common past, remembrance, commemoration, interpretation and reinterpretation".[114] James V. Wertsch and Henry L. Roediger III also observe that collective

---

112   Interview with Hriday Pal.

113   In this connection, it needs to be pointed out that the attempts to bring about *Hinduization* of the *Namasudras* is not an entirely new phenomenon. Bharat Sevashram Sangha in the 1930s and the Hindu Mahasabha in the 1940s made serious attempts to mobilize the *Namasudras* and other *dalit* groups in Bengal and many *dalits* responded positively to such attempts. See, Sarbani Bandyopadhyay, "Another History: Bhadralok Responses to Dalit Political Assertion in Colonial Bengal," in *The Politics of Caste in West Bengal,* eds. Uday Chandra, Geir Heierstad and Kenneth Bo Nielsen (New Delhi: Routledge, 2016), 51-75 and Sekhar Bandyopadhyay, *Caste, Culture and Hegemony: Social Dominance in Colonial Bengal* (New Delhi: Sage, 2004), 191-239.

114   Cited in Philip Schlesinger, "On National Identity: Some Conceptions and Misconceptions Criticized," *Social Science Information* 26, no. 2 (1987): 235.

remembering invariably entails some identity project that strives to construct a collective identity based on victimhood apart from many other factors.[115] In a similar vein Chris Weedon & Glenn Jordan see collective memory as something that signifies narratives of past experience constituted by and on behalf of specific groups within which they find meaningful forms of identification. It "works via the interpellation of individuals within specific narratives of the past that give them a sense of individual and shared identity and belonging".[116] This is why perhaps a person like Krittibas Thakur, who is otherwise extremely critical of *Manuvaad* and *Hinduization* of the *Matua* movement, also expresses concern about the perceived threat that the *Matua* community anticipates from the Muslims. He narrates not only with disappointment but also with a great deal of apprehension how merciless atrocities were committed in Bangladesh on the *Matuas* after the demolition of Babri mosque in India in early 1990s. This apprehension of a repeat of religious persecution, heightened through the politicisation of the memory of past events is quietly facilitating the evaporation of the difference between outcastes and caste Hindus in the *Namasudra* consciousness, by supplanting the sense of caste consciousness with a feeling of Hindu belongingness. Subir Mondal, a TMC leader while criticizing the BJP for fooling the *Matuas* with the promise of citizenship, also attributes the success of BJP's *Matua* mobilization to the *Matua* community's historical memory of a troubled relationship with the Muslims.

> We do talk about secularism, and we should. But all this talk about secularism can't hide the ghastly and outrageous atrocities that have been committed on the *Matuas* on a sustained basis only because of their religious identity. I visited many refugee colonies after 1971 and the horrors they suffered are simply unimaginable. Many of their relatives simply disappeared never to be found again. In my view many among the *Matuas* are supporting the BJP not only out of any simple resentment against the Muslims but also out of quest for revenge for the past. They believe that the BJP through NRC-CAA will throw the Muslims out of the country.[117]

Subir's explanation is suggestive of the fact that the politics that is being played out is exploiting the historical anxieties of the *Matuas*, leading to *Hinduization*

---

115   James V. Wertsch and Henry L. Roediger III, "Collective Memory: Conceptual Foundations and Theoretical Approaches," *Memory* 16, no. 3 (2008): 320.

116   Chris Weedon and Glenn Jordan, "Collective Memory: Theory and Politics," *Social Semiotics* 22, no. 2 (2012): 143, 146.

117   Interview with Subir Mondal.

of *Matua* consciousness and further othering of the Muslims. As a result, the Muslims have replaced the caste Hindus as the main adversary in the *Namsudra* consciousness. This change in political outlook is crucial for comprehending the growing inclination of the *Matua* refugees towards the politics of *Hindutva*, which aims to obscures caste divisions for the sake of Hindu consolidation. In North India, as Badri Narayan has highlighted, the *Hindutva* outreach to the lower-caste groups in rural micro-politics has resorted to cultural construction of local *dalit* heroes as Hindu avatars and crusaders against medieval Muslim invaders.[118] While this largely approximates what historian Eric Hobsbawm famously called 'invention of tradition',[119] the 'politics of memory' that is being currently played out in West Bengal, far from being rooted in a distant and mythical micro-tradition draws upon a more real, tangible and subjectively felt collective experience. As a result, the BJP's narrative seems to be making significant inroads into the political consciousness of the *Matuas*, propelling the emergence of an overarching Hindu identity capable of subsuming their caste identity. Political articulation of lower-caste identity is generally seen as an impediment to Hindu consolidation. But identity of a caste can also be reciprocally articulated by stressing its Hindu credentials- by putting forth its unique caste culture as an expression of *Hindutva*. In Rajasthan, for instance, the BJP has been able to present *Hindutva* as a version of *Rajput* values.[120] To mobilize the *Matuas* the BJP seems to be following the same playbook. Its strategy seems to be to amplify the Hindu roots and Hindu affiliation of the *Matua* tradition and also to emphasize how *Matuas* share a common destiny with the larger Hindu society. Therefore, it is not at all surprising that an unmistakable shift has occurred in the locus of their conscious identification from caste to religion. In this connection, it needs to be pointed out that to a considerable extent this shift is being driven by strategic imperatives. Citizenship is a key issue for the *Matuas* and in the current circumstances rallying behind the BJP is seen by many of them to be a smart strategy. Recently, in the context of BJP's rising popularity among the *Matuas*, Sekhar Bandyopadhyay has reminded us that the *Namasudras* have historically transacted their support with the mainstream political parties for strategic considerations.[121] Undeniably, this is a fact

---

118   Badri Narayan, *Fascinating Hindutva: Saffron Politics and Dalit Mobilisation* (New Delhi: Sage, 2009).

119   Eric Hobsbawm and Terence Ranger, *The Invention of Tradition* (New York: Cambridge University Press, 2012).

120   C.J Fuller, "Introduction," in *Caste Today,* ed. C.J Fuller (Delhi: Oxford University Press, 1996), 24–25.

121   Sekhar Bandyopadhyay, "Bengal's Star Caste," *Indian Express,* April 1, 2021.

of recent political history. The *Namasudra* community, at different times in the past, supported different political parties for fulfilment of their interests, exhibiting strategic political behaviour. Their recent move towards the BJP is also largely dictated by strategic imperatives relating to the CAA.Their support for the BJP in the first place, arose out of strategic necessities as the party promised to satisfy their demand for citizenship through legislative intervention in the form of the CAA. But in the process the political narrative presented by the BJP to justify the CAA has also gained acceptance among the members of the community. At one level this appears to be a strategic political alignment as formal endorsement of the BJP's political narrative about the citizenship issue and the history associated with it can potentially put an end to their woes satisfying their principal demand. However, what appears as a strategic shift in their political allegiance also entails a shift in their communal self-perception. We have already analysed how a visible transformation in their political language and thinking due to politicisation of their collective historical memory is being fuelled by their increasing political interaction with the BJP. Therefore, in case of the *Matuas* the strategic shift in their political allegiance and their changing perception of communal belongingness are closely aligned. Hence, the story about the correspondence between the *Namasudras* and the BJP appears to be a more complex and multi-layered one that requires greater scrutiny.

It is possible to make sense of the fluctuations in the communal self-understanding of the *Matuas* by taking into consideration the nature of identity politics. Identity politics expresses the interests of a certain social category which is used to generate a sense of identity. But in so doing identity politics prioritizes one out of a plethora of identities available to a group of individuals. In other words, an identity based social grouping reflects politicisation of one identity category over others for the sake of fulfillment of common goals. Therefore, identity politics bases itself on a "caricatured version of the world in which one characteristic of a group is over-determined".[122] In other words, in identity politics the members of the concerned group are supposed to act on the basis of only one aspect of their life. But people's conceptions of themselves along the lines of collective identity are situational and changeable. Joshua Gamson while highlighting the post-modern impulse to take apart and blur group identities in the context of queer movement, makes a larger point that identities are much more unstable and fluid than identity

---

122   Hugo Gorringe, "You Build Your House, We'll Build Ours: The Attractions and Pitfalls of Dalit Identity Politics," *Social Identities* 11, no. 6 (2005): 656.

based movements tend to assume.[123] Joane Nagel also brings out this fluctuating nature of the identity centric solidarities in her study on the dynamics
of ethnic identity. She observes that an individual is always in possession of
a portfolio of ethnic identities that are more or less salient in various situations and vis-a-vis various audiences. As audiences change, the socially defined
array of ethnic choices open to an individual also changes. Hence, an individual's choice of an ethnic identity during the process of social interaction
depends partly on where and with whom the interaction is taking place. An
individual of Cuban ancestry may be a Latino vis-a-vis non-Spanish-speaking
ethnic groups, a Cuban American vis-a-vis other Spanish-speaking groups, a
Marielito vis-a-vis other Cubans, and white vis-a-vis African Americans. Thus,
the choice of an ethnic identity is determined by an individual's perception of
its meaning in relation to different audiences and its salience and utility in the
prevailing social context.[124] This conveys the strategic dimensions of collective identity. Yen Espiritu's study particularly focuses on the strategic value of
identity with respect to a layering of Asian-American identity. While the larger
Asian pan-ethnic identity represents one level of identification, especially vis-
a-vis non-Asians, national origin (e.g., Japanese, Chinese, Vietnamese) remains
an important basis of identification and organization both vis-a-vis other
Asians as well as the larger society. This, according to Espiritu, reflects the tendency of people to select from a diverse array of pan-ethnic and nationality-
based identities, in accordance with perceived strategic utility and symbolic
appropriateness of those identities in different settings and with regard to
different audiences. She observes that the larger Asian-American pan-ethnic
identity tends to emerge as the primary locus of identification where large
group size appears advantageous in grabbing resources and political power.
However, she also notes that Asian-American pan-ethnicity tends to be tran-
sient, often giving way to smaller, culturally distinct nationality-based Asian
ethnicities.[125] Hugo Gorringe's study on *dalit* movement in Tamil Nadu also
shows how particularism is an offshoot of identity politics. He demonstrates
how *dalit* movement in Tamil Nadu originally envisaged as a united movement
of the marginalized or a trans-caste movement based on the umbrella category
of *dalit,* has effectively got converted into a movement to mobilize particular

123   Joshua Gamson, "Must Identity Movements Self-Destruct? A Queer Dilemma," *Social
      Problems* 42, no. 3 (1995): 390–407.
124   Joane Nagel, "Constructing Ethnicity: Creating and Recreating Ethnic Identity and
      Culture," *Social Problems* 41, no. 1 (1994): 154–156.
125   Yen Espiritu, *Asian American Panethnicity: Bridging Institutions and Identities*
      (Philadelphia: Temple University Press, 1992).

caste and sub-castes. In this context, his study presents a larger point that in identity politics each collective actor is riven by fissures that must be papered over or temporarily silenced to enable coordinated action. On occasions there is consensus as to the primary node of mobilization, but this consensus tends to relapse to particularism, implying continual reduction of wider struggle into narrower splinter groups. Similarly, if situation and issues demand, solidarities can flourish around larger groupings too.[126] This points to the shifting terrain of identity politics rooted in strategic considerations. But as Nagel points out quite convincingly that, it is not only the perception of strategic utility which regulates the shifting terrain of identity politics, but socio-political circumstances or structural factors also play a very crucial role. She shows that identity centric loyalties are constructed not from within but are also shaped and constrained by political policies, institutions and ethnically linked resource policies. The latitude available to an individual to choose identities strategically and consciously often remains limited. According to Nagel people often develop identification along ethnic lines owing to everyday experience relating to inter-ethnic interaction. But she finds that formal ethnic labels and political policies regulating ethnicity are even more powerful sources of identity since the state today is the dominant social institution. She particularly mentions the role of immigration policy that by regulating immigrant population and creating official ethnic labels shape patterns of ethnic identification and create conditions for ethnic mobilization.[127] Arguing on similar lines Chandran Kukathas, notes that identity groups are not fixed and unchanging entities in the moral and political universe, as their boundaries shift with a change in socio-political context. Citing the example of the *Malays*, he points out that the Malays in Malaysia emerged as a distinct and cohesive identity because of categorisation by the colonial authorities and also because of the appearance of Chinese immigrants.[128]

With these theoretical insights we can again come back to the analysis of *Matua* mobilization in West Bengal and attempt to contextualize it. The BJP has accommodated the *Namasudras* on its own terms, i.e. by largely practicing its trademark *Hindutva* politics in pursuance of a known and established political template without making any significant alteration in it. This has propped up religion as the primary axis of identification instead of caste in the field of political contestation. It is possible to make sense of this shift

126   Gorringe, "You Build Your House," 653–672.
127   Nagel, "Constructing Ethnicity," 156–158.
128   Chandran Kukathas, "Are There Any Cultural Rights?," *Political Theory* 20, no. 1 (1992): 110–111.

from one identity to another as the primary source of communal belongingness, if in line with the theoretical insights we have drawn about identity politics, loyalties based on collective identities are seen as dynamic and
constantly evolving phenomena structured not only by a calculation of their
strategic utility but also by constantly evolving political and social scenario.
The utility, boundaries and meaning of solidarities arising out of religion,
caste, ethnicity, race, or any other identity are always in a flux as they are
constantly negotiated and revised in response to shifts in political and institutional environment.

The political behaviour of the *Namasudras* has indeed been motivated
by situational imperatives or contextual necessities. This time too they have
responded strategically to the prevailing political situation. However, while
doing so they have embraced a shift in the prime locus of their group identification, demonstrating in the process, little inhibitions towards assertion
of Hindu identity and its prioritization over other communal attachments.
Since they do not posit themselves outside the larger Hindu fold and, define
their identity only in opposition to Brahmanism not Hinduism, in a religiously
polarized political and communal space their sense of Hindu belongingness
can very well override their caste consciousness. Our theoretical exploration
of identity politics suggests that individuals tend to cohere around a particular identity in opposition to an 'other'. In other words, identity-based solidarities are often situational. One identity can override the others becoming the
primary base of identification in response to a situation in which an actor is
embedded. However, this response need not be fully strategic. As Nagel points
out, seeing identity only as a strategic choice runs the risk of emphasizing
agency at the expense of structure. In practical terms, people enjoy limited latitude to make conscious decision with regard to identity choices in a particular
situation. In other words, an individual may choose an identity strategically
for his or her self-description but the choice is often limited by socio-political
environment. This is because identity-based solidarities are also propped up by
demographic, political, social, and economic processes. While different identity categories are available to an individual for developing solidarity at a particular time and place, it is often the social, economic, and political situation
of the time and the place that dictates which identity he or she derives his or
her primary sense of belongingness from. Everyday experience of social life by
enforcing social ascription and more importantly political policies by promoting identity labels with regard to matters like immigration and resource distribution often lay groundwork for a particular identity category to emerge as

the primary site of communal allegiance for a group of people.[129] Interestingly, the CAA is a policy of regulating immigrant population of different religious identities. It has promoted labels like 'religiously persecuted Hindus' which draws its rationale from the collective memory associated with everyday experience of conflict prone communal relations of the past.[130] Therefore, in the present political scenario where the *Namasudras* are labelled as 'persecuted Hindus' and are pitted against the 'Muslim other' through the invocation of a collective historical memory their recourse to their religious identity for self-identification and association with the larger society is not simply a conscious strategic move. It also involves an act of reflexive absorption and internalization of a particular communal consciousness. Hence, the political alignment of the *Namasudra* community with the BJP goes beyond simple strategic calculation. It also entails a change in their self-perception and communal consciousness, with religion emerging as the primary axis of their identification instead of caste.

Therefore, in the light of the analytical insights and ethnographic evidences presented in this chapter, we can conclude that the current pattern of mobilization of the *Namasudras* does not fit into the traditional template of caste politics in which the lower or backward castes are pitted against the upper or dominant castes. In other words, in conventional caste politics both the unit of mobilization and the unit of opposition are caste categories: *Mahars* versus *Brahmans* or *Jatavs* versus *Yadavs*. But in the emerging template, caste is relevant only as a unit of mobilization while the feeling of exclusion and opposition fuelling such mobilization is not directed towards any caste category (such as 'upper caste' or 'dominant caste') but towards the religious category of Muslims. As a result, the logic of caste-based mobilization appears to be disconnected from caste consciousness. Therefore, though this seems like caste politics, it is primarily a more flexible variety of *Hindutva* politics, where caste identity only plays a supporting role that serves to strengthen and buttress the Hindu consciousness of the groups mobilized along caste lines.

---

129   Nagel, "Constructing Ethnicity," 156–158.
130   It needs to be highlighted that the provisions of the CAA do not contain the word 'persecuted Hindus'. However, the Statement of Objects and Reasons (SoR) talks about the religious persecution of Hindus and other non-Muslim communities in Pakistan, Bangladesh and Afghanistan. Moreover, the representatives of the government and of the BJP have been consistently using the label 'persecuted Hindus' while discussing the CAA in public forums and platforms. As a result, the label 'persecuted Hindus' has become elevated to a formal and official categorization.

Hence, the recent shift in the electoral preference of the *Matua* community involves not only a strategic change in their political allegiance but also a fundamental transformation in their sense of identity and communal belongingness. A narrative of communal self-perception is prone to internalization and is not as readily changeable as political allegiance. Nevertheless, it is not immutable. From a theoretical point of view, just like any political solidarity forged by identity concerns, communal solidarity configured by *Hindutva,* or the politics of Hindu identity can't be be expected to remain perpetually stable and enduring. As already outlined, the idea that identity-based loyalty is stable enough to provide secure and solid political ground for relatively durable political action is problematic. Any identity around which identity politics is organized never enjoys a stable and static pre-eminence over other identities and can be superseded by any other identity with a change in the prevailing situation. In other words, in identity politics tension between different identities of the participants is never fully resolved and in a changed situation the same group of individuals may come to derive a greater sense of solidarity and a more effective strategic script for political action from an entirely different identity or a reinterpreted version of the same identity. Therefore, the possibility of a further transformation of the *Namasudra* consciousness in response to a changed political or institutional situation, in which the higher castes or any other entity emerge as an oppositional category can never be ruled out, particularly in view of the tendency of larger groups such as one with pan-Hindu solidarity, to break down into narrower caste specific groups over a period of time. In other words, in case of the *Matuas,* the possibility of caste based solidarity overriding their religious identity in a changed socio-political scenario can't be ruled out.

Analysing Patterns of Political Representation
Continuity or Change

We have already seen in the previous chapter how the steady electoral decline of the organized Left in West Bengal politics Left Front has sparked off anticipation about the enhanced role of caste in mainstream party politics of the state.[1] This anticipation draws heavily from the increasing political correspondence between Matua Mahasangha and mainstream political parties and also from other relatively minor developments like the formation of Social Justice Forum based on *dalit*-Muslim alliance. Some scholars see in these developments a potential for the rise of caste as an important factor in the electoral politics of the state. These developments were analysed in the previous chapter in detail. But to form a more concrete idea about the actual impact of these developments, it is important to assess their effects on the trends of political representation. In other words, it is imperative to examine the merit of the 'rise of caste thesis' through a scrutiny of trends relating to political representation, which is an important index of the rise of caste based political actors and forces in mainstream party politics. This chapter presents a detailed analysis of the trends of political representation of lower castes in legislature and Council of Ministers in West Bengal. However, it needs to be pointed out that the political representation of lower castes can be used as an analytical tool to assess the importance of caste as a political factor only in institutional politics at the macro level. To locate the phenomenon of politicisation of caste identity in micro politics one needs to focus upon the dynamics of political mobilization at the grassroots. Chapter 2 contains a detailed analysis of the role of caste in political mobilization. The findings of this chapter concerning the political representation of the lower castes are only relevant with regard to the impact of caste factor on the domain of macro politics.

---

1 Parts of this chapter appeared in Ayan Guha, "Caste Question in West Bengal Politics: Continuing Inconsequentiality or Rising Relevance?" *Contemporary South Asia* 29, no. 3 (2021): 376–400.

1   Explaining 'Rise of Caste' Hypothesis

The main advocate of the view that West Bengal is witnessing a resurgence
of caste politics is Praskanva Sinharay. According to him since the electoral
decline of the Left Front, three new trends in the interaction between community and organized politics have emerged. One is seen in the increasing
tendency to privilege community affiliation over party affiliation while working within a political party. Another trend relates to the growing inclination
towards articulation of identity-based demands by aligning with mainstream
political parties, as has been observed in the case of the *Matuas*. Lastly, efforts
to establish independent identity based political platforms are also being
made. Such efforts found manifestation in Abdur Rezzak Mollah's attempt to
create an exclusive organization for the *dalits* and Muslims. Sinharay however,
mainly bases his argument on the emergence of Matua Mahasangha, an organization of the *Matuas* (belonging mostly to lower caste *Namasudra* community) as an important political player.[2]

While Sinharay is confident about the arrival of a 'new politics of caste'
in West Bengal, other scholars appear to be more cautious in endorsing the
'rise of caste' thesis. One viewpoint has tended to suggest that the upper caste
parties dominating the political scene of West Bengal still have vested interests in making the language of caste illegitimate and therefore, they will continue to work towards sustaining an order of hegemonic control of the upper
castes.[3] Another powerful perspective has pointed out that the TMC has more
or less co-opted the Left's mode of functioning leading to continuing marginalization of social identities like caste in mainstream party politics. It is an
accepted proposition in scholarship on West Bengal that Left politics in West
Bengal instituted a new kind of sociability, known as 'party society', marked
by overwhelming social penetration of political parties into every sphere of
everyday life. Under such a form of sociability "a field of political transactions
is opened up which is within the reach of most villagers and where matters
of local interests can be sorted out on a day-to-day basis" and the party domi-
nates "the socio-political sphere to the extent that other competing channels
of public transactions are either weak or non-existent". In 'party society', party

2   Praskanva Sinharay, "A New Politics of Caste," *Economic and Political Weekly* 47, no. 34
    (2012): 26–27; Praskanva Sinharay, "The West Bengal's Election Story: The Caste Question in
    Lok Sabha Elections," *Economic and Political Weekly* 49, no. 16 (2014): 10–12.
3   Sarbani Bandyopadhyay, "Caste and Politics in Bengal," *Economic and Political Weekly* 47,
    no. 50 (2012): 71–73; Dwaipayan Sen, "An Absent-minded Casteism?," *Seminar*, 645 (May 2013).

acts as an intermediary between the government and the communities clos-
ing off all other alternative channels of social mediation and interaction. In
the process it establishes itself as the single most important institution of the
rural social life. As a result, people's unquestionable allegiance to the party
grows at the expense of their allegiance to competing social institutions such
as caste and religion.[4] Thus, in 'party society', party acts as the most fundamental and elementary institution of social life and monopolizes every inch
of social space leaving little room for autonomous functioning of communities and social bodies. Every other social institution from caste councils and
religious bodies to schools, sporting clubs, traders' associations are either
eliminated or subordinated to the overarching authority of the party. It is the
operation of the 'party society' during the Left rule in rural West Bengal that
accounted for the marginal position of other social institutions such as landed
patriarchs, caste councils or religious bodies. Political parties monopolized
the entire social space taking over the roles of these social organizations. The
'party society' might have been an original contribution of the CPI(M) but
the current politics of the state demonstrates that the rules of the party society are meticulously followed by all political parties. This is because in West
Bengal there is a modular form of party activity to which all parties aspire,
dictated by the socially established role that a party and its functionaries are
expected to perform in rural life.[5] According to Partha Chatterjee "the recent
political transition has not or not as yet meant a reassertion of the autonomy
of local social institutions. Rather, the Trinamool Congress, in the districts
of Southern Bengal, where it is now dominant, appears to be keen to adopt
the Left Front model of the dominance of the political over the social and
exclude the Communist Party of India- (Marxist)- CPI(M) from local power".[6]
Dwaipayan Bhattacharyya has also argued that the end of the CPI(M) rule has
not resulted in the termination of coercive structure of 'party society'; it has
only passed into the hands of the TMC which has exhibited utter ruthlessness

---

4 Dwaipayan Bhattacharyya, "Party Society, Its Consolidation and Crisis: Understanding
   Political Change in Rural West Bengal," in *Theorising the Present: Essays for Partha Chatterjee*,
   eds. Anjan Ghosh, Tapati Guha Thakurta and Janaki Nair (New Delhi: Oxford University
   Press, 2011), 226–250.
5 Partha Chatterjee, "The Coming Crisis in West Bengal," *Economic and Political Weekly* 44, no. 9
   (2009): 42–45.
6 Partha Chatterjee, "Partition and the Mysterious Disappearance of Caste in Bengal," in
   Politics of Caste in West Bengal, eds. Uday Chandra, Geir Heierstad and Kenneth Bo Nielsen
   (New Delhi: Routledge, 2016), 96.

in marginalizing autonomous voices of dissent in rural localities.[7] I have also argued elsewhere that in post-2011 West Bengal party still remains the principal cleavage in rural life. This can easily be inferred from the fact that in West Bengal violence still occurs mainly and quite frequently over political matters relating to elections and party allegiance and rarely over caste and communal disputes.[8] Based on their exhaustive field research Glyn Williams and Sailaja Nandigama have also argued that 'party society' has not emanated from the CPI(M) itself, but from institutionalization of party-politicised *Panchayat* rule ridden with inter-party competition for power. Unlike many other states in India, candidates in West Bengal's *Panchayat* elections are permitted to stand as representatives of political parties. As a result, party politics has deeply infiltrated everyday life in rural West Bengal.[9] Thus, the central contention of this line of argument is that even after the electoral decline of the Left Front, the pivotal position of political parties in rural society remains more or less intact. This accounts for the political insignificance of other social institutions such as landed patriarchs, caste councils or religious bodies. They still remain subordinate to the over-arching authority of the all powerful institution of political party. The resulting scenario is that of continuing inconsequentiality of caste in mainstream party politics.

All these critiques of the 'rise of caste thesis' have not gone to the extent of proclaiming a radical break from the past while engaging with the nature of post-Left politics. However, none of these critiques have scrutinised the 'rise of caste thesis' through the important prism of political representation which is a primary indicator of the rise of caste as a significant factor in mainstream macro politics. In this connection, this chapter intends to underline that the 'rise of caste thesis' has ignored possibly the most important indicator of the rise of caste factor in institutional macro level politics, which is political representation. An empirical analysis of the trends of political representation of the lower castes shows that the rise of the lower castes is yet to occur in West Bengal.

---

7   Dwaipayan Bhattacharyya, *Government as Practice: Democratic Left in a Transforming India* (New Delhi: Cambridge University Press, 2017), 148–49.
8   Ayan Guha, "Caste and Politics in West Bengal: Traditional Limitations and Contemporary Developments," *Contemporary Voice of Dalit* 9, no. 1 (2017): 34–35.
9   Glyn Williams and Sailaja Nandigama, "Managing Political Space: Authority, Marginalised People's Agency and Governance in West Bengal," *International Development Planning Review* 40, no. 1 (2018): 20.

2   Two Concepts of Representation: A Brief Theoretical Exploration

Identity politics, to a significant extent, revolves around the issue of representation, intending to facilitate the articulation of opinions, resentment and concerns of the groups mobilized on the basis of their identities. Representation is
a major theme in democratic theory. Hanna Pitkin who is generally credited for
bringing the issue of representation at the centre-stage of democratic theory
has made a distinction between four forms of representation: (1) formalistic,
where a representative is legally empowered to act for another; (2) descriptive,
where a representative stands for a group by virtue of sharing similar charac-
teristics such as race, sex, ethnicity, or residence; (3) symbolic, where a leader
stands for certain symbols such as national unity; and (4) substantive, where
a representative seeks to advance a group's policy preferences and interests.
Of these forms substantive representation and descriptive representation have
become the two broad conceptual categories through which the entire issue of
political representation is generally viewed. The descriptive form of representation is associated with the identity of the representative. Here the criterion
to assess representation is the extent of resemblance between the representative and the represented. According to Pitkin, the concept of descriptive
representation is woefully limited and inadequate because it focuses on the
composition of a political institution rather than its activities. Pitkin favours
substantive form of representation which is based on the concept of function-
ality of the representative. In case of substantive representation, the representative has to be responsive to the represented. What matters is what the
representative does, not who he or she is.[10] So, the concept of substantive representation is based upon the idea of universal citizenship: a representative
can effectively represent any social group irrespective of whether he or she
belongs to that social group or not. Therefore, a male can represent a female, a
white man a black man and an upper caste a lower caste.

However, it is often argued that substantive form of representation can't
succeed in a diverse and heterogeneous society which contains historically
marginalized and discriminated social groups. Descriptive form of representation is often considered necessary in such a society. A compelling statement of
the concept of descriptive representation is represented by Anne Phillips' idea
of 'politics of presence'. Phillips has critically engaged with the argument that
emphasis on the identity of a representative diverts attention from whether
he or she is acting in the interests of the represented. In her view even if the

---

10   Hanna Pitkin, *The Concept of Representation* (Los Angeles: University of Press, 1967).

entry of a greater number of members of marginalized groups in political institutions fails to influence policies, their representation should be encouraged
to reverse their previous exclusion and to publically acknowledge equal worth
of all citizens. Providing adequate political representation to the members of
marginalized groups is the surest way of securing recognition and dignity for
them. The blacks and the women cannot enjoy equal dignity and equal political status until their representatives join government bodies. Finally, what
gets represented depends on who represents. A range of ideas are blocked by
the hegemonic culture or dominant norm which controls what could or could
not be expressed. Greater political representation of the excluded groups will
ensure that perspectives shaped by their unique experiences will find a voice
in the political process. According to Phillips female politicians represent
women's interests much better than male politicians because the former share
life experiences with women voters. As a result of enhanced political representation of the marginalized groups the dominant and exclusionary norms will
come under greater challenge.[11]

Marion Young also in several of her works has advocated descriptive representation, highlighting the inadequacy of the concept of universal citizenship
that requires citizens to transcend their particular identities and ignore interests and concerns relating to their identities in public life for the sake of con-
forming to a general will. For Young, the idea of universal citizenship excludes
those groups who are incapable and unwilling to adopt a general point of
view, which is nothing but a discourse of the dominant. Some groups are privileged and are in a position to promote their values and ways of life as ideal
norms which all individuals are expected to conform to. Therefore, commonly
accepted public norms that are claimed to be neutral are not neutral but stand
for the values of the dominant groups. Hence, in a society where some groups
are privileged and some are marginalized, the idea of universal citizenship
leads to the perpetuation of social exclusion of the marginalized groups. Young
points out that, different social groups have different needs, perceptions and
cultural and historical experiences which shape their political reasoning and
policy perspectives. Therefore, there should be special efforts directed towards
ensuring adequate representation of the marginalized groups.[12] In her words,
"I feel represented when at least some of those discussing and voting on policies understand and express the kind of social experience I have because of

---

11   See, Anne Phillips, *Politics of Presence* (New York: Clarendon, 1995).
12   Marion Iris Young, *Justice and the Politics of Difference* (Princeton, NJ: Princeton University
         Press, 1990); Marion Iris Young, "Polity and Group Difference: A Critique of the Ideal of
         Universal Citizenship," *Ethics* 99, no. 2 (1989): 250–274.

my social group position and the history of social group relations".[13] Melissa Williams has also argued on the same lines. According to her historically disadvantaged groups must have a 'voice' in legislative decision-making since legislative process is deliberative in nature. So, legislative institutions must be equipped with adequate presence of individuals who have direct access to historically excluded perspectives. For example, she feels that women must have sufficient representation in legislatures because "women's perceptions, concerns, and needs are inaccessible" to men.[14] Therefore, adequate representation of marginalized groups in legislatures is required to facilitate "the discursive exchange of the perspectives of all relevant social groups before a decision is reached". This will "harmonize the competing interests of different social groups such that no group's interests are permanently frustrated".[15]

Jane Mansbridge's advocacy of descriptive representation also deserves particular attention in this context. Mansbridge has pointed out that descriptive representation is not universally necessary but it is needed in certain contexts. These contexts are 1) existence of distrust between marginalized groups and privileged groups; 2) existence of a situation where political preferences of the marginalized groups have not been fully formed; 3) existence of low level of *de facto* legitimacy of the political system in the eyes of the members of marginalized groups due to their past discrimination; and 4) existence of a situation where ruling ability of marginalized groups is widely questioned.[16] Therefore, even if we don't lend blanket support to the idea of descriptive representation, it can at least be argued that, in some specific situations descriptive representation is indeed necessary. Following Mansbridge we can argue that, if one group is historically dominant and the other historically subordinate there is likely to be distrust between them. In conditions of such long lasting historical distrust, voters from a subordinate group can forge bonds of trust only with those representatives who share their experiences of subordination. Williams also emphasizes the important factor of trust. For Williams, trust is the cornerstone for democratic accountability. Williams shows that consistent patterns of betrayal of African-Americans by privileged white citizens give them good reason for distrusting white representatives and institutions dominated by the whites. For Williams, relationships of distrust can be "at least partially mended

---

13   Marion Iris Young, *Inclusion and Democracy* (Oxford: Oxford University Press, 2000), 134.

14   Melissa Williams, *Trust, and Memory: Marginalized Groups and the Failings of Liberal Representation* (Princeton, NJ: Princeton University, 1998), 133.

15   Williams, *Trust, and Memory,* 147–48.

16   Jane Mansbridge, "Should Blacks Represent Blacks and Women Represent Women? A Contingent 'Yes'," *The Journal of Politics* 61 (1999): 628–57.

if the disadvantaged group is represented by its own members". Williams also highlights the importance of past experiences or 'memory' in this context. A shared memory of oppression partly defines a group's collective agency and therefore, possession of shared experience of marginalization justifies certain institutional mechanisms to guarantee presence or representation.[17]

From this perspective, it can be argued that, historical discrimination faced by the lower castes and the resulting distrust they still harbour about the motives of the higher castes make a strong case for greater descriptive representation of the *dalits*. Further, their long exclusion from political power has created a notion that they are somehow unable to rule; a negative social perception which, as Mansbridge has pointed out, is often faced by the marginalized groups. Descriptive representation can only challenge such negative social perceptions about them. Further, in the context of the *dalits*, descriptive representation is also necessary to enhance the legitimacy of the political system in their eyes since greater participation by *dalit* leaders in political institutions is likely to create a feeling of inclusion among the *dalits*. This will also facilitate achievement of outcomes which scholars like Phillips, Young and Williams consider necessary for marginalized groups like the *dalits*: expression of historically excluded *dalit* perspectives in democratic deliberation and social affirmation of their equal worth and dignity.

3   Mapping Trends of Political Representation in West Bengal

Caste based identity politics by promoting collective political action premised on caste centric solidarities intends to bring unrepresented or inadequately represented caste groups into political limelight, raise their core concerns in public domain, forestall their stigmatised and inglorious social portrayal and most importantly unlock the portals of institutional politics for them. Critics of identity politics frequently and sometime justifiably contest politicisation of caste identity but there are some virtues of this mode of political organisation that also need to be acknowledged. It is highly unlikely that *dalit* issues would have attained much prominence without the emergence of *dalit* politics, one of the core objectives of which has been enhancement of political representation of the *dalits*.

The Constitution of India has provided for reservation of seats in legislatures for the lower castes. However, the real progress in the direction of

---

17   Williams, *Trust, and Memory*, 14.

achieving descriptive representation for marginalized caste groups began to occur with the emergence of caste based political parties in North India. They played an instrumental role in politicisation of lower caste identity leading to the rise of *dalit* politics as well as the politics of *Mandal* based on the OBC (Other Backward classes) identity. The political assertion of socially and politically disadvantaged caste groups led to a significant rise in their political representation in legislatures as well as in other political bodies. In other words, increase in political representation of the lower caste groups manifested their political rise and indicated a real and effective emergence of caste politics. For example, in Uttar Pradesh (UP) Assembly the representation of the OBCs increased from 9 percent in 1952 to 27.52 percent in 2002. During the same period the representation of the upper castes went down from 58 percent in 1952 to 35.38 percent in 2002. On the other hand, the representation of the *Jatavs* (a Scheduled caste community which mobilized by Bahujan Samaj Party (BSP) played an instrumental role in the emergence of *dalit* politics in UP) increased from 2.35 percent in 1974 to 12.29 percent in 2002.[18] Similarly, due to karpoori Thakur's mobilization of the backward castes in Bihar in the 1970s their representation in unreserved seats in Bihar Assembly increased from 30.5 percent in 1962 to 38.5 percent in 1977. The mainstay of backward caste politics, the *Yadavs* emerged as the second largest caste group in Bihar Assembly (next only to *Rajputs*) occupying 21 percent of unreserved seats by 1977, though they accounted for only 11 percent of total population of Bihar.[19] In the 1980s the *Yadavs* emerged as the single largest caste group in Bihar Assembly with as many as 41 *Yadav* legislators.[20] Overall, the percentage of upper caste MLAs decreased from 46 percent in 1952 to 30 percent in 2005 in Bihar. During the same period the percentage of backward caste MLAs increased from 19.53 percent to 34.5 percent, while the percentage of SC MLAs increased from 13.9 percent to 16.9 percent.[21]

---

18   Jasmine Zerinini, "The Marginalization of the Savarnas in Uttar Pradesh?," in *Rise of the Plebeians?The Changing Face of Indian Legislative Assemblies*, eds. Christophe Jaffrelot and Sanjay Kumar (New Delhi: Routledge, 2009), 35–37.

19   Harry W Blair, "Rising Kulaks and Backward Classes in Bihar: Social Change in the Late 1970s," *Economic and Political Weekly* 15, no. 2 (1980): 67.

20   Francine R. Frankel, "Caste, Land and Dominance in Bihar: Breakdown of the Brahminical Social Order," in *Dominance and State Power in Modern India, Vol I*, eds. Francine Frankel and M.S.A. Rao (Delhi: Oxford University Press, 1989), 119.

21   Cyril Robin, "Bihar: The New Stronghold of OBC Politics," in *Rise of the Plebeians? The Changing Face of Indian Legislative Assemblies,* eds. Christophe Jaffrelot and Sanjay Kumar (New Delhi: Routledge, 2009), 100.

In this way, the signs of the emergence of caste politics became visible in the rising political representation of the politically mobilized caste groups. Thus, the emergence of caste politics has entailed caste-based mobilization along with the rise of political representation of the caste groups mobilized along caste lines. Hence, from an analytical point of view effective inauguration of caste politics in macro political domain is inextricably linked with the rising political representation of the lower castes. Caste politics or politicisation of caste identity in various parts of India, particularly since the late 1970s, has got manifested in the rising political representation of the lower castes, which has been hailed as 'second democratic upsurge',[22] 'silent revolution'[23] and 'rise of plebeians'[24] and 'politics of direct appeal'.[25] Thus, political trends in various parts of India have so far demonstrated that rise in lower caste political representation is the most veritable sign of the emergence of caste as an influential factor in institutional politics at the macro level. Hence, for making a reasonable assessment of the rise of caste politics, it is imperative to find out as to whether lower castes have started to become mobilized into political participation in West Bengal in the same way as in other states, which are strongholds of caste politics.

The 'rise of caste thesis' has committed a major analytical oversight by not investigating the existing trends relating to lower caste political representation. However, Sinharay, the main advocate of the 'rise of caste thesis' has made an important observation relating to lower caste political representation. He claims to have discovered an increasing tendency in recent times to give greater importance to the community identity of the candidates rather than their party identity during election campaigns. According to him party banners are no longer the only identity of the candidates in the fray. For instance, in 2014 Lok Sabha election candidates such as Manohar Tirkey of the Left Front, Dasarath Tirkey of the TMC and Birendra Bara of the BJP were known

22   Yogendra Yadav, "Understanding the second democratic upsurge: Trends of Bahujan Participation in electoral politics in the 1990s," in *Transforming India: Social and Political Dynamics of Democracy,* eds. Francine R. Frankel, Zoya Hassan, Rajeev Bhargava and Balveer Arora (New Delhi: Oxford University Press, 2000), 120–145.

23   Christophe Jaffrelot, *India's Silent Revolution: The Rise of the Lower Castes in North India* (Delhi: Permanent Black, 2003).

24   Christophe Jafferlot, "Introduction," in *Rise of the Plebeians? The Changing Face of Indian Legislative Assemblies,* eds. Christophe Jaffrelot and Sanjay Kumar (New Delhi: Routledge, 2009), 1–23.

25   Sanjay Reddy, "A Rising Tide of Demands: India's Public Institutions and the Democratic Revolution," in *Public Institutions in India: Performance and Design,* eds. Devesh Kapur and Pratap Bhanu Mehta (New Delhi: Oxford University Press, 2005).

more by their *Oraon* origin while Joseph Munda of the Congress was primarily identified with a protestant Christian lineage.[26] But, this tendency is not something new and existed even during the long rule of the Left Front. All political parties, including the CPI(M) rarely made any large-scale use of caste or any other social identity for the purpose of organized electoral mobilization. But this does not imply that parties did not at all take into account geographical concentration of different communities. Stephanie Tawa Lama Rewal's study on the profile of West Bengal MLAS (Members of Legislative Assembly) from 1952 to 2001 has revealed that political parties have indeed given some importance to the regional concentration of different communities. 59.4 percent of all middle caste MLAS came from the southwestern region, especially from the districts of Midnapore, Hoogly and Howrah where the *Mahishyas*, who constitute the single largest middle caste group of West Bengal are concentrated. The Scheduled Tribe dominated districts of Darjeeling and Jalpaiguri supplied 53.6 percent of all Scheduled Tribe MLAS. Similarly, 44.1 percent of the Muslim MLAS hailed from southeastern districts of Nadia, Murshidabad and 24 Parganas, where Muslims have a sizeable presence. Moreover, 28.3 percent of the upper caste MLAS got elected from the *bhadralok* stronghold of Greater Kolkata.[27] Atul Kohli has also pointed out that the CPI(M) gave sufficient consideration to the fact that eastern districts are populated by Biharis and Jharkhandis, that Darjeeling is dominated by *Gurkhas*, that interior areas have concentration of tribal population, and that districts such as Burdwan are inhabited by land-holding agricultural castes. Thus, in West Bengal too, while selecting candidates for elections, sufficient care has always been taken by political parties to ensure that their candidates are able to attract support on the basis of primordial loyalties. But "none of this in West Bengal, however, adds up to the 'backward castes' movement of a Bihar type, or the concern with the 'dominant castes' in Karnataka".[28]

Therefore, what needs to looked at in this context is the magnitude and proportion of political representation secured by the lower castes. The 'rise of caste thesis' while making a sweeping generalisation has not bothered to make a comparison between the trends of lower caste political representation during the Left rule and the same during the post-Left era. To discover

26   Sinharay, "The West Bengal's Election Story,"11.

27   Stéphanie Tawa Lama-Rewal, "The Resilient Bhadralok: A Profile of the West Bengal MLAS," in *Rise of the Plebeians? The Changing Face of Indian Legislative Assemblies*, eds. Christophe Jaffrelot and Sanjay Kumar, (New Delhi: Routledge, 2009), 379–80.

28   Atul Kohli, *The State and Poverty in India: The Politics of Reform* (Cambridge: Cambridge University Press, 2006), 104.

the actual impact of caste factor on mainstream institutional politics, it is imperative to make this comparison by undertaking a thorough data centric analysis of patterns of political representation. But before embarking upon an analysis of political representation, it is necessary to furnish a few disclaimers. All information concerning caste background of political functionaries is not available. Therefore, it is not always possible to ascertain which caste or sub-caste a political representative belongs to due to non-availability of data. Still, it is possible to draw sufficient insights about the broad patterns of political representation of the lower castes from the limited amount of available data.

The percentage of SC MLAs in West Bengal has so far varied between 19.64 percent and 24.49 percent (see Table 5). Available data does not show any considerable increase in the proportion of SC MLAs since 2011. Most importantly, an overwhelming proportion of SC MLAs (94.44 percent in 2011 and 98.55 percent in 2016) continues to get elected from reserved seats (see Table 5). What is even more striking is that in 2016 Assembly elections, the number of SC candidates who got elected from unreserved seats was actually the lowest, i.e. only one (see Table 5). SC MLAs from all the three major parties have mostly come from reserved seats (see Tables 6, 7 and 8). Interestingly, the percentage of SC MLAs elected from the CPI(M) has remained higher than the percentage of SC MLAs elected from the TMC (see Tables 7 and 8). So, there is little evidence to suggest that the political ascent of the TMC has led to the political rise of the lower castes in mainstream electoral politics.

However, data concerning elected representatives may not offer conclusive evidence in this regard. It is also imperative to look at the relevant data concerning candidates' caste background to assess the commitment of political parties towards ensuring political representation of the *dalits*. An analysis of last three Assembly elections shows that the percentage of SC candidates has remained around 30 percent (see Table 9). A sizeable proportion of SC candidates (from 34 to 37 percent) has contested from unreserved constituencies (see Table 9). But this does not imply that the lower castes are not facing political exclusion. Most of the SC candidates who contested from unreserved seats did not belong to the major political parties of the state. They were mostly independent candidates or belonged to marginal political players such as the Bahujan Samaj Party (BSP). The SC candidates of three major political parties contesting from unreserved seats accounted for only a meagre proportion of total number of SC candidates contesting from unreserved seats (see Tables 10, 11 and 12). For instance, in 2016 Assembly elections the percentage of SC candidates contesting from unreserved seats from the INC (Indian National Congress), CPI(M) and TMC were 0, 10.87 and 2.86 percent respectively (see Tables 10, 11 and 12). This reflects lack of commitment of all major political

TABLE 5   SC MLAs in assembly elections (1952–2016)

	1952	1957	1962	1967	1969	1971	1972	1977	1982	1987	1991	1996	2001	2006	2011	2016
Total no. of MLAs	238	252	252	280	280	280	280	294	294	294	294	294	294	294	294	294
Total number of SC MLAs	47	52	59	60	55	56	60	65	62	63	66	68	62	66	72	69
Percentage of SC MLAs of total MLAs	19.75	20.63	23.41	21.43	19.64	20	21.43	22.11	21.09	21.43	22.45	23.13	21.09	22.44	24.49	23.47
Total number of SC MLAs elected from reserved seats	41	42	42	54	54	54	54	59	59	59	59	59	59	59	68	68
Percentage of SC MLAs elected from reserved seats out of total SC MLAs	87.23	80.77	71.19	90.00	98.19	96.43	90.00	90.77	95.16	93.65	89.39	86.76	95.16	89.39	94.44	98.55
Total number of SC MLAs elected from unreserved seats	06	10	17	06	01	02	06	06	03	04	07	09	03	07	04	01

TABLE 5   SC MLAS in assembly elections (1952–2016) (cont.)

	1952	1957	1962	1967	1969	1971	1972	1977	1982	1987	1991	1996	2001	2006	2011	2016
Percentage of SC MLAs elected from unreserved seats out of total SC MLAs	12.77	19.23	26.67	5.17	1.81	3.57	10.00	9.23	4.84	6.35	10.61	13.24	4.84	10.61	5.56	1.45

SOURCE: DATA FROM 1952 TO 2001 HAS BEEN CALCULATED FROM STÉPHANIE TAWA LAMA-REWAL, "THE RESILIENT BHADRALOK: A PROFILE OF THE WEST BENGAL MLAS", IN *RISE OF THE PLEBEIANS? THE CHANGING FACE OF INDIAN LEGISLATIVE ASSEMBLIES*, EDS. CHRISTOPHE JAFFRELOT AND SANJAY KUMAR, (NEW DELHI: ROUTLEDGE, 2009). DATA FROM 2006 TO 2016 HAS BEEN CALCULATED FROM ELECTION COMMISSION OF INDIA'S STATISTICAL REPORTS ON GENERAL ELECTIONS, 2006, 2011 AND 2016 TO LEGISLATIVE ASSEMBLY OF WEST BENGAL.

TABLE 6   SC MLAS of Indian National Congress (INC) in assembly elections (1952–2016)

Year	Total MLAS	Total SC MLAS	SC MLAS from reserved seats	SC MLAS from unreserved seats	% of SC MLAS	% of SC MLAS in reserved seats out of total SC MLAS of INC	% of SC MLAS in unreserved seats out of total SC MLAS of INC
1962	157	40	31	09	25.5	77.50	22.50
1967	127	24	23	01	18.9	95.83	4.17
1969	55	12	12	0	21.8	100	0
1971	103	19	19	0	18.4	100	0
1972	216	47	45	02	21.8	95.74	4.26
1977	20	03	03	0	15	100	0
1982	82	06	04	02	7.3	66.67	33.33
1987	40	03	03	0	7.5	100	0
1991	43	01	00	01	2.3	100	0
1996	82	10	08	02	12.2	80	20.00
2001	26	04	03	01	15.4	75	25.00
2006	21	02	02	0	9.52	100	0
2011	42	11	10	01	26.19	90.91	9.09
2016	44	08	08	0	18.18	100	0

SOURCE: DATA FROM 1962 TO 2001 HAS BEEN CALCULATED FROM LAMA-REWAL, STEPHANIE TAWA (2009). DATA FROM 2006 TO 2011 HAS BEEN CALCULATED FROM ELECTION COMMISSION OF INDIA'S STATISTICAL REPORTS ON GENERAL ELECTIONS, 2006, 2011 AND 2016 TO LEGISLATIVE ASSEMBLY OF WEST BENGAL

parties to the cause of *dalit* representation. Furthermore, contrary to common perception, the TMC has not fared any better than the CPI(M) when it comes to giving representation to the lower castes. The proportion of SC candidates of the TMC who contested from unreserved constituencies was much lower than the proportion of SC candidates of the CPI(M) who contested from unreserved constituencies in Assembly elections of 2011 and 2016. (see Tables 11 and 12).

Data relating to parliamentary elections also brings out a similar picture of severe and continuing political exclusion of the lower castes in West Bengal. The proportion of SC MPs (Members of Parliament) to total MPs has remained close to the proportion of SCs to total population due to the system of reserved

TABLE 7   SC MLAS of CPI(M) in assembly elections (1967–2016)

Year	Total MLAS	Total SC MLAS	SC MLAS from reserved seats	SC MLAS from unreserved seats	% of SC MLAS	% of SC MLAS in reserved seats out of total SC MLAS of CPI(M)	% of SC MLAS in unreserved seats out of total SC MLAS of CPI(M)
1967	43	09	07	02	20.9	77.78	22.22
1969	80	16	14	02	20.0	87.50	12.50
1971	113	25	23	02	22.1	71.88	28.12
1977	178	45	39	06	25.3	86.67	13.33
1982	174	46	42	04	26.4	91.30	8.70
1987	187	48	44	04	25.7	91.67	8.39
1991	188	52	47	05	27.7	90.39	9.61
1996	157	46	40	06	29.3	86.95	13.05
2001	143	38	37	01	26.6	97.37	2.63
2006	176	47	43	04	26.00	91.49	8.51
2011	40	11	11	0	27.5	100	0
2016	26	09	09	0	34.6	100	0

SOURCE: DATA FROM 1962 TO 2001 HAS BEEN CALCULATED FROM LAMA-REWAL, STEPH-
ANIE TAWA (2009). DATA FROM 2006 TO 2011 HAS BEEN CALCULATED FROM ELECTION
COMMISSION OF INDIA'S STATISTICAL REPORTS ON GENERAL ELECTIONS, 2006, 2011 AND
2016 TO LEGISLATIVE ASSEMBLY OF WEST BENGAL

seats (see Table 13). But the declining strength of the Left Front has not brought about any increase in the political representation of the lower castes. In the last three Lok Sabha elections not a single SC candidate got elected from unreserved seats in West Bengal (see Tables 13, 14, 15 and 16).

Available data, however, suggests that both overall percentage of SC candidates and percentage of SC candidates contesting from unreserved constituencies in Lok Sabha elections have remained sizeable (Table 17). But most of the SC candidates fought as independent candidates or belonged to marginal political players like the BSP. The mainstream political parties have shown little interests in enhancing representation of lower castes by giving SC candidates the opportunity to contest from unreserved seats. In the three consecutive

TABLE 8   SC MLAS of TMC in assembly elections (2001–2016)

Year	Total MLAS	Total SC MLAS	SC MLAS from reserved seats	SC MLAS from unreserved seats	% of SC MLAS	% of SC MLAS in reserved seats out of total SC MLAS of TMC	% of SC MLAS in unreserved seats out of total SC MLAS of TMC
2001	60	07	07	0	11.67	100	0
2006	30	03	02	01	0	66.67	33.33
2011	184	39	37	02	21.19	94.87	5.13
2016	211	50	49	01	23.70	98.0	02.0

SOURCE: DATA OF 2001 HAS BEEN CALCULATED FROM LAMA-REWAL, STEPHANIE TAWA (2009). DATA FROM 2006 TO 2011 HAS BEEN CALCULATED FROM ELECTION COMMISSION OF INDIA'S STATISTICAL REPORTS ON GENERAL ELECTIONS, 2006, 2011 AND 2016 TO LEGISLATIVE ASSEMBLY OF WEST BENGAL

Lok Sabha elections of 2004, 2009 and 2014 not a single SC candidate of the INC fought from unreserved seats (see Table 18). In each of the parliamentary elections of 2004, 2014 and 2019 only one SC candidate contested from unreserved constituencies on a CPI(M) ticket. In 2009 not a single SC candidate of the CPI(M) contested from unreserved seats (see Table 19). In the last three parliamentary elections, not a single SC candidate of the TMC contested from unreserved constituencies (see Table 20).

In this context, we should also take into consideration the trends of SC representation in the Council of Ministers. The SCs have consistently failed to achieve adequate representation in West Bengal's Cabinet of Ministers. During the regime of the Left Front from 1977 to 2011 the SCs remained severely under-represented in the Cabinet of Ministers. The highest proportion of representation they achieved was 14 percent in 1987 (see Table 21). Even this was below their share in total population, which is around 23 percent. Thus, the SCs never obtained adequate and proportionate representation in the Cabinet of Ministers during the long rule of the Left Front. Francesca Jensenius' estimate of average percentage of SC representation in the Cabinet of Ministers of major states between the period 1977 and 2007 shows how SC representation in West Bengal's Cabinet remained excessively low compared

TABLE 9   SC candidates in assembly elections (2006–2016)

	2006	2011	2016
Total number of candidates	1654	1792	1961
Total number of SC candidates	496	565	614
Percentage of SC candidates of total candidates	29.99	31.53	31.31
Number of SC candidates in unreserved seats	184	192	226
Percentage of SC candidates in unreserved seats out of total SC candidates	37.10	33.98	36.81
Number of SC candidates in reserved seats	312	373	388
Percentage of SC candidates in reserved seats out of total SC candidates	62.90	66.02	63.19

SOURCE: ELECTION COMMISSION OF INDIA'S STATISTICAL REPORTS ON GENERAL ELEC-
TIONS, 2006, 2011 AND 2016 TO LEGISLATIVE ASSEMBLY OF WEST BENGAL

to SC representation in the Cabinets of other states.[29] The average percentage of SCs in the Assembly in West Bengal remained close to the percentage of SC population due to the constitutionally mandated system of reservation. But the gap between percentage of SCs in the Assembly and percentage of SCs in the Cabinet in West Bengal was not only unusually large but also highest among all states. While this gap was 11.4 percent in West Bengal, in all other states barring Orissa (5.4 percent) and Tamil Nadu (8.1 percent) this gap was less than 5 percent (see Table 22). Thus, SC representation in West Bengal Cabinets remained disproportionately low during the Left rule. Most importantly, this situation has not undergone any change during the TMC regime. Despite much discussion and anticipation about the political rise of the *dalits* in West Bengal particularly the *Namasudras,* on account of the decline of the Left, the representation of the SCs in the Cabinet of Ministers has not

---

29   Francesca R. Jensenius, "Power, Performance and Bias: Evaluating the Electoral Quotas for Scheduled Castes in India" (PhD dissertation, University of California, Berkeley, 2013), 82–83.

TABLE 10 SC candidates of INC in assembly elections (2006–2016)

Year	Total candidates	Total sc candidates	sc candidates in reserved seats	sc candidates in unreserved seats	% of sc candidates	% of sc candidates in reserved seats out of total sc candidates of INC	% of sc candidates in unreserved seats out of total sc candidates of INC
2006	262	55	52	03	20.99	94.55	5.45
2011	66	19	18	01	28.78	94.74	5.26
2016	92	14	14	0	15.21	100	0

SOURCE: ELECTION COMMISSION OF INDIA'S STATISTICAL REPORTS ON GENERAL ELECTIONS, 2006, 2011 AND 2016 TO LEGISLATIVE ASSEMBLY OF WEST BENGAL

TABLE 11 SC candidates of CPI(M) in assembly elections (2006–2016)

Year	Total candidates	Total sc candidates	sc candidates in reserved seats	sc candidates in unreserved seats	% of sc candidates	% of sc candidates in reserved seats out of total sc candidates of CPI(M)	% of sc candidates in unreserved seats out of total sc candidates of CPI(M)
2006	212	51	46	05	24.06	90.2	9.80
2011	213	59	51	08	27.70	86.44	13.56
2016	148	46	41	05	31.08	89.13	10.87

SOURCE: ELECTION COMMISSION OF INDIA'S STATISTICAL REPORTS ON GENERAL ELECTIONS, 2006, 2011 AND 2016 TO LEGISLATIVE ASSEMBLY OF WEST BENGAL

TABLE 12   SC candidates of TMC in assembly elections (2006–2016)

Year	Total candidates	Total SC candidates	SC candidates in reserved seats	SC candidates in unreserved seats	% of SC candidates	% of SC candidates in reserved seats out of total SC candidates of TMC	% of SC candidates in unreserved seats out of total SC candidates of TMC
2006	257	55	48	07	21.40	87.27	12.73
2011	226	51	49	02	22.57	96.08	3.92
2016	293	70	68	02	23.89	97.14	2.86

SOURCE: ELECTION COMMISSION OF INDIA'S STATISTICAL REPORTS ON GENERAL ELECTIONS, 2006, 2011 AND 2016 TO LEGISLATIVE ASSEMBLY OF WEST BENGAL

TABLE 13   SC MPs in Lok Sabha elections (2004–2019)

	2004	2009	2014	2019
Total number of elected SC MPs	09	10	10	10
Number of SC MPs elected from reserved seats	08	10	10	10
Number of SC MPs elected from unreserved seats	01	0	0	0
Percentage of SC MPs of total MPs	19.05	23.81	23.81	23.81
Percentage of SC MPs elected from reserved seats out of total SC MPs	88.89	100	100	100
Percentage of SC MPs elected from unreserved seats out of total SC MPs	11.11	0	0	0

SOURCE: ELECTION COMMISSION OF INDIA'S STATISTICAL REPORTS ON GENERAL ELEC-
TIONS, 2004, 2009, 2014 AND 2019

TABLE 14   SC MPs of INC (2004–2019)

Year	Total MPS	Total SC MPS	SC MPs in reserved seats	SC MPs in unreserved seats	% of SC MPS	% of SC MPs in reserved seats out of total SC MPs of INC	% of SC MPs in unreserved seats out of total SC MPs of INC
2004	06	0	0	0	0	0	0
2009	06	0	0	0	0	0	0
2014	04	0	0	0	0	0	0
2019	02	0	0	0	0	0	0

SOURCE: ELECTION COMMISSION OF INDIA'S STATISTICAL REPORTS ON GENERAL ELEC-
TIONS, 2004, 2009, 2014 AND 2019

TABLE 15   SC MPs of CPI(M)- (2004–2019)

Year	Total MPs	Total SC MPs	SC MPs in reserved seats	SC MPs in unreserved seats	% of SC MPs	% of SC MPs in reserved seats out of total SC MPs of CPI(M)	% of SC MPs in unreserved seats out of total SC MPs of CPI(M)
2004	26	06	05	01	23.08	83.33	16.67
2009	09	05	05	0	55.56	100	0
2014	02	0	0	0	0	0	0
2019	0	0	0	0	0	0	0

SOURCE: ELECTION COMMISSION OF INDIA'S STATISTICAL REPORTS ON GENERAL ELEC-
TIONS, 2004, 2009, 2014 AND 2019

TABLE 16   SC MPs of TMC (2004–2019)

Year	Total MPs	Total SC MPs	SC MPs in reserved seats	SC MPs in unreserved seats	% of SC MPs	% of SC MPs in reserved seats out of total SC MPs of TMC	% of SC MPs in unreserved seats out of total SC MPs of TMC
2004	01	0	0	0	0	0	0
2009	19	03	03	0	15.79	100	0
2014	34	10	10	0	29.41	100	0
2019	22	5	5	0	22.73	100	0

SOURCE: ELECTION COMMISSION OF INDIA'S STATISTICAL REPORTS ON GENERAL ELEC-
TIONS, 2004, 2009, 2014 AND 2019

TABLE 17   Candidates in Lok Sabha elections (2004–2019)

	2004	2009	2014	2019
Total candidates	355	368	472	467
Total SC candidates	114	121	154	148
Percentage of SC candidates	32.11	32.88	32.63	31.69
SC candidates in unreserved seats	60	47	60	59
Percentage of SC candidates in unreserved seats out of total SC candidates	52.33	38.84	38.96	39.86
SC candidates in reserved seats	54	74	94	89
Percentage of SC candidates in reserved seats out of total SC candidates	47.37	61.16	61.04	60.13

SOURCE: ELECTION COMMISSION OF INDIA'S STATISTICAL REPORTS ON GENERAL ELEC-
TIONS, 2004, 2009, 2014 AND 2019

TABLE 18   Candidates of INC in Lok Sabha elections (2004–2019)

Year	SC candidates	SC candidates in reserved seats	SC candidates in unreserved seats	% of SC candidates in reserved seats out of total SC candidates of INC	% of SC candidates in unreserved seats out of total SC candidates of INC
2004	07	07	0	100	0
2009	03	03	0	100	0
2014	10	10	0	100	0
2019	13	10	03	76.92	23.08

SOURCE: ELECTION COMMISSION OF INDIA'S STATISTICAL REPORTS ON GENERAL ELEC-
TIONS, 2004, 2009, 2014 AND 2019

TABLE 19   Candidates of CPI(M) in Lok Sabha elections (2004–2019)

Year	SC candidates	SC candidates in reserved seats	SC candidates in unreserved seats	% of SC candidates in reserved seats out of total SC candidates of CPI(M)	% of SC candidates in unreserved seats out of total SC candidates of CPI(M)
2004	06	05	01	83.33	16.67
2009	08	08	0	100	0
2014	09	08	01	88.89	11.11
2019	09	08	01	88.89	11.11

SOURCE: ELECTION COMMISSION OF INDIA'S STATISTICAL REPORTS ON GENERAL ELECTIONS, 2004, 2009, 2014 AND 2019

TABLE 20   Candidates of TMC in Lok Sabha elections (2004–2019)

Year	SC candidates	SC candidates in reserved seats	SC candidates in unreserved seats	% of SC candidates in reserved seats out of total SC candidates of TMC	% of SC candidates in unreserved seats out of total SC candidates of TMC
2004	06	04	02	66.67	33.33
2009	06	06	0	100	0
2014	10	10	0	100	0
2019	10	10	0	100	0

SOURCE: ELECTION COMMISSION OF INDIA'S STATISTICAL REPORTS ON GENERAL ELECTIONS, 2004, 2009, 2014 AND 2019

TABLE 21   Percentage of scheduled caste (SC) cabinet
            ministers in West Bengal (1977–2006)

Year	Percentage
1977	0
1982	4.3
1987	14.3
1991	9.7
1996	9.1
2001	11.8
2006	12.1

SOURCE: KUMAR RANA, "PROBLEMS AND PROSPECTS
OF DALIT EMANCIPATION IN WEST BENGAL," *VOICE OF
DALIT* 1, NO. 2 (2008): 177

increased. In the first TMC government (2011–2016) only three SC Ministers
[Dr Upen Biswas (Backward Classes Welfare) and Shri Ujjal Biswas (Technical
Education and Training) of the *Namasudra* caste, and Binay Krishna Barman
(Forest) of the *Rajbanshi* caste] were appointed. This number became only
two (Binay Krishna Barman in charge of Department of Forests and Ashima
Patra, Minister of State in charge of Technical Education) in the second TMC
government formed in 2016 accounting for only 6 percent of the total strength
of the Ministry.[30]

4   Decoding Political Outlook towards Representation

As discussed previously, descriptive representation is concerned with the
identities of the political representatives. Hence, descriptive representation is
intimately linked to identity politics and also provides a justification for it. The
fundamental rationale behind identity politics, when practised by marginalized communities is generally to increase their political representation. On the
other hand, substantive representation is non-identitarian, concerned only

---

30   Rup Kumar Barman, "Right-Left-Right and Caste Politics: The Scheduled Castes in West
      Bengal Assembly Elections (from 1920 to 2016)," *Contemporary Voice of Dalit* 10, no. 2
      (2018): 230.

TABLE 22   Cabinet membership for SCs across India (1977–2007)

State	Size of the assembly	Percent SCs in the assembly	Average percent SCs in cabinet	Average size of cabinet
Andhra Pradesh	294	14	13.3	25
Bihar[a]	324	15.6	14.9	34
Gujarat	182	8.3	8.2	22
Haryana	90	18.9	15	17
Himachal Pradesh	68	24.6	21.3	12
Karnataka	224	14.9	17.1	25
Kerala	140	9.4	6.4	18
Madhya Pradesh[b]	320	17.1	13.2	28
Maharashtra	288	6.8	6	26
Orissa	147	19.5	14.1	23
Punjab	117	24.8	17.6	22
Rajasthan	200	18.8	16.9	24
Tamil Nadu	234	18.2	10.1	20
Uttar Pradesh[c]	419	21.4	16.2	33
West Bengal	294	21.3	9.9	41
Total	3341	16.7	13.2	25

a   In 2000 Bihar was split into Bihar and Jharkhand, and only Bihar with 243 constituencies is included in this dataset for the years after that

b   In 2000 Madhya Pradesh was split into Madhya Pradesh and Chhattisgarh, and only Madhya Pradesh with 230 constituencies is included in this dataset for the years after that

c   In 2000 Uttar Pradesh was split into Uttar Pradesh and Uttaranchal, and only the 403 constituencies of Uttar Pradesh is included in this data for the years after that

SOURCE: JENSENIUS, FRANCESCA R. "POWER, PERFORMANCE AND BIAS: EVALUATING THE ELECTORAL QUOTAS FOR SCHEDULED CASTES IN INDIA," PHD DISSERTATION (UNIVERSITY OF CALIFORNIA, BERKELEY, 2013), 83

with functioning of the representative rather than his or her identity. An analysis of the CPI(M)'s party agenda and programmes clearly suggests that the party stands for a non-identitarian model of politics that relies on class based mobilization and tends to dismiss descriptive representation seen through the prism of caste or any other identity. It finds caste based political mobilization not only a futile political exercise but also a harmful distraction from the real goal of class politics. The CPI(M) Programme updated in 2000 says-

> Many caste leaders and certain leaders of bourgeois political parties seek to utilise the polarisation on caste lines for narrow electoral gains and are hostile to building up the common movement of the oppressed sections of all castes. They ignore the basic class issues of land, wages and fight against landlordism, which is the basis for overthrowing the old order.

Similarly, the Political Resolution of the 18th Congress of the CPI(M) held in 2005 says-

> The intensification of the caste appeal and fragmentation of the working people on caste lines is a serious challenge to the Left and democratic movement. Taking up caste oppression, forging the common movement of the oppressed of all castes and taking up class issues of common concern must be combined with a bold campaign to highlight the pernicious effects of caste-based politics. The Party should work out concrete tactics in different areas taking into account the caste and class configurations. Electoral exigencies should not come in the way of the Party's independent campaign against caste-based politics.

Thus, it appears that in the ideological discourse of the CPI(M) caste politics is seen as an impediment to the growth of class consciousness and successful organization of class based political struggle. The real form of social organisation for the party appears to be 'class' that in its view provides a modern and real basis for classifying, organizing and mobilizing people.

Due to their preoccupation with a class centric approach, caste issues have always failed to attract adequate attention from Indian Communists. They have never felt the need to build any separate organization or front to represent the *dalits* or organize struggles on caste issues. The Communist parties have built various mass fronts like the Centre of Indian Trade Unions (CITU), All India Kisan Sabha (AIKS), Students' Federation of India (SFI) and even cultural wings like the Indian People's Theatre Association (IPTA). However, they have never established any such platforms for the *dalits*. During national movement Jagjivan Ram's Depressed Classes League or Harijan League received patronage from Gandhi and Congress while Hindu Mahasabha had links with Depressed Classes Association. But the Communists had no front of their own on caste issues. They did not also establish any connection with any existing *dalit* organization. For a considerably long period of time caste related concerns such as abolition of untouchability were also not included in political programmes of the Communist Party of India (CPI) or the workers' and peasants' organizations [such as All India Trade Union Congress (AITUC), All India Kisan Sabha (AIKS) or Workers' and Peasants' parties (WPP)] which had been under Communist control and influence. The AITUC till 1942 did not include abolition of caste discrimination as an objective in its Constitution and AIKS made no mention of caste or untouchability in any of its programmes until 1945. Similarly, not until the second Congress of the CPI in 1948 caste issue was taken up with much seriousness. In the 'Political Thesis' of the party, abolition of caste discrimination was included as an objective but at the same time the 'Political Thesis' denounced Ambedkar as 'separatist', 'opportunistic' and pro-British for keeping the untouchable masses away from general democratic revolution. According to Gail Omvedt, Indian Communists have tended to ignore caste issues because of their overwhelmingly upper caste background. The leadership of the Left parties has always remained dominated by the higher castes. According to Omvedt the problem is not that the Communist movement in India originated as a Brahman-dominated movement but that it remained Brahman-dominated. She gives the example of South African Communist Party to make her point. It was originally dominated by white workers and often adopted a racist position against the blacks. But later its increasing recruitment of many African leaders led to a transformation of the party agenda, which ultimately incorporated issues and problems affecting the blacks. But in case of Indian Communist parties, this kind of transformation has never taken place. The social background of the Left leadership has remained largely unaltered.[31] This possibly explains why Left parties have demonstrated little efforts to enhance *dalit* representation.

The neglect of the caste question by the Indian Marxists and also their lack of efforts to increase *dalit* representation by encouraging caste based political mobilization can also be attributed to their inadequate and myopic conceptualization of caste. When confronted with the question of caste, the Indian Communists have demonstrated a great deal of uneasiness and ambiguity. The dominant tendency among the Indian Communists is to consider caste as a part of the superstructure, which is determined by the materials relations of production at the base or class relations. In the CPI(M)'s political discourse,

---

31   Gail Omvedt, *Dalits and the Democratic Revolution: Dr. Ambedkar and the Dalit Movement in Colonial India* (New Delhi: Sage, 1994), 180–184.

for instance, class is seen as a more relevant, progressive and legitimate category while the question of caste is perceived as a mere part of the super-structure.[32] B.T Ranadive[33] who exercised a great deal of influence over the development of the CPI(M)'s conceptual approach towards the question of caste saw caste as an "ideology and the superstructure of the earlier feudal age". He linked caste system with the semi-feudal economic relations and struggle against caste with agrarian reform. In his view caste system in India is sustained by feudal land relations. It represents nothing but the social consciousness generated by feudalism. According to Ranadive the colonial rule did not want a full-scale social transformation of the feudal order as the rise of a powerful indigenous *bourgeoisie* was not in its interest. Therefore, it kept the existing rural land relations intact as far as possible and only superimposed on them minimum modern capitalist relations. After independence the Congress party, instead of attempting to demolish the feudal economic relations also made a compromise with the feudal and semi-feudal landlords. Ranadive, therefore, recommends that only agrarian struggle, directed against feudal rural land relations can destroy caste system.[34] Influenced by such thinking the Communist politics in India has mostly tended to see caste as an element of the superstructure and a legacy of feudalism. The CPI(M)'s Memorandum on National Integration submitted in 1968 states:

> It (caste atrocity) is a common practice, throughout the country – the legacy of the evil practice of untouchability and social oppression and brutality that persists in our rural areas, even after 20 years of independence and in spite of our laws and commissions for Scheduled Castes and Tribes. It is the result of the growth of feudal and semi-feudal landlordism and of the 'new rich', on the same feudal caste and social basis, and of their grip over the village economy and life. It is a reflection of the failure of the government to liquidate the medieval feudal economic base, of its failure to abolish landlordism, give land to the tiller and assure him land and employment, fair wages, and decent living conditions (house sites, education and medical services).[35]

---

32   Partha Chatterjee, *The Nation and Its Fragments: Colonial and Postcolonial Histories* (Princeton: Princeton University Press, 1993), 173–74.

33   B T Ranadive was the General Secretary of the undivided Communist Party of India during 1948–50. Later he became a member of the Politbureau of the CPI(M) when the Party was formed in 1964. He remained a member of the Politbureau till his death in 1990.

34   B.T. Ranadive, *Caste, Class and Property Relations* (Calcutta: National Book Agency, 1991).

35   Community Party of India (Marxist), "Memorandum on National Integration," 1968.

Arguing on similar lines Sitaram Yechury, currently the General Secretary of the CPI(M) and also an influential leader and ideologue of the party, in his writings, has attributed the failure to abolish casteism to the continuing survival of feudal land relations. In his words, "The inability to eliminate the vestiges of feudalism meant, at the level of the super-structure, the existence and perpetuation of the social consciousness associated with feudalism. The feelings of communalism and casteism continued to dominate the social order".[36] Accordingly, the Communists have suggested economic remedies for abolition of the caste system. As a result, for *dalit* empowerment enhancement of political representation of lower castes and caste based political mobilization do not appear necessary to them. They mainly recommend agrarian reforms relating to land and wage as the solution to the problem of caste discrimination and caste prejudice. Resolution adopted at the All India Convention on Problems of Dalits in 2006 also declared that only overhauling of the land structure could solve the caste problem. It states –

> There has been no basic change in caste system after nearly 60 years of independence after independence as the *bourgeoisie* compromised with landlordism fostered caste prejudices. After independence also, the basic structure of land relations, overhauling of which would have given a blow to untouchability and the caste system has not been changed.[37]

This tendency to treat caste as a super-structural form linked to feudal relations of production has led to efforts to subsume caste into a feeling of class, causing neglect of caste related issues. This is primarily the reason why from an ideological point of view the Left parties have never felt comfortable with politicisation of caste identity. They have advocated non-identitarian class centric political mobilization with little focus on the efforts to raise caste consciousness and to increase the political representation of the lower castes.

In scholarly literature which broadly endorses the theoretical framework of Marxism, the tendency to see caste as an element of superstructure is also quite prominent. In this approach specific forms of caste relations are seen to be contingent on productive organization. For instance, Dipankar Gupta has attempted to relate *varna* and *jati* to the mode of production. *Varna* and *jati* are, according to him, reflective of specific socio-economic formations. *Varna*

---

36   Sitaram Yechury, "Communalism, Religion and Marxism," *Marxist* 10/11, no. 4/1 (1992–93).
37   Communist Party of India (Marxist), "Resolution adopted at All India Convention on Problems of Dalits," New Delhi, February 22, 2006.

is a system of differentiation that prevailed in the epoch of Asiatic mode of production characterized by general exploitation by the state. The *jati* system that developed in the epoch of feudalism was characterized by localized exploitation in a closed village economy.[38] However, to overcome the tendency of economic determinism in Marxist analysis of caste, some scholars, have tried to follow a slightly different trajectory in their conceptualization of caste within the broader theoretical framework of Marxist thought. Rather than seeing caste a super-structural form associated with a particular mode of production, they find it more appropriate to regard caste as the Indian form of material relations at the base and therefore, the Indian version of class. According to Gail Omvedt in pre-capitalist society of India castes were the forms in which classes existed. *Jatis* had functioned as the basic units of production and exploitation. However, she has not fully abandoned social reality of class in favour of caste in Indian context. She argues that classes came into existence due to the introduction of capitalist relations of production by the British rule. In other words, class got separated from caste as the introduction of capitalist production caused a separation between the social and economic levels. As class as an entity was brought into existence by capitalism during the colonial rule, it functions only in capitalist core areas of factory production. Peasants and tribal communities are class-like but their relations of exploitation are interwoven with pre-capitalist community features.[39]

However, this position also fails to provide an entirely satisfactory conceptualization of caste. Partha Chatterjee has identified a serious analytical difficulty associated with this approach. He has pointed out that in Omvedt's analysis the separation between economic and social levels occurs not due to any immanent development, but as a result of the external intervention of colonialism. Therefore, "to the extent that the new conditions of capitalist production are treated as external, a duality between two structures of class and caste becomes unavoidable."[40] However, in the context of our discussion, what is more pertinent is to recognize the non- recognition by the Left of the independent reality of caste. In Omvedt's analysis for example, the inability to overcome class-centrism finds clear manifestation in the emphasis placed upon the external dynamics of colonialism and also in the efforts to carve out

---

38 Dipankar Gupta, "From *Varna* to *Jati*: The Indian Caste System, from the Asiatic to the Feudal Mode of Production," *Journal of Contemporary Asia* 10, vol. 3 (1980): 249–271.

39 Gail Omvedt, "An Introductory Essay," in *Land, Caste and Politics in Indian States,* ed. Gail Omvedt (Delhi: Author's Guild Publications,1982), 9–50.

40 Partha Chatterjee, "Caste and Subaltern Consciousness," *Subaltern Studies* 6 (1994):167–209.

a social sphere, i.e. the conditions of capitalist relations of production, where class is the pre-dominant social reality.

Due to the inability to overcome class-centricism at the theoretical level, the Communist political praxis also ended up exclusively focusing on the problems of the broad category of proletarian class within which the *dalits* were accommodated either as landless labourers or poor workers. In an interview to Scheduled Castes and Tribes Commission in 1979 the then Chief Minister of West Bengal, Jyoti Basu said that the Left Front government would provide benefits to the lower castes not on the basis of their caste identity but on the basis of the poverty and economic exploitation faced them, by effectively implementing progressive rural development measures.[41] A committee set up by the West Bengal government to look into the question of caste backwardness in August 1980 maintained that, "Poverty and low levels of living standards rather than caste should, in our opinion, be the most important criteria for identifying backwardness". This committee also rejected reservation or quota in government services for the OBCs.[42] Jyoti Basu rejecting the need to identify the backward classes on the lines of caste famously stated before the Mandal Commission that in West Bengal there were only two castes – the rich and the poor.[43] But Gour Mohan Shar, General Secretary, West Bengal Swarnakar Sabha in his submission before the Mandal Commission opposed Basu's view that there were only two castes, i.e., the rich and the poor noting that caste system is as deeply entrenched in West Bengal as in other parts of the country.[44] Furthermore, in 1991 Mandal Commission Action Committee headed by a senior Left Front Minister and Chairman of the State Forward Bloc, Bhakti Bhusan Mandal claimed that at least 50 percent of total population of West Bengal belonged to the other backward classes.[45] However, officially the CPI(M) remained reluctant to unequivocally endorse OBC reservation on the basis of caste for quite a long period of time. This attitude of the party is reflective of its political strategy to reject caste as a unit of mobilization in favour of class. The CPI(M) has all along remained averse to caste based identity politics, stressing the need to address what it views as the central faultline in Indian society: the divide between the rich and the poor.

---

41   Atig Ghosh, "Left Front Government in West Bengal (1971–1982)," *Policies and Practices* 93 (2017): 22.

42   Government of India, *Report of the Backward Classes Commission, Volume I* (New Delhi: Government of India, 1980), 11.

43   Anjan Ghosh, "Cast(e) out in Bengal," *Seminar* 508 (May 2021).

44   Government of India, *Report of the Backward Classes Commission, Volume I*, 49.

45   Sweta Kushry, "Mandal Commission and the Left Front in West Bengal," *Economic and Political* Weekly 26, no. 8 (1991): 419–20.

It is this dismissive approach towards caste based identity politics that has over the years built an unfavourable political and ideological disposition to the idea of descriptive representation. Stephanie Tawa Lama-Rewal while doing research about the caste identity of political leaders in West Bengal has found out that the party men and elected leaders generally demonstrate an apparent lack of information regarding their own and others' caste identity.[46] Expressing the logic of substantive representation the leaders of the party have often argued that it is not right to presume that only *dalit* leaders can effectively represent the *dalits* masses. While explaining the lack of *dalit* representation in an interview Sitaram Yechury said that Kanshi Ram[47] once asked him "why there wasn't a single *dalit* minister in the West Bengal government. I was shocked, so I said let me find out. I discovered many *dalits* and tribals. Kanti Biswas was the education minister for many years in West Bengal. I had no idea he was *dalit*. We used to travel all across the country in the same coupe. I did not know he was *dalit* till Kanshi Ram asked this. The point was these things were never part of our consciousness".[48] During the Left regime it was this claim of casteless political consciousness that by giving credence to the logic of substantive representation shaped public perception in favour of non-essentiality of greater *dalit* representation for *dalit* empowerment. This in effect, nullified the fundamental rationale behind caste-based identity politics.

It is often contended by the 'crisis of representation' thesis that people have lost their faith in political parties to effectively represent their interests and that they now turn to civil society organisations instead of political parties. However, studies on Indian scenario have highlighted that people still consider political parties as the most important avenues to secure representation of their interests. Though there is some amount of disillusionment with political parties, this has not led to "the institutionalization of trust in newer forms of representation such as the non-governmental sector".[49] Furthermore, since the civil society organizations are largely dominated by middle classes, for the poorer population political parties still offer the principal possibility to secure representation.[50] Therefore, political representation is still considered

---

46   Lama-Rewal, "The Resilient Bhadralok," 362.
47   Kanshi Ram is a *dalit* politician who founded Bahujan Samaj Party (BSP) which has been spearheading *dalit* politics since the late 1980s in India's most populous state, Uttar Pradesh.
48   Saba Naqvi and Panini Anand, "Yechury interview," *Outlook*, April 17, 2013.
49   Neera Chandhoke, "Revisiting the Crisis of Representation Thesis: the Indian context," *Democratization* 12, no. 3 (2005): 326.
50   John Harriss, "Antinomies of Empowerment: Observations on Civil Society, Politics and Urban Governance in India," *Economic and Political Weekly* 42, no. 26 (2007): 2716–2724.

extremely crucial particularly for hitherto unrepresented or inadequately represented groups like the *dalits* and the backward castes. Political representation has remained a core concern of all forms of identity politics including caste politics. In fact, one of the fundamental objectives of identity politics is to achieve for concerned groups adequate political representation seen in descriptive terms. But, the CPI(M) in West Bengal has consistently argued against identity politics, emphasizing the need to address what it views as the central faultline in Indian society: the divide between the rich and the poor. Accordingly, the party has not felt it necessary to encourage greater political representation of the *dalits* and instead recommended agrarian reforms relating to land and wage as the ultimate solution to the caste question. Standing for a model of substantive representation, the party leaders have often argued that it is not right to presume that only *dalit* leaders can effectively represent the *dalits*. Since the electoral decline of the Left Front some sporadic and limited attempts have been made to politically mobilize the *dalits* particularly the *Namasudras* along the lines of caste. However, any real and meaningful emergence of caste politics must be accompanied by an overall shift from substantive representation to descriptive representation of the mobilized groups.

In order to find out whether such a shift has taken place or not a detailed investigation has been undertaken in this chapter of the trends of *dalit* political representation in West Bengal since such trends, as politics in other parts of the country have shown us, manifest the actuals signs indicative of the effective emergence of caste politics. This investigation has clearly revealed that the political decline of the Left Front has not brought about any notable increase in the political representation of the *dalits* in descriptive terms. In other words, there is yet to be any shift from substantive to descriptive model of representation. In view of the absence of such a shift, it is difficult to endorse the contention that caste has finally come to impact mainstream electoral politics of West Bengal. Since substantive representation stands for non-identitarian politics, it is currently premature to expect the emergence of full-fledged caste based identity politics in West Bengal without some fundamental change in the prevailing notions about political representation. This finding makes it imperative to explore the reasons for continuing inconsequentiality of caste in West Bengal's mainstream electoral politics. The remaining chapters of the book will attempt to identify the structural factors which contribute to the relative insignificance of caste in the formal electoral politics of West Bengal.

Caste and Politics of Numbers

Delving Deep into Demography

In the ongoing debate about the role of caste in West Bengal politics, the demographic scenario of the state has not been subjected to any systematic and exhaustive analytical treatment.[1] The findings of an essay by Partha Chatterjee which came out more than two decades ago are still widely referred to.[2] An elaborate scrutiny of the demographic scenario based on the updated data of the Socio-Economic Caste Census (SECC) of 2011 still remains an unfulfilled imperative. Therefore, there is clearly a need for an updated analysis of caste demography of West Bengal. In recognition of this need this chapter closely engages with various demographic dimensions of the caste question in West Bengal on the basis of latest and updated demographic data. For certain information we still have to depend on the 1931 census[3] but such information can also give us valuable insights if they are analysed in the light of the latest data and are subjected to a more detailed analytical investigation. Further, some comparison with the demographic scenario of other states may also prove useful. Thus, several analytical avenues may open up if existing demographic analysis is enriched with a comparative perspective and also expanded with additional and updated data. Therefore, to analyse caste demography of West Bengal I have collected updated data from the latest SECC of 2011. Whenever there is non-availability of updated information, I have attempted to correlate such data with relevant information from the census of 1931. Furthermore, for putting things into perspective data concerning caste demography of West Bengal has also been correlated with comparable data relating to caste demography of other states. Such a comparative approach has so far remained largely unexplored. All these efforts have generated new findings and also new evidences

---

1   Parts of this chapter first appeared in Ayan Guha, "Caste Question in West Bengal Politics: Continuing Inconsequentiality or Rising Relevance?" *Contemporary South Asia* 29, no. 3 (2021): 376–400 and Ayan Guha, "Caste and Politics in West Bengal: Traditional Limitations and Contemporary Developments," *Contemporary Voice of Dalit* 9, no. 1 (2017): 27–36.

2   See, the chapter "Caste and Politics in West Bengal" in Partha Chatterjee, *The Present History of West Bengal* (New Delhi: Oxford University Press, 1997), 69–86.

3   1931 was the last time when census exercise undertook caste-wise enumeration before SECC of 2011. Caste related data of SECC has not fully been released.

in support of already exiting findings. The broad argument presented here is that the political assertion of caste identity in West Bengal faces a number of demographic handicaps.

1   Demographic Fragmentation of Caste Groups

Caste politics in India has demonstrated two patterns. First, caste identity of a dominant caste has been politically nurtured for electoral success. *Jats* in Haryana, *Yadavs* in Uttar Pradesh (UP), *Kammas* and *Reddys* in Andhra Pradesh, *Vokkaligas* and *Lingayats* in Karnataka and *Patidars* in Gujarat are examples of such dominant castes.[4] In current political scenario different parties have become champions of a specific caste or a cluster of caste groups, and different castes or caste coalitions have come to identify themselves with particular political parties. For example, the *Yadvas* are known to solidly back the Samajwadi Party in UP and Rashtriya Janata Dal in Bihar. Similarly, the *dalits*, particularly the *Jatavs* in UP strongly support the BSP. The same can be said more or less about the *Kurmis* in relation to Janata Dal (United) in Bihar and the *Kammas* in relation to Telegu Desam Party in Andhra Pradesh. On the other hand, efforts have been made to consolidate a *bahujan samaj* comprising several caste groups with more or less identical demands and placed more or less at similar level of socio-economic development. For example, in the 1970s in Bihar, Karpoori Thakur made a political alliance of the backward castes, including *Yadavs, Kurmis* and *Koeris*.[5] In the 1970s in Uttar Pradesh Charan Singh stitched together a coalition called AJGAR, consisting of *Ahir (Yadav), Jat, Gujjar* and *Rajput*.[6] Mayawati's Bahujan Samaj Party (BSP) also did the same in Uttar Pradesh by attempting to build an alliance of all the ex-untouchable castes. Madhavsinh Solanki in Gujarat formed a large non-upper caste coalition, Known as KHAM which was made up of the *Kshatriyas* (consisting of low caste *Kolis* and *Rajputs*), *Harijans, Adivasis* and Muslims in the early 1980s.[7]

4   Susan Bayly, *Caste, Society and Politics in India from Eighteenth Century to Modern Age* (New Delhi: Cambridge University Press, 2011), 323.

5   See, Pradip Kumar Bose, "Mobility and Conflict: Social Roots of Caste Violence in Bihar," in *Social Stratification,* ed. Dipankar Gupta (New Delhi: Oxford University Press, 2014), 369–384.

6   Christophe Jaffrelot, *India's Silent Revolution: The Rise of the Low Castes in North Indian Politics* (New Delhi: Permanent Black, 2003), 288–89.

7   Christophe Jaffrelot , "Quota for Patels? The Neo-Middle-Class Syndrome and the (Partial) Return of Caste Politics in Gujarat," *Studies in Indian Politics* 4, no. 2 (2016): 219.

Due to such developments in last three to four decades there has been a significant increase in the political representation of the lower and intermediate castes. The phenomenon has famously been described as *mandalization* of politics. However, West Bengal has so far bucked this trend of steady political rise of the lower and intermediate castes. This is perhaps because in West Bengal the two patterns of caste politics mentioned above have much lesser political prospects due to some peculiar demographic dynamics. An analysis of demographic scenario will point out that there are no dominant castes in West Bengal.[8] As a result, while endorsement of the interests of particular caste groups provides rich dividends to political parties in various states, in West Bengal such a strategy has never seemed politically prudent.

The latest 2011 census gives us information about the Scheduled Castes (SCs). However, there is no updated data regarding other caste categories. Therefore, we have to rely on the 1931 census for information concerning the upper and intermediate castes. The present proportion of population of various castes will not be exactly the same, but it is also not likely to be vastly different. Their proportion has been calculated by taking into account only those districts of undivided Bengal, which now fall within the jurisdiction of present-day West Bengal. Data of 1931 census presented here however, does not reflect the Partition induced marginal adjustments which were made with regard to the boundaries of districts like Nadia and Dinajpur. Furthermore, population statistics of the areas of Manbhum district of Bihar, which came to form Purulia district of post colonial West Bengal are also not included in the figures of the 1931 census presented here.

The numerically significant Scheduled Castes in West Bengal are *Rajbanshi, Namasudra, Bagdi, Pod* and *Bauri.* The numerically significant intermediate castes are *Mahishya, Sadgope, Goala, Tanti, Tili, Teli* (See Tables 24 and 27). If considered in terms of the proportion to total population the demographic strength of these castes don't match that of the so-called dominant castes such as *Yadav* in UP (8.7%), *Yadav* in Bihar (15%), *Jat* in Haryana (25%), *Patidar* in Gujarat(13%), *Maratha-Kunbi* in Maharashtra (32%), *Lingayat* (15%) and *Vokkaliga* (11%) in Karnataka and politically assertive SCs such as *Mahar* (5.86) in Maharashtra and *Jatav* (9.92) in UP (See Table 23). In comparison, the largest

---

8   The idea of the dominant caste propounded first by sociologist M N Srinivas in 1959 applies to any caste which is numerically strong, politically influential and also holds the substantial economic power in the form of ownership of land. Moreover, its ritual rank is not too low. Later he also added other criteria of dominance such as the number of educated persons in a caste and the occupations they pursue. See, M.N Srinivas, "The Dominant Caste in Rampura," *American Anthropologist* 61, no. 1 (1959):1–16.

TABLE 23   Population percentage of dominant castes in various Indian States

Caste	State	Percentage of state population
Yadav	Uttar Pradesh	8.7
Yadav	post 2000 Bihar	15
Jat	Rajasthan	9
Jat	Haryana	25
Patidar	Gujarat	13
Maratha-Kunbi	Maharshtra	31.19
Lingayat	Karnataka	15.3
Vokkaliga	Karnataka	10.8
Kamma	Andhra Pradesh (before formation of Telengana)	5
Reddy	Andhra Pradesh (before formation of Telengana)	8

SOURCE: CHRISTOPHE JAFFRELOT AND SANJAY KUMAR, EDS., *RISE OF THE PLEBEIANS? THE CHANGING FACE OF INDIAN LEGISLATIVE ASSEMBLIES* (NEW DELHI: ROUTLEDGE, 2009), 32, 66, 165, 215, 246, 279; RAVEEN THUKRAL, "NON-JAT VOTERS HOLD THE KEY TO HARYANA", *SUNDAY GUARDIAN*. HTTP://WWW.SUNDAY-GUARDIAN.COM/ANALYSIS/NON-JAT-VOTERS-HOLD-THE-KEY-TO-HARYANA

SC in West Bengal, the *Rajbanshis* constitute only 4.17 percent of the total population of the state as per the 2011 census (see Table 24).

The middle castes also suffer from limited demographic strength. We don't have updated data concerning the total population of the intermediate castes. But it is possible to arrive at a rough estimatation. As per 2011 census SCs, STs and Muslims constitute 23.51, 5.80 and 27.01 percent of the total state population respectively. This means that the upper and middle castes together account for 43.68 percent of the total population. As per the 1931 census three upper castes- Brahman, *Baidya and Kayastha* account for 7.45 percent of the population of the state (see Table 25). Following partition and migration from districts of eastern Bengal which were the strongholds of upper castes, (particularly the *Kayasthas* who were concentrated in large numbers in Dacca, Mymensingh, Chittagong, Bakarganj and Noakhali), the proportion of upper castes in districts such as Nadia, 24 Parganas, Jalpaiguri and Coochbehar has possibly increased a little. Therefore, we can assume that upper caste

TABLE 24   Population statistics of numerically significant lower castes of West Bengal as per census, 2001 and census, 2011

Castes	Number of persons (2001)	Percentage of state sc population (2001)	Number of persons (2011)	Percentage of state sc population (2011)	Percentage of state population (2001)	Percentage of state population (2011)
All scs	18452555	100	21463270	100	23.02	23.51
Rajbanshi	3386617	18.35	3801677	17.71	4.22	4.17
Namasudra	3212393	17.41	3504642	16.33	4.01	3.84
Bagdi	2740385	14.85	3058265	14.25	3.42	3.35
Pod	2216513	12.01	2450260	11.42	2.76	2.68
Bauri	1091022	5.91	1228635	5.72	1.36	1.35
Chamar/ Muchi	995756	5.40	1039591	4.84	1.24	1.14
Jalia Kaibartta	409303	2.22	569448	2.65	0.51	0.62

SOURCE: 2001 AND 2011 CENSUS DATA

TABLE 25   Population share of upper castes of West Bengal

Caste	Percentage
Brahman	4.76
Baidya	0.21
Kayastha	2.46

SOURCE: CENSUS, 1931, VOL. V, PART II, IMPERIAL TABLE XVII

TABLE 26   Estimated broad caste/community composition of West Bengal (in percentage)

Higher castes	9–11
Intermediate castes	32–34
Scheduled castes	23.51
Scheduled tribes	5.80
Muslims	27.01
Others[a]	2.45

a Others includes Christians (0.72 percent), Sikhs (0.07 percent), Buddhists (0.31 percent), Jains (0.07 percent), any other religion (1.03 percent) and those who have not stated their religion (0.25 percent)
SOURCE: CENSUS, 2011, HTTPS://WWW.CENSUS2011.CO.IN/DATA/RELIGION/STATE/19-WEST-BENGAL.HTML

TABLE 27   Population proportion of numerically significant middle castes

Caste	Percentage of total population
Mahishya	9.78
Sadgope	2.61
Gop	2.27
Tanti	1.37
Teli	1.14
Tili	0.80
Kamar	0.74
Kumhar	0.66

SOURCE: CENSUS, 1931, VOL. V, PART II, IMPERIAL TABLE XVII

population will be close to 10 to 11 percent. Hence, the total population of the middle castes is likely to be in the range of 32 to 34 percent, which is significant (see Table 26). But there are too many middle castes. Therefore, though the middle castes constitute a significant proportion of the total population of the state, they are severely fragmented. Fragmentation of the intermediate castes is so severe that barring the *Mahishya* caste no other intermediate caste accounts for more than 3 percent of the total state population (see Table 27). The share of each of these intermediate castes to total population is negligible.

2   Geographic Concentration of Caste Groups

In West Bengal the only caste which is to some extent comparable to the dominant castes of other states in terms of its demographic size and proportion to total population is the *Mahishya* caste. With regard to the *Mahishyas* we have to rely upon the 1931 census. If we look at the 1931 census figures, we shall find that the *Mahishyas*, who constitute the largest single middle caste in South Bengal, inhabit a comparatively large stretch of South Bengal consisting of Midnapore, Howrah, Hoogly and 24 Parganas. However, their numerical presence is not much prominent in other districts of South Bengal such as Purulia, Birbhum, Bankura, Burdwan, Kolkata, Nadia, Murshidabad. Still, their population size is large in districts where they are concentrated. They constitute 31.56 percent of Midnapore's population, almost 25 percent of Howrah's population, almost 16 percent of Hoogly's population and approximately 12 percent of South 24 Parganas' population. Overall they seem to be present in considerable numbers in South Bengal. Therefore, the *Mahishyas* are the only caste whose geographical spread as well as demographic strength in several districts seem to be significant. But the *Mahishyas* are not socially and politically organized. The lack of political mobilization of the *Mahishyas* despite their relatively substantial demographic strength suggests that there are factors other than demography which also need to be taken into consideration. However, even in terms of demography too there are certain handicaps which the *Mahishyas* face despite their large size. The demographic spread of the *Mahishyas* is limited compared to the dominant castes of other states.

Each of the so-called dominant castes of other states is more or less spread over the entire state or concentrated in a large stretch of area within the state. But unlike dominant castes of other parts of the country, the *Mahishyas* or no lower or middle caste of West Bengal has comparable presence over a large region or sub-region within the state. This point requires some illustration through presentation of actual data. For example, the *Jatavs* cover the whole of UP. According to the 1931 census, if we exclude Uttaranchal and the Gonda district, the *Jatavs* constitute a minimum of 6.4 percent (Pilbhit) and a maximum of 19.6 percent (Azamgarh and Ballia) of each district's population.[9] The *Yadavs* in Bihar are, more or less, present in all parts of the state. As per the 1931 census they account for 14 percent of the population of North Bihar and 15.7 percent of the population of South Bihar.[10] They constitute more than 25 percent of the population of districts such as Bhagalpur, Gaya, Hazaribag, Patna, Saharsha, Saran, Vaishali, Nalanda and Rohtas.[11] Similarly, the *Yadavs* in UP have a wide presence in the state. They are mostly concentrated in Agra- Kanpur belt of central UP and in eastern UP. They are a strong force in Mainpuri, Etawah, Etah, Firozabad, Kannauj, Farrukhabad, Badaun, Faizabad, Ghazipur, Jaunpur, Azamgarh. Also in western UP, which is considered as a *Jat* belt, the *Yadavs* have a fair presence.[12] Similarly spread across all 48 Lok Sabha seats to varying extents , the *Maratha-Kunbi* caste group in Maharashtra enjoys overwhelming dominance in three regions, western Maharashtra, Marathwada and North Maharashtra.[13] Similarly barring the eastern tribal belt, the *Patidars* are spread all over Gujarat, with a higher concentration in North Gujarat and Saurashtra peninsula.[14] In the South Indian state of Karnataka the *Lingayats* are numerically significant in Bombay-Karnataka and Hyderabad Karnataka regions. They are mainly concentrated in northern and central Karnataka (Belgaum, Bagalkot, Bidar, Bijapur, Chikkodi, Chitradurga, Davangere, Dharwad and Haveri). The *Vokkaligas* are numerically strong in the Old Mysore region which accounts for almost half of the Assembly seats. They are mainly concentrated in the south districts with a few variants among agriculturists in the coastal and northern districts such as Mandya, Chikaballapur, Hassan, Bangalore Rural, Bangalore North, Bangalore South and Mysore.[15] In

---

9   Jasmine Zerinini, "The Marginalization of the Savarnas in Uttar Pradesh," in *Rise of the Plebians? The Changing Face of Indian Legislative Assemblies*, eds. Christophe Jaffrelot and Sanjay Kumar (New Delhi: Routledge, 2009), 31.

10   Cyril Robin, "Bihar: The New Stronghold of OBC Politics," in *Rise of the Plebians? The Changing Face of Indian Legislative Assemblies*, eds. Christophe Jaffrelot and Sanjay Kumar (New Delhi: Routledge, 2009), 67.

11   Bose, "Mobility and Conflict", 371.

12   Indian Express Bureau, "Lok Sabha Polls: The Caste Constituency", *Indian Express*, April 29, 2014, http://indianexpress.com/article/india/politics/lok-sabha-polls-the-caste-constituency.

13   Indian Express Bureau, "Lok Sabha Polls: The Caste Constituency."

14   Indian Express Bureau, "Lok Sabha Polls: The Caste Constituency."

15   Sandeep Shastri, "Legislators in Karnataka: Well- entrenched Dominant Castes," in *Rise of the Plebians? The Changing Face of Indian Legislative Assemblies*, eds. Christophe Jaffrelot and Sanjay Kumar (New Delhi: Routledge, 2009), 248; Indian Express Bureau, "Lok Sabha Polls: The Caste Constituency."

Andhra Pradesh (prior to the separation of Telengana) while the *Reddys* were spread throughout the state, they predominated in the Southern Andhra districts, the Rayalseema and Telengana areas. The *Kammas* were concentrated in the deltaic region covering the districts of Nellore, Chittor, Anantapur and Khammam.[16] Thus, all these castes have a very large geographic spread. The castes like *Maratha-Kunbi* in Maharashtra, *Yadavs* in U.P and *Patidars* in Gujarat are spread all over the state. Other dominant castes predominate over a large region or sub-region of a state consisting of many districts.

In contrast, in West Bengal the geographical spread of numerically important lower and middle castes is limited. Though the *Mahishyas* have a relatively considerable geographical spread in comparison to other caste groups, almost 45 percent of the *Mahishyas* are concentrated in Midnapore alone and 24 Parganas and Howrah along with Midnapore account for close to 75 percent of the total *Mahishya* population (see Table 28). Other middle castes are also handicapped by this limitation. Three to four South Bengal districts account for 55 to 60 percent population of other middle castes like *Sadgope, Gop, Tanti and Tili*. In some cases, even 30 to 35 percent of the population of a middle caste is concentrated in one single district. For example, Midnapore accounts for more than 30 percent population of the *Tanti* caste and Bankura accounts for almost 34 percent population of the *Tili* caste (see Table 28). Furthermore, except the *Mahishyas*, the other intermediate castes contribute negligible proportion to the total population of the districts where they are concentrated. Apart from the *Mahishyas,* none of the other middle castes comprises 10 percent of the population of any district (see Table 29).

Similarly, none of the SCs also has a state wise presence or presence over a considerably large region within the state. The *Rajbanshis*, numerically the largest *dalit* caste are spread only over a stretch of North Bengal. Almost 65 percent of the total population of the caste is concentrated in the three small North Bengal districts, namely, Cooch Behar, Jalpaiguri and Uttar Dinajpur. Similarly, more than 50 percent of the total population of the *Namasudras* are concentrated in two South Bengal districts of Nadia and North 24 Parganas which are adjacent to one another. The *Bagdis* though distributed more evenly than other castes in southern part of Bengal are mostly found in Hoogly and North 24 Parganas. In case of the *Pods,* also more than 62 percent of the total population of the caste inhabit only one district, namely, South 24 Parganas.

---

16   Anne Vaugier-Chatterjee, "Two Dominant Castes in Andhra Pradesh," in *Rise of the Plebians? The Changing Face of Indian Legislative Assemblies,* eds. Christophe Jaffrelot and Sanjay Kumar (New Delhi: Routledge, 2009), 279.

TABLE 28   District wise population breakup of numerically significant middle castes of
            West Bengal

Caste	Proportion of district population of each caste of its total state population (in percentage)
Mahishya	Midnapore (44.17), 24 Parganas (16.47), Howrah (13.69)
Sadgope	Midnapore (20.57), Burdwan (18.65), Birbhum (14.67)
Gop	24 Parganas (15.30), Burdwan (14.71), Bankura (13.93), Nadia (11.72)
Tanti	Midnapore (30.16), Hoogly (9.91), 24 Parganas (9.47), Bankura (8.76)
Teli	Midnapore (19.03), Burdwan (14.05), Birbhum (9.71)
Tili	Bankura (33.44), Midnapore (13.75), Hoogly (13.45)

SOURCE: CENSUS, 1931, VOL. V, PART II, IMPERIAL TABLE XVII

Similarly, two adjacent western districts, Bankura and Purulia account for close to half of the total *Bauri* population. The *Muchis* are also found mostly in North 24 Parganas and Birbhum (see Table 30). Thus, none of the lower castes is evenly distributed across the state.

Thus, there are no castes in West Bengal remotely comparable to the so-called dominant castes of other states in terms of demographic strength and geographical spread. None of the middle and lower castes is spread over a large geographical area in West Bengal. Only in some particular geographical pockets certain castes enjoy numerical preponderance. In other words, there are no castes in West Bengal comparable to the *Yadavs* in Uttar Pradesh, *Jats* in Haryana, *Vokkaligas* and *Lingayats* in Karnataka, and the *Kammas* and *Reddys* in Andhra Pradesh. Thus, an analysis of demographic situation of West Bengal brings to light the severe fragmentation of the middle castes and limited geographic spread of major lower and middle castes. These factors have proved obstructive to caste based political mobilization. This has been witnessed also in case of Madhya Pradesh where insignificant demographic strength of individual SCs and OBCs and limited extent of their territorial concentration have

TABLE 29   District wise population share of numerically significant middle castes of
             West Bengal

Caste	Share of population of each caste in total district population (in percentage)
Mahishya	Midnapore (31.56), Howrah (24.92), Hoogly (15.74), 24 Parganas (12.14), Nadia (6.49), Murshidabad (5.48)
Sadgope	Birbhum (8.20), Burdwan (6.31), Hoogly (4.89), Bankura (3.95), Midnapore (3.92), Mushidabad (3.82)
Gop	Bankura (5.82), Burdwan (4.34), 24 Parganas (2.62)
Tanti	Midnapore (3.03), Bankura (2.21)
Teli	Bankura (2.79), Birbhum (2.38), Burdwan (2.08), Midnapore (1.58)
Tili	Bankura (4.93), Hoogly (1.93), Midnapore (0.80)

SOURCE: CENSUS, 1931, VOL. V, PART II, IMPERIAL TABLE XVII

blocked avenues of political mobilization along caste lines unlike in other
states of North India.[17]

3   Demography and Political Aggregation of Caste Interests

It is rarely possible for a single caste group to enable a political party to win
elections on the basis of votes of its members. Given that the support of
a single caste group can't ensure electoral success, it becomes essential to
build multi-caste alliances. In other words, caste-based movements are often
required to embrace a less exclusivist or particularistic politics for achieving
electoral success. The successful example of *bahujan* politics in UP based on

---

17   Christophe Jaffrelot, "The Uneven Rise of Lower Castes in the Politics of Madhya Pradesh,"
       in *Rise of the Plebians? The Changing Face of Indian Legislative Assemblies,* eds. Christophe
       Jaffrelot and Sanjay Kumar (New Delhi: Routledge, 2009), 103–148.

TABLE 30 District wise population statistics of numerically large lower castes of West Bengal in major districts of their concentration

Caste	Percentage share of district population of each caste of its total population	Percentage share of each caste of total district population
Rajbanshi	Cooch Behar (27.97), Jalpaiguri (24.27), Uttar Dinajpur (13.10)	Cooch Behar (37.72), Jalpaiguri (23.82)
Namasudra	Nadia (25.77), North 24 Parganas (24.43), Jalpaiguri (9.73)	Nadia (17.48), North 24 Parganas (8.56)
Bagdi	Hoogly (20.61), Paschim Midnapur (12.12)	Hoogly (11.42), Paschim Midnapur (7.62)
Pod	South 24 Parganas (62.17), Nadia (19.32)	South 24 Parganas (18.66), North 24 Parganas (4.73)
Bauri	Bankura (28.50), Purulia (19.76)	Bankura (9.74), Purulia (8.29)
Chamar/ Muchi	North 24 Parganas (24.56), Birbhum (15.54)	Birbhum (4.61), North 24 Parganas (3.31)

SOURCE: PRIMARY CENSUS ABSTRACT DATA, 2011, TABLE A-10 (APPENDIX)

the support of the *dalits* and backward castes has demonstrated the practical necessity of lower caste political mobilization to transcend the caste categories upon which it is originally based and build an alliance of like-minded caste groups. However, in West Bengal there is limited scope for *bahujan* politics that involves building of a common agenda of social justice by various lower caste groups. In West Bengal such political aggregation of caste interests has been hampered by a mismatch between political and economic demands of major lower caste groups and bridging this mismatch has become extremely difficult due to demographic factors. Caste fragmentation hinders the creation of caste coalitions, particularly in a situation where the demands of different caste groups do not match. In this regard, first the mismatch between political and economic demands of major lower caste groups requires some explanation.

As has been highlighted in Chapter 3, the principal demands of the *Namasudras* are refugee rehabilitation and citizenship rights. These demands are peculiar to the *Namasudras* only. They do not concern other communities. On the other hand, the largest SC community, the *Rajbanshis* have long been demanding a separate province for them within the Indian Union. Their principal demand is territorial and cultural autonomy. This demand has absolutely no relevance for the *Namasudra*s and other caste groups. Rather, the demands of the *Rajbanshis* are contradictory to those of the *Namasudras*. This aspect needs to be explained in some detail.

The *Rajbanshi* community forms the main support base of the two movements for separate states in North Bengal within the Indian Union, the Kamtapur movement led by Kamtapur People's Party (KPP) and Greater Cooch Behar movement led by Greater Cooch Behar Democratic Party (GCDP). The demands and grievances expressed by both these movements are more or less similar. The KPP demands a separate state of Kamtapur consisting of the six North Bengal districts (Malda, Uttar Dinajpur, Dakshin Dinajpur, Jalpaiguri, Cooch Behar and Darjeeling excluding the hills of Darjeeling), as it claims that this region originally belonged to the *Kamtapuris* (the original inhabitants of the region), predominantly *Rajbanshis*. The GCDP's demand is the formation of a separate Greater Cooch Behar State comprising Cooch Behar, Darjeeling, Jalpaiguri, North and South Dinajpur districts and the undivided Goalpara district of Assam. The GCDP argues that inclusion of the erstwhile princely state of Cooch Behar in West Bengal in 1950 violated agreement between the King of Cooch Behar and the Government of India.

The *Rajbanshis* are among the earliest settlers in North Bengal, along with certain other ethnic groups. Their native language is *Rajbanshi* or *Kamtapuri*. Their demand for territorial autonomy in the form of separate statehood arises from the loss of land, economic opportunities and cultural identity caused by massive influx of Bengali refugees from East Pakistan (later Bangladesh).[18] Rup Kumar Barman has shown that average population growth rate of North Bengal has consistently remained higher than that of the whole of West Bengal in each decadal census from 1951 to 2001.[19] Census data also suggests that the percentage of *Rajbanshi* population has decreased over the years in two districts where the *Rajbanshis* are mainly concentrated, Jalpaiguri and Cooch Behar (See Table 31). Other reasons behind the demand for statehood are North Bengal's underdevelopment and the economic backwardness of the *Rajbanshis* owing to consistent governmental neglect. Since the *Rajbanshis* are the earliest settlers of the region, a good number of them were *jotedars* and other forms of subtenants and the remaining were *adhihar*s (sharecroppers).

---

18   Jyotiprasad Chatterjee and Supriyo Basu, *Left Front and After: Understanding the Dynamics of Poriborton in West Bengal* (New Delhi: Sage, 2020), 162.

19   Rup Kumar Barman, "Partition of Bengal and Struggle for Existence of the Scheduled Castes: Impact of the Partition (1947) on the Rajbanshis of North Bengal," *Voice of Dalit* 2, no. 2 (2009): 152.

Many rich *Rajbanshis* lost their land due to transfer of land to the Bengali refugees from the East Pakistan/ Bangladesh through implementation of land ceiling acts after independence.[20] On the other hand, many *Rajbanshi adhihars* also lost cultivating rights on land with pressure on land increasing due to continuous influx of non-*Rajbanshi adhihars*. They also failed to derive much benefit from government's policy of land reforms due its relative lack of success in Coochbehar and Jalpaiguri. The mushrooming of unauthorized tea gardens from the late 1980s also contributed to the growth of landlessness by eating away a good part of the land cultivated by the *Rajbanshis*.[21] As a result, economic situation of the *Rajbanshis* has sharply deteriorated over the years on account of their continuing alienation from land.

Thus, the movements for separate states in North Bengal have been motivated by strong anti-refugee sentiments. The declining ratio of *Rajbanshi* population in the districts of North Bengal is a major issue of concern for the members of the community. Influx of outsiders (mainly immigrant Bengalis locally known as *bhatias*) is widely perceived as a threat to the livelihood and culture of the original inhabitants of the region. Time and again demands have been raised for expulsion of the outsiders who came after the Partition in 1947. Therefore, it is quite apparent that the demands of the two largest lower caste communities of West Bengal are quite opposite. While the *Namasudras* want proper rehabilitation and resettlement of the Hindu Bengali refugees from Bangladesh, the demand for territorial and cultural autonomy of the *Rajbanshis* arises from their opposition to the resettlement and rehabilitation of Bengali refugees from Bangladesh. As a result, while the *Namasudras* are demanding implementation of the CAA, the *Ranbanshis* are opposed to it. The *Rajbanshis* are afraid that the CAA will encourage migration of Hindu Bengalis from Bangladesh further endangering the culture and livelihood of the *Rajbanshis*. However, they are in favour of a citizenship screening drive akin to Assam's National Register of Citizens (NRC) in order to put a check on migration from Bangladesh.[22] Therefore, it is difficult to build a broad alliance of all lower caste groups by devising some common socio-political agenda as

---

20   Arun Kumar Jana, "Backwardness and Political Articulation of Backwardness in the North Bengal Region of West Bengal," in *Rethinking State Politics in India*, ed. Ashutosh Kumar (New Delhi: Routledge, 2011), 182–183.

21   Arun Kumar Jana, "Development (?) and Identity Politics in West Bengal: The Kamtapur Movement in North Bengal," in *Globalization and Politics of Identity in India*, eds. Bhupinder Brar, Ashutosh Kumar and Ronki Ram (New Delhi: Pearson, 2008), 113.

22   Suvojit Bagchi, "Rajbongshis Oppose CAA, but Back NRC in North Bengal," December 18, 2019, https://www.thehindu.com/news/national/rajbongshis-oppose-caa-but-back -nrc-in-north-bengal/article30341447.ece; Snigdhendu Bhattacharya, "TMC, BJP Woo

TABLE 31   District-wise percentage of Rajbanshi population

District	1951	1961	1971	1981	1991	2001	2011
Jalpaiguri	32.68	35.19	32.03	29	23.42	3401173	23.82
Cooch Behar	47	46	46.84	40.96	39.86	2479155	37.72

SOURCE: CENSUS (1951–2011)

there is absence of common issues which can forge political unity among different marginalized castes.

In such a scenario where demands of different caste groups are dissimilar, a common *dalit* political agenda can only be formulated by conceding disproportionate prominence to any particular caste group and the recognition by other caste groups of its pre-eminent position. But caste demography of West Bengal rules out such an outcome. This can be best understood by comparing the West Bengal scenario with that of UP where *dalit* politics has arguably achieved its greatest success. In UP the *Jatavs* who account for 56.3 percent of the total *dalit* population and 9.92 percent of the total state population according to the 2011 census have spearheaded *dalit* politics by rallying behind the Bahujan Samaj Party (BSP). Their massive demographic clout vis-a-vis other *dalit* groups such as *Pasi* and *Dhobi* has enabled them to dictate the trajectory of *dalit* politics. Due to their colossal numerical preponderance, they have faced little difficulty in setting the agenda of *dalit* politics. The *Mahars* who account for 57.5 percent of the total SC population of Maharashtra has also dictated *dalit* politics in Maharashtra riding on their numerical strength. In contrast, no *dalit* group in West Bengal enjoys such massive demographic advantage over other lower caste groups. The *Rajbanshis, Namasudras, Bagdis* and *Pods* account for 18.35, 17.41, 14.58 and 12.01 percent of total Scheduled Caste population respectively. Thus, the major *dalit* groups possess comparable demographic strength. Therefore, no lower caste group is in a position to dictate the agenda of *dalit* politics by asserting its hold over other lower caste groups through utilization of its demographic strength. As a result, different lower caste groups are only left with the option of particularistic mobilization that can only have limited impact on electoral politics.

Rajbangshi Voters, Bengal's Largest SC Group, Ahead of Polls," *Wire*, February 13, 2021, https://thewire.in/politics/bjp-bengal-elections-amit-shah-koch-rajbangshi-tmc-greater-cooch-behar.

Absence of caste politics in West Bengal has been attributed in this chapter to some specific aspects of demography. Through an exhaustive analysis of latest demographic data, it has been argued that that political assertion of caste identity in West Bengal faces a number of demographic handicaps such as absence of a dominant caste, demographic fragmentation of the intermediate castes, limited geographical spread of major lower and intermediate castes and unfavourable pattern of population distribution for political aggregation of caste interests. Thus, several aspects of West Bengal's caste demography are inimical to the growth of caste politics. However, the insignificance of caste in institutional politics of West Bengal is a complex and multifaceted issue. Caste demography alone can't account for the complex phenomenon of marginalization of caste factor in West Bengal politics. As has already been pointed out, non-articulation of caste identity by the *Mahishyas*, who come closest to being qualified as a dominant caste suggests that there are possibly some intangible cultural factors which are also at play. Hence, it is imperative to direct our analytical efforts towards dissection of the relationship between caste and dynamics of political culture. Chapters 6 and 7 will analyse the role of political culture in the context of caste as political category in West Bengal.

Material Basis of Caste

Putting Political Economy into Perspective

Political economy often provides an important backdrop in which dynamics of caste undergo politicisation.[1] Andre Beteille in his seminal study on a Tamil Nadu village has demonstrated that caste, class and power have now become differentiated axes of stratification. As a result of growing occupational diversification caste identity of an individual unlike in earlier times no longer necessarily determines his or her position in the class or power hierarchy. Beteille has also pointed out that the composition of landownership has become more heterogeneous in terms of caste.[2] Yet, caste dynamics have not completely ceased to operate in the economic sphere. Though rural occupations have now to a large extent become free from caste restrictions, there still remains a marked tendency for certain castes to cluster in particular occupations. In other words, the phenomenon of certain castes being disproportionately represented in particular occupations still persists.[3] Divya Vaid's study based on the individual-level National Election Study 2004 CSDS (Centre for Developing Societies) data set with approximately 27,000 respondents, has found that a tentative correspondence exists between castes and classes at the extremes of the caste system. For example, priests are still predominantly Brahmans, and sweepers are often from the lowest castes. It is in the middle of the hierarchy where all the fluidity and mobility occur.[4] Therefore, there remain massive barriers to the entry by the lower castes into certain occupations and economic activities. G.K Karanth has observed that despite growing occupational diversification, lower caste individuals still face much greater difficulty

---

1 Parts of this chapter first appeared in Ayan Guha, "Caste Question in West Bengal Politics: Continuing Inconsequentiality or Rising Relevance?" *Contemporary South Asia* 29, no. 3 (2021): 376–400 and Ayan Guha "Beyond Conspiracy and Coordinated Ascendancy: Revisiting Caste Question in West Bengal under the Left Front Rule (1977–2011)", *Contemporary Voice of Dalit* 13, no. 1 (2021): 50–65.

2 André Béteille, *Caste, Class, and Power: Changing Patterns of Stratification in a Tanjore Village* (New Delhi: Oxford University Press, 1965).

3 M.N Panini, "The Political Economy of Caste," in *Caste: Its Twentieth Century Avatar*, ed. M.N Srinivas (Gurgaon: Penguin, 1997), 28–68.

4 Divya Vaid, "The Caste-Class Association in India: An Empirical Analysis," *Asian Survey* 52, no. 2 (2012): 95–422.

in changing their traditional occupations compared to the upper castes. This is largely due to the continuing social, economic and political pressure exerted by the higher castes on the *dalit*s in order to keep them entangled in traditional patron-client networks, reproducing the economic dependency of the *dalit*s on the higher caste patrons.[5] A number of studies have pointed out that even qualified *dalit*s continue to face discrimination in hiring processes in formal, urban labour market.[6]

Thus, the lower castes face significant constrains in achieving upward economic mobility. This implies that there is still a strong link between caste and economic dynamics. It has been pointed out that if there is considerable correlation between caste hierarchy and possession of material resources, social protests and political mobilization tend be organised on the basis of primordial identity even when the main source of deprivation as well as the objective of political action remain economic. Hence, in case of West Bengal, the material context of political inaction of the *dalits* deserves some investigation. The economic situation of the lower castes in West Bengal has not remained unexplored in the existing scholarship. For instance, Barbara Harriss-White's study on the rural agro-based commercial economy of West Bengal has highlighted that, though those who operate in the grain markets claim to be ignorant about the caste identity of their employees and vehemently deny the role of caste in everyday economic life, the Scheduled Castes and Scheduled Tribes are routinely denied trade licenses and institutional credit. She has found that no lower caste individual owns rice mills and that very few lower caste individuals own husking mills.[7] But despite such scholarly exploration of the economic handicaps faced by the lower castes in West Bengal, the link between the material situation of the lower castes and absence of large-scale *dalit* mobilization has not been explicitly explored. Simply put, while analysing the absence of caste-based identity politics in West Bengal, little scholarly attention has been devoted to the political economy of the state.

---

5   G.K Karanth, "Caste in Contemporary Rural India," in *Caste: Its Twentieth Century Avatar*, ed. M.N Srinivas (Gurgaon: Penguin, 1997), 91–92.

6   See, Ashwini Deshpande and Katherine Newman, "Where the Path Leads: The Role of Caste in Post-University Employment Expectations," *Economic and Political Weekly* 42, no. 41 (2007): 4133–4140; Surinder S. Jodhka and Katherine Newman, "In the Name of Globalisation: Meritocracy, Productivity and the Hidden Language of Caste," *Economic and Political Weekly* 42, no. 41 (2007): 4125–4132; Sukhadeo Thorat and Paul Attewell, "The Legacy of Social Exclusion: A Correspondence Study of Job Discrimination in India," *Economic and Political Weekly* 42, no. 41 (2007): 4141–4145.

7   Barbara Harriss-White, "West Bengal's Rural Commercial Capital," *International Critical Thought* 3, no. 1 (2013): 29–30.

1   **Caste and Economic Aspects of Identity Politics**

Politics of identity is largely concerned with recognition/respect. According to Charles Taylor we define our identity always in dialogue with, sometimes in struggle against, the things our significant others want to see in us. Because our identities are formed dialogically, we are dependent on the recognition by others. In this highly influential perspective identity is largely seen to be shaped by the presence and absence of recognition, and hence non-recognition or misrecognition is viewed as source of oppression.[8] By implication, identity politics, therefore, tends to be construed as a socio-political mobilization organized by a group of people with the goal to gain recognition and respect for their shared social identity. But identity politics is not entirely divorced from the issue of economic development. Rather, the quest for economic empowerment is often found to act as a significant motive behind identity politics. The main aim of identity politics often is to secure social justice for people belonging to oppressed identities. Social justice is generally perceived to have cultural as well as economic connotations. Social justice which identity politics seeks to achieve has been conceptualized in terms of *both* cultural recognition (respect for and revaluation of degraded identities) and economic redistribution. In other words, identity politics is a system of politics within which there are two inter-related components: the politics of recognition/respect and the politics of limited economic distribution, though the former being the dominant component influences the latter.[9] Critiques of identity politics often argue that identity politics tends to remain preoccupied only with dignity and cultural recognition bypassing economic welfare and material bases of injustice. In the United States critics like Todd Gitlin and Richard Rorty who view themselves as part of the progressive Left have expressed concerns that the rise of the cultural Left with its emphasis on identity politics renders struggles for economic justice insignificant.[10] Critics in the United Kingdom and Europe have also expressed similar concerns. Brian Barry, for instance, has also observed that identity politics erodes social solidarity, political consensus and public support necessary for a redistributive welfare state. The more we emphasize our cultural differences, the less likely we are to work together to

---

8   Charles Taylor, "The Politics of Recognition," in *Multiculturalism: Examining the Politics of Recognition*, ed. Amy Gutmann (Princeton: Princeton University Press, 1994), 25–73.

9   Raju Das, "Identity Politics: A Marxist View," *Class, Race and Corporate Power* 8, no. 1 (2020).

10   Todd Gitlin, *The Twilight of Common Dreams: Why America is Wracked by Culture Wars* (New York: Metropolitan Books, 1995); Richard Rorty, *Achieving Our Country: Leftist Thought in Twentieth-Century America* (Cambridge, MA: Harvard University Press, 1998).

fight economic inequality.[11] However, identity politics' preoccupation with cultural recognition has been justified by its proponents through the claim that it is not possible to address economic inequalities suffered by a group of people sharing an oppressed identity without first addressing their cultural misrecognition. According to Axel Honneth economic injustices are rooted in a cultural order, and therefore, cultural recognition gained through identity politics will ultimately lead to rectification of economic injustices.[12] On the contrary, Nancy Fraser has pointed out that *both* politics of redistribution and politics of recognition are required to secure social justice for bivalent categories like gender or race, which involve interconnected cultural and economic realities and face both cultural disrespect and economic exploitation. She calls for a politics of recognition that can be coherently combined with the politics of economic equality.[13]

Caste in India, like gender in Fraser's account, is a bivalent category. For the *dalits* the lived reality of caste entails exploitation involving an overlapping mix of interrelated cultural and economic experiences. Mobilization for *dalit* emancipation, however, is largely focused on gaining socio-cultural recognition through contestation of untouchability, political and bureaucratic representation and acquisition of state power. The path to attain equality in economic terms has also been generally visualized through attainment of recognition rooted in representation and governmental power by prominent *dalit* leaders like Kanshi Ram and Mayawati.[14] During the *Mandal* debate too the demand for OBC (Other Backward Castes) reservation in education and government jobs was made not with the objectives to achieve material well-being and to redress economic inequalities, but to achieve social respect, social status and power. The motivation to secure a government job was not only about having employment; it also meant having a share in state power as a means to enhance "an individual's as well as a community's social status and

---

11   Brian Barry, *Culture and Equality: An Egalitarian Critique of Multiculturalism* (Cambridge, MA: Harvard University Press, 2001).

12   Axel Honneth, *The Struggle for Recognition: The Grammar of Social Conflicts* (Cambridge: Polity, 1995); Nancy Fraser and Axel Honneth, *Redistribution or Recognition: A Political-Philosophical Exchange* (London:Verso, 2003).

13   Nancy Fraser, *Justice Interrupts: Critical Reflections on the "Postsocialist" Condition* (New York: Routledge, 1997).

14   Gail Omvedt, *Dalits and the Democratic Revolution: Dr. Ambedkar and the Dalit Movement in Colonial India* (New Delhi: Sage, 1994), 246; Badri Narayan, *The Making of the Dalit Public in North India: Uttar Pradesh 1950–Present* (New Delhi: Oxford University Press, 2011), 99.

honour".[15] The Mandal Commission accordingly, defined backwardness by giving disproportionately greater importance to social factors downplaying economic criteria.[16] Similarly, the agenda of India's most successful *dalit* based political party, Bahujan Samaj Party (BSP) in Uttar Pradesh is largely based on the notion of *swabhiman* (self-respect). Its leadership has argued that "self-respect is more important to *dalit*s than material gains" while regarding capture of state power as the primary means of securing dignity for the *dalit*s. The governments led by the BSP in U.P rolled out mainly symbolic initiatives like Periyar Mela, Ambedkar parks and statues. No clear and detailed economic agenda for *dalit* empowerment has come out of BSP ideology.[17] The underlying presumption is that the achievement of political power will ultimately bring about economic empowerment of the lower castes. As a result, redistribution has become reducible to a claim over recognition and representation in the mainstream discourse of *dalit* politics. This corresponds to Honneth's rationale behind identity politics which suggests that identity and redistribution are not mutually exclusive. Due to deep penetration of cultural prejudices into the economic system, economic inequality can only be rectified by addressing identity-based misrecognition. *Dalit* politics to a considerable degree has achieved dignity and recognition for the lower castes through greater representation. It has successfully pursued what Anne Phillips calls a 'politics of presence'.[18] Despite this there is a widespread view that caste-based identity politics has largely remained trapped in a narrative of symbolic change and has failed to generate proportionate and adequate economic empowerment of the lower castes.[19]

---

15   Sambaiah Gundimeda, *Dalit Politics in Contemporary India* (Abingdon: Routledge, 2016), 111.

16   Dipankar Gupta, "Caste and Politics: Identity over System," *Annual Review of Anthropology* 34 (2005): 424.

17   Sudha Pai, *"Dalit* Question and Political Response: Comparative Study of Uttar Pradesh and Madhya Pradesh," *Economic and Political Weekly* 39, no. 11 (2004): 1141–1150.

18   See, Anne Phillips, *The Politics of Presence* (Oxford: Clarendon Press, 1995).

19   See, Craig Jeffrey, "A Fist Is Stronger than Five Fingers': Caste and Dominance in Rural North India," *Transactions of the Institute of British Geographers* 26, no. 2 (2001): 217–236; Sudha, Pai, *Dalit Assertion and the Unfinished Democratic Revolution: The Bahujan Samaj Party in Uttar Pradesh* (New Delhi: Sage, 2002); Cyril Robin, "Bihar: The New Stronghold of OBC Politics," in *Rise of the Plebeians? The Changing Face of Indian Legislative Assemblies*, eds. Christophe Jaffrelot, and Sanjay Kumar (New Delhi: Routledge, 2009) 2729–2739; Anand Teltumbde, "Bathani Tola and the Cartoon Controversy," *Economic and Political Weekly* 47, no. 22 (2012): 10–11; Zoya Hasan, "Democracy and Development in Uttar Pradesh," in *Development Failure and Identity Politics in Uttar Pradesh*, eds. Roger Jeffery, Craig Jeffrey and Jens Lerche (New Delhi: Sage, 2014), 239–256.

Though economic demands have been neglected by the dominant discourse of caste politics, they have acted as strong catalysts to caste mobilization at the grassroots. Rajni Kothari and Rushikesh Maru have shown how common economic interests arising out of resentment against the dominant caste of *Patidars* played a pivotal part in the formation of Gujarat Kshatriya Sabha, a caste federation consisting of upper caste Rajputs on the one hand, and some cultivating castes on the other.[20] Economic motivations have caused formation of several caste associations. Robert Hardgrave has described how caste associations such as Nadar Mahajan Sangam are not geared towards the preservation of caste traditions and customs, but towards the general welfare of the community.[21] Similarly, Lloyd I. Rudolph and Susanne Hoeber Rudolph have discussed how the Vanniya Kula Kshatrya Sangham, a caste association of the *Vanniyars* functioned as an economic interest group focusing mainly on economic issues in its resolutions. Some of its prominent demands were better irrigation, electricity for agricultural areas, better roads, expansion of the Krishna Pennar multi-purpose water project, relief to tenants for rain failure and making tillers owners of the soil.[22] Thus, caste politics has often emerged out of a material basis and caste identity has been used to articulate economic demands. Hugo Gorringe has pointed out that in Tamil Nadu land reforms and redemption of *panchami* land (forest and wastelands) were principal demands of the *dalit* movement.[23] Similarly, Suryakant Waghmore has highlighted how in Maharashta's Marathwada the demand to cultivate *gaairan* land (common grazing land) acted as a catalyst to *dalit* mobilization.[24] Nicolas Jaoul has also described how in UP at the behest of the *Ambedkarites* symbolic politics was integrated with material demands like effective ownership of communal plots of land. Ambedkar's statues were erected by local Ambedkar committees on communal village land which was supposed to have been redistributed to the landless by the government under the Twenty Points Scheme against poverty. BSP's grassroot workers organized cycle processions from village to village shouting slogans such as *jo zameen sarkari hai, wo zameen hamari hai*

---

20   Rajni Kothari and Rushikesh Maru, "Caste and Secularism in India: Case Study of a Caste Federation." *Journal of Asian Studies* 25, no. 1 (1965): 33–50.

21   Robert Hardgrave, *The Nadars of Tamilnad: The Political Culture of a Community in Change* (Berkeley: University of California Press, 1969), 262.

22   Lloyd I. Rudolph and Susanne Hoeber Rudolph, "The Political Role of India's Caste Associations," *Pacific Affairs*, 85, no. 2 (2012): 351.

23   Hugo Gorringe, *Untouchable Citizens: Dalit Movements and Democratisation in Tamil Nadu* (New Delhi: Sage, 2005), 158.

24   Suryakant Waghmore, *Civility against Caste: Dalit Politics and Citizenship in Western India* (New Delhi: Sage, 2013), 91–115.

(government's land is our land). Thus, *dalit* villagers at the grassroots linked political symbols with economic demands that were omitted from the BSP agenda.[25] Though material issues have not been given enough importance by the parties claiming to champion the interests of the lower castes, the expectation of distributive justice and economic benefits has played an important role in motivating the *dalit*s to mobilize politically as a united force. Craig Jeffrey, Patricia Jeffery, and Roger Jeffery through their field research in UP have found out the presence of widespread disillusionment with the BSP's agenda of *dalit* politics that disproportionately emphasizes capture of political power to the exclusion of livelihood issues. The common *dalit* masses believe that respect and recognition are impossible to achieve without ensuring *dalit*s' access to economic resources.[26] The contemporary *dalit* movement in Gujarat led by leaders like Jignesh Mevani has also raised concrete economic demands like allotment of land and loan waiver, amplifying the scope of *dalit* politics from one aiming at dignity, respect and identity, to one also focusing on livelihood issues. Mevani has explicitly expressed the need to move away from *asmita* (dignity) to *astitva* (livelihood).[27] Therefore, in view of the fact that economic deprivation has often acted as a stimulus to *dalit* politics, it is imperative to find out the connection between the absence of large-scale *dalit* mobilization and dynamics of political economy in West Bengal. In other words, the material context of the lack of *dalit* political assertion needs to be extensively explored.

2 Caste and Patterns of Landholding

Historically, Bengali landholders belonged to diverse caste backgrounds. The *zamindars* primarily belonged to the upper castes. But many *zamindars*, even those influential among them, belonged to intermediate castes such as *Teli, Subarnabanik, Tambuli* or even *Sadgope* or *Mahishya*. While the traditional gentry mostly belonged to the upper castes, the *jotedars* who were in actual control of the village land and economy mainly came from lower and middle

25   Nicolas Jaoul, "Learning the Use of Symbolic Means: *Dalits*, Ambedkar Statues and the State in Uttar Pradesh," *Contributions to Indian Sociology* 40, no. 2 (2006):175–207.

26   Craig Jeffrey, Patricia Jeffery and Roger Jeffery, "*Dalit* Revolution? New Politicians in Uttar Pradesh, India," *Journal of Asian Studies* 67, no. 4 (2008): 1365–1396.

27   Anand Teltmunde, "Fire of Una Ignites Saffron Udupi," *Economic and Political Weekly* 71, no. 44/45; Saroj Giri, "From Uprising to Movement: Dalit Resistance in Gujarat," *Economic & Political Weekly* 52, no 33 (2017): 15–17; Ayan Guha, "A New Caste Agenda," *Statesman*, December 18, 2017; Neera Chandoke, "Three Cheers for Civil Society," *Hindu*, January 18, 2018.

ranking peasant castes, such as *Sadgope, Namasudra, Aguri* and *kaivarta*.[28]
Thus, if the *zamindars* belonged characteristically to the Brahman, *Kayastha*
and *Baidya* castes, the typical *jotedars* were characteristically *Mahishya*
or *Rajbanshi* by caste, though the association was in neither case perfect.[29]
According to Sugata Bose in colonial times the agrarian structure of the western part of the undivided Bengal province (which currently constitutes West
Bengal) was constitutive of a three-tiered peasant smallholding- demesne
labour complex. The first tier was occupied by a rent receiving non-cultivating
gentry section mostly belonging to the upper castes. The middle tier consisted of a numerically large segment of owner cultivators mostly belonging to
respectable peasant castes such as *Aguri, Sadgope, Mahishya* and *Namasudra*.
A large pool of primarily untouchable landless labourers lay at the bottom.[30]

This agrarian structure seems to exhibit some degree of continuity, particularly if the middle and lower tiers of the economic structure are concerned.
After the late nineteenth century a broad segment of middle-caste peasant
smallholders, or owner-cultivators, gradually emerged. The influence of the
middle-caste peasantry became further consolidated when post independence
land reforms abolished *zamindari* system and removed whatever influence the
zamindars had over the middle peasants. This segment experienced upward
social mobility at the expense of the *zamindars* and some managed to achieve
significant clout and influence in rural society. After the Communist government came to power the middle peasants also reaped benefits from its agrarian policies and moved in to occupy local positions in the Communist parties
and their unions.[31] The upper and middle peasantry came to dominate various
tiers of the *panchayat* as well as the Left parties.[32] During the rule of the Left
Front they functioned as a new agrarian elite enjoying economic and political
hegemony.[33] In contemporary West Bengal, the upper caste educated Bengalis

---

28   Rajat Ray and Ratna Ray, "Zamindars and Jotedars: A Study of Rural Politics in Bengal,"
      Modern Asian Studies 9, no. 1 (1975): 84.
29   Andre Beteille , *Marxism and Class Analysis* (New Delhi: Oxford University Press,
      2013), 230.
30   Sugata Bose, *Agrarian Bengal. Economy Social Structure and Politics, 1919–1947.*
      (Cambridge: Cambridge University Press, 2008), 3–33.
31   Kenneth Bo Nielsen, "Orchestrating Anti-Dispossession Politics: Caste and Movement
      Leadership in Rural West Bengal," *Journal of Contemporary Asia* 50, no. 5 (2020): 764–765.
32   Dayabati Roy, *Rural Politics in India: Political Stratification and Governance in West Bengal*
      (Delhi: Cambridge University Press, 2014), 40.
33   Ritanjan Das and Zaad Mahmood, "Contradictions, Negotiations and Reform: The Story
      of Left Policy Transition in West Bengal," *Journal of South Asian Development* 10, no. 2
      (2015): 212.

are mostly concentrated in urban areas and they have little landed property.[34] In districts, the landownership remains primarily in the hands of intermediate castes and even some upwardly mobile lower castes such as the *Namasudras*. For example, while in Burdwan, the *Aguris* constitute the main landholding caste, in Midnapur and Howrah, the *Mahishyas* are the principal landholding caste.[35] Thus, the rural middle classes or middle peasants who own a fair amount of land in most cases belong to diverse caste backgrounds. This landholding pattern has prevented crystallization of political demands along caste lines. The lack of homogeneity of the caste identities of the landholding class has prevented their conversion into a cohesive political bloc which is potentially capable of being mobilized in favour of any political party.

3   Caste and Relative Deprivation

In analysing the rise of the *dalit* movement, the concept of relative deprivation has been used by scholars to unearth manifest as well as underlying motivations behind *dalit* mobilization. But in the analyses of the absence of *dalit* politics in West Bengal, the important factor of relative deprivation faced by the lower castes has remained entirely unexplored. It is not possible to grasp the actual extent of relative deprivation in economic terms. Nevertheless, an attempt can be made to arrive at some broad understanding in this regard.

Simply put, the concept of relative deprivation is based upon the idea that people often tend to see deprivation in relative rather than in absolute sense. The concept of relative deprivation first emerged from a study on American soldiers in World War II made by Samuel Stouffer and his associates. They discovered that the army units, in which the rate of promotion was fastest, were actually the ones where maximum people were dissatisfied with the promotions, often due to the reason that they themselves did not get promoted.[36] Although Stouffer and his associates were first to use the notion of relative deprivation, it was Robert K. Merton who systematically developed

---

34   Partha Chatterjee, *The Present History of West Bengal* (New Delhi: Oxford University Press, 1997), 81.

35   Atul Kohli, "From Breakdown to Order: West Bengal," in *State and Politics in India*, ed. Partha Chatterjee (New Delhi: Oxford University Press, 1997), 339; John Echeverri-Gent, "Public Participation and Poverty Alleviation: The Experience of Reform Communists in India's West Bengal," *World Development* 20, no. 10 (1992): 1411.

36   Samuel Stouffer et al, *The American Soldier, Vol. 1: Adjustment During Army Life*. (Princeton, NJ: Princeton University Press, 1949).

the concept in relation to the idea of reference group. Applying the concept to analyse social mobility he makes the argument that "men frequently orient themselves to groups other than their own in shaping their behaviour and evaluations and it is the problems centered about this fact of orientation to non-membership groups that constitute the distinctive concern of reference group theory".[37] It is the tendency to compare their own situation with that of other non-membership groups that gives rise to a feeling of relative deprivation in people's minds. Today much of the conceptualization of relative deprivation is typically based on the notion of reference group.[38] However, relative deprivation has also been interpreted as a negative discrepancy between expectations and reality by some scholars. They have defined it as a perception that achievements are failing to match expectations.[39] Others define relative deprivation somewhat more narrowly using the conceptual framework of reference group. Here relative deprivation arises out of the widespread perception that one's membership group is in a disadvantageous position, relative to some other group. Since my analysis here is only concerned with the material basis of the collective mentality of the *dalit*s, I shall also apply the concept of relative deprivation through the well-known framework of reference group theory. To be precise, what is relevant for my analysis is group based relative deprivation or what W.G Runciman calls 'fraternal relative deprivation'. Following Merton, W.G. Runciman also based his formulation of relative deprivation on reference group theory. More importantly, Runciman made a crucial distinction between egoistic (individual) and fraternal (group) relative deprivation. Egoistic relative deprivation arises out of interpersonal comparisons. A person develops the feeling of egoistic relative deprivation when he comes to believe that he is personally deprived. Similarly, a person may also believe that a social group to which she belongs is deprived in comparison to a reference group. In that case fraternal relative deprivation will arise. Fraternal relative deprivation is thus, based upon intergroup comparisons.[40] It would be useful here

---

37   Robert K Merton, *Social Theory and Social Structure* (Glencoe, Free Press, 1968), 288.

38   Joan Neff Gurney and Kathleen J. Tierney, "Relative Deprivation and Social Movements: A Critical Look at Twenty Years of Theory and Research," *The Sociological Quarterly* 23, no. 1 (1982): 40.

39   See, David Aberle, *The Peyote Religion among the Navaho* (New York: Wenner-Gren Foundation for Anthropological Research, 1966); Ted Gurr, *Why Men Rebel* (Princeton: Princeton University Press, 1970); Denton Morrison, "Some Notes Toward Theory on Relative Deprivation, Social Movements, and Social Change," in *Social Movements: A Reader*, ed. R. R. Evans (Chicago: Rand McNally, 1973), 103–116.

40   W.G Runciman, *Relative Deprivation and Social Justice* (Berkeley: University of California Press, 1966).

to briefly explore the concept of reference group. Ralph Turner distinguishes between two kinds of reference group: identification group and valuation group. Identification group is the source of an individual's perspectives and values. In case of an identification group, a person takes the role of a member while adopting the group's standpoints as his own. On the other hand, an individual also compares himself with certain groups or notes the impression he is making on them or in some other way takes account of them. These groups might be called valuation groups.[41] It is possible to make a further distinction between positive and negative valuation groups. Gerald D. Berreman's study on the Nikolski Aleuts reveals that an individual may value any particular valuation group positively or negatively. The positive valuation group constitutes a reference group of imitation whose social conduct and culture are considered as proper and worth following. Berreman points out that, white men for the Nikolski Aleuts form a positive reference group. The Nikolski people want to be respected by the whites and they tend to evaluate themselves by reference to white men's standards. They have therefore adopted many of white men's values, perspectives, and behaviours. Most aspects of the native culture, ridiculed by whites, are for them negatively valued as most of the Nikolski Aleuts identify with their membership group of modern, white-oriented Aleuts. In other words, the traditional Aleut society constitutes a negative valuation group. But at the same time, they are alienated from their positively valued reference group as the whites are keen to maintain some amount of social distance from the Nikolski Aleuts. The Nikolski Aleuts are therefore, denied full access to the white life and its advantages. This gives rise to a feeling of relative, if not absolute deprivation, creating a fertile ground for the emergence of nativistic movements.[42] It is this feeling of group based relative deprivation or what Runciman calls 'fraternal relative deprivation' that creates support for political protest.[43] In this perspective relative deprivation has a role to play in the emergence of movements like the American Civil Rights Movement or *dalit* movement.

The sociological analysis of the rise of *dalit* movement has been to an extent inspired by the theory of relative deprivation. The analysis of *dalit* movement

41 Ralph H Turner, "Role-Taking, Role Standpoint, and Reference-Group Behaviour," *American Journal of Sociology* 61, no. 4 (1956): 327- 328.

42 Gerald D Berreman, "Aleut Reference Group Alienation, Mobility, and Acculturation," *American Anthropologist* 66, no. 2 (1964): 231–250.

43 Smith J. Heather, Thomas F. Pettigrew, Gina M. Pippin and Silvana Bialosiewicz, "Relative Deprivation: A Theoretical and Meta-Analytic Review," *Personality and Social Psychology Review* 16, no. 3 (2012): 204.

through the framework of relative deprivation is based upon the assumption that *dalit* movement or politics emerges when *dalit* groups find themselves socially and materially deprived in comparison to their reference groups, whose social and economic success they aspire to achieve. Gopal Guru has pointed out that the educated and employed *dalits* belonging to the *Mahars* and *Mangs* of Maharashtra, feel relatively deprived both socially and materially in comparison to the upper castes. The political activism of these *dalit* groups is rooted in their feeling of relative deprivation.[44] Owen Lynch's study on the *Jatav* caste of Agra has also utilized the framework of relative deprivation. Lynch has identified three reference groups: reference group of imitation whose behaviour is emulated, reference group of identification with which an individual identifies and finally a negative reference group which stands as one's enemy or as the denier of the claims of one's own group. The reference group for identification for the *Jatavs* is the Scheduled Castes, their reference group of imitation is the liberal leaders of the independence movement, and the Brahmans and wealthy Punjabi businessmen constitute the reference group of negation. Lynch argues that relationship of the *Jatavs* with their negative reference group is one of relative deprivation. The perception that the economic privileges enjoyed by the Brahmans and the Punjabis have been accumulated through exploitation of the lower castes is one of the main motivating factors behind their political activism.[45] Hugo Gorringe has also pointed out that in Tamil Nadu in the 1980s the *Vanniyars* were mobilized by the *Pattali Makkal Katchi* (PMK) by raising the issue of relative caste deprivation of the *Vanniyars* vis-à-vis the *dalits*. The *Vanniyars* harboured a feeling that unlike the *dalit*s they had not been provided government benefits in proportion to their population. They mobilized in the 1980s claiming the status of a 'Most Backward Caste' so as to gain access to a greater share of state resources.[46] Several others scholars have also attempted to link the emergence of *dalit* politics with relative deprivation.[47] T.K Oommen has rightly pointed out that although deprivation can't be perceived solely in terms of material conditions,

---

44   Gopal Guru, "*Dalit* Movement in Mainstream Sociology," *Economic and Political Weekly* 28, no. 14 (1993): 571.

45   Owen M. Lynch, *The Politics of Untouchability* (Delhi: Gautam Book Centre, 2015), 86–95.

46   Hugo Gorringe, *Panthers in Parliament: Dalits, Caste and Political Power in South India* (New Delhi: Oxford University Press, 2017): 54–57.

47   Harold Issac, *India's Ex-Untouchables* (Bombay: Asia Publishing House, 1964); M. S. A Rao, *Social Movements in India, Vol 1* (Delhi: Manohar, 1982); Barbara Joshi, "Recent Developments in Inter-Regional Mobilisation of *Dalit* Protest in India," *South Asia Bulletin* 7 (1987): 112–135.

lack of material resources has remained an influential motive behind the political mobilization of the poorer among the depressed classes.[48]

In this connection, we could look at some of the relevant economic indicators which can reflect the extent of relative deprivation faced by the Scheduled Castes (scs) and the Other Backward Classes (obcs) in West Bengal. There is scarcity of data which can effectively capture community-wise economic conditions. However, the limited data which is available can still give us some idea about the extent of material deprivation suffered by the lower castes vis-à-vis other sections of society. One of the most important aspects of political economy that can be studied to obtain some idea about the material basis of relative deprivation is landholding structure. Landholding patterns must be taken into consideration because, particularly in rural areas, land is not only the most important economic resource but also often a source of dignity. Hugo Gorringe, writing in the context of Tamil Nadu, has pointed out that for the *dalit*s, the demand for land extends beyond economics. It is tied with dignity and social status. In this sense, land or any such economic demand is itself an aspect of the struggle for recognition.[49] The *dalits* also perceive a close connection between land politics and caste politics. This is because control over land is closely associated with the caste system. The domination of the higher castes over the *dalits* is maintained, to a large extent, through their ownership of land on which the *dalit* cultivators depend for their livelihood.[50] The importance of land as a resource in the rural society of West Bengal has been highlighted by Sarasij Majumder's study on the Singur movement. It has found that landownership provides significant social and economic leverage that enables a person to make financial arrangements for educating a male child for a non-farming career. Further, it also offers possibility to enjoy leisure, to obtain a dowry on the marriage market, to exercise control over landless labourers and to conduct hard negotiation with the land broker, and also to reap benefits from speculative value of land. As a result, people are generally reluctant to part away with their land. While there is a thriving land market in rural West Bengal, selling of land is a social taboo as it is mostly undertaken only in circumstances of economic hardship. Land is thus a material and symbolic marker of distinction.[51]

---

48   T. K. Oommen, "Sociological Issues in the Analysis of Social Movements in Independent India," *Sociological Bulletin* 26, no. 1 (1977): 21.

49   Gorringe, *Untouchable Citizens*, 159, 173.

50   Gorringe, *Panthers in Parliament*, 88–89.

51   Sarasij Majumder,"Who Wants to Marry a Farmer? Neoliberal industrialization and the Politics of Land and Work in Rural West Bengal," *Focaal – Journal of Global and Historical Anthropology* 64 (2012): 89.

4   Land and Agrarian Politics

Compared to other states West Bengal's rural economy is characterized by much greater incidence of small landholdings. The agrarian economy of West Bengal has historically seen a much greater incidence of small and marginal landholdings compared to other states. The average size of holdings in 1953–1954 was 3.01 acres in West Bengal, while the corresponding national level figure was 6.25 acres. In the country as a whole, holdings above 15-acres accounted for 10 percent of total holdings and 52.51 percent of agricultural land, while for West Bengal the corresponding figures were 2.60 percent and 26 percent.[52] The land reforms undertaken by the Left Front government led to further proliferation of small and marginal landholdings, since it proved to be far more significant in terms of the number of households that were recipients of land compared to total quantum of distributed land. The recipients had mostly received small plots of land which later turned out to be economically non-viable as a source of livelihood. For understanding the link between proliferation of small landholdings and land reform it is important to engage with the Left Front's agrarian politics.

According to Atul Kohli the CPI(M) followed a clear class-based mobilization strategy. The party attempted to mobilize the lower and lower-middle classes like the agricultural workers and small and marginal farmers by claiming to represent their interests.[53] Such a claim found manifestation in Central Committee resolutions on Tasks on the Kisan Front (1967), Central Agrarian Issues (1973) and the political resolution adopted at the Tenth Congress of the CPI(M) held in Jalandhar in April 1978. However, over the years the ideological orientation of the CPI(M) gradually changed from revolutionary to reformist direction.[54] The recognition that electoral calculations had to be given primacy by abandoning theoretical orthodoxy gradually dawned upon the party. Consequently, the CPI(M) did not focus its attention only on extreme lower rungs of the rural society. It tried to build an all-inclusive alliance of rural classes minus the large landowners or *jotedars*. As a result, the unity between

52   Sunil Sengupta, "West Bengal Land Reforms and Agrarian Scene," *Economic and Political Weekly* 16, vol. 25/26 (1981): 69–70.

53   Atul Kohli, "Parliamentary Communism and Agrarian Reform: The Evidence from India's Bengal," *Asian Survey* 23, no. 7 (1983): 791.

54   Atul Kohli, "From Elite Radicalism to Democratic Consolidation: The Rise of Reform Communism in West Bengal," in *Dominance and State Power in Modern India: Decline of A Social Order, Vol II*, eds. M. S. A. Rao and Francine F. Frankel (New Delhi: Oxford University Press, 1990), 367–416.

the middle peasants on one hand and agricultural labourers and sharecroppers on other hand was emphasized. Even though the agricultural labourers working on the land of the relatively affluent rich and middle peasants routinely found themselves at loggerheads with the latter, it was CPI(M)'s electoral agenda to keep both employers and workers on their side. In the process, the party in rural areas ultimately came to be dominated by none other than the middle peasants.[55] The term 'middle class peasant' generally refers to middle and rich peasants whose status and position in society are largely based upon their relatively large landholdings, their relatively high or pure ritual status, their engagement in mostly non-manual work and lifestyle or upon an accepted claim to such status.[56] They mostly belong to the middle peasant castes such as *Sadgope, Aguri, Mahishya* and even some upwardly mobile lower castes such as *Namasudra*.[57] Thus, the rural middle classes or middle peasants own fair amount of land and they in most cases belong to intermediate castes.

The CPI(M)'s political strategy of building multi-class rural alliance exhibited a clear bias in favour of the middle peasants. Such bias got reflected in the neglect of the interests of agricultural labourers. No separate organization was set up for the agricultural workers within the West Bengal Kisan Sabha, despite the formation of such an organization within the All India Kisan Sabha in 1981. The reason for this lay in the political need to protect the interests of the middle peasantry who employed hired labour to get their land cultivated. However, the Left Front also needed to prevent alienation of marginal farmers, sharecroppers, and agricultural workers. The most volatile issue that often exposed conflict of interests between the landholding peasants and their hired agricultural labourers was the rate of wage.[58] Under such circumstances, the party in order to maintain its pro-poor image must be seen to be waging a struggle in favour of the agricultural workers. But unlike in earlier times, the party was

---

55   Ben Rogaly, "Containing Conflict and Reaping Votes: Management of Rural Labour Relations in West Bengal," *Economic and Political Weekly* 33, vol. 42/43 (1998): 2729–2739; Dipankar Basu, "Political Economy of 'Middleness': Behind Violence in Rural West Bengal," *Economic and Political Weekly* 36, vol. 16 (2001): 1333–1344.

56   A.E Ruud, "Land and power: The Marxist conquest of Rural Bengal," *Modern Asian Studies* 28, no. 2 (1994): 360.

57   Kohli, "From Breakdown to Order," 339; Echeverri-Gent, "Public Participation and Poverty Alleviation," 1411.

58   Various field studies have pointed out that casual labour hiring is quite common among medium- and small farmers, particularly because of the tendency of farmers belonging to ritually pure caste groups to avoid manual labour on grounds of custom, caste status and so on. For instance, see, Pranab Bardhan and Asok Rudra, "Labour Employment and Wages in Agriculture: Results of a Survey in West Bengal," *Economic and Political Weekly* 15, no. 45/46 (1980): 1943.

now in power and therefore, it had to ensure that such struggle contributed to raising of class consciousness in the direction of party's interests without disrupting the general political stability of the countryside and without alienating the support of the influential class of middle peasantry. As a result, such struggle ultimately ended in negotiation-oriented consensus politics at the behest of the party. Dwaipayan Bhattacharyya has argued that the "CPI(M) excelled in what may be regarded as the 'politics of middleness', a consensus-evoking unifying politics of meditation between several sectional interests". Illustrating the operation of such politics in a village, he has pointed out that every wage negotiation started with a strike. The agricultural labourers usually demanded a rate which the party fixed for them. The party regarded such strikes as manifestations of class struggle against the landowners. The landowners usually agreed at the end of the negotiation to raise the wage up to a rate lower than the official rate with the full consent of the party. The workers ended their strike and resumed their work with a sense of gratitude towards the party. With the help of such 'politics of mediation', a united peasant alliance was maintained.[59] This kept the size of the anti-party forces sufficiently low.

Furthermore, during land redistribution and land seizure, only the landlords were targeted while middle peasants were left off the hook. Rather, in the initial phase of land grab movement, middle and small peasants and agricultural labourers fought unitedly against the big landowners or so-called *jotedar*s, their common enemy and therefore, their united front was given an oppositional identity. There is little unanimity regarding the meaning of the term *jotedar* among scholars. One meaning of the term is substantial farmer. Such a meaning has emerged from District Gazetteers of North Bengal districts in colonial times and accounts of colonial officials.[60] According to Rajat Ray and Ratna Ray, in villages beyond their residence the *zamindars* had little control over cultivable lands and effective control over land at the village level was wielded by a dominant class of village landholders, popularly referred to as *jotedar*s. They held huge tracts of village land and got them cultivated by sharecroppers and agricultural labourers.[61] However, colonial accounts

59   Dwaipayan Bhattacharyya, "Politics of Middleness: The Changing Character of the Communist Party of India (Marxist) in Rural West Bengal," in *Sonar Bangla? Agricultural Growth and Agrarian Change in West Bengal and Bangladesh*, eds. Ben Rogaly, Barbara Harriss White and Sugato Bose (New Delhi: Sage, 1999), 279–300.

60   See, F. Buchanan-Hamilton, *A Geographical, Statistical and Historical Description of the District, a Zillah of Dinajpur in The Province, or Soubah of Bengal* (Baptist Mission Press, 1833); L. S. S. O'Malley, *Darjeeling District Gazetteer* (Government of West Bengal, 1907), 147–148.

61   Ray and Ray, "Zamindars and Jotedars," 81–102.

of other districts portray *jotedar*s simply as tenants.[62] Therefore, it has been pointed out that powerful *jotedar*s capable of competing with or even surpassing the authority of the *zamindars*, was not a universal phenomenon and remained confined mostly to the frontier areas in North Bengal and parts of the 24 Parganas newly brought under cultivation.[63] Hence, there are local variations in the usage of the term. Even in some villages of Bardhaman district, the term *jotedar* is used to refer to the sharecroppers. However, in contemporary political discourse, *jotedar* has become an undifferentiated social category indicative of large landowners. The leftist political strategy had a role in shaping the popular conception of the term *jotedar*. Though the *jotedar* was not a homogenous social or economic category, the term *jotedar* was made synonymous with large landowners in the late 1960s in the political discourse promoted by the Communists. The *jotedar*s were endowed with the unity of a class possessing more or less similar interests and economic capabilities. This was done keeping in mind the objective of mobilizing a large segment of rural population and raising their class consciousness by projecting before them a common class enemy in the form of *jotedar*s.[64] In this background, the multiclass alliance was justified on the ground that unity among all categories of peasants was the only way through which "struggles are won, by isolating the main enemy, by splitting the main enemy, by splitting the ranks of the opposing vested interests, and dealing with them one at a time, and by always trying to keep the majority in the rural society on the side of those struggling through these united fronts".[65] In this way, the inclusive category of peasant class was discovered as a unit of electoral mobilization, and the entire mobilization pattern was given a class-oriented direction. Consequently, the electoral rhetoric exclusively focused on the problems of the broad category of proletarian class within which the *dalit*s were accommodated either as landless labourers or poor workers. In such a political scenario, caste identity did not matter much. The lower castes saw themselves primarily as peasants and not as *dalit*s. A.E Ruud has pointed out that the Left parties placed before the rural masses the

62   L. S. S. O'Malley, *Bankura District Gazetteer* (Government of West Bengal, 1908),102; J. C. K Peterson, *Burdwan District Gazetteer* (Government of West Bengal, 1910), 155.

63   Bose, "Agrarian Bengal," 3–33; Joya Chatterjee, *Bengal Divided: Hindu Communalism and Partition* (New Delhi: Cambridge University Press, 2002), 58.

64   Andre Beteille , *Studies in Agrarian Social Structure* (Delhi: Oxford University Press, 1974), 117–41.

65   Biplab Dasgupta, "Agricultural Labour under Colonial, Semi-Capitalist and Capitalist Conditions: A Case Study of West Bengal," *Economic and Political Weekly* 19, no. 39 (1984): 146.

desired *chasi* (peasant) way of life, the *chasi* model.[66] Thus, the peasant identity became the locus of conscious identification for the ritually pure middle farmers as well as *dalit* agricultural workers and provided them an orientation to act together out of supposedly common economic interests.

Thus, the CPI(M) maintained a multi-class peasant alliance in which the ritually pure middle peasants clearly dictated the terms. Since the middle peasants mostly belonged to the intermediate castes, the strategy of empowering the middle peasants ended up benefitting the intermediate castes more than others. Does this mean that the political mobilization strategy of the CPI(M) was motivated by some caste bias? There is little to suggest that there was any upper caste conspiracy dictating its political agenda. The primary motive behind the middle peasant orientation of the multi-class rural social coalition forged by the CPI(M) was political. The party simply acted in conformity with its political interests of broadening its support base. It was the political potential of the middle peasantry which enabled this section of the rural populace to gain favourable treatment from the party. Harekrishna Konar, known to be a radical voice within the party, recognizing the importance of the support of relatively well-off and better-educated middle peasantry said in a speech he delivered at a meeting of college and university teachers on July 24, 1969: "As the combination of monopoly capital and feudalism aided by imperialism is a formidable force, the number of enemies must be kept to the minimum as far as practicable. So the middle peasants must be made a close ally, otherwise our strength will sag".[67] This understanding mainly came from the recognition that the middle peasants constitute a numerically significant group in rural areas. Tony Beck has found that in rural West Bengal resources are largely controlled by a group of middle peasant households who wield political power at the local level. In his estimate, the wealthiest 20 percent households belonging to the middle peasant category control about 45 to 50 percent of the village land.[68] Biplab Dasgupta has also estimated that numerically the middle peasants account for 15 to 20 percent of the population in many villages, unlike

---

66   A. E. Ruud, "From Untouchable to Communist: Wealth and Status among Supporters of the Communist Party (Marxist) in Rural West Bengal," in *Sonar Bangla? Agricultural Growth and Agrarian Change in West Bengal and Bangladesh,* eds. Ben Rogaly, Barbara Hariss-White and Sugata Bose (New Delhi: Sage, 1999), 253–78.

67   Harekrishna Konar, "Present Stage of Peasant Movement," *The Marxist,* 41 (2015), https://www.cpim.org/content/present-stage-peasant-movement.

68   Tony Beck, "Common Property Resource Access by Poor and Class Conflict in West Bengal," *Economic and Political Weekly* 29, no. 4 (1994): 187–189+191–197.

the richer section which would generally amount to 3 percent to 5 percent.[69] Moreover, the middle peasants generally remain in close proximity with the poorer sections both physically and psychologically, and by virtue of this proximity they often wield considerable influence on the political opinions of their dependent sharecroppers and the landless labourers. The relatively higher social status of the middle peasants also places them in a favourable position to command respect and support from those at the bottom of the social hierarchy.[70] It is, therefore, easier for the political parties to reach out to the rural masses through the leadership of the relatively affluent, politically articulate and socially aware middle peasants. The importance accorded to the middle peasants could also be attributed to the fact that they were also in a better position to deal with government officials mostly belonging to similar social and caste backgrounds. Above all, they were better educated than the poor rural masses. Therefore, they were considered better equipped to perform leadership functions. Binoy Chowdhury, a highly respected CPI(M) Kisan Sabha leader said, "These middle peasants, they are educated, they are vocal; so they would sometimes lead, due to certain traditions. They enjoyed more clout with the local people who are mostly illiterate".[71] Thus, in the political mobilization strategy of the Left Front, the middle and rich peasants had an important political role. General Secretary of the CPI(M) from 1992–2004, Harkishan Singh Surjeet stated quite unequivocally,

> The poor peasants are the most trustworthy ally of the working class in the people's democratic revolution while the middle peasants too have an important role to play in this revolution. Then there remain the strata of rich peasants who, because of their position in the system of production, are inclined to gravitate towards the class of landlords. Yet, to write off the rich peasants would be a mistake and against the interests of the revolution. Our Party, the CPI(M), has thoroughly debated this question and come to the correct conclusion that the rich peasants, though they remain a vacillating section, can be won over to the side of the working class at certain junctures.[72]

---

69   Biplab Dasgupta, "Sharecropping in West Bengal: From Independence to Operation Barga," *Economic and Political Weekly* 19, vol. 26 (1954): 91.

70   Echeverri-Gent, "Public Participation and Poverty Alleviation," 1411.

71   Cited in A.E. Ruud, "Land and Power: The Marxist Conquest of Rural Bengal," *Modern Asian Studies* 28, no. 2 (1994): 374.

72   Harkishan Singh Surajeet, "The CPI(M) Programme: Updated in Tune with Changing Times," *The Marxist* 16, vol. 3–4 (2000), http://cpim.org/content/programme-updated -changing-times.

This is fully in line with the official programme of the party. The updated party programme (2000) of the CPI(M) while declaring agricultural labourers and poor peasants as the 'basic allies of the working class' goes on to say:

> The middle peasantry, too, are the victims of the depredations of usurious capital, of feudal and capitalist landlords in the countryside and of the capitalist market controlled by MNCs and big *bourgeoisie*. Landlord domination in rural life so affects their social position in innumerable ways as to make them reliable allies in the people's democratic front. The rich peasantry is an influential section of the peasantry. The *bourgeois*-landlord agrarian policies have undoubtedly benefited certain sections of them and they also gained under the rule of the post-independence regimes. They are inclined to join the capitalist landlord class by virtue of their engaging agricultural labourers on hire for work in their farms. But, attacked by constant price fluctuations and subjected to ravages of the market under the grip of monopoly traders and MNCs they come up against the *bourgeois*-landlord government. At certain junctures, they can also be brought into the people's democratic front and play a role in the people's democratic revolution despite their vacillating character.[73]

Therefore, it is not entirely surprising, that with the political rise of the CPI(M), institutional power in rural society shifted not from the higher to the lower classes such as sharecroppers or landless farmers, but from the former to an in-between group belonging to middle peasant backgrounds or to such petty *bourgeois* background as teaching. In Atul Kohli's study conducted in districts of Burdwan and Midnapore, 8.3 percent of *Panchayat* members have less than 2 acres, 69 percent have 2–5 acres, 19.4 percent have 6–10 acres and 2.8 percent have over 10 acres of land. None of them uses only family labour on their land. A total of 83.3 percent use hired labour and 16.7 percent use sharecroppers.[74] Thus, the *Panchayat* leaders mostly belonged to the middle peasants, and they generally came from the intermediate castes. John Echeverri-Gent's study on Gram *Panchayats* in Midnapore district found that middle castes accounted for 23 out of 36 *Panchayat Pradhans* (Chairpersons) and 15 *Pradhans* came from the locally dominant *Mahishya* caste.[75]

---

73   Communist Party of India (Marxist), *Party Programme*, 35.
74   Atul Kohli, *The State and Poverty in India: The Politics of Reform* (Cambridge: Cambridge University Press, 2006), 111–113.
75   Echeverri-Gent, "Public Participation and Poverty Alleviation," 1411.

The reason for disproportionate importance given to the ritually pure middle peasants by the CPI(M) was purely political. The support and the leadership role of the middle peasantry were deemed crucial for the political success of the party. After the second consecutive victory of the Left Front, it was also declared by the West Bengal unit of Kisan Sabha that this victory would have never been possible without the support of an influential section of the middle peasants.[76] This situation underwent some change after the enactment in 1992 of the 73rd Constitutional Amendment Act which reserved seats for the Scheduled Castes (SCs) and Scheduled Tribes (STs) in proportion to their population in *Panchayat* bodies. As a result, the numerical representation of the SCs and STs in *Panchayat* bodies enhanced significantly. Social composition of *Panchayat* members elected in the first *Panchayat* elections in 1993 after the enactment of 73rd Amendment Act and social composition of *Panchayat* members elected in the last *Panchayat* elections held during the period Left rule in 2008 presented, respectively, in Tables 32 and Table 33 show that since the enactment of 73rd Amendment Act, SCs and STs have enjoyed proportionate representation in *Panchayat* bodies. Still, the lower-caste *Panchayat* functionaries failed to act autonomously as the real power rested with the *bhadralok* dominated party. While making decisions they were always controlled and guided by party leaders of higher social and ritual status.[77] Sukanta Bhattacharyya's field research in a Bardhaman village has captured the changes in the social patterns of representation and their impact. During 1978–83, out of five members returned to the *Panchayat* four were *Aguris* (next to Brahmans in the caste hierarchy) and one was a *Bagdi* (at the bottom of the caste hierarchy). The *Panchayat Pradhan* (chairman) was an *Aguri*. In the 1993 elections patterns of caste representation underwent some change. Two *Bagdis*, two *Aguris* and one *Dhoba* were elected and a *Bagdi* became the *Panchayat Pradhan*. However, the increased political representation secured by the lower castes did not result in their proportionate political empowerment since the real power or leadership still largely remained in the hands of ritually pure middle peasants.[78] Though the numerical strength of the lower castes and lower classes gradually increased in local bodies, decision-making power remained in the hands of party leaders invariably belonging to the upper castes. Dayabati Roy through her field

---

76   West Bengal Pradeshik Kisan Sabha, *Shompadkiya Report and Prastab* (Pandua, Hoogly 1982), 122.

77   Poromesh Acharya, "Panchayats and Left Politics in West Bengal," *Economic and Political weekly* 28, no. 22 (1993): 1080.

78   Sukanta Bhattacharya, "Caste, Class and Politics in West Bengal," *Economic and Political Weekly* 38, no. 3 (2003): 242–246.

study has shown that in the contemporary rural power structure, based on the practices of grassroots democracy and caste-wise reservations, the upper caste domination seems to be largely continuing in new forms. In the village Kalipur where Roy carried out her field study, the Scheduled Caste *Pradhan* was crucially dependent on the higher caste party leaders both in managing village affairs and running the *Panchayat*. The actual power of the *Panchayat*, including its decision-making authority, rested mainly with the zonal secretary of the CPI(M). The *Pradhan* attended the office only to sign on the dotted lines as and when required by the party bosses. In village politics as well, the *Pradhan* did not seem to hold any real power. The two upper caste party leaders from the neighbouring village, one Brahman and another *Kayastha* exercised real power over village affairs.[79] Thus, the real power rested with the party and the privileged social strata of middle peasants which controlled the *panchayats*. Thus, the increased political representation of the lower castes did not result in their proportionate political empowerment since the real power remained in the hands of ritually pure middle peasants. Thus, the dominance of the rural middle classes belonging mostly to intermediate castes remained unscathed despite implementation of reservation for lower castes in the institutions of local governance in the rural areas.

Thus, in the rural areas the CPI(M) promoted the interest of the middle peasants. In this respect, the class-based mobilization strategy of the CPI(M) may apparently seem similar to the peasant politics of the type pursued by Charan Singh in Uttar Pradesh. Christophe Jaffrelot has pointed out that Charan Singh tried to subsume caste identities into a feeling of class or at least into one of a peasant movement. But this strategy was, to a great extent, determined by caste considerations. Charan Singh claimed to represent the interests of the land-owning peasants by forming a multi-caste alliance of *Ahirs*, *Jats*, *Gujjars* and *Rajputs* (known as AJGAR) who were relatively well-off landowning peasants. However, one purpose was to push forward the interests of the *Jats and* place them on a dominant position, vis-à-vis other castes. But the *Jats* consisted only 1.2% of the population of the state and on their own they were in no position to play any meaningful political role. Therefore, to promote the interest of the *Jats*, Charan Singh had to work through a multi-caste alliance and class idioms of *kisan* (peasant) politics were invoked to bring landowning castes on a single platform.[80] Thus, caste dynamics remained hidden in class

---

79   Dayabati Roy, "Caste and Power: An Ethnography in West Bengal, India," *Modern Asian Studies* 46, no. 4 (2012): 947–74.

80   Christophe Jaffrelot, "The Rise of the Other Backward Classes in the Hindi Belt," *Journal of Asian Studies* 59, no. 1 (2000): 86–108.

TABLE 32 Social composition of panchayat members elected in 1993 in West Bengal
(percentage of total members in 8 districts)

	Gram panchayats	Panchayat samitis	Zilla parishads
SC women	14.4	14.5	13.3
SC men	24.1	25.3	24.5
Total SCs	38.5	39.8	37.8
ST women	3.0	3.2	3.2
ST men	4.4	3.9	3.8
Total STs	7.4	7.1	7.0
Total women	35.5	34.6	36.1

Note: 8 districts are Jalpaiguri, Uttar Dinajpur, Dakshin Dinajpur, Nadia, Hoogly, Bardhaman,
South 24 Parganas and Birbhum
SOURCE: GOVERNMENT OF WEST BENGAL, DEVELOPMENT AND PLANNING DEPARTMENT,
WEST BENGAL HUMAN DEVELOPMENT REPORT 2004 (KOLKATA: GOVERNMENT OF WEST
BENGAL, 2004), 63

TABLE 33 Social composition of panchayat members elected in 2008 in West Bengal
(percentage of total members)

	Gram panchayats	Panchayat samitis	Zilla parishads	Total
SC	35.86	35.39	34.40	35.76
ST	8.52	8.21	8.52	8.47
OBC	5.74	5.60	4.26	5.70
General Hindu	25.94	27.86	32.57	26.35
Muslims	23.38	22.41	19.63	23.17
Other minorities	0.56	0.53	0.61	0.55

SOURCE: GOVERNMENT OF WEST BENGAL, DEPARTMENT OF PANCHAYATS AND RURAL
DEVELOPMENT, *INFORMATION ON WEST BENGAL PANCHAYATS, THEIR MEMBERS AND FUNC-
TIONARIES* (KOLKATA: GOVERNMENT OF WEST BENGAL, AUGUST 2010), 111–114

politics. However, this was not exactly the case during the Left rule in West
Bengal. While Charan Singh was himself a *Jat*, the higher organs of the party
and government in West Bengal were dominated by upper castes, not intermediate castes. While many *Panchayat* functionaries and party leaders at the rural
level came from the intermediate castes, the higher organs of the party and
the government remained dominated by the upper castes. As already pointed

out, almost invariably they belonged to the three upper castes – Brahman, *Kayastha* and *Baidya*. These castes have enjoyed representation disproportionately higher than their demographic strength in higher organs of the party and Council of Ministers while the representation of the intermediate castes has remained below their demographic weight quite consistently.[81]

Thus, while the middle peasantry remained dominant in the countryside, it does not mean that party was a mere instrument in their hands. Through the model of democratic centralism, the state-level CPI(M) leadership belonging mostly to Hindu *bhadralok* middle class possessed the main controlling power within the party. The party itself had power which was disassociated from its class character.[82] As a result, the dominance of the intermediate castes at the village level did not automatically translate into their dominance over state politics. But the party to maintain its rural dominance had to ensure that its agrarian policies would not be injurious to the economic interests of the middle peasants. It was this political consideration that imposed some serious constraints on the landmark land reform initiatives of the Left Front government.

Land reforms in West Bengal had two dimensions, *barga* and *patta*. The former, famously known as Operation *Barga,* called for registration of sharecroppers and grant of security to the sharecroppers from arbitrary eviction. The latter type of reform or *patta* involved acquisition of ceiling surplus land and their redistribution among the landless farmers.[83] Taken together, *barga* and *patta* covered 41.3 percent of the rural population of West Bengal up to 2002. A substantial number of beneficiaries belonged to socially deprived sections, i.e. *dalit*s and *adivasis*. Up to 2002, the SCs accounted for 30.5 percent of the registered sharecroppers and 37.1 percent of *pattadars*. The corresponding

---

81   See, Stéphanie Tawa Lama-Rewal, "The Resilient Bhadralok: A Profile of the West Bengal MLAs," in *Rise of the Plebeians?*, eds. Christophe Jaffrelot and Sanjay Kumar (New Delhi: Routledge, 2009), 388–390.

82   Ben Rogaly, "Containing Conflict and Reaping Votes: Management of Rural Labour Relations in West Bengal," *Economic and Political Weekly* 33, no. 42/43 (1998): 2731.

83   The extent of success achieved by Left Front's agrarian policies particularly land reform has provoked a great deal of academic debate. A number of scholars have highlighted the positive impact of the Left Front's landmark land reform initiatives by emphasizing the role of land reforms in raising agricultural productivity and in reducing rural poverty. See, T.J Nossiter, *Marxists State Governments in India: Politics, Economy and Society* (London: Pinter Publishers, 1988); John Harriss, "What is Happening in Rural West Bengal? Agrarian Reforms, Growth and Distribution," *Economic and Political Weekly* 28, no. 24 (1993): 1237–1247; Debabrata Bandyopadhyay, "Not a Gramscian Pantomime," *Economic and Political Weekly* 32, no. 12 (1997): 581–584; Vikas Rawal and Madhura

figures for the STs were 11 percent and 19.3 percent, respectively.[84] Till 30th November, 2006 of all *pattadars*, 37.41 percent were *dalit*s and 18.59 percent were *adivasis*.[85]

Thus, a considerably large number of rural households came to possess land and a substantial proportion of them were *dalit*s and *Adivasis*. But an analysis of available data points out that the land distribution initiative was far more significant in terms of the number of households that were recipients of land, rather than total quantum of distributed land. The size of the distributed plots was quite small. According to G.K Lieten there was limited prospect of recovering excess land in West Bengal. The number of large landholdings was quite low. The average size of holdings was much smaller compared to other states. Therefore, the only available option was to distribute vested land among as many families as possible so as to enable them to 'walk on two legs'.[86] However, the fact remains that the option of lowering the land ceiling in order to maximize the average land area per beneficiary was not explored. West Bengal Land Reforms (Amendment) Act, 1972 passed by the Congress Government enforced ceiling on the basis of a family of five members: 12.36 acres (five standard hectares) of irrigated land or 17.30 acres of non-irrigated land. The Left Front after coming to power in 1977 did not

---

Swaminathan, "Changing Trajectories: Agricultural Growth in West Bengal, 1950 to 1966," *Economic and Political Weekly* 33, no. 40 (1998): 2595–2602; Abhijit V Banerjee, Paul J. Gertler, and Maitreesh Ghatak, "Empowerment and Efficiency: Tenancy Reform in West Bengal," *Journal of Political Economy* 110, no. 2 (2002): 239–80; G.K Lieten, *Power, Politics and Rural Development: Essays on India* (New Delhi: Manohar, 2003); Anil Kumar Chakraborti, *Beneficiaries of Land Reforms: The West Bengal Scenario* (Kolkata: State Institute of Panchayat and Rural Development, 2003). On the other hand, there is also an expanding body of literature which is critical of the land reforms undertaken by the Left Front. Scholars critical of the Left Front's agrarian development programmes have mainly highlighted the fact that the size of the plots distributed to the beneficiaries was so small that they later turned out to be economically non-viable source of livelihood. See, Madhusudan Ghosh, "Agricultural Development, Agrarian Structure and Rural Poverty in West Bengal," *Economic and Political Weekly* 33, no. 47/48 (1998): 2987–2995; Sunil Sengupta and Haris Gazdar, "Agrarian Politics and Rural Development in West Bengal," in *Indian Development: Selected Regional Perspectives*, eds. Jean Dreze and Amartya Sen (New Delhi: Oxford University Press, 1998): 129–204. Abhirup Sarkar, "Political Economy of West Bengal: A Puzzle and a Hypothesis," *Economic and Political Weekly* 41, no. 4 (2006): 341–348.

84   Government of West Bengal, *West Bengal Human Development Report 2004* (Development and Planning Department, 2004), 34–35.

85   Government of West Bengal. *West Bengal Economic Review 2006–07* (Development & Planning Department, Bureau of Applied Economics and Statistics, 2007), 103.

86   G. K Lieten, "De-peasantisation Discontinued: Land Reforms in West Bengal," *Economic and Political Weekly* 25, no. 40 (1990): 2265–68.

lower land ceiling which would have made more land available for redistribution.[87] Ross Mallick has estimated that acquisition of land over 5 acres would make available 44 percent of cultivable land for redistribution and would provide positive gains to 87 percent of agricultural households. This step would, therefore, enable the government to provide land with ownership rights to the tenants or *bargadars*. However, land ceiling was not lowered as such a step would inevitably hit the interests of the relatively affluent sections of the peasantry. In other words, further redistribution would adversely affect the members of the *Panchayat* and Kisan Sabha who mostly owned middle-sized holdings and used sharecroppers and agricultural workers to get their land cultivated. P. Sundarayya, the then General Secretary of the CPI(M) in 1973 advocated lowering the ceiling limit, confiscation of all land of the landlords including that below the ceiling level and conferring ownership rights on the tenants but his proposals did not become acceptable to the members of the CPI(M) from West Bengal. Sundarayya, who later resigned from the party attributed the stand taken by the West Bengal unit of the CPI(M) to "the rich and middle peasant composition of the party and their orientation to these classes".[88] The original central Committee resolutions on Tasks on the Kisan Front (1967) and Central Agrarian Issues (1973) which were to a great extent shaped by the thinking of the then General Secretary, P. Sundarayya called for putting an end to sharecropping by transferring land under tenancy to the actual cultivators. But the Left Front did not implement these resolutions in West Bengal because of its middle peasant orientation.[89]

Thus, the Left Front's agrarian reform initiatives paved the way for proliferation of economically unsustainable small holdings due to the political strategy of privileging the interests of the middle peasants over those of the rural poor. As already pointed out, according to the 2006–2007 West Bengal Economic Review of all the beneficiaries of land redistribution, 37.41 percent were *dalits* and 18.59 percent were *adivasis*. But the size of new holdings was too small to be economically viable. Most beneficiaries obtained small plots, less than one acre in size, substantially below the average size of holdings.[90] By June, 1990 3.64 lakh hectares of surplus agricultural land was distributed

87   Ratan Khasnabis, "Economy of West Bengal," *Economic and Political Weekly* 43, no. 52 (2009): 109.

88   Ross Mallick, *Development Policy of a Communist Government: West Bengal since 1977* (Cambridge: Cambridge University Press, 2008), 39–41.

89   Dwaipayan Bhattacharyya, *Government as Practice: Democratic Left in a Transforming India* (New Delhi: Cambridge University Press, 2017), 71.

90   Mallick. *Development Policy of a Communist Government,* 44.

among 18.91 lakh families. The average land area allotted per beneficiary turned out to be 0.192 ha.[91] A large field survey carried out in 89 villages spread across 15 districts of the state has reported that while only 4 percent of cultivable land was distributed, almost 15 percent of total households or one in every three landless households received some land.[92] West Bengal Development Report, 2010 also notes that West Bengal accounts for highest incidence of marginalisation of landholdings among the major agricultural producing states in India. The report attributes the higher incidence of land-holdings in the marginal class to land reforms and mounting demographic pressure on land.[93] According to the estimates of Lieten, around three-fourth of the additional households in the smaller size category is accounted for by new landowners (beneficiaries of land reforms), and the rest by the rate of growth of rural population.[94] Thus, one important effect of land reform was a rapid proliferation of small holdings. The number of marginal and small operational holdings has increased remarkably over the years (see tables 34, 35 and 36). As a result, most landholdings, whether held by *dalits* or non-*dalits*, are today small and marginal (see Table 37). Accordingly, there is little difference in the average size of all holdings (0.74 ha), average size of Non-Schedule Caste and Non-Schedule Tribe holdings (0.79 ha) and average size of Schedule Caste holdings (0.63 ha) (see Table 38). Therefore, if landown-ership is concerned there appears little prospect for the development of the feeling of relative deprivation among the *dalits* vis-a-vis the other castes. As outlined, this situation has emerged out of the agrarian politics practiced by the Left.

Further, in West Bengal landlessness is not a problem which is predom-inantly faced by the *dalits*. In West Bengal, 46.5 perecnt of households do not own land other than homesteads, while the proportion of landless *dalit* households is 54.1 percent (see Table 39). Therefore, the gap between the percentage of total landless households and the percentage of landless *dalit* households is only 7.6 percent, while in other states such a gap is much more pronounced (34.6 percent in Haryana, 32 percent in Punjab, 28.6 percent in

91   Madhusudan Ghosh, "Agricultural Development, Agrarian Structure and Rural Poverty in West Bengal," *Economic and Political Weekly* 33, no. 47/48 (1998): 2989.

92   Pranab Bardhan and Dilip Mookherjee, "Poverty Alleviation Efforts of Panchayats in West Bengal," *Economic and Political Weekly* 39, no. 9 (2004): 967.

93   Planning Commission, *West Bengal Development Report* (New Delhi: Academic Foundation, 2010), 49.

94   Lieten, "De-peasantisation Discontinued," 2268.

TABLE 34   Percentage distribution of different sizes of holdings and areas of holdings in West Bengal

Size class	Percentage of holdings (1970–71)	Percentage of areas (1970–71)	Percentage of holdings (1981–82)	Percentage of areas (1981–82)	Percentage of holdings (1991–92)	Percentage of areas (1991–92)	Percentage of holdings (2002–03)	Percentage of areas (2002–03)
Marginal	61.2	24.8	74.3	29.3	80.7	40	88.8	58.3
Small	22.8	28.9	15.8	28.8	13.4	30.7	8.9	26.7
Semi-medium	12.9	31.1	8.1	28.3	5	22.1	2.1	12.2
Medium	3	14.6	1.7	11.4	0.9	7.3	0.2	2.7
Large	0.1	0.6	0.1	2.3	0	0	0	0

Note:
Marginal: Holding less than 1.01 hectare
Small: Holding between 1.01 hectare and 2.00 hectares
Semi-medium: Holding between 2.01 hectares and 4.00 hectares
Medium: Holding between 4.01 hectares and 10.00 hectares
Large: Holding greater than or equal to 10 hectares
SOURCE: PLANNING COMMISSION, *WEST BENGAL DEVELOPMENT REPORT 2010* (NEW DELHI: GOVERNMENT OF INDIA, 2010), 50

TABLE 35   Percentage distribution of households for different size category of ownership holdings in West Bengal

Year	Marginal	Small	Semi-medium	Medium	Large
2003	92.06	5.70	1.40	0.20	0.00
1992	85.88	9.48	3.94	0.71	0.00
1982	81.60	11.50	5.54	1.28	0.08
1971–72	77.62	12.64	7.30	2.39	0.05

SOURCE: GOVERNMENT OF INDIA, MINISTRY OF STATISTICS AND PROGRAMME IMPLEMEN-TATION, NATIONAL SAMPLE SURVEY ORGANIZATION, *REPORT NO. 491, HOUSEHOLD OWNER-SHIP HOLDINGS IN INDIA, 59TH ROUND*, DECEMBER 2003-JANUARY 2004, 19

TABLE 36   Percentage of area under different size category of ownership holdings in West Bengal

Year	Marginal	Small	Semi-medium	Medium	Large
2003	58.23	25.71	11.88	4.02	0.00
1992	41.29	28.11	22.98	7.62	0.00
1982	30.33	28.77	27.23	12.12	1.54
1971–72	27.28	25.69	27.72	18.61	0.70

SOURCE: GOVERNMENT OF INDIA, MINISTRY OF STATISTICS AND PROGRAMME IMPLEMEN-TATION, NATIONAL SAMPLE SURVEY ORGANIZATION, *REPORT NO. 491, HOUSEHOLD OWNER-SHIP HOLDINGS IN INDIA, 59TH* ROUND, DECEMBER 2003-JANUARY 2004, 19

TABLE 37   Average size of holdings of different social groups of West Bengal

Type of holdings	Average size (in hectare)
All holdings	0.74
SC holdings	0.63
Non-SC and non-ST holdings	0.79

SOURCE: AGRICULTURAL CENSUS, 2010–11

TABLE 38   Percentage distribution of holdings and areas of holdings by different social groups of West Bengal

Size class	Percentage of all holdings	Percentage of sc holdings	Percentage of areas of sc holdings	Percentage of non-sc and st holdings	Percentage of areas of non-sc and st holdings
Marginal	82.16	86.6	62.11	80.33	52.04
Small	13.76	10.89	26.82	14.93	30.39
Semi-medium	3.75	2.39	10.15	4.34	15.1
Medium	0.32	0.12	0.91	0.41	2.46
Large	0.01	0	0	0	0.01

SOURCE: AGRICULTURAL CENSUS, 2010–11

Bihar, 24.8 percent in Maharashtra, 22.9 percent in Gujarat, 19.7 percent in Rajasthan, 17.1 percent in Karnataka, 17.1 percent in Kerala, 17 percent in Jharkhand, 17.1 percent in Kerala, 14.2 percent in Tamil Nadu). Furthermore, this gap in West Bengal is even half of the national level gap of 14.9 percent. This suggests that the *dalit*s and non-*dalit*s are more or less similarly placed in terms of possession of landholdings in West Bengal. Hence, landlessness does not appear to be a problem that can galvanize the entire *dalit* community in support of common agrarian demands. This is because almost half of the lower caste households possess some amount of land. On the other hand, non-possession of land by an equally large section of the *dalit*s has also prevented the conversion of the entire *dalit* community into a more or less small landholding class, with broadly similar agrarian interests. Thus, the patterns of distribution of landholdings have restricted the scope for the *dalit*s to develop common economic demands and articulate those demands through the assertion of *dalit* identity. Therefore, the non-articulation of *dalit* identity appears to have some basis in the structure of land distribution.

TABLE 39   Households that do not own any land other than homesteads as a proportion of
             all households, by social group, rural India, 2003 in percent

States	Adivasi	*Dalit*	Non *dalit*/adivasi	All
Andhra Pradesh	48.7	64.5	49.6	53.2
Arunachal Pradesh	4.5	53.6	93.8	23.5
Assam	27.6	49.8	40.9	40.3
Bihar	22.1	72.3	35.3	43.7
Chattisgarh	18.4	31.5	31.0	26.2
Delhi	100.0	99.7	97.3	98.1
Goa	0.0	N.A	59.0	57.1
Gujarat	34.3	67.0	43.1	44.1
Haryana	100.0	84.1	34.9	49.5
Himachal Pradesh	14.5	22.7	23.5	22.7
Jammu & Kashmir	44.1	21.8	8.9	11.0
Jharkhand	18.7	41.7	24.9	24.7
Karnataka	54.0	57.5	34.7	40.4
Kerala	66.1	85.4	66.1	68.3
Madhya Pradesh	41.1	35.6	30.8	34.0
Maharashtra	61.2	69.6	35.5	44.8
Manipur	11.0	41.6	45.6	30.2
Meghalaya	25.4	59.2	60.9	29.0
Mizoram	15.0	100.0	6.0	14.9
Nagaland	9.3	N.A	100.0	15.5
Orissa	33.3	52.8	35.9	38.5
Punjab	98.9	88.9	36.5	56.9
Rajasthan	6.8	39.3	17.0	19.6
Sikkim	35.5	65.1	46.7	44.4
Tamil Nadu	66.7	78.7	59.5	64.5
Tripura	48.5	67.4	62.1	59.4
Uttar Pradesh	51.8	33.9	23.2	26.3
Uttaranchal	60.9	33.7	25.2	27.7
West Bengal	48.8	54.1	42.8	46.5
India	35.5	56.5	37.8	41.6

SOURCE: UNIT LEVEL DATA, NSS LAND AND LIVESTOCK HOLDINGS SURVEY, 59TH ROUND
TAKEN FROM APARAJITA BAKSHI, "SOCIAL INEQUALITY IN LAND OWNERSHIP IN INDIA: A
STUDY WITH PARTICULAR REFERENCE TO WEST BENGAL," *SOCIAL SCIENTIST* 36, NO. 9/10
(2008): 101

5   Other Economic Indicators

Apart from landholding some other vital economic indicators can also be taken
into consideration to understand the phenomenon of relative deprivation. The
economic indicators which have been taken into account for this purpose have
been chosen carefully. One purpose is to discover overall economic well-being
or material standard of living of the lower castes relative to that of other castes.
For this, monthly per capita consumption expenditure (MPCE) from the NSS
Consumer Expenditure Survey has been taken into account. Economic indicators concerning income are possibly the best measure to discover standard of
living but information concerning income is difficult to collect in a developing country like India. In developing countries, expenditure serves as a good
proxy for income for several reasons. Firstly, at low levels of income, savings are
negligible resulting in a close correspondence between income and consumption expenditure. Secondly, wage or earnings data, even when reliable, may not
account for days of employment and seasonality of work. Moreover, wage or
earnings data in the NSS is reported only for those who are employed in regular
salaried jobs or as casual labour and not for those who are self-employed. Wage
data for casual workers are often missing or unreliable. Thirdly, payment is often
in kind and wage data typically accounts only for the monetary component of
earnings. Finally, like in the case of agricultural households, a household is both
a production and consumption unit and it is difficult to distinguish between
receipts and outflows.[95] The gap between the monthly per capita consumption
expenditure (MPCE) of the General Category households and the MPCE of SC
households in rural areas is much lower in West Bengal in comparison to other
states with large concentration of the SCs. The gap between the MPCE of the
General Category households and the MPCE of OBC (Other Backward Classes)
households in rural areas is almost negligible in West Bengal, while such gap is
much more pronounced in other states (see Table 40).

Another economic indicator which can be considered important in this
regard is rural poverty ratio. It provides direct evidence of the community wise
proportion of people suffering from extreme economic hardships. Rural poverty and rural MPCE have been taken into account, as in West Bengal the lower
caste population is largely concentrated in rural areas.[96] In West Bengal the

---

95   Smriti Sharma, "Caste-Based Crimes and Economic Status: Evidence from India," *Journal
        of Comparative Economics* 43 (2015): 208–209.

96   Partha Chatterjee, "Partition and the Mysterious Disappearance of Caste in Bengal,"
        in *Politics of Caste in West Bengal*, eds. Uday Chandra, Geir Heierstad, and Kenneth Bo
        Nielsen (New Delhi: Routledge, 2016), 96.

gap between the rural poverty ratio of the General category and that of the sc category is only 2 percent. This gap is higher in all other states except Jammu and Kashmir. Furthermore, West Bengal is the only state apart from Assam where the percentage of poor rural obcs is less than that of rural poor belonging to the General category. Additionally, the gap between the percentage of

TABLE 40   Monthly per capita expenditure (MPCE) in rupees in major states (rural) by social groups

State	SC	OBC	Others (excluding SCS, STS and OBCs)	Gap between others and SCS	Gap between others and OBCs
Andhra Pradesh	1155	1184	1571	416	387
Bihar	697	759	927	230	168
Chhatisgarh	709	831	904	195	73
Gujarat	1088	1038	1590	502	552
Haryana	1165	1375	1835	670	460
Jharkhand	780	852	971	191	119
Karnataka	934	1021	1121	187	100
Kerala	1400	1706	2295	895	589
Madhya Pradesh	839	969	1269	430	300
Maharshtra	1031	1135	1309	278	174
Odisha	757	862	1018	261	156
Punjab	1271	1723	2069	798	346
Rajasthan	986	1289	1316	330	27
Tamil Nadu	1003	1220	1350	347	130
Uttar Pradesh	804	880	1086	282	206
Uttarakhand	1064	1410	2106	1042	696
West Bengal	897	951	992	95	41
All India	929	1036	1281	352	245

SOURCE: NATIONAL SAMPLE SURVEY ORGANIZATION, MINISTRY OF STATISTICS AND PRO-GRAMME IMPLEMENTATION, GOVERNMENT OF INDIA, *HOUSEHOLD CONSUMER EXPEN-DITURE ACROSS SOCIO-ECONOMIC GROUPS*, REPORT NO. 544, 66TH ROUND (OCTOBER 2012), 18

poor rural OBCs and that of the rural poor of the General category is as high as 9 percent (see Table 41). Thus, the relative economic deprivation faced by the lower and backward castes in West Bengal does not seem to be as acute as in other states. Therefore, it is quite likely that the low level of relative economic deprivation faced by lower castes has not augured well for the conscious deployment of caste as a political vocabulary of socio-economic marginalization in West Bengal.

TABLE 41   State-wise rural poverty ratios across social groups, 2004–05

States	SC	OBC	Others	Gap between SCs and others	Gap between OBCs and others
Andhra Pradesh	15.4	9.5	4.1	11.3	5.4
Assam	27.7	18.8	25.4	2.3	- 6.6
Bihar	64.0	37.8	26.6	38.2	11.2
Gujarat	21.8	19.1	4.8	17.0	14.3
Haryana	26.8	13.9	4.2	22.6	9.7
Himachal Pradesh	19.6	9.1	6.4	13.2	2.7
Jammu and Kashmir	5.2	10.0	3.3	1.9	6.7
Karnataka	31.8	20.9	13.8	18.0	7.1
Kerala	21.6	13.7	6.6	15.0	7.1
Maharashtra	44.8	23.9	18.9	25.9	5.0
Madhya Pradesh	42.8	29.6	13.4	29.4	16.2
Odisha	50.2	36.9	23.4	26.8	13.5
Punjab	14.6	10.6	2.2	12.4	8.4
Rajasthan	28.7	13.1	8.2	20.5	4.9
Tamil Nadu	31.2	19.8	19.1	12.1	0.7
Uttar Pradesh	44.8	32.9	19.7	25.1	13.2
West Bengal	29.5	18.3	27.5	2.0	- 9.2
Chhattisgarh	32.7	33.9	29.2	3.5	4.7
Jharkhand	57.9	40.2	37.1	20.8	3.1
Uttarakhand	54.2	44.8	33.5	20.7	11.3
All India	36.8	26.7	16.1	20.7	10.6

SOURCE: MINISTRY OF SOCIAL JUSTICE AND EMPOWERMENT, GOVERNMENT OF INDIA

6 Economic Development and Politics of Caste Coalition

It is rarely possible for a single caste to garner enough votes to make a political party win elections. Therefore, political parties try to build coalitions of different caste groups for electoral purposes. But when different caste groups come together and form a political coalition they do so if their political and economic interests coincide.[97] It is generally the case that the interests of different caste groups coincide, only when they are positioned more or less at the similar socio-economic level. Therefore, for electoral purposes efforts are generally made to mobilize together castes positioned at more or less similar levels of socio-economic development.[98]

Hence, we have mostly seen castes with similar level of socio-economic position to come together to form socio-political coalition. In pre-independence Bihar Triveni Sangh was formed as a caste coalition and political party in 1934 based upon the commonalities of interests of three prominent middle peasant castes of Bihar, namely *Yadav, Koeri* and *Kurmi*.[99] Charan Singh in the 1970s in Uttar Pradesh successfully build a coalition of cultivating castes, popularly known as AJGAR, an acronym where A stood for *Ahir (Yadav)*, J for *Jat*, G for *Gujjar* and R for *Rajput*.[100] In the 1970s Congress Chief Minister Devraj Urs in Karnataka achieved political power by managing to form a caste alliance of non-*Vokkaligas* and non-*Lingayats*, the lower OBCs and other marginalized groups.[101] Karpoori Thakur in Bihar also managed to form a caste coalition of all OBCs (lower and upper) and other marginalized groups in the 1970s.[102] Madhavsinh Solanki, a four-time Congress Chief Minister of Gujarat owed his political success to his successful stitching together of a large non-upper caste coalition, known as KHAM which was made of *Kshatriyas (Kolis* and *Rajputs)*

---

97 Gupta, "Caste and Politics," 421.

98 Anil Bhatt, "Politics and Social Mobility in India," *Contribution to Indian Sociology* 5 (1971): 109.

99 Omprakash Kashyap, "Triveni Sangh: First Hints of the Power of Organization," *Forward Press*, 2016, https://www.forwardpress.in/2016/10/triveni-sangh-first-hints-of-the-power -of-organization/.

100 Jaffrelot, "The Rise of the Other Backward Classes," 93.

101 James Manor, "Pragmatic Progressives in Regional Politics: The Case of Devaraj Urs," *Economic and Political Weekly* 15, no. 5/7 (1980): 201–203+205+207+209+211+213; James Manor, "Karnataka: Caste, Class, Dominance and Politics in a Cohesive Society," in *Dominance and State Power in Modern India, Vol I,* eds. Fancine F. Frankel and M.S. A Rao (Delhi: Oxford University Press, 1990), 322–61.

102 Jagpal Singh, "Karpoori Thakur: A Socialist Leader in the Hindi Belt," *Economic and Political Weekly* 50, no. 3 (2015): 54–60.

Harijans (Scheduled Castes), *Adivasis* and Muslims in the 1980s.[103] Mayawati's *bahujan* politics in the 1990s in UP also successfully formed a coalition of all *dalit* communities.

In West Bengal there is limited scope for this kind of political aggregation of the interests of the lower castes due to their uneven economic development. Development indicators suggest high level of disparity in the economic conditions of major lower caste groups. While the level of illiteracy is still high among the *Bagdis, Chamars and Bauris*, literacy rate of the *Namasudras* and *Pods* have reached close to 80 percent (see Table 42). The broad occupational pattern of the major lower caste groups also brings out the same scenario of uneven development (see Table 43). The dependence of the *Namasudras* on agriculture has come down from 56.7 percent in 1991 to 40.89 percent in 2011, while the dependence of the Pods on agriculture has decreased from 69.5 percent in 1991 to 44.68 percent in 2011. These two large *dalit* groups which are concentrated in the vicinity of Kolkata have experienced considerable social mobility, while other lower caste groups have lagged behind.[104] The dependence of other major lower caste groups on agriculture is still pretty high (see Table 43). Therefore, due to wide mismatch in the economic conditions of various lower caste groups, their economic needs and priorities are likely to be vastly different. Ranabir Samaddar has pointed out that while the *Namasudras* and *Pods* possess the basic education to concentrate on demands for jobs, better educational facilities and reservation, the members of communities like *Bagdi, Chamar* and *Bauri* are mostly not in a position to do so.[105] Such a situation provides little incentive to the lower castes to come together and build a common agenda of socio-economic demands for collective political action. Due to dissimilarities in the demands of various caste groups, patronage to one particular caste group may politically alienate the others. The closeness of the TMC with the Matua Mahasangha after the election of Mamata Banerjee as the new Chief Minister in 2011 reportedly enraged the *Pods*.[106] The prospects of caste politics based on aggregation of interests of different lower caste groups in such a scenario are likely to be quite limited. In other words, in West Bengal it is difficult to forge a common front of all the depressed groups along the lines of caste on the basis of some common agenda.

---

103   Christophe Jaffrelot, "Quota for Patels? The Neo-middle-class Syndrome and the (partial) Return of Caste Politics in Gujarat," *Studies in Indian Politics* 4, no. 2 (2016): 219.

104   Chatterjee, "Partition and the Mysterious Disappearance of Caste in Bengal," 100.

105   Ranabir Samaddar, "Whatever has Happened to Caste in West Bengal," *Economic and Political Weekly* 47, no. 36 (2013):78–79.

106   Sarbani Bandyopadhyay, "Caste and Politics in Bengal," *Economic and Political Weekly* 47, no. 50 (2012): 73.

TABLE 42 Status of literacy among major scheduled castes of West Bengal as per census, 2001 and census, 2011

Caste	Literacy rate (2001)	Literacy rate (2011)
Rajbanshi	60.14	70.66
Namasudra	71.93	79.52
Bagdi	47.72	61.41
Pod	72.10	79.75
Bauri	37.47	50.50
Chamar/Muchi	46.99	60.04

SOURCE: WEST BENGAL, DATA HIGHLIGHTS: THE SCHEDULED CASTES, CENSUS OF INDIA, 2001 AVAILABLE AT HTTP://CENSUSINDIA.GOV.IN/TABLES_PUBLISHED/SCST/DH_SC_WES TBENGAL.PDF; PRIMARY CENSUS ABSTRACT DATA, 2011, TABLE A-10

TABLE 43 Dependence on agriculture of major scheduled castes of West Bengal as per census, 2011

Caste	Per cent of population dependent on agriculture
Rajbanshi	63.45
Namasudra	40.89
Bagdi	69.64
Pod	44.68
Bauri	60.78
Chamar/Muchi	51.39

SOURCE: PRIMARY CENSUS ABSTRACT DATA, 2011, TABLE A-10

Political economy has remained a neglected theme in the academic literature relating to the role of caste in West Bengal politics. There is no dearth of studies on the political economy of West Bengal particularly on the agrarian policies of the Left Front like its remarkable land reform initiative. However, no explicit attempts have been made to explore whether there are any links between the agrarian politics and policies on one hand and marginalization of caste factor in mainstream party politics on the other hand. In this context, this chapter has attempted to highlight how various aspects of political economy have played a role in influencing the operation of caste as a political category in West Bengal. It is quite likely that there are many other unexplored aspects of political economy which have relevance with regard to the role of caste in institutional politics. Therefore, there is a promising scope for future scholarship to pursue a more serious academic scrutiny of the relationship between the politics of caste in West Bengal and several crucial dimensions of the political economy of the state.

CHAPTER 6

Micro-politics in Rural Society

Social Imagination, Political Culture and Economic Reality at the Grassroots

In recent times due to the impact of modernization the caste system has undergone significant changes. A number of studies have pointed out that the ritual and occupational basis of caste has broken down to a significant extent.[1] This has resulted in the improvement of socio-economic status of some upwardly mobile lower and middle castes.[2] Furthermore, democratic politics has led to political empowerment of the previously marginalized caste groups. Caste, primarily a ritual concept has been politicised to pursue secular rather than traditional ritual concerns of its members. Terming this process as de-ritualization or secularization of the caste system, a case has been advocated in favour of emancipatory and developmental potential of caste-based identity politics. It has been argued that though caste is an embodiment of unequal social relationships and hierarchy, politicisation of caste identity in an electoral democracy could enable the lower castes to challenge cultural prejudice and subordination.[3]

As we have already seen, in West Bengal democratic politics under the impact of a great deal of political maneuvering by the Left parties led to

---

1   Dipankar Gupta, "Whither the Indian Village: Culture and Agriculture in Rural India," *Economic and Political Weekly* 40, no. 8 (2005): 751–58; M.N Srinivas, "An Obituary on Caste as a System," *Economic and Political Weekly* 38, no. 5 (2003): 455–59; D. L Seth, "Caste and Class: Social Reality and Political Representation," in *Caste and Democratic Politics in India*, ed. Ghanshyam Shah (New Delhi: Permanent Black, 2002), 209–233.

2   R. L Hardgrave, "Political Participation and Primordial Solidarity: The Nadars of Tamilnad," in *Caste in Indian Politics*, ed. Rajni Kothari (New Delhi: Orient Longman, 1970), 96–120; William L. Rowe, "The New Cauhans: A Caste Mobility Movement in North India," in *Social Stratification*, ed. Dipankar Gupta (New Delhi: Oxford University Press, 2014), 326–338.

3   See, Rajni Kothari, "Introduction," in *Caste in Indian Politics*, ed. Rajni Kothari (New Delhi: Orient Longman, 1970), 3–25; Rajni Kothari, "Rise of the Dalits and the Renewed Debate on Caste," *Economic and Political Weekly* 29, no. 26 (1994): 1589–1594; Lloyd Rudolph, "The Modernity of Tradition: The Democratic Incarnation of Caste in India," *The American Political Science Review* 59, no. 4 (1965): 975–989; Lloyd Rudolph and Susanne Hoeber Rudolph, "The Political Role of India's Caste Associations," *Pacific Affairs* 85, no. 2 (2012): 335–353; D. L Sheth, "Secularisation of Caste and Making of New Middle Class," *Economic and Political Weekly* 34, no. 34/35 (1999): 2502–2510; Ashutosh Varshney, "Is India Becoming More Democratic," *The Journal of Asian Studies* 59, no. 1 (2000): 3–25.

political buttressing of the competing identity of class that overshadowed community identities like caste in process of political mobilization. Does this imply irrelevance of caste in ground level political and social dynamics? Has caste been completely abandoned as a form of identity for engendering political solidarity and for spawning social association? For finding answers to these questions, it is important to redirect our gaze to ground level social setting. This chapter attempts to do so by studying the socio-political situation of a village, called Mekhlapur situated in the *Matua* belt of Nadia district of West Bengal.

The primary objective here is to understand the link between the role of caste in micro-politics and non-politicisation of caste identity in formal party politics. An exploration of this link also involves consideration of broader and more general questions relating to caste mobilization such as a) whether social mobility among the lower castes necessarily creates better prospects for their political mobilization on caste lines, b) what is the role of political culture in furthering the cause of *dalit* politics and c) how far the weakening of the ritual basis of caste affects the role of caste in sustaining patron- client network in the realm of economy and in maintaining traditional notions and perceptions about caste identity in the realm of inter-caste relations.

The findings from this village can't be generalized to the state or the country as a whole. But it is possible to draw some valuable insights by studying the ground situation of this particular village due to several reasons which also influenced my selection of this village for field research. First, Mekhlapur is a prototype of typical Bengali villages where upper castes are found in very few numbers. Partha Chatterjee has pointed out that the steady flight of the upper caste households from rural areas to urban centres in search of urban occupations since the early 1980s has led to a situation where now-a-days it is difficult to find upper caste families in most villages in West Bengal.[4] Second, this village is largely populated by the *Namasudras* and *Bagdi*s, who are respectively the second largest and third largest Scheduled Caste (SC) groups of West Bengal. Third, almost all the *Namasudras* in the village belong to the *Matua* sect. As has already been discussed in Chapter 2, in recent times the politics of the state has seen mobilization of the *Matuas* under their organization Matua Mahasangha. Based on the recent political assertion of the *Matua-Namasudra* community, it has been argued that a 'new politics of caste' has set foot on the political scene of West Bengal. This village situated in the *Matua* belt running

---

4   Partha Chatterjee, "Partition and the Mysterious Disappearance of Caste in Bengal," in *Politics of Caste in West Bengal,* eds. Uday Chandra, Geir Heierstad and Kenneth Bo Nielsen (New Delhi: Routledge, 2016), 96.

through the districts of Nadia and North 24 Parganas is only a few kilometers away from the *Matua* citadel, Thakurnagar.

1 Existing Findings about Micro-Dynamics of Caste in West Bengal: An Overview

According to Uday Chandra and Kenneth Bo Nielsen any judgment regarding the role of caste in West Bengal politics will depend on how one defines politics. They have argued that the insignificance of caste in party politics does not mean that it is of no value in informal, micro politics at the grassroots constituted by "local relations of power and influence".[5] Partha Chatterjee (1997: 84) has also observed that "the absence of caste articulation of political demands does not mean that caste authority and caste linkages have not proved useful to various political parties as instruments of gathering electoral support in the relatively un-mobilized areas ..... In apparently uninstitutionalised world of what may be called 'politics among the people', caste categories have continued to provide many of the basic signifying terms through which collective identities and social relations are still perceived".[6] Therefore, for a holistic understanding of the role of caste in politics, caste dynamics in the informal domain of micro-politics at the grassroots need to be taken into account. Several studies have attempted to provide a glimpse of the micro-politics of West Bengal. All of these studies have located undercurrents of caste in social and political dynamics at the village level, thereby confirming the role of caste in local politics and social relations. However, different studies have uncovered different dimensions of this role. Before proceeding further, it is imperative to briefly look at the major findings of these studies regarding the role of caste at the micro level.

First, it has been pointed out that caste bias and caste stereotypes exist in rural society and play a major role in shaping *de facto* power relations at the local level. Caste dynamics impact power relations by continually reproducing prejudiced and stereotypical perspectives about caste identity, which in turn determine political role of individuals. Dayabati Roy's fieldwork in two villages of Bardhaman district has revealed that lower caste political leaders face difficulty in gaining respectability and legitimacy due to continuing presence

---

5   Uday Chandra and Kenneth Bo Nielsen, "The Importance of Caste in Bengal," *Economic and Political Weekly* 47, no. 44 (2012): 59–62.

6   Partha Chatterjee, *The Present History of West Bengal* (New Delhi: Oxford University Press, 1997), 82, 84.

of long held negative social images traditionally associated with their caste identity. This has created a situation where the lower caste *Panchayat* functionaries fail to act autonomously and exercise effective power despite holding official positions. *De facto* power rests with upper caste party leaders who control lower caste *Panchayat Pradhan*s operating from behind the scene.[7] Glyn Williams and Sailaja Nandigama have also noted a general tendency among Scheduled Caste and Scheduled Tribe households to bank upon the extensive social networks of their more influential high-caste neighbours for seeking various kinds of assistance from the party.[8] Kenneth Bo Nielsen's study on the Singur movement[9] has shown that caste stereotypes and prejudices even influence assignment of political role in popular politics and political movements. He has found that the image of the *Bauris* as idle, insensible and irresponsible relegated them to the position of foot soldiers in the Singur movement. The movement was largely led by the individuals belonging to the socially respectable and ritually pure *Mahishya* caste. Their leadership derived legitimacy from the fact that the *Mahishya* identity was associated with *bhadralok* cum *chasi* lifestyle entailing a fusion between peasant ethics and *bhadralok* norms.[10] Further, the political dominance enjoyed by certain castes like the *Mahishyas* does not emanate today from their ritual status but from their accumulated historical advantages. The dominant castes reproduce their dominance by translating their socio-economic privileges acquired over decades and centuries into political connections and social and economic capital, while at the same time obfuscating the caste roots of their dominance.[11]

Another important finding offered by the existing literature is that the political parties do not shy away from mobilizing caste groups locally despite the absence of efforts directed towards bringing about large scale statewide political mobilization along caste lines. At the village level political parties

---

7   Dayabati Roy, "Caste and Power: An Ethnography in West Bengal, India," *Modern Asian Studies* 46, no. 4 (2012): 947–74.

8   Glyn Williams and Sailaja Nandigama, "Managing Political Space: Authority, Marginalised People's Agency and Governance in West Bengal," *International Development Planning Review* 40, no. 1 (2018): 17.

9   Singur is located in Hoogly district of West Bengal. In 2006 a movement started in Singur to protest against forcible acquisition of fertile farmland for a proposed car factory by Tata Motors. In the face of huge protests the plan to set up the factory was cancelled in 2008.

10 Kenneth Bo Nielsen, "The Politics of Caste and Class in Singur's Anti-land Acquisition Struggle," in *Politics of Caste in West Bengal,* eds. Uday Chandra, Geir Heiestad and Kenneth Bo Nielsen (New Delhi: Routledge, 2016), 125–146.

11 Kenneth Bo Nielsen, "Orchestrating Anti-Dispossession Politics: Caste and Movement Leadership in Rural West Bengal," *Journal of Contemporary Asia* 50, no. 5 (2020): 761–784.

often strike with particular caste groups purely localized alliances, which do not extend to other areas. A.E Ruud has demonstrated how in two villages in Bardhaman district the CPI-M maintained a mutually beneficial alliance with the *Bagdi* caste.[12] Another major finding is that in local politics caste also plays some role in shaping political loyalties. Glyn Williams' study on the dynamics of micro politics in three Birbhum villages has suggested that the centre stage of local politics is often occupied by informal networks of *dols* (groups) formed on the basis of caste and kinship affiliations. The voting preference of a person is often dictated by the leaders of such *dols*.[13]

Thus, all these existing studies have discovered operation of caste dynamics in micro politics. This leads to the obvious question: why micro-level caste dynamics do not spill over to the mainstream macro politics. While answer to this question may be found in a range of factors spread over multiple realms, one significant factor could very well be traced to political culture or the dominant value system which generally has a strong bearing on patterns of political mobilization. The existing studies on West Bengal's micro-politics have scarcely addressed this important factor. But interestingly many of these studies have come up with one common observation, which in my opinion sufficiently provokes an academic examination of the role of social and political values in shaping the political role of caste in rural society. Several ethnographic studies have highlighted that, caste despite being pervasive in social and political processes at the local level rarely finds open and explicit political articulation. The party men and elected leaders demonstrate an apparent lack of information regarding their own and others' caste identity.[14] People often hesitate to mention their caste names before field researchers.[15] Further, the representation of the lower castes is articulated primarily in class rather than in caste idioms such as *Khetmajur* or agricultural labourers.[16] The upper caste antipathy to the lower caste individuals also gets ventilated through secular

12   Arild Engelsen Ruud, "From Untouchable to Communist: Wealth and Status among Supporters of the Communist Party (Marxist) in Rural West Bengal," in *Sonar Bangla? Agricultural Growth and Agrarian Change in West Bengal and Bangladesh,* eds. Ben Rogaly, Barbara Hariss-White and Sugata Bose (New Delhi: Sage, 1999), 253–78.

13   Glyn Williams, "Panchayati Raj and the Changing Micro Politics of West Bengal," in *Sonar Bangla? Agricultural Growth and Agrarian Change in West Bengal and Bangladesh,* eds. Ben Rogaly, Barbara Hariss-White and Sugata Bose (New Delhi: Sage, 1999), 229–252.

14   Stéphanie Tawa Lama-Rewal, "The Resilient Bhadralok: A Profile of the West Bengal MLAs," in *Rise of the Plebeians? The Changing Face of Indian Legislative Assemblies,* eds. Christophe Jaffrelot and Sanjay Kumar (New Delhi: Routledge, 2009), 362.

15   Chatterjee, *The Present History of West Bengal,* 84.

16   Nielsen, "The Politics of Caste and Class," 132.

expressions such as *faltu* or worthless.[17] The employers in rural commercial economy also express their ignorance about the caste identity of their employees and deny its significance in operation of economic activities.[18]

This *prima facie* suggests that while caste sentiments do exist, their form of operation is extremely subtle. This makes the working of caste in informal politics an extremely complex affair. Thus, the existing studies have brought to the fore the deeply intricate nature of micro level caste dynamics, thereby, somehow indicating the need for further ethnographic investigation. It is in this backdrop that this chapter attempts to undertake an academic scrutiny of West Bengal's micro-politics, devoting a great deal of attention to the vexed question of political articulation of caste consciousness. Since the mode of collective political articulation is shaped by cultural attitudes imbibed through political socialization, an analytical exploration of political culture and dominant social values forms a major focus of this chapter.

2   A Note on Methodology

This study is based upon ethnographic research carried out in 2016–17. Data presented in this study has been mostly gathered through open-minded, non-structured, unrecorded and informal conversation with individuals, known as 'key informants' in social anthropology. Key informants were those with whom lengthy discussions were undertaken on several issues. Sufficient care was taken to ensure that the sample of informants remained representative in terms of both caste and class. The *Panchayat Pradhan* of the village and her husband acted as the most important 'key informants'. Conversation was also conducted with many ordinary villagers. They were asked specific questions regarding issues which only concerned them. A great deal of information was also obtained through direct observation of behaviour and actions in accordance with the participant observation method.

The primary point of access to the village was provided by the most influential politician of the village who happens to be the spouse of the *Panchayat Pradhan* of the locality. However, no guidance was obtained from him in selection of key informants. Efforts were made first to establish some sort of personal rapport with them before starting communication regarding village affairs. They talked only after receiving the assurance that the views expressed

17   Roy, "Caste and Power," 959.
18   Barbara Harriss-White, "West Bengal's Rural Commercial Capital," *International Critical Thought* 3, no. 1 (2013): 29–30.

by them won't be passed on to any other person in the village. Further, conversation with the villagers was conducted on strict condition that the source of information would remain undisclosed. Therefore, the names of the informants and names of the all the villages and the particular areas mentioned in this chapter have been anonymised.

3   Geography and Demography of the Village under Study

Mekhlapur lies along the border between Nadia and North 24 Parganas, two South Bengal districts. It falls under the jurisdiction of Beliadanga Gram *Panchayat*.[19] Beliadanga consists of eight wards. Mekhlapur is a *Panchayat* ward. It consists of a few *paras* (localities). Most of the *paras* are multi-caste habitations except the *Bagdi para* lying at one end of the village, where only people from *Bagdi* caste live.

Mekhlapur has some 150 households with a population of around 600.[20] It is largely populated by the *Namasudras,* who are the largest caste group in the village. There is a small stretch lying along the border of the village where only *Bagdi* families live. The *Bagdi para* overlaps the area of two villages, Mekhlapur and Sepani. Among the upper castes I could find only a few *Kayastha* households. There were a few *Mahishya* (intermediate caste) households also. The number of upper caste households has decreased over the years. Earlier there used to be a relatively larger number of upper caste households. They held large estates. Land reforms resulted in substantial reduction not only in the size of their landholdings but also in the social prestige and authority associated with landholding. Thereafter, most of them gradually disposed of their remaining land and settled in urban areas.[21]

4   Caste and Class: Converging, Diverging and Intersecting Identities

The bulk of the population of the village derives their income from agricultural activities. The traditional occupation of the *Namasudras* was agriculture. It apparently seems that their dependence on traditional occupation still remains intact. However, a close investigation reveals that the nature of their

---

19   Real name of the *Panchayat* area has not been used.
20   This information has been obtained from the *Panchayat Pradhan*. It has been further cross-checked with the voter list.
21   Conversation with *Panchayat Pradhan*'s husband, Jiban Biswas.

engagement with agriculture has changed. Most importantly, agriculture no longer remains the sole source of livelihood for many.

The upper caste households are not poor, but they are not among the largest landowners. Rather, their economic standing is no better than the general *Namasudra* households in terms of landholding and income from agriculture. The *Namasudra* inhabitants remained mostly unaffected by land reforms. They had migrated from former East Pakistan (now Bangladesh) with a relatively meagre amount of resources and managed to acquire small landholdings. As a result, they retained whatever land they had possessed even after land reforms. A large section of the *Namasudras* is small and middle landholders though some of them are marginal landowners or landless farmers too. Most of the landless households belong to the *Bagdi* community. An overwhelmingly large number of the *Bagdi* households possess no land for cultivation. The upper and middle caste households generally possess sufficient land, but they are not among the largest landholders of the village. But many of them have invested their wealth and savings on purchasing property in urban areas.

Thus, the *Namasudras* in this village constitute the landowning section despite their low ritual status. Further, many members of the *Namasudra* households have been able to secure employment in organized professional sector. On the other hand, the low ritual status of the *Bagdis* complements their low economic status. The *Bagdis* are engaged mostly in their traditional occupation which is fishing. Most of the *Bagdis* in this village are illiterate. Only a handful of them have studied beyond the tenth standard. Due to lack of formal education the *Bagdis* in this village are not in a position to look for white-collar employment in public and private sectors unlike the *Namasudras*.

It has been pointed out that *dalits* often fail to make transition to urban economy due to their "relative isolation, low levels of education, poor health, lack of financial resources, and lack of experience of anything other than agricultural labour". But some *dalit* communities, like the *Namasudras* of Mekhlapur appear to have benefited greatly from urban exposure.[22] One of the reasons as to why the *Namasudras* have become more mobile in class terms is because their cultural capital and social connections had been historically stronger than those of the *Bagdis*. Among the lower castes in colonial Bengal the *Namasudras* were most well-off, well-organized and politically connected. When the Government of India Act of 1919 made provision for the inclusion of a representative of the depressed classes among the nominated non-official

---

22   Judith Heyer, "The Marginalisation of Dalits in a Modernising Economy," in *The Comparative Political Economy of Development: Africa and South Asia*, eds. Barbara. Harriss-White and Judith Heyer (London: Routledge, 2010), 236.

members of the Bengal Legislative Council, a *Namasudra* was nominated by the Bengal Government because suitable candidates could be found only among the *Namasudras* given their better educational standards.[23] The earlier generations of the *Namasudras* of Mekhlapur mostly migrated from three villages situated in Faridpur district of current Bangladesh. They migrated relatively earlier, in the 1950s and early 1960s. As a result, they are now in a relatively stable and settled condition. Conversation with several *Namasudra* individuals also suggests that displacement significantly stimulated their urge to fight for their advancement, contributing immensely to their subsequent upward mobility. Most of them were in a state of impoverishment when they arrived in West Bengal from East Pakistan. But there were some individuals, who had a fair amount of cultural and economic resources, and they used their resources for the betterment of the other members of the community. For instance, the family of Nabakrishna Biswas was quite affluent and Nabakrishna Biswas, using his political connections did a great deal in providing relief assistance to other *Namasudra* migrants who had settled in Mekhlapur.[24] Most importantly, being an educated and wealthy person he used his resources for dissemination of education in the village.[25] Thus, the common *Namasudras* benefited because of cultural capital, political connections and economic resources of some of the members of their community.

However, not all members of the *Namasudra* community have been able to achieve economic mobility. Some members of the community still possess no land and work as agricultural labourers. On the other hand, a numerically significant and socially compact middle class has emerged among the *Namasudra* community. Thus, the *Namasudra* community is experiencing considerable economic differentiation. But, on the whole, the *Namasudras* in this area can be regarded as an upwardly mobile community. D. L Sheth has pointed out that since the mid 1970s due to affirmative action programme, a sizeable number of members of the lower castes have achieved the status of middle class. This has led to the emergence of a 'new middle class'.[26] The findings of this field study confirm this observation. Therefore, the earlier coincidence between caste and class can no longer be taken as a given phenomenon. However, for the *Bagdis*

---

23   Sekhar Bandyopadhyay, *Caste, Protest and Identity in Colonial India: The Namasudras of Bengal, 1872–1947* (New Delhi: Oxford University Press, 2011), 109.

24   Nabakrishna Biswas was in the Congress party.

25   Detailed discussion about Nabakrishna Biswas has been made in the later part of this chapter.

26   D. L Sheth, "Secularisation of Caste and Making of New Middle Class," *Economic and Political Weekly* 34, no. 34/35 (1999): 2502–2510.

the coincidence between caste and class remains largely intact. Such a complex caste-class nexus has influenced village politics. This issue will be taken up in the later part of this chapter.

5   Cultural Dynamics of Caste

Evidence from Mekhlapur suggest that the ritual basis of caste has considerably weakened. According to Haradhan Biswas, a 62-year-old *Namasudra* peasant, during their childhood the *Namasudras* were not allowed inside the upper caste households and the upper castes people would not take food and drink water in *Namasudra* households. Haradhan could still remember that he and his friends would roam about freely in the village fields and spacious courtyards of residential buildings but were specifically instructed by their elders not to step inside some particular houses. While as children they could not understand the reasons behind such instructions, after becoming adults they came to realize the real reasons behind such instructions. However, such a situation is no longer prevalent. Political leaders belonging both to the CPI(M) and the Congress party worked for the removal of caste rules and norms.[27] However, while untouchability has mostly withered away, the cultural dynamics of caste still operate in disguised forms.

Kenneth Bo Nielsen has described in the context of Singur movement how stereotypes associated with caste identity can result in political exclusion.[28] Such stereotypes can also lead to social segregation and economic distress for different caste groups. The prevalence of casteist hiring practices has been reported by several scholars. For instance, a study by Samantha Agarwal and Michael Levien has shown how in the labour maket spawned by Special Economic zones *dalits* are discriminated by upper caste brokers and employers who either refuse to hire them or slot them into the lowest-paying and symbolically 'dirtiest' work such as sanitation.[29] But impediments to occupational diversification of the *dalits* could also be more subtle. Ramnarayan Rawat has shown how inaccurate historical representation of the *Chamars* as leather workers led to their economic marginalization in North India. Contesting the easy association of the *Chamars* with leatherwork, he has presented evidences to demonstrate that a majority of the *Chamars* were engaged in agriculture,

---

27   Conversation with some elderly 'key informants'.
28   Nielsen, "The politics of Caste and Class in Singur's Anti-land Acquisition Struggle,"125–146.
29   Samantha Agarwal and Michael Levien, "Dalits and Dispossession: A Comparison," *Journal of Contemporary Asia* 50, no.5 (2020): 719.

while the leather industry in Uttar Pradesh during the nineteeth century was dominated laregely by the Muslims. The increase in the number of *Chamars* in leather industry afterwards was not because of any tradition but because this was one of the few employment opportunities available to them. But the general presumption of a necessary association between leatherwork and *Chamar* identity severely limited economic avenues for the *Chamars* in the labour market, preventing their occupational diversification.[30] Similar situation can be observed in Mekhlapur too, where a certain kind of negative cultural typecasting of the *Bagdis* has obstructed their occupational diversification.

Though the *Bagdis* of the village are mostly engaged in fishing, few *Bagdi* individuals also work as agricultural labourers. However, the bulk of agricultural labourers come from an adjoining village, inhabited by many tribal people. The landowners prefer to hire tribal agricultural workers who are known to be physically strong. The *Bagdis* are also considered physically sturdy. But the landowners generally avoid employing them since they are considered rowdy and ill-tempered by nature. Thus, stereotypes linked to caste identity have influenced hiring decisions in a manner which obstructs occupational diversification of the *Bagdis*.

Therefore, a common grievance of the *Bagdis* is that the outsiders are favoured over them, when it comes to hiring agricultural workers. Many *Namasudras* counter this allegation by denying that the *Bagdi para* constitutes a part of the village. Many *Bagdis* have also become increasingly prone to considering *Bagdi para* as a separate village. Thus, cultural images associated with caste identity have impacted social imagination of spatial frontiers. The fact that formal conception of space does not always necessarily coincide with lived reality of space has been highlighted by Henri Lefebvre's analysis of how space is socially produced. Lefebvre distinguishes among spatial practices (perceived space), representations of space (conceived space), and representational space (lived space). Spatial practices denote the ways people generate, use and perceive space. Representations of space are officially defined space conceived by engineers, cartographers, architects, and bankers through plans, designs, drawings, and maps. Representations of space tend to be, connected to formal or institutional apparatuses of power. Representational space, on the other hand, are lived spaces produced and modified over time and through use; spaces which are invested with symbolism and meaning. Lefebvre argues that this is "space as directly lived through its associations and images and

---

30   Ramnarayan Rawat, *Reconsidering Untouchability: Chamars and Dalit History in North India* (Ranikhet: Permanent Black, 2012).

symbols, and hence the space of inhabitants and users". Lefebvre has shown that space is produced out of the dynamic interaction and mutual interdependency between all these three elements. This suggests that the idea of space can be socially produced, and that social relations and circumstances may have a bearing on the meaning and idea of space.[31] While Mekhlapur being a *Panchayat* ward can be seen as a *representation of space, Bagdi para* stands for *representational space* which is produced out of social experience mediated by the working of caste dynamics. Thus, caste based social relations and lived space can unite in everyday life.

A number of studies have highlighted that space has the potential to be a unifying factor in *dalit* politics. Jaoul has pointed out that symbolic appropriation of public spaces through erection of Ambedkar statues in Uttar Pradesh (UP) has created *dalit* unity around the symbol of Ambedkar statues.[32] Maxine Loynd's study on the significance of Bahujan Samaj Prerna Kendra in Lucknow has shown how built space by articulating a new vision of the moral, political and spatial order can "mediate an experience of belonging to an imagined *dalit* community, united across space, time and class".[33] But the social meaning of space can also create social fissures. The disagreement between the *Namasudras* and *Bagdis* concerning the boundaries of Mekhlapur suggests that space can be also imagined by the *dalit* communities in a manner which is inimical to *dalit* unity and by implication inimical also to the political articulation of a unified *dalit* identity. Thus, the way space is imagined by the *dalits* themselves can also have some bearing on the prospects of *dalit* mobilization.

The *Kayastha* landowners don't participate directly in agricultural activities and fully rely on agricultural labourers. They stick to the *bhadralok* mode of social behaviour by abstaining from all sorts of manual labour. In this connection, an exploration of *bhadralok* culture and its significance for everyday micro-politics is necessary. According to J.H Broomfield *bhadralok* is a status group in a Weberian sense since the most important attribute of this group is social honour.[34] S.N Mukherjee has described the *bhadralok* as a social class, generally equating it with middle class.[35] An overwhelming majority

---

31   Henri Lefebvre, *The Production of Space*, trans. Donald Nicholson-Smith (Oxford: Blackwell, 1991), 33, 38–39.

32   Nicolas Jaoul, "Learning the Use of Symbolic Means: Dalits, Ambedkar Statues and the State in Uttar Pradesh," *Contributions to Indian Sociology* 40, no. 2 (2006): 175–207.

33   Maxine Loynd, "Understanding the Bahujan Samaj Prerna Kendra: Space, Place and Political Mobilisation," *Asian Studies Review* 33, no. 4, (2009): 479.

34   J. H. Broomfield, *Elite Conflict in a Plural Society* (Bombay: Oxford University Press, 1968).

35   S.N. Mukherjee, *Calcutta: Myths and History* (Calcutta: Subarnarekha, 1977).

of the *bhadralok* belonged to the three upper castes, Brahman, *Kayastha* and *Baidya* during the colonial era.[36] As a result, the term *bhadralok* has become synonymous with upper caste Hindu Bengali identity. However, technically the *bhadralok* is a non-ascriptive group. Though most of the members of this group belong to the three upper castes of Bengal, being an upper caste does not automatically qualify a person to be a *bhadralok*. Similarly, anyone of any caste can achieve *bhadralok* status by adhering to a particular style of life and social behaviour. According to Broomfield the *bhadralok* are "distinguished by many aspects of their behaviour-their deportment, their speech, their dress, their style of housing, their eating habits, their occupations and their associations – and quite as fundamentally by their cultural values and their sense of social propriety".[37] Being a *bhadralok* is more about adhering to a certain set of values and observance of certain social norms such as preference for higher learning, engagement in urban profession, involvement in various intellectual, artistic, and literary activities, attachment to Bengali language and literature and aversion for manual labour.[38]

These values and norms can be seen as equivalent of a culture (*bhadralok* culture in this case), if in accordance with Talcott Parsons' analysis, culture is seen as being embodied in norms and values. According to Parsons culture is a patterned and ordered system of symbols that provide objects of orientation to actors and therefore it has a significant bearing on the action and behaviour of individuals.[39] It is this link between *bhadralok* culture and social behaviour that constitutes the major concern of our analysis. Clifford Geertz argues that it is through the "behaviour – or, more precisely, social action – that cultural forms find articulation."[40] In this regard, Geertz urges us to have a deep and rooted understanding of the semiotics – symbols and meanings of culture, since he sees culture to be a system of conceptions which are communicated symbolically. Culture for him is a "historically transmitted pattern of meanings embodied in symbols, a system of inherited conceptions expressed in symbolic forms by means of which men communicate, perpetuate, and develop their knowledge about and attitude toward life"[41] where symbol can be "any

---

36   See, John McGuire, *The Making of a Colonial Mind: A Quantitative Study of the Bhadralok in Calcutta, 1857–1885* (Canberra: Australian National University, 1983).

37   Broomfield, *Elite Conflict in a Plural Society*, 5–6.

38   A detailed analysis of *bhadralok* identity has been presented in Chapter 7.

39   Talcott Parsons, *The Structure of Social Action* (New York: McGraw-Hill, 1937).

40   Clifford Geertz, *The Interpretation of Cultures* (New York: Basic Books, 1973), 17.

41   Clifford Geertz, "Religion as a cultural system," in *Anthropological Approaches to the Study of Religion*, ed. Michael Banton (London: Tavistock, 1966), 3.

object, event, quality, or relation which serves as a vehicle for a conception ....
the conception is the symbol's meaning".[42] An application of Geertz's concept
of culture can lead us to approach norms and values associated with *bhadralok*
culture as a system of shared symbols and meanings capable of influencing
social behaviour. Culture, on this view, must be interpreted through investigation of symbols. Since symbols get reflected in social behaviour, it is through
an analysis of social behaviour that cultural dynamics can be comprehended.
In other words, human behaviour will only make sense, if it is understood as
functioning symbolically in a particular context. In this connection, Geertz
stresses the vital fact that symbols are tangible and concrete embodiments of
ideas, attitudes, or beliefs. Meanings are not 'in people's heads'; symbols and
meanings are shared by social actors- between, not in them; they are public,
not private. In other words, culture is public because meaning is public. Thus,
in Geertz's analysis the "construction, apprehension, and utilization of symbolic forms" are social events.[43] Applying Geertz's paradigm, *bhadralok* culture
can be seen in semiotic terms, a sort of public act in which people express
themselves using various signs and symbols which have pre-ascribed cultural
meaning. Hence, we can identify the influence of *bhadralok* culture on everyday practices and mental outlook of the rural masses by treating their action
or behaviour as the fundamental text of culture.

The social behaviour of the *Namasudras* of Mekhlapur suggests their growing socialization in the *bhadralok* culture but various complexities are involved
in the process of absorption and observance of *bhadralok* culture. Those who
own land among the *Namasudras* cultivate their land through a mix of family labour and hired labour. However, they mostly refuse to acknowledge that
they themselves directly participate in cultivation. But their neighbours and
the agricultural labourers they employ tell a different story. From their versions I came to know about the direct participation of many of the *Namasudra*
landholders in cultivation. This behavioural pattern can be described as an
expression of what M.N Srinivas calls 'dual culture', i.e. an adherence to traditional norms in one context and modern and egalitarian values in another context.[44] G.K Karanth's contention that a dual culture with respect to caste based
practices may emerge due to exposure to urban culture and education also
appears quite illuminating in this context.[45] F.G Bailey's distinction between

---

42   Geertz, "Religion as a Cultural System," 5.

43   Geertz, *The Interpretation of Cultures*, 9–13, 91–94.

44   See, M.N. Srinivas, *Dual Culture of India* (Raman Memorial Lecture, Banglore, 1977).

45   See, G.K, Karanth, "Caste in Contemporary Rural India," in *Caste: Its Twentieth Century
        Avatar* ed. M.N Srinivas (Gurgaon: Penguin, 1997), 98.

normative and pragmatic rules of behaviour also seems analytically useful here. Normative rules, according to Bailey, correspond to culturally defined ideal modes of conduct which are commonly shared and internalized by the members of a group. Pragmatic rules on the other hand, are deviations from ideal rules in practical life, for the sake of tactical and situational adaptation.[46] The *bhadralok* norms function as normative rules in this context. One of the key features of the *bhadralok* value system is its dislike for manual labour. In *bhadralok* consciousness manual work bears some sort of social stigma.[47] In actual practice some *Namasudra* landowners sometimes deviate from, what Bailey calls normative rules, by directly participating in agricultural activities. But they accept the *bhadralok* norms as the embodiment of the ideal form of social conduct worthy of emulation. Hence, they do not publicly acknowledge the occasional pursuance of what Bailey calls pragmatic rules or practical deviation from *bhadralok* norms in this context. In this regard, it also needs to pointed out that, *bhadralok* culture is a code of conduct not only in the sense of how one should comport oneself but also perhaps more importantly, what are the things that one should admire and worship.[48] Hence, so long as one favours intellectual activities over manual work and seek to perform the former, that person carries within himself a *bhadralok* consciousness despite occasional deviation from the *bhadralok* mode of social behaviour.

Such innovative adaptation with *bhadralok* norms can be seen in other contexts too. In rural Bengal the Left parties successfully attempted to achieve some kind of fusion between peasant ethics and *bhadralok* values. A.E Ruud has pointed out that the Left parties placed before the rural masses the desired *chasi* (peasant) way of life or the *chasi* model which provided some scope to the untouchable communities to gain greater respectability by reforming their lifestyle. This model while endorsing the hard work of peasant life assimilated *bhadralok* values such as greater sexual discipline, cleanliness in attire, sophisticated mannerism, engagement with the culture of learning, adherence to civility and abandonment of moral vices like drinking, brawling etc.[49] Thus, cultivation despite being manual labour was allowed entry into the realm of respectability, if it carried with it other social codes and symbols of *bhadralok* culture. However, evidences from Mekhlapur suggest that this fusion between

---

46   F.G Bailey, *Stratagems and Spoils: A Social Anthropology of Politics* (New York: Schocken Books, 1969).
47   Broomfield, *Elite Conflict in a Plural Society,* 5.
48   Parimal Ghosh, "Where Have All the 'Bhadraloks' Gone?," *Economic and Political Weekly* 39, no. 3 (2004): 248.
49   Arild Engelsen Ruud, "From Untouchable to Communist," 253–278.

peasant ethics and *bhadralok* norms is steadily losing its social appeal. There is now a growing desire among the upwardly mobile sections among the lower castes to move towards a purer version of *bhadralok* values. The refusal of many *Namasudra* landowners to acknowledge their participation in cultivation activities arises out of this desire. This brings to light changing nature of the value system in rural Bengal. Moreover, the younger members of the community have little interest in agriculture, and they avoid direct participation in cultivation work.

The desire to emulate purer *bhadralok* norms has arisen due to greater exposure of younger people to urban culture. Exposure to urban culture has come in the form of urban education and urban employment. It is evident that a section of the *Namasudra* community has experienced considerable prosperity. Almost half of the *Namasudra* households have a family member who is employed in government or private job outside the village, in cities and towns of West Bengal and even in other states of India. Some have even gone abroad to Gulf countries. The extended family of Rathin Biswas is a case in point. The grandfather of Rathin Biswas came from former East Pakistan after the Partition in 1947 and settled in Mekhlapur. He had two sons, Govardhan Biswas and Govinda Biswas. Govinda Biswas, the father of Rathin Biswas became employed in a Group D job in an office of the Ministry of Defence. Govardhan Biswas got employment in a local post office as a clerk. The family thereafter made efforts to educate their children. One son of Govardhan Biswas studied hotel management in an institute in Kolkata and is now working in a Dubai hotel. His other son is working in a post office in a nearby town. One of the daughter-in laws of Govardhan Biswas has recently got a Group-D job in railways.

Rathin Biswas primarily draws his income from agriculture. He is an educated person who went to a college, situated in the suburbs of Kolkata. However, he has failed to land up a job. Despite fair amount of income, he draws from agriculture, he has decided to utilize his education. Side by side with the supervision of agricultural activities, he works as a private tutor. He sees private tuition as an alternative source of social respectability. "I earn enough from my land. I don't need to offer private tuition for money. I don't charge a single penny from many of my students who are financially weak. But I want to be known as an educated person. Money is not everything. It is respect also which counts", says Rathin. Rathin is a well known in the village for his tuition classes and is well respected too.

Despite experiencing prosperity many elderly *Namasudras* still work on the fields out of an emotional attachment to land while the aspirational youths find cultivation work to be demeaning . As per the information provided by a few tribal agricultural labourers employed by a well off *Namasudra* landowner Govardhan Biswas, he often works with them side by side on his own field. On the other hand, his nephew Rathin Biswas, despite having ample time in his hand does not perform any cultivation work with his own hands. He runs a coaching centre to earn respect rather than money. Thus, the younger villagers' conception of being a *bhadralok* or a respected individual does not entail the work of cultivation. Being exposed to urban culture owing to their stint outside the village for educational and occupational purposes, their understanding of respect is somehow different from that of their elderly family members. Under the influence of the younger members of the family, the older people's attitude towards cultivation has also become ambiguous. While they often work on their fields out of an emotional connect with their land, they also feel ashamed to divulge their participation in manual work. Thus, while the impact of *bhadralok* values on both younger and older generations is evident; such values are experienced and absorbed differently by them.

In this context, it is quite evident that in the changing village society, education and jobs in the organized sector have become new symbols of social respectability. The people of the younger generations are concentrating their energies on socio-economic upliftment by following the trajectory of social mobility dictated by *bhadralok* norms. This trajectory calls for education and urban employment in respectable white-collar professions. Thus, it appears quite clearly that the *bhadralok* values have deeply penetrated the *Namasudra* consciousness. The key to understanding non-politicisation of caste identity in West Bengal lies in such widespread penetration of *bhadralok* values into the social consciousness of lower caste groups like the *Namasudras*. This has created the absence of what has been termed as 'counterpublic' by Rita Felski and 'subaltern counterpublic' by Nancy Fraser. Counterpublic is an alternative cultural realm constituted by individuals belonging to a subordinated social group. Fraser defines 'subaltern counterpublic' as a parallel discursive arena formed by subordinated social groups where they "invent and circulate counter discourses which in turn permit them to formulate oppositional interpretations of their identities, interests, and needs".[50] Felski also points out that it is through participation in counterpublic that the marginalized people resist the homogenising tendency of the dominant culture and forge a common identity based upon shared experience. Felski stresses the fact that some form

---

50   Nancy Fraser, "Rethinking the Public Sphere: A Contribution to the Critique of Actually Existing Democracy," *Social Text*, no. 25/26 (1990): 67.

of solidarity based upon collective identity is a necessary precondition for the emergence and effectiveness of an oppositional movement.[51]

In this connection, a brief discussion of the contrasting trajectory of *dalit* politics in UP, where *dalit* mobilization has achieved great success can give us valuable insights. Badri Narayan's study on politicisation of *dalit* identity in UP has brought forth the significance of a *dalit* public sphere as an alternative space where historical experiences of humiliation and aspirations for dignity circulate in the form of stories and enable the formulation of a *dalit* political identity. The stories of oppression and recounting of heroic deeds of *dalit* icons like Ambedkar and Phule provide an alternative normative framework, representative of a *dalit* public sphere found in places such as tea shops in the *chamar patti* which are only frequented by lower caste individuals. Badri Narayan thus, brings out the significance of the emergence of a separate *dalit* public sphere as an important pre-condition for the rise of *dalit* politics.[52] Eva Maria-Hardtmann also emphasizes the crucial role of an alternative cultural space outside the dominant public sphere in the creation and articulation of a *dalit* political identity. It stands for a counter- discourse or a counterculture that provides the site for the construction of *dalit* identity. This only becomes possible when *dalit* groups despite their many differences make use of their 'common points of references' and tacit knowledge of the 'other' to arrive at a common agenda, formulating an alternative discourse to the dominant reasoning and sensibility.[53]

In this context, it is also important to highlight the requisite conditions necessary for the creation of a *dalit* public sphere. According to Badri Narayan *dalit* public sphere was brought into existence due to the efforts of an upwardly mobile, educated *dalit* middle class who transmitted alternative political consciousness to the *dalit* masses. They tried to shatter the dominant narrative through a steady production of alternative literature. Through this alternative literature many lower caste heroes and icons who had allegedly remained unsung due to dominance of upper caste value system were created as symbols of *dalit* pride and glory. In contrast, in West Bengal the normative critique of the dominant socio-cultural narrative in the form of a counter discourse has failed to gain ground among a vast majority of *dalit* masses. Such a counter

51   Rita Felski, *Beyond Feminist Aesthetics: Feminist Literature and Social Change* (Cambridge: Harvard University Press, 1989).

52   Badri Narayan, *The Making of the Dalit Public in North India: Uttar Pradesh, 1950–Present* (New Delhi: Oxford University Press, 2011).

53   Eva MariaHardtmann, *The Dalit movement in India: Local practices, global Connections* (New Delhi: Oxford University Press, 2009), 226–227.

discourse is not entirely absent but it is not widespread. It is pertinent to high-light that in the last few decades there has been an outpouring of Bengali liter-ature about *dalit* issues authored by *dalit* writers. Contemporary Bengali *dalit* writers consider *Matua Sahitya* (literature) as the earliest form of *dalit* litera-ture in Bengali.[54] *Dalit* literature is generally recognized as a deeply political project while *Matua Sahitya* contains a heavy dose of religious writing. But this religious writing can also be seen as a political discourse where religious and secular themes blend with one another.[55] According to *dalit* writer Nakul Mallik, Tarak Chandra Sarkar, the author of Harichand Thakur's hagiography *Sri Sri Harililamrita* was the pioneer of *Kabigaan* tradition which vehemently decried caste based discrimination and Brahmanical domination.[56] Earliest written *dalit* literature in Bengali also appeared in the pages of journals such as *Namasudra Suhird, Namasudra Hitaishi* and *Pataka* founded by *Namasudra* leaders belonging to the *Matua* sect.[57] However, over the years *Matua* move-ment while retaining its anti-Brahmanical character has undergone a steady process of *Hinduization* and in the process it has absorbed many of the norms and ideas of the dominant culture.[58] Furthermore, the non-emergence of an oppositional *dalit* discourse in the form of a full-fledged body of Bengali *dalit* literature till the late twentieth century was also prevented due to the unwill-ingness of mainstream Bengali literature and dominant *bhadralok* culture to acknowledge the different reality of *dalit* experience.[59]

Organized *dalit* literature of the modern variety or to be specific *dalit* liter-ature as a movement in Bengal took off almost twenty years after it had made its first appearance in Maharashtra in the early 1970s. The beginning of Bengali *Dalit Sahitya* as a literary movement is generally associated with developments like the foundation of Bangiya Dalit Lekhak Parishad (Bengal Dalit Writers Association) in 1987 by Nakul Mallik and establishment in 1992 of Bangla Dalit

---

54   Jaydeep Sarangi and Bidisha Pal, "Bangla Dalit Womanist Speaks: Interview with Bengali Dalit Writer Kalyani Thakur Charal," *Writers in Conversation* 7, no. 2 (2020): 4.

55   Sipra Mukherjee, "Creating Their Own Gods: Literature from the Margins of Bengal," in Joshil K. Abraham and Judith Misrahi-Barak (eds.), *Dalit Literatures in India* (New Delhi: Routledge, 2018), 138–52.

56   Many members of the *kabiyāl* troupes of West Bengal today are also followers of the *Matua* faith. See, Carola Erika Lorea, *Folklore, Religion and the Songs of a Bengali Madman: A Journey between Performance and the Politics of Cultural Representation* (Leiden: Brill, 2016), 171, 195.

57   Jaydeep Sarangi, "Towards the Cultural Banner of Bangla Dalit Literary Movement: An Interview with Nakul Mallik", *Writers in Conversation* 5, no. 2 (2018): 7.

58   For an analysis of *Hinduization* of *Matua* movement see chapter 2.

59   Runa Chakraborty Paunksnis, "Bengali Dalit Literature and the Politics of Recognition," *South Asia: Journal of South Asian Studies* (2021): DOI: 10.1080/00856401.2021.1962496.

Sahitya Sanstha (The Literary Association of Bengali Dalits) by a group of Bengali *dalit* writers who also promoted the journal *Chaturtha Dunia* (Fourth World) as a vibrant forum for *dalit* literature. In last few years a few Bengali *dalit* writers like Manoranjan Byapari and Kalyani Thakur Charal have gained recognition in literary circle. Manoranjan Byapari has rightly observed that "at the beginning of the twenty first century it is clear that *dalit* literature in Bangla can no longer be wished away or consigned to invisibility or relegated to the margins. Whether one likes it or not, this sapling has taken root in the soil".[60] Still, mainstream Bengali readership is largely unfamiliar with the work of Bengali *dalit* authors. Unlike in states like UP and Maharashtra where *dalit* literature has become immensely popular, in West Bengal there is little awareness about Bengali *dalit* literature even among the *dalits*. Mainstream Bengali literature written by *bhadralok* writers is immensely popular among rural population cutting across castes and communities. The reluctance of dominant *bhadralok* culture to acknowledge the prevalence of caste bias does play a role in preventing the Bengali *dalit* literature from gaining adequate recognition and popularity. However, at the same time the absorption of *bhadralok* culture by the *dalits* is also to a considerable extent responsible for a *dalit* counterpublic not taking deeper roots. Well known Bengali *dalit* writer Nakul Mallik also acknowledges this: "Most of them (Bengali *dalits*) have lost the power of independent thought and the will to fight. They are still hanging on to the ideas of the privileged classes, whose thought neither endorses political independence of *dalits* nor leaves space for their literature".[61] The *Namasudras* of Mekhlapur have never read any *dalit* literature and very few of them have heard about Bengali *dalit* authors. But relatively educated among them with college degrees have read several works of Rabindranath Tagore and other mainstream Bengali authors. A.E Ruud's through his field research has pointed out the immense popularity of the works of *bhadralok* writers like Saratchandra Chattopadhyay, Tarashankar Bandyopadhyay, Bibhutibhusan Bandyopadhyay and Manik Bandyopadhay among the rural masses.[62] While in UP and Maharashtra the upwardly mobile sections among the lower castes worked towards the creation of a *dalit* counter-culture, their counterparts in West Bengal such as the affluent *Namasudras* (as witnessed in Mekhlapur) have chosen to emulate the *bhadralok* value system, not to counter it. The widespread acceptance of *bhadralok* social norms and cultural codes by the upwardly mobile sections of

---

60   Manoranjan Byapari and Meenakshi Mukherjee, "Is There Dalit Writing in Bangla?" *Economic and Political Weekly* 42, no. 41 (2007): 4120.

61   Sarangi, "Towards the Cultural Banner of Bangla Dalit Literary Movement," 17.

62   Ruud, *Poetics of Village Politics*, 88–95.

the lower castes has ruled out the possibility of the emergence of a *dalit* public sphere as a pervasive entity and a vibrant site for alternative ideas.

6   Locating Caste in Politics at the Grassroots

Beliadanga Gram *Panchayat* since its formation has seen keen political contest between the CPI(M) and the TMC. TMC leader Shefali Biswas who got elected from Mekhlapur is the Gram *Panchayat Pradhan* of Beliadanga. Former *Pradhan* Nandolal Biswas also belonged to Mekhlapur.

During the CPI(M) era the party was led by Binoy Bain who fully controlled village politics. But in *Panchayat* the party was represented by quiet and unassuming Nandolal Biswas. Nandolal simply followed the guidelines he received from Binoy. Binoy owed his position to the backing of party leaders at the district level. He rarely acted independently. He simply carried out the directions he received from the upper caste party members at the district level. Now there seems to be no division between the actual leader and a formal functionary in institutional power structure.[63] The most influential political person now in the village is Jiban Biswas, whose wife Shefali Biswas is the *Panchayat Pradhan*. Shefali is basically a proxy of Jiban, who is the real power behind the throne.[64] Thus, the family of Jiban Biswas is today the power centre of the village. According to Jiban's key associates, he does seek the advice of his party on key issues but very rarely the party dictates him on petty village matters. Due to greater autonomy which the leader now enjoys in his functioning, community preferences rather than party diktats can now get reflected much more effectively in the decisions of the village leader. Therefore, apparently the community now has a better chance of representation. This is in line with Dwaipayan Bhattacharyya anticipation that the decline of the CPI(M) is likely to undermine "the autonomy of all existing parties and bring them under the control of locally constituted networks of caste, ethnic, and religious associations".[65]

---

63   This information has been shared by several ground level political workers.

64   This inference is based on author's personal observation of the ways of functioning of both Jiban and Shefali. Moreover, almost all the informants have described Shefali as a proxy of Jiban, highlighting the fact that it is Jiban who calls the all shots on behalf of his wife. He could not himself contest elections as Mekhlapur *Panchayat* ward is reserved for women candidates.

65   Dwaipayan Bhattacharyya, "Party Society, Its Consolidation and Crisis: Understanding Political Change in Rural West Bengal," in *Theorising the Present: Essays for Partha Chatterjee*, eds. Anjan Ghosh, Tapati Guha Thakurta and Janaki Nair (New Delhi: Oxford University Press, 2011), 245.

However, a close investigation reveals that Jiban functions primarily as a party-man enabling the party to wield supreme control over all village affairs. He decides the formation of the local school committees in consultation with his higher party bosses. Even the local *Durga puja* (annual worship of Goddess *Durga*) committee members take directions from him. The amount of contri-bution that each household needs to make for organizing the *puja* is decided by the *puja* committee in consultation with Jiban.

Furthermore, in local politics the so-called lower castes seem to play by the *bhadralok* rules, whereby caste matters little. This is evident in attempts by the lower caste leaders to gain political support only through means considered legitimate by the *bhadralok* culture rather than through explicit caste linkages. Education is one such important means.[66] Nabakrishna Biswas, a *Namasudra* played an instrumental role in dissemination of education in Mekhlapur and surrounding areas, and it is through his efforts that two schools, one primary school and another secondary school were set up in this area in the 1950s. Both these schools were named after the grandfather of Nabakrishna Biswas. Nabakrishna Biswas also set up another school in a neighbouring area, named after his grandmother. Nabakrishna commanded enormous respect in the vil-lage. Nabakrishna joined the Congress party and became an influential leader in the village. Many of his family members got involved in politics and later gained political capital from his legacy.[67] His grandson Jiban Biswas con-trols village politics today. The members of the Biswas family have become important actors in village politics not because they represent the numerically dominant caste in the village. Their political appeal lies in the fact that they have played an instrumental role in dissemination of education in the village. Therefore, they derive political legitimacy from the fact that they appear to primarily represent a progressive parlance of political modernity, not a tradi-tional loyalty like caste.

Moreover, the *Namasudra* community has remained politically fragmented. The members of the community don't cast their votes in support of a single candidate.[68] Both Nandolal and Shefali have their own group of followers among the *Namasudra* community. As a result, factors other than caste have become important. The *Namasudras* no longer constitute a homogenous lot

---

66   The *Namasudra* community has always strived to gain education. Their focus on dissemi-nation of education heavily draws on the teachings of Guruchand Thakur, who had urged the *Namasudras* to gain education in order to escape from socio-economic subordination.

67   This information has been collected from some elederly informants in the locality and also from Jiban Biswas.

68   Conversation with Jiban Biswas and several political workers.

socially and economically. When they migrated to West Bengal, barring a very few affluent individuals like Nabakrishna Biswas, all of them, more or less, were confronted by similar economic plight. However, such a situation no longer prevails. A sizeable section of the community has enthusiastically responded to the efforts of the government to disseminate education and managed to obtain government and private jobs in the organized sector. But the economic success of the upwardly mobile individuals has created social distance between them and the others within the same community. Having undergone socialization into *bhadralok* culture, the upwardly mobile *Namasudras* increasingly find less educated and less prosperous members of their own community to be uncultured and uncivilized. As a result, economically prosperous and educated individuals have mostly distanced themselves, from those who have lagged behind, by cutting down social interaction with the latter. This disconnect is deeply damaging for the emergence of a *dalit* political identity, which requires conscious efforts to bind together different sections of the *dalit* community on the basis of a common agenda. Jaoul has shown how in UP the Ambedkarite middle class has made sincere attempts to reconcile upward mobility with group solidarity. The affluent members of the *dalit* community patronize and fund activities like celebration of Ambedkar's birthday while the *dalit* organizers treat the affluent members of the community with utmost respect and importance during such occasions.[69] Thus, *dalit* festivals offer opportunities for contact between the *dalit* elite and the grassroots leaders, and during these events the former make public statements declaring their allegiance to their community. This builds a solidarity that acts a link connecting the subaltern arenas of participation and the institutional public sphere.[70] In this way the tendency of the *dalit* middle class to distance themselves from the larger community is warded off. In Mekhlapur such efforts seem to be absent. The author has been told by many relatively poor *Namasudra* peasants that those in possession of government jobs no longer bother about the problems of their relatively poorer caste fellows. One can hear frequent cribbing that people like Nabakrishna Biswas have become a lost species. When I enquired about the possible solution, the general response was one of utter despondency: '*Kichhu hobena, ebhabei cholbe*' (Nothing will happen, things will go on like this).

---

69   Nicolas Jaoul, "Citizenship in Religious Clothing? Navayana Buddhism and Dalit Emancipation in Late 1990s Uttar Pradesh," *Focaal* 76 (2016): 56–57.

70   Nicolas Jaoul, "Dalit Processions: Street Politics and Democratization in India," in *Staging Politics: Power and Performance in Asia and Africa,* eds. J.C. Strauss and D.B. Cruise O'Brien (London: I.B.Tauris, 2007),190–91.

It is generally assumed that the emergence of an educated and relatively well-off *dalit* middle class creates favourable condition for *dalit* political mobilization. Hugo Gorringe has shown in the context of Tamil Nadu that the emerging *dalit* middle class offered both resources and educated leadership contributing to the emergence of the *Pallar* political party- Puthiya Tamizhagam (PT) and *Paraiyar* political party- the Dalit Panthers of India.[71] Sudha Pai has also attributed the success of *dalit* politics in UP to doubling of the rate of literacy between 1981 and 1991. During this period UP witnessed one of the highest rates of enrolment in its private, unaided schools. This along with reservation in public employment paved the way for the emergence of a small middle-class among the *dalit*s in UP, especially among the *Jatavs*, who acted as the vanguard of *dalit* politics[72] However, evidences from Mekhlapur suggest that economic enrichment and educational attainments of some sections of the *dalit*s may not necessarily further the cause of *dalit* politics. The exposure to *bhadralok* values has significantly blunted the sense of caste solidarity of the upwardly mobile sections of the *Namasudra* community in Mekhlapur. As a result, caste loyalties do not seem to provide a common basis for bringing the entire community on a single platform for collective social and political action. This brings to light the crucial role of cultural outlook and social values, which determine the way in which economic resources and cultural capital are utilized for political purposes in actual practice. Rising wealth and intellectual attainments among the lower castes can lead to their effective political mobilization, only if they become favourably disposed to a value system conducive to the conversion of economic and cultural resources into *dalit* political agency.

However, recent attempts to invoke the *Matua* identity have made some impact in the village. Conduct of marriage ceremonies as per *Matua* rites without the aid of the Brahman priests has become more frequent. Thakurnagar, the *Matua* citadel is only a few Kilometres away from Mekhlapur and many villagers visit Thakurnagar during *Matua* festivals. Jiban arranges buses during *Matua* festivals like *Baruni Mela* (birth anniversary of Harichand Thakur) to enable the villagers to travel to Thakurnagar. But Jiban, a 35-year-old college educated young politician went to Thakurnagar only once in his life. According to him young men like him are not much enthusiastic about such festivals and are more concerned with real issues. However, they have regard for the religious

---

71   See, Hugo Gorringe, *Untouchable Citizens: Dalit Movements and Democratisation in Tamil Nadu* (New Delhi: Sage, 2005).

72   Sudha Pai, *Dalit Assertion and the Unfinished Democratic Revolution: The Bahujan Samaj Party in Uttar Pradesh* (New Delhi: Sage, 2002), 82–83.

sentiments of their elders and therefore, provide them necessary assistance to facilitate their religious pursuits.

Therefore, in such a situation what is the role of *Matua* identity in political mobilization? According to Jiban it has created more divisions than unity. There are two *Matua dols* (groups) led by two *dolpatis* (group leader) in the village.[73] They follow the same religious practices and sing and dance on the same religious festivals but they have provided refuge to mutually antagonistic individuals. If a person has a problem with his neighbour, he joins the rival *dol* of his neighbour. What are the reasons for such personal differences? According to Jiban economic prosperity and white-collar employment gained by some have created divisions between the affluent and the less affluent. Thus, in the present scenario the limited utility of caste identity in political mobilization of the *Namasudras* is well understood by politicians like Jiban.

However, an intimate investigation of the mode of social and political interaction will divulge the covert forms into which caste has disguised itself. Persisting in the realm of social consciousness in the guise of traditional conceptions and cultural attitudes, caste continues to influence the way in which political functions of individuals are shaped and political actions are conducted. As has already been pointed out, *Bagdi* identity has come to be associated with unruly behaviour and ignorance. We have already seen how such cultural typecasting prevents the *Bagdis* from taking up their desired economic functions and makes them cling on to their traditional economic role. However, such cultural typecasting has political effects too. Actually, the economic and political effects of such cultural typecasting reinforce each other. The image of the *Bagdis* as disorderly, empty-headed and rowdy has excluded them from any meaningful political role. They are not considered fit for political leadership because unlike the *Namasudras* they are not educated and articulate. No *Bagdi* has ever contested for any elected post from this village. None of the political parties have any *Bagdi* leader of some importance and stature.

As already pointed out the unruly image of the *Bagdis* has blocked their economic mobility. With little chance to get hired as agricultural labourers, they have little option but to engage in fishing, which they consider to be less profitable than cultivation. According to some of the *Bagdi* villagers, agricultural labour assures a fixed sum of money and there is also possibility of

---

73   Religious minded *Matuas* organize themselves into *dols* (groups) to collectively perform congregational religious activities like *kirtan* (a genre of religious performance arts involving singing and dancing in the praise of Hindu God Lord *Krishna* and his lady love, Radha).

working overtime. Moreover, the employer also has to provide food to the agricultural labourers during the work of cultivation. On the other hand, fishing does not assure guaranteed income. On several days there is no income at all.[74] The engagement of the *Bagdis* in fishing has also made them dependent on the affluent *Namasudra* households who own large village ponds. This has created caste-based patron-client network. One can find a nexus of multiple factors working here. The affluent *Namasudra* leaders try to win over the *Bagdi* support through economic concessions. Jiban owns a large pond where he allows the *Bagdis* to fish at concessional rates. This has helped him to earn the goodwill of the *Bagdis* who voted for his wife in the last *Panchayat* elections.[75] Thus, cultural typecasting of a caste has blocked its economic mobility making it dependent on the politically powerful for patronage. The economic dependence operating through the patron-client network, in turn reinforces caste based cultural stereotypes. To an extent this approximates what Balmurli Natrajan has termed 'culturalization of caste'. Natrajan's study of an artisan caste called *Jhariya Kumhar* from the central plains of Chhattisgarh has shown how through culturalization of caste, symbolic or super-structural elements play a role in reproduction of productive relations.[76] Evidence from Mekhlapur also suggest that culturalization of caste is at work through logics of patronage and dependence, albeit without the ritual trappings of older caste hierarchies. Cultural stereotypes and stigma are shaping boundaries between castes in times when ritual hierarchies are crumbling down. Geir Heierstad's study on the *Kumars* (potter caste) of Kolkata has also shown that for the *Kumars* caste is no longer an identity that regulates commensality and ritual interaction. It is a label or a marketing brand which they use to sell their products (*murtis* or images of Gods and Goddesses particularly the images of Goddess *Durga*) in an immensely competitive market. By showcasing their products as embodiments of an authentic tradition and glorious legacy, inherited by them from their predecessors, they bring caste as a raw material into production and marketing. This has led to commodification of caste, which is a modern phenomenon shaped by the logic of capitalism.[77] Castes are thus operating sociologically, more or less, as cultures with their in-group and out-group

---

74   Conversation with a group of *Bagdi* fishermen who sell fish at the nearby market.

75   Conversation with a group of *Bagdi* fishermen and with Jiban, Nandolal and Binoy.

76   Balmurli Natrajan, *The Culturalization of Caste in India: Identity and Inequality in Multicultural Age* (London: Routledge, 2011), 121–134.

77   See, Geir Heierstad, *Caste, Entrepreneurship and the Illusions of Tradition: Branding the Potters of Kolkata* (London: Anthem, 2017).

socio-economic dynamics. In Mekhlapur this has ensured that economic as well as political relations remain segregated along caste lines. Thus, caste plays a role in defining power relations between groups. But it does not act as a political vocabulary of marginalization. As a result, it does not provide any organizational basis of political mobilization.

A.E Ruud has recently claimed that patron-client relationship which sustained caste as a practice is disintegrating with the declining hold of the upper castes.[78] However, this field study finds out that caste-based patronage still exists despite the declining influence of the upper castes. The wealthy members of the upwardly mobile lower castes, as exemplified by the family of Jiban Biswas, have emerged as the new patrons of the disadvantaged groups. It has often been argued that violent backlash against the *dalit* community has mostly come from those castes which are categorised as OBCS (Other Backward Classes). Analysing the Khairlanji incident Teltumbde has pointed out that violence against *dalit*s is now mostly committed by the backward castes.[79] Sudha Pai has also highlighted that in UP most of the atrocities against the untouchable communities have been committed by the *Yadavs* and *Kurmis*.[80] Sambaiah Gundimeda has also demonstrated that in UP the BSP's two-pronged agenda of social justice for the *dalit*s- horizontalisation of vertical social order and democratisation of undemocratic political order has faced severe challenge and opposition from the OBCS.[81] However, evidences from Mekhlapur suggest that an upwardly mobile *dalit* community may also act like a so-called dominant backward caste in trying to keep other untouchable communities under its grip. The political elites of the village mostly belonging to the *Namasudra* community seem to have developed a stake in preventing democratisation of undemocratic political order, which could lead to greater political representation of the *Bagdis* at their costs. They look down upon the *Bagdis* and even less educated and less successful individuals among their own community as uncultured, uncivilised and therefore unsuitable for any meaningful political role. This proves the continuing relevance of Ambedkar's assertion that the caste system is marked by an "ascending scale of reverence and a

78   Arild Engelsen Ruud, "From Client to Supporter: Economic Change and the Slow Change of Social Identity in Rural West Bengal," in *Politics of Caste in West Bengal*, eds. Uday Chandra, Geir Heierstad and Kenneth Bo Nielsen (New Delhi: Routledge, 2016), 213.

79   Anand Teltumbde, "Khairlanji and its Aftermath: Exploding Some Myths," *Economic and Political Weekly* 42, no. 12 (2007): 1019– 25.

80   Pai, *Dalit Assertion and the Unfinished Democratic Revolution*, 167.

81   Sambaiah Gundimeda, *Dalit Politics in Contemporary India* (Abingdon: Routledge, 2016), 110–112, 140.

descending scale of contempt".[82] Even castes within the broader *dalit* category look down upon others who they perceive to be beneath them in social status.

7   Summing Up

The crucial role of the *dalit* middle class in providing social and political agency for *dalit* politics is frequently emphasized. But in Mekhlapur social mobility among the *Namasudras* has not proved conducive to caste mobilization. This brings to light the determining role of political culture in shaping political prospects of expanding economic resources and cultural capital of the rising *dalit* middle class.

This field study further demonstrates that caste is not overtly deployed as a conscious vocabulary of socio-political marginalization in rural West Bengal due to overall dominance of *bhadralok* culture. *Bhadralok* values seem to have become entrenched in the rural social psyche preventing the rise of a *dalit* public sphere, the crucial role of which in the emergence of *dalit* politics has been highlighted by a number of studies.[83] The *bhadralok* value system might not have filtered down from the upwardly mobile sections of the *dalit* community into the actual life practices of those at the bottom of the socio-economic ladder. But its legitimization by the upwardly mobile sections has led to its internalization as the model code of conduct by all groups placed at different layers of the socio-economic spectrum. And it is this very model that, by relying upon secular criteria like education and occupation rather than traditional loyalties like caste identity, has robbed the idiom of caste of much of its political possibilities.

Does this mean that caste is an insignificant political factor? If we presume that caste plays a role in politics only when it provides a basis for politically organizing people and expressing interests and grievances of specific communities, then indeed caste does not matter in West Bengal politics. This is because in West Bengal caste is a silent factor. It does not provide an effective platform for open political mobilization and a vocal idiom for ventilation of demands for redistribution of political and economic resources. But its apparent muteness does not make it insignificant in grassroot politics. It silently performs the key function of shaping political and economic power relations

---

82   B.R Ambedkar, *Who are the Shudras? How They Came to be the Fourth Varna in Indo-Aryan Society* (Bombay: Thacker & Co, 1946), 26.

83   Narayan, *The Making of the Dalit Public in North India;* Hardtmann, *The Dalit Movement in India.*

between groups and communities. As a result, power relations remain segregated along caste lines.

In Mekhlapur the socialization of a sizeable section of the *Namasudra* community into the *bhadralok* value system has made it difficult to organize them on caste lines. However, the attempts to politically mobilize the support of the *Bagdis* have yielded greater success. But such support has been mobilized not by evoking caste sentiments or by articulating caste-oriented demands but by offering unstable economic patronage. Interestingly, it is caste-based profiling that has made the *Bagdis* dependents on such patronage, resulting in the creation and continual reproduction of largely caste based patron-client network. Hence, in view of the evidences gathered from Mekhlapur, it is difficult to agree to Ruud's contention that caste no longer plays any significant role in patronage system in rural Bengal.[84]

Overall, it can be argued that caste is not irrelevant in grassroot politics. Caste in rural society has disguised itself into unapparent forms. It now operates mostly as a part of unconsciously inherited social perceptions and cultural attitudes. This enables it to act as a significant factor in the allotment of political roles to individuals, conduct of political activity, operation of patron-client relationship and even social imagination of spatial frontiers. In other words, caste stereotypes and caste feelings existing at the ground level do influence political and economic activities, but they do so imperceptibly without much public articulation, making the interaction between caste and politics an immensely complex affair in contemporary West Bengal.

Therefore, caste does play an important political role in rural West Bengal. But unlike in other states, in West Bengal's micro-politics, there is an intriguing absence of social dialogue about everyday experiences of caste. What accounts for this lack of political articulation of caste experiences can be found in political culture and social outlook embodied in the dominant *bhadralok* value system. Drawing theoretical insights from Geertz, *bhadralok* culture in our analysis has been conceptualized in semiotic terms, a sort of public act in which people express themselves using various signs and symbols which have pre-ascribed cultural meaning. This analytical approach has unveiled deep and growing penetration of *bhadralok* values in social consciousness of lower caste groups. In other words, the social acceptance of *bhadralok* culture is profound and pervasive. The pervasive influence of *bhadralok* culture has led to an absence of sustained social dialogue on caste practices and experiences, preventing the emergence of a counter culture in the form of an effective *dalit*

---

84   Ruud, "From Client to Supporter," 193–215.

public sphere. This in turn hinders the emergence of caste as political idiom of marginalization and protest. As a result, caste while remaining present in socio-economic relations and cultural processes fails to find a channel for political articulation. Unlike in many other states which are strongholds of caste politics, in West Bengal transportation of local dynamics of caste from micro politics to state level mainstream macro politics has effectively been thwarted by the non-emergence of a vibrant and pervasive *dalit* public sphere, which could have acted as a link between micro and macro levels of politics.

To sum up, this study has come up with three main findings: (1) *bhadralok* culture seems to have become entrenched in rural society in post-colonial West Bengal, preventing the emergence of an alternative *dalit* public sphere, which could have facilitated politicisation of *dalit* identity; (2) significant class divisions have emerged among upwardly mobile untouchable groups such as the *Namasudras* which, on the whole, are now in a position to act as dominant castes at the village level, and better-off families within these groups have begun emulating *bhadralok* norms; and (3) despite the absence of overt caste based political mobilization and weakening of the ritual basis of caste, groups are stereotyped and stigmatized in caste terms and such stigmatization by producing political and economic effects carves out a covert role for caste in political and economic processes. It is the interrelated nature of these dynamics that shapes the role of caste in rural West Bengal.

CHAPTER 7

Unmasking Political Culture

Cultural Dynamics in Mainstream Politics

In several accounts relating to the interaction between caste and politics in West Bengal the role of political culture has been acknowledged but not with much attendant scrutiny or analysis. Part of the reason for this lies in the intangible and nebulous nature of regional political cultures that are difficult to capture in academic analysis, which demands tangible and concrete evidences as well as conformity to rigid methodologies. Therefore, though scholarly instinct has often hinted towards the invisible hand of political culture, a full and thorough unveiling of the impact of West Bengal's political culture on the political trajectory of caste has eluded academic inspection. This is perhaps the reason why the existing literature despite being equipped with an awareness of the importance of political culture in shaping identity related political concerns fails to give sufficient clarity as to how the dominant or mainstream political culture of the state has influenced the political role of caste in institutional politics. In other words, despite some hints here and there, the role of political culture in non-crystallization of political demands along the lines of caste has not been explicitly explored and adequately addressed.

The politics of West Bengal is intimately linked to what is generally referred to as *bhadralok* culture. *Bhadralok* is a unique social group that emerged in nineteenth century colonial Bengal. The members of this group played a crucial role in nineteenth century Bengal renaissance. In popular perception the *bhadralok* identity has become inalienable from the idea of Bengal renaissance. Bengal renaissance is normally associated with various forms of *bhadralok* directed social activism; education, social and religious reform, revivalism, philanthropy, and patriotic politics.[1] Being the first group to receive western education and imbibe western modernity, the *bhadralok* established their firm control over nationalist politics and the worlds of culture and literature in colonial Bengal, fashioning in the process the social and political culture of Bengal. It is widely believed that nineteenth century *bhadralok* culture laid the foundations for the Bengal of today.[2] Being

---

1 Sumit Sarkar, "Calcutta and the Bengal Renaissance," *in Calcutta: The Living City, Vol I,* ed. Sukanta Chaudhuri (Calcutta: Oxford University Press, 1990), 104.

2 Sumit Sarkar, *Writing Social History* (New Delhi: Oxford University Press, 2013),185.

a hegemonic social force, it has shaped the template of legitimate political conduct in West Bengal. Therefore, the evolving relationship between the political dynamics of caste and *bhadralok* culture demands a close scholarly examination. Given the intangible nature of political culture, such an examination, however, runs the risk of occasional deviations from the standard and established pattern of academic analysis. Hence, my attempt in this chapter is to show without bothering too much about protocols of method, how the hegemonic influence of the dominant value system in the form of *bhadralok* culture, has impacted the making of the dominant political lexicon and established pattern of political praxis, which have a bearing on the mode of articulation of the political idiom of caste in West Bengal. Thus, this chapter scrutinizes the political culture of West Bengal and its impact on the prospects of caste as a political resource. To be specific, it attempts to understand the role of political culture in marginalization of caste question in institutionalized party politics of West Bengal.

At the outset, I shall inquire the historical link between *bhadralok* norms and mainstream political culture. This inquiry will begin with a critical engagement with the meaning and evolution of the *bhadralok* as a sociological category and the process of establishment of *bhadralok* hegemony. Thereafter, I shall inspect the general political and ideological orientation of the *bhadralok,* analysing how and why the *bhadralok* culture developed leftist leanings. This will logically lead to the next part of the discussion, which will investigate the evolving intercourse between *bhadralok* ideology and mainstream politics in an attempt to find out how *bhadralok* values have influenced the mainstream political culture of West Bengal. In this regard, I shall explore the recent political history of West Bengal in order to show that the electoral decline of the Left has not brought about any fundamental change in the general political culture of the state. My investigation will reveal that the TMC has more or less co-opted the Left's mode of functioning, resulting in the perpetuation an established pattern of political template informed by a complex interplay between *bhadralok* norms and Left-wing political discourse. In this context, I shall argue that the prolongation of the political template originally associated with Left politics suggests entrenched institutionalization of a Left minded political culture, which tends to limit the political role of caste by privileging the discourse of class over that of caste. The concluding section will briefly consider the possibility of a structural transformation of the prevailing political culture as a result of the recent rise of *Hindutva* politics in the state.

1   *Bhadralok*: Decoding the Sociological Category

Nineteenth century saw the rise of a group of educated Bengalis mainly located in Calcutta and but also in other towns of Bengal. They came to describe themselves as 'middle class' in English, but would also use a more expressive word, *bhadralok* ('gentleman' or 'a man of good breeding') when referring to themselves in Bengali.[3] The precise nature of the *bhadralok* as a social category is debatable. It is commonly perceived as either a caste club or a social class. Interestingly, the concept of *bhadralok* as a social category includes both caste and class elements. Therefore, scholars have used the prisms of both caste and class to conceptualize what it entails to be a *bhadralok*. But due to a variety of constitutive ingredients which are uniquely intrinsic to the *bhadralok* identity, it can't be solely reduced to a single caste or class category. Therefore, we can attempt to make sense of the *bhadralok* as a social group through the familiar prisms of caste and class only to a limited extent .

John F. Broomfield, who has produced the most well-known and authoritative work on the colonial *bhadralok* has avoided conflating the *bhadralok* identity with either caste or class. He believes that the *bhadralok* constitute a status group in a Weberian sense, since the most important attribute of this group is social honour. He finds wealth not to be an essential criterion for attainment of the *bhadralok* status. According to him the colonial *bhadralok* were distinguished by their distinctive and more sophisticated speech and attire, abstinence from manual labour, a sense of common pride in achievements of Bengali culture and more fundamentally by their cultural values and a sense of social propriety. Thus, Broomfield highlights several cultural markers of the *Bhadralok* identity. More importantly, he suggests that these cultural markers could be acquired by anyone through western education.[4] Hence, for Broomfield the *bhadralok* is mainly a cultural identity, with liberal western education being the hallmark of that identity. It is therefore, an open status group not based on any ascriptive status like caste but on achieved status that comes with education and cultural refinement.

However, caste dynamics can't be completely ignored while conceptualizing the *bhadralok* as a social category. Technically, the *bhadralok* in the colonial era was a non-ascriptive category. Anyone could gain entry into the privileged coterie of the *bhadralok* through exposure to western education, modern occupations and a particular style of life. But as pointed out by a number of studies,

---

3   Marcus F. Franda, "West Bengal," in *State Politics in India*, ed. Myron Weiner (Princeton: Princeton University Press, 1968), 263.

4   J.H Broomfield, *Elite Conflict in a Plural Society* (Bombay: Oxford University Press, 1968), 5–8.

the members of the *bhadralok* were primarily drawn from the three upper castes of Bengal, Brahmans, *Baidyas* and *Kayasthas*. Sumit Sarkar, for instance, despite recognising the existence of several strata within the *bhadralok* category identifies the *bhadralok* with higher castes. Because of the preponderance of the higher castes among the *bhadralok*, the term *bhadralok* over a period of time became synonymous with the Bengali higher caste identity in public discourse and it came to be applied to non-upper caste individuals only by analogy.[5] However, the linkage between *bhadralok* status and caste identity is riddled with complexities. Several historically informed accounts have presented a much more complicated picture of the complex interconnection between them .

John McGuire's quantitative estimates of the *bhadralok* in a number of socially important sectors reveal that in the second half of the nineteenth century the *bhadralok* were drawn from a wide range of *jatis* but there was clear predominance of some specific *jatis* among the *bhadralok*. These *jatis* included the Brahmans, *Baidyas* and *Kayasthas*, whose representation in the *bhadralok* society was quite substantial. However, quite a considerable number of individuals from a few intermediate castes, like the *Subarnabaniks* also managed to attain *bhadralok* status. McGuire shows that their representation in important social positions was quite significant.[6] Broomfield also points out that individuals from castes like the *Subarnabanik* and *Gandhabanik* quite frequently made entry into the *bhadralok* society as they managed to acquire English education and profitable business associations.[7] While acknowledging the practical difficulties faced by individuals from the lower castes in gaining admission to the *bhadralok* circle due to lack of access to western education, Broomfield

---

5   Pradip Sinha, "Social Changes," in *The History of Bengal* (1757–1905), ed. N.K Sinha (Calcutta: University of Calcutta, 1967), 410.

6   The educational organizers belonged to as many as 18 *jatis*, the press organizers as many as 12 *jatis* and organizers of voluntary associations as many as 18 *jatis*. But clearly, some *jatis* were numerically more dominant than others in important social spheres. In 1869, in Hindu College there were 184 *Kayastha*, 100 *Subarnabanik*, 87 Brahman, 13 *Vaidya*, 9 *Khettri* and 31 *Navasakha* students. Between 1857 and 1885 of educational organizers 29 percent were *Radhi Kayasthas*, 27 percent were *Saptagram Subarnabaniks* and 20 percent were *Radhi* Brahmans. Of the press organizers 30 percent were *Radhi* Brahmans, 20 percent were *Saptagram Subarnabaniks*, 17 percent were *Radhi Baidyas* and 7 percent were *Dakshin Radhi Kayasthas* in 1885. Between 1857 and 1885 the organizers of voluntary associations were composed mainly of the *Radhi* Brahmans (28 percent), *Dakshin Radhi Kayasthas* (26 percent) and *Saptagram Subarnabaniks* (percent). See, John McGuire, *The Making of a Colonial Mind: A Quantitative Study of the Bhadralok in Calcutta, 1857–1885* (Canberra: Australian National University, 1983), 22, 47, 54, 63, 78.

7   Broomfield, *Elite Conflict*, 7.

emphasizes that the membership in *bhadralok* society was in no way ascriptive. If a lower caste individual could gain urban professional employment on the basis of western education and was able to successfully acclimatise himself with the cultural values and lifestyle characteristic of the *bhadralok* status , he would gain acceptance as a *bhadralok*.[8] Several other studies also indicate that, due to expanding opportunities of economic mobility in nineteenth century, it became increasingly possible for lower caste individuals to achieve the status of *bhadralok*. For instance, Anindita Ghosh's study on low life print culture of colonial Calcutta highlights the emergence from mid-nineteenth century onwards of a sizeable body of printer-publishers, authors and readers of relatively plebeian origin who can be classified as 'petty *bhadralok*' or 'lesser *bhadralok*'. The Battala area of North Calcutta became a major centre for production of popular books with concentration of numerous small presses. Many of the entrepreneurs of this printing and publishing industry of Batttala belonged to low caste groups of smiths and artisans who were skilled in metal working. They manned these cheap presses and also remained connected with the trade as printers, publishers, authors and artists. The *Karmakars, Shils* and *Lahars* were prominent castes involved in this business.[9]

S.N Mukherjee's extensive research on caste and class situation of colonial Calcutta also underlines that the *bhadralok* was an open *de facto* social group. While many individuals from the three upper castes because of their prior socio-economic advantages managed to swell the ranks of the *bhadralok*, their attainment of the *bhadralok* status was not just because of their higher caste identity. Mukherjee emphasizes that while men like Motilal Seal, a *Subarnabanik* (unclean *Sudra*) and Guruchand Basak, a weaver of low ritual status were leading *bhadralok* of Calcutta in nineteenth century, majority of the higher caste people, for not being equipped with requisite academic and cultural qualifications, were not considered as *bhadralok*. He points out that only individuals sharing a common economic position, a similar level of education and a similar style of living were treated as *bhadralok*.[10]

Interestingly, Mukherjee's refutation of the *bhadralok* as a caste aristocracy leads him to describe the *bhadralok* as a social class. As class is an open social category, he finds it useful to make sense of the *bhadralok* as a social group. Apparently, the categorization of the *bhadralok* as a social class, poses some

---

8   Broomfield, *Elite Conflict,* 9.

9   Anindita Ghosh, "Revisiting the 'Bengal Renaissance': Literary Bengali and Low-Life Print in Colonial Calcutta," *Economic and Political Weekly* 37, no. 42 (2002), 4329–4338.

10   S.N Mukherjee, "The Bhadraloks of Bengal," in *Social Stratification,* ed. Dipankar Gupta (New Delhi: Oxford University Press, 2014), 179–180.

difficulty, since the *bhadralok* comprise of individuals belonging to different economic strata. From the contemporary accounts like *Kalikata Kamalalaya* written by Bhabani Charan Bandyopadhyay, the editor of one of the earliest Bengali newspapers *Samachar Chandrika*, it becomes quite clear that the *bhadralok* was not a unified category in economic terms. *Kalikata Kamalalaya* published in 1823 is an analysis of the social of life of colonial Calcutta presented in the form of a dialogue between a newcomer to the city and a local person. It provides us with an elaborate classification of the *bhadralok*. As described in *Kalikata Kamalalaya* the topmost tier of the *bhadarlok* category was occupied by the *abhijat* (aristocratic) *bhadralok* consisting of big *zamindars*, wealthy merchants and *diwans* dependent on rental income and profits from trading activities run in collaboration with the British. According to Bhabani Charan they had a lot of free time at their disposal and utilized it by engaging in activities ranging from learning and religious discussion to womanizing. The petty landholders, shopkeepers, those employed in bureaucracy and commercial enterprises and other self-employed professionals like doctors, lawyers and journalists were positioned at the intermediate level of the *bhadralok* society. They were not extremely rich but had reasonably sound economic standing. The lowest rung of the *bhadralok* category was populated by struggling poor migrants from districts earning livelihood from low level government and private jobs.[11] Thus, Bhabani Charan's account makes it quite evident that individuals categorized as *bhadralok* were not members of a single class. S.N Mukherjee attempts to overcome the analytical difficulty of defining the *bhadralok* through the analytical prism of class, by neither conceptualizing class as a homogenous economic category nor denying the centrality of cultural norms as the essential signifiers of *bhadralok* identity. Mukherjee argues that the Marxist category of class is an inclusive one; it denotes a combination of 'economic power, market chances, occupational prestige and style of life' as well as consciousness on the part of its members of their separate existence and exclusiveness from other social groups. For him, the distinction between 'class situation' and 'status situation' is more theoretical than real, as it is often the case that the rich enjoy high status in society. Hence, honour can be knit to a class situation; the style of life and consumption of goods are linked with acquisition of goods. Therefore, he sees class as a *de facto* social group, the members of which hold a common position along some continuum of the economy, enjoy similar type of lifestyle and possess the consciousness of a

---

11   Bhabani Charan Bandyopadhyay, *Kalikata Kamalalaya* (Calcutta: Samacharchandrika Press, 1823), 8–17.

class. All these commonalities unified the rich *abhijat bhadralok* and a middle income *bhadralok* group. According to Mukherjee the *abhijat bhadralok* (big zamindars, merchants and top administrators) constituted a highly rich but subservient capitalist class who became wealthy and powerful because of their business dealings and association with the British. They were not a part of the traditional elite or old nobility but a new group of upstarts who rose to prominence by sheer hard work and struggle. Then there was a middle-income group or *grihasta bhadralok* consisting of small *zamindars*, small merchants, shopkeepers and more importantly white-collar professionals who imitated the lifestyle of the *abhijat bhadralok* and accepted their leadership. The line of demarcation between these two groups was not clear as they were both referred to as 'educated natives' by the British. As both these groups acquired English education, followed similar lifestyle or cultural norms and emerged and flourished under British patronage having little association with old aristocracy, Mukherjee considers both of them as a 'new middle class'.[12]

Like Mukherjee, Sumit Sarkar also equates the '*bhadralok*' with the 'middle class' and uses the two terms interchangeably. But he also takes care to emphasize that the middle class or the *bhadralok* in economic terms was not a homogenous group. The *bhadralok* category included a wide spectrum of individuals from the low-paid clerks, humble school teachers to the affluent professionals. Within the category of *bhadralok* or colonial middle class Sarkar distinguishes between a highly successful group of religious and social reformers, writers, journalists, lawyers, doctors, teachers and politicians and a much less successful group of declining traditional literati, jobless graduates, obscure hack writers, humble school teachers and poor clerks.[13] While English education brought reasonable economic and professional success to some, most could only manage to acquire humble clerical jobs in government and mercantile offices.[14] According to Sarkar this created a cultural divide within the *bhadralok,* giving rise to high and low cultures. The more affluent *bhadralok* mostly focused upon higher education, religious reform, philanthropy, and nationalist politics. But the less successful *bhadralok* became attracted to the low-life literature churned out by the printing presses like those of Battala in North Calcutta as well as *bazar* painting of Kalighat, which expressed their

---

12   S.N Mukherjee, *Calcutta: Myths and History* (Calcutta: Subarnalekha, 1977), 25–27.
13   Sarkar, *Writing Social History*, 190–191.
14   Sumit Sarkar, "Kaliyuga, 'Chakri' and 'Bhakti': Ramakrishna and His Times," *Economic and Political Weekly* 27, no. 29 (1992): 1544.

anguish and frustration resulting out of their lack of economic success.[15] Still both these groups were united into the same social category of *bhadralok* by some shared values. Tithi Bhattacharya's work illustrates more explicitly the importance of shared culture as the main unifying factor among the economically diverse groups within the *bhadralok* category. She finds that the *bhadralok* was composed of a landed rentier class and a class of *petty-bourgeoisie* dependent on income from salaries and urban professions. Further, there were two rungs within the class of *petty bourgeoisie*: the bottom rung of lowly clerks and the top layer of relatively high-ranking officials of colonial bureaucracy. The two main groups, the rentier class and the *petty bourgeoisie* were united by the common ideology of education that also made them identify with a common culture. Though the *bhadralok* came from diverse social and economic backgrounds, culture or at least the rhetoric about culture, was something that gave them a unified identity.[16] Himani Bannerji also points out that in both its form and content, western education or the new knowledge operated as an ideology and played a crucial role in shaping the world- view of Bengali non-menial classes. "It provided the language, the organization of discourse, and many of the terms of reference in which were encoded both the social practices and the worldviews" of the *bhadralok*.[17] Highlighting the importance of culture in the construction of *bhadralok* identity, Parimal Ghosh emphasizes that the *bhadralok* shared an agreement about their self-perception. Despite belonging to different socio-economic strata, they broadly agreed as to what constituted a *bhadralok*. More importantly, they believed in a common moral code of conduct. But this code was less about actual observance and more about what to admire and aspire for. Ghosh argues that it did not matter whether one had actually read literary stalwarts like Rabindranath Tagore or Bankim Chandra Chatterjee, but an admiration for them and an acknowledgement of their greatness were sufficient. Similarly, it did not matter if one's politics was casteist, or communal, but it was important to agree that secularism was desirable. Ghosh further points out that with increasing entry of individuals from lower castes and classes into the *bhadralok* category due to economic changes after independence, the defining element of the *bhadralok* status is

---

15   Sumit Sarkar, "The Kalki Avatar of Bikrampur: A Village Scandal in Early Twentieth Century Bengal," in *Subaltern Studies, Volume VI*, ed. Ranajit Guha (New Delhi: Oxford University Press, 1994), 6, 36–37.

16   Tithi Bhattacharya, *The Sentinels of Culture: Class, Education and the Colonial Intellectual in Bengal* (New Delhi: Oxford University Press, 2005), 51–52, 60.

17   Himani Bannerji, "The Mirror of Class-Class Subjectivity and Politics in 19th Century Bengal," *Economic and Political Weekly* 24, no. 19 (1989): 1045.

now acknowledged to be a belief in a code of conduct, in which primacy is given to a sense of admiration for higher education or college degrees. Thus, it is psychological identification with a code of conduct which places a person in the category of *bhadralok*.[18]

Therefore, what comes out of the entire discussion is the fact that, though membership of a certain caste or class makes it easier for an individual to enter into the charmed circle of the *bhadralok*, the social category of *bhadralok* has never been a homogenous one in terms of both caste and class. "There were internal differences on the basis of subtly different levels of social, economic, educational or professional criteria, which also contextually intersected and overlapped."[19] The *bhadralok* is therefore, primarily a cultural identity. What fundamentally defines the *bhadralok* is acceptance of what is commonly referred to as the *bhadralok* culture, an embodiment of a set values, norms, and a code of conduct. Hence, one acquires *bhadralok* identity by identifying with a particular culture. Broadly speaking, the essential ingredients of this culture are keenness to attain higher education, abstinence from manual work, civil and sophisticated modes of articulation, apparent fondness for intellectual and artistic activities and admiration for and pride in Bengali cultural and literary achievements.

2   Emergence and Evolution of the *Bhadralok*

The *bhadralok* were a product of the economic changes brought about by the British rule. The British rule generated commercial and business opportunities for a section of the local merchants in the second half of the eighteenth century. For collection of indigenous goods for export, transportation of imported commodities to local markets and management of investment on an alien land, the British needed help of local agents or middlemen. Therefore, in the initial decades of the British rule many ambitious men flourished by acting as *banias* or agents of the European private traders and *diwans* or intermediaries for East India administration. They became wealthy and prosperous by venturing into comprador type of business activities. Kantababu, Darpanarayan

---

18   Parimal Ghosh, "Where Have All the 'Bhadraloks' Gone?," *Economic and Political Weekly* 39, no. 3 (2004): 247–251.

19   Swarupa Gupta, *Notions of Nationhood in Bengal: Perspectives on Samaj, c. 1867–1905* (Leiden: Brill, 2009), 49.

Tagore, Ram Chandra Dutta, Ramdulal Dey, Motilal Seal and Nabakrishna Deb were some of the most prominent 'comprador-rajas' of colonial Calcutta of late eighteenth and early nineteenth century.[20]

Beginning in 1780 many Agency Houses started their operations in Calcutta. Alexander & Company, Palmer & Company, Colvin & Company, Fairlie-Fergusson & Company, Cruttenden-Mackillop & Company, and Mackintosh & Company were some of the largest and well-known Agencies Houses which started their operations in India under the patronage of the East India Company.[21] These Agency Houses started off as agents for remittance and investment of private savings of the company servants but gradually diversified their activities by building and operating ships, setting up banks and insurance companies and undertaking ventures in mining, manufacturing and plantation projects. Their number steadily increased over the first half of the nineteenth century. In the absence of large-scale banking facilities and due to preoccupation of British money with domestic economy these Agency Houses were in dire need of finances. In this situation the filthy rich *banias* became the financiers and decided to invest their accumulated capital in business activities. Their importance grew further with increasing reluctance by the British to invest capital in India, caused by financial crisis of 1830–33 when all leading Agency Houses collapsed.[22] They were replaced by a new kind of business organization in the form of Managing Agency Houses, which took over the management of various joint stock companies. Managing Agency Houses undertook all management functions of the managed companies, including establishing and running the business as well as raising finances. They also used to hold a limited number of shares of their managed companies.[23] In 1834 Dwarakanath Tagore, one of the wealthiest merchants of Calcutta in partnership with William Carr, an indigo trader set up Carr, Tagore and Company which was one of the most energetic Managing Agency Houses. He purchased a coal mine and steamboat in its name and then forming joint stock companies with his British and Indian business partners placed their management in the hands of

20   Pradip Sinha, *Calcutta in Urban History* (Calcutta: Firma KLM, 1978), 16–18.

21   B.B Misra, *The Indian Middle Classes: Their Growth in Modern Times* (New Delhi: Oxford University Press, 1960), 89.

22   Bhattacharya, *The Sentinels of Culture*, 42–44.

23   Umakanth Varottil, "Corporate Law in Colonial India: Rise and Demise of the Managing Agency System," in *Colonial Adventures: Commercial Law and Practice in the Making,* eds. Serge Dauchy, Heikki Pihlajamäki, Albrecht Cordes, and Dave De ruysscher (Leiden: Brill, 2021), 246.

his firm. This became a standard template for business operation with respect to Managing Agency Houses.[24] Another leading merchant of Calcutta Motilal Seal started a firm in partnership with the Europeans and set up the Oswald and Seal Company after the crisis of 1830–33.[25] Thus, these ambitious men first worked as brokers and middlemen attached to the Europeans and their firms, learnt trading lessons, amassed a huge amount of wealth, and then set up firms and businesses of their own independently or in collaboration with the British. They came to constitute a subservient capitalist class with significant stake in trade and commerce. However, by the middle of the nineteenth century, the indigenous entrepreneurs had lost their interest in trade and commerce. This was partly caused by the worldwide commercial crisis of 1847 and consequent crash of the Union Bank of Bengal in 1847–48, that affected several prominent families of Calcutta. These commercial failures shook the trust of the indigenous businessmen in the European style of business. Another important factor was diminishing dependence of the Agency Houses on indigenous capital due to the increasing availability of British finance capital. This occurred as a result of the development of a monopoly through the system of Managing Agency Houses which now started to act as links with the major finance groups in the city of London and which provided the channel for the import of British finance capital.[26] Calcutta's foreign trade, its shipping, banking, insurance and even its manufacturing industry of jute and cotton came to be entirely run by the European Agency Houses. It was European capital which launched these jute and cotton mills which were developing along the banks of the river Hooghly in late nineteenth century. On the other hand, internal trade came to be dominated by men from other Indian provinces, mainly the *Marwaris* who began to operate in Calcutta's Barabazaar area.[27] In the face of competition from British finance capital the indigenous entrepreneurs preferred to withdraw their capital from business activities and reinvest it in land. They began to purchase *zamindaris*, intermediate tenures, or urban real estate. One example is the *zamindari* of the Mukherji family of Uttarpara in Hugli. The failure of the Agency Houses, wiping off a large part of the family's fortunes, marked

---

24   Blair B. Kling, "The Origin of the Managing Agency System in India," *Journal of Asian Studies* 26, 1 (1966): 37–47.

25   Bhattacharya, *The Sentinels of Culture*, 43.

26   McGuire, *The Making of a Colonial Mind*, 13–14.

27   Anil Seal, *The Emergence of Indian Nationalism* (Cambridge: Cambridge University Press, 2007), 50.

a turning point, and the purchase of land became a more secure investment option for this family.[28]

This move by the indigenous entrepreneurs to invest in land was also motivated by the growing attractiveness of landed property after the introduction of Permanent Settlement in 1793. With the introduction of Permanent Settlement, the landlords acquired perpetual and hereditary proprietary rights over land subject to the payment of a fixed revenue to the British Government. The rights of hereditary succession of the heirs or lawful successors of the landlords were also recognized.[29] The permanence of the system created a sense of economic security and made land a stable and profitable source of income. In other words, it offered to the landholders the prospects of earning substantial surpluses after rent collection and payments to the government.

As a result, land value and agricultural prices subsequently soared. Land prices started to increase from 1806–07 onwards and continued to increase till the economic depression caused by the commercial failures between 1830 and 1834. Again, the general depression caused by the failure of the Union Bank in 1847–48 adversely affected the land prices. But after 1857 the land prices started to pick up and until about the end of the first world war, the highest prices prevailed between 1859 and 1879.[30] In this economic atmosphere, investment in land became a highly lucrative option. This attracted to land many of Calcutta's wealthy merchants who started to purchase *zamindaris*. Further, the initial assessment of revenue under Permanent Settlement was quite high and many of the existing *zamindari* establishments were not able to immediately start achieving the target level of rent collection. Consequently, many old *zamindaris* fell into the hands of more commercially oriented landlords or city based wealthy merchants when the government confiscated many *zamindaris* for revenue arrears and put them up for auction.[31]

The opportunities to invest in land further expanded with increasing sub-infeudation of land. Sub-infeudation was the product of a practice started by a few *zamindari* houses to sub-let their land for meeting the revenue demand. This practice was given legal recognition by the Patni Regulation of 1819. This

28   B.B Chaudhuri, "Land Market in Eastern India, 1793–1940 Part II: The Changing Composition of the Landed Society," *The Indian Economic & Social History Review* 12, no. 2 (1975): 144–45.

29   Sekhar Bandyopadhyay, *From Plassey to Partition and After: A History of Modern India* (New Delhi: Orient BlackSwan, 2016), 84.

30   B.B Chaudhuri, "Land Market in Eastern India, 1793–1940, Part I: The Movement of Land Prices," *The Indian Economic & Social History Review* 12, no. 1 (1975), 14, 27, 39.

31   Partha Chatterjee, "The Colonial State and Peasant Resistance in Bengal 1920–1947," *Past and Present* 110 (1986): 173.

threw open different levels of intermediate land tenures and rent-collecting rights for sale, giving impetus to sub-infeudation of land.[32] The great bulk of purchasers of such intermediate tenures came from Calcutta's merchant class, which gradually became a non-productive class of rent receivers rather than agricultural entrepreneurs. With their gradual dissociation from comprador type of business activities they no longer remained filthy rich with a luxurious lifestyle of the previous times but retained a reasonable amount of economic affluence, extracting substantial rents from *zamindaris* and intermediate tenures.[33] But in the later decades of the nineteenth century the returns from land began to dip and it became increasingly difficult for the rentier class to sustain their affluence by remaining solely dependent on land. While sub infeudation expanded at a rapid rate increasing the number of intermediaries, agricultural productivity remained stagnant, and population grew much more rapidly than at any previous time. Furthermore, in the second half of the nineteenth century significant curbs were imposed through legislative measures like the Rent Act of 1859 and Bengal Tenancy Act of 1885 on rent enhancements and eviction of tenants.[34] This came to adversely affect the process of appropriation of surplus product in the form of rent by the city-based rentier class.[35]

All these factors led to a decrease in profit from land. In such circumstances, it became increasingly necessary for the rentier class to supplement their income from land by some other source of income. As a result, the members of this class increasingly concentrated their energies on acquiring English education in the hope of obtaining jobs in government and private sectors. Though the rent they were earning from land was no longer sufficient to maintain their earlier affluence, it was just adequate to gain entry into elite educational institutions of Calcutta like Hindu College. At that time, an entry into these intuitions guaranteed a place in colonial bureaucracy.[36] This group successfully

---

32   Amit Bhaduri, "The Evolution of Land Relations in Eastern India under British Rule," *Indian Economic and Social History Review* 13 (1976): 47.

33   Bhattacharya, *The Sentinels of Culture*, 51–53.

34   The Rent Act of 1859 conferred occupancy rights on tenants who had held land for twelve years and also imposed some restrictions on enhancement of rent. The said twelve years rule was continued in the Bengal Tenancy Act of 1885, but it went one step further by extending this principle to the extent that any person who had continuously cultivated any plot of land as a *raiyat* (tenant) in any particular village for twelve years became a settled *raiyat* of the village with occupancy rights. See for details, N K Sinha, "Agrarian Economy and Agrarian Relations in Bengal- 1859–1885," in *History of Bengal, 1757–1905*, ed. N.K Sinha (Calcutta: Calcutta University Press, 1967), 295–298, 304–305.

35   Alan Smalley, "The Colonial State and Agrarian Structure in Bengal," *Journal of Contemporary Asia* 13 (1983): 186–87.

36   Bhattacharya, *The Sentinels of Culture*, 63.

supplemented their rental earning, but in the process they ended up gradually disassociating themselves from agricultural production. Ratnalekha Ray has described how Pal Chaudhuris of Mahesganj, had to cope with decrease in rental income by engaging in diverse economic activities and by seeking alternative means of livelihood including modern urban occupations.[37] Similarly, N. K Bose has documented the change in the livelihood patterns of the famous Sinha family of Raipur in Birbhum district. S. P Sinha or Lord Sinha, a famous lawyer and a moderate Congressman who was the first Indian to be appointed as Advocate-General of Bengal in 1908, and the first Indian to become a member of the Governor-General's Executive Council in 1909 belonged to this family. His ancestor Lalmohan had settled a large number of weavers in Raipur and adjoining areas and later Lalmohan's son Shyamkishore began to supply coarse cloth to the British by acting as a *bania* (business agent) of John Cheap, an employee of British East India Company. In the process the Sinha family became wealthy and bought the *zamindari* of Rajnagar in Birbhum district from the ruling family of Rajnagar. Later the members of this family became engaged in indigo trade in collaboration with the British. But with declining profit from indigo trade and diminishing income from the *zamindari* as it broke up into many branches, the succeeding generations migrated to Calcutta and became engaged in professions like medicine, law and civil service.[38]

On the other hand, simultaneous to the rise of a rentier class, there emerged a salaried class among the *bhadralok*. The expansion of colonial bureaucracy created several salaried positions which demanded college degrees. This led many ambitious individuals from rural areas to flock to cities and towns in search of educational and professional opportunities. They were mainly from families of petty landowners. With their meagre income they were in no position to afford the fees of the prestigious Presidency College. Still, they did their best to educate their children in English. They used to send their children to missionary colleges with less fees, or, from the 1870s onwards to *bhadralok* controlled colleges which charged even cheaper fees.[39] Thus, English education gradually became for this class of *bhadalok* the most important and often the sole material means of subsistence. However, job opportunities were not plentiful. Only a few could manage to grab respectable well-paying positions, while

37   Ratnalekha Ray, "The Changing Fortunes of the Bengali Gentry under Colonial Rule – Pal Chaudhuris of Mahesganj, 1800–1950," *Modern Asian Studies* 21, no. 3 (1987): 511–19.

38   Nirmal Kumar Bose, *The Structure of Hindu Society*, trans. Andre Beteille (New Delhi: Orient Longman, 1996), 142–46.

39   McGuire, *The Making of a Colonial Mind*, 53.

the majority had to remain content with ill-paid clerical jobs in the lower rungs of bureaucracy and commercial enterprises.

Thus, the more affluent rentier class as well as small landowners came to rely on western education for livelihood though in different degrees. Their dependence on land also lessened over time. By 1891 the great majority of educated and professional men had clearly cut loose from dependence on agriculture; only about 7 percent of government officers and clerks, 10 percent of lawyers, 10 percent of teachers, and less than one percent of literary men had a connection with land.[40] Thus, the *bhadralok* gradually evolved from being a landed class to a primarily professional class. Pressed by economic necessities, individuals belonging to the *bhadralok* category despite holding different class positions became united in their efforts to achieve English education and to imbibe a set of cultural norms produced by English education. This created a sense of cultural oneness amidst increasing caste and class fluidities, giving rise to a unified cultural identity in the form of *bhadralok identity*.

3   From Culture to Politics: Tracing the Roots of *Bhadralok* Hegemony

The story of the emergence of *bhadralok* hegemony and that of the marriage between *bhadralok* culture and Left politics are intimately interlinked. Both the stories started to unfold together more evidently in the early decades of the twentieth century. It was under the influence of radical Socialist and Marxist ideas that the *bhadralok* started to realise the necessity to build bridges with the masses. This realisation led to conscious efforts to bring about acculturation of the masses into *bhadralok* culture, creating a fertile condition for the genesis of *bhadralok* hegemony. The hegemony of the *bhadralok* could not have become entrenched without the construction of a social and political discourse supportive of that hegemony. The *bhadralok* found such a political discourse in Left-wing ideology.

As already highlighted, the *bhadralok* is an open and non-ascriptive group. But since acquisition of western education, which was a necessary criterion for the attainment of *bhadralok* status, was dependent upon the economic capacity to access educational avenues, the opportunities for the lower orders of the society to acquire *bhadralok* status were quite limited in practical terms throughout the nineteenth century. Education was not only costly, but

---

40   *1891 Census, Bengal,* IV, table XVII, 836–52, taken from Anil Seal, *The Emergence of Indian Nationalism* (Cambridge: Cambridge University Press, 2007), 57.

the system of education was often non-inclusive. The private schools were mainly meant for the education of the children of the indigenous elite and it was difficult for the children of the normal families to obtain admission in those schools. Sanskrit College till 1854 admitted only higher caste students.[41] Hindu College opened itself for non-Hindus only in 1855 when it was renamed as Presidency College and became a government institution. Thus, the education system "was controlled by the *bhadralok* primarily in the interests of the *bhadralok*".[42] A common apprehension which perturbed various sections of the *bhadralok* was that the dissemination of higher education among the lower orders would enable them to shun their traditional occupations and rise above their social station. Bengali tracts relating to the issue of education ranging from the high culture of Vidyasagar to the cheap tracts of unknown authors expressed this common fear. While some members of the *bhadralok* community opposed spread of education among lower classes, majority of them were in favour of controlled and limited spread of particularized education among the lower classes.[43]

On the other hand, the new culture promoted by western education proved particularly hostile to folk or popular culture. Before the arrival of the British, the elite and the masses shared a common cultural life. Cultural acts like *palagan* (musical play), *kirtan* (devotional chorus song), *jatra* (folk theatre), *sangs* (pantomime), *khemta* and *kheur* (popular and apparently vulgar song and dance forms), *panchali* (religious ballad song) *tarja* (poetic duel), and *kabigaan* (musical duel) mostly performed by the lower caste poets, singers and dancers were common sources of enjoyment for both rich landlords and poor peasants. But the emerging *bhadralok* culture equipped with Victorian sensibilities found the content and style of these folk cultural forms obscene. Since the middle of the nineteenth century attempts were made to censor such indigenous cultural expressions through legislation and public campaign. Consequently, *jatra* gave way to modern theatre and play which increasingly came to portray events and characters from ancient Sanskrit classics. Similarly, traditional lyrical verses like *kathakata* and *panchali* presenting erotic and sensual love affairs of mythological characters was replaced by a new genre of poetry represented by Madhusudan Dutta, Hemchandra Bandyopadhyay and Nabinchandra Sen. This new form of poetry was composed in a sankritized

---

41   At the beginning, only the Brahmans and *Baidyas* were allowed admission in Sanskrit College. The *Kayasthas* were allowed in January 1851 and ultimately the college decided to open its doors to all respectable Hindus in December 1854.

42   Broomfield, *Elite Conflict*, 9.

43   Bhattacharya, *The Sentinels of Culture*, 91, 161, 183.

Bengali, and it dug up characters from ancient Indian history and epics and presented them in the style of Greek epics. Thus, the new literature gave up sensual love in favour of romantic love.[44] In this way, in the nineteenth century western educated *bhadralok* self-consciously withdrew themselves from the indigenous cultural space inhabited by a vast multitude of the impoverished and ignorant masses, preferring to erect rigid aesthetic walls in order to separate their cultural arena from that of the lower orders.

Therefore, during much of the nineteenth century *bhadralok* culture remained socially secluded with the *bhadralok* steadfastly attempting to keep a safe distance from the masses and jealously preventing percolation of learning and traits of cultural refinement down the social ladder. Tagore in one of his political essays entitled *Byadhi o Pratikar* (The Disease and its Remedy) which he wrote in 1907 castigated this elitist mentality of the *bhadralok*, blaming it for the lack of participation of the lower classes in the Swadeshi movement:

> When suddenly the English educated urbanite goes to the peasant and says 'we are brothers' the peasant does not understand what it means. Those who we usually call 'that damn peasant', those people whose everyday life is of no concern to us, those people who are no more to us than some statistics in government reports, those whom we do not stand by in their life misery-those are the people we suddenly call upon as our brothers who must buy (*khadi*) cloth at a higher price and face baton charge by the *Gurkha* (policeman) when we want to fight the government, and that kind of call fails to convince anyone.[45]

However, at the same time liberal education also exposed a section of the *bhadralok* to the radical and egalitarian ideas of the west. Towards the end of the nineteenth century some vague Socialist ideas started to influence the Bengali mind. This became manifest in Bengali *bhadralok's* increasing concern for the toiling masses. Egalitarian ideas started to influence prominent Bengali *bhadralok* such as Bankim Chandra Chatterjee and Vivekananda as the nineteenth century drew towards an end. In his essay *'Samya'* (equality) Bankim

---

44   See, Sumanta Banerjee, *The Parlour and the Streets: Elite and Popular Culture in Nineteenth Century Calcutta* (Calcutta: Seagull, 1998), 78–198; Sumanta Banerjee, "Bogey of the Bawdy Changing Concept of 'Obscenity' in 19th Century Bengali Culture," *Economic and Political Weekly* 22, no. 29 (1987): 1197–1206; Anindita Ghosh, "Singing in a New World: Street Songs and Urban Experience in Colonial Calcutta," *History Workshop Journal* 7 (2013), 111–136.

45   Sabyasachi Bhattacharya, *Rabindranath Tagore- An Interpretation* (Penguine, Gurgaon, 2011), 95.

Chandra Chatterjee discussed the ideas of equality as enunciated by Utopian Socialists like Louis Blanc, Robert Owen and Saint Simon and traced them back to Rousseau. Describing Communism as a 'fruit of the tree' grown out of the seed sown by Rousseau he called the Utopian Socialists as 'wise and perceptive'. Bankim discussed their ideas to make a case for the elimination of unjust artificial inequalities which he associated in Indian context with three kinds of differences: between the Brahman and the *Sudra*, between the foreigner and the Indian, and above all between the rich and the poor. He also included in this essay a moving account of the oppression of a poor peasant Paran Madal to present a practical picture of the inequality existing between rich *zamindars* and poor peasants. Bankim's fundamental purpose for recapitulating the arguments of European egalitarianism was to advocate equal rights, which he expressed in the following words:

> No one should … think "I am a big man by birth, others are small men by birth". You have not been born in a superior class because of any qualities you possess; he who is born in an inferior class is not because of any faults of his. Therefore, the lowly born is as entitled to the pleasures of earth as you are. Do not place hindrances in the path of his happiness; remember that he is your brother – your equal. Against principles of justice and because of faults inherent in legal systems, there are those who inherit property from their ancestors as well as titles that connote kingship and immense power. They need to remember that Paran Mandal, who is a Bengali farmer, is their brother and their equal. No man has control over his birth. Paran Mandal was not lowly born because of inferior qualities. The property that the king enjoys alone, is property to which Paran Mandal also has a right. Through principles of justice.[46]

Swami Vivekananda also thematized the question of equality via the figure of the *Sudra* or the low caste.[47] In such thematization the influence of Socialist ideas becomes quite evident if we consider the following passage from his essay *Bartaman Bharat* (India at Present):

---

46   Bankim Chandra Chattopadhyay, transl. Bibek Deboy, *Samya* (New Delhi: Liberty Institute, 2002), 31.

47   Prathama Banerjee, "Between the Political and the Nonpolitical: the Vivekananda Moment and a Critique of the Social in Colonial Bengal, 1890s–1910s," *Social History* 39, no. 3 (2014), 336.

A time will come when there will be the rising of the *Sudra* class, with their *Sudra-hood*; that is to say, not like that as at present when the *Sudras* are becoming great by acquiring the characteristic qualities of the *Vaishya* or the *Kshatriya*, but a time will come when the *Sudras* of every country, with their inborn *Sudra* nature and habits – not becoming in essence *Vaishya* or *Kshatriya*, but remaining as *Sudras* – will gain absolute supremacy in every society. The first glow of the dawn of this new power has already begun to break slowly upon the Western world, and the thoughtful are at their wits' end to reflect upon the final issue of this fresh phenomenon. Socialism, Anarchism, Nihilism, and other like sects are the vanguard of the social revolution that is to follow.[48]

Expression of such sentiments in favour of radical egalitarian outlook reflected the changing political mood of time. Nevertheless, they were not identical with a full grown belief in or any systematic advocacy of the ideology of Marxism or Socialism. As K.M Pannikar observes, in nineteenth century the general critique of inequality and poverty was situated within a *bourgeois* perspective. While inequality was decried, the ameliorative measures suggested for betterment of the condition of the poor did not call for denouncement of the very system and structure responsible for the genesis and reproduction of such inequality. With regard to Swamy Vivekananda, Pannikar argues that Vivekananda, despite being able to visualise a future rightly belonging to the *Sudras* and to identify God with the poor, ended up offering knowledge and spiritual enlightenment as solutions.[49] It was not until the start of the twentieth century and more specifically till the 1920s, that radical Socialist and Communist ideas and organizations began to make some real headway in Bengal, giving rise to a strong Socialist/Marxist political tradition. It is this tradition that subsequently exerted indelible influence on *bhadralok* culture and identity.

Most of the early Communist stalwarts of India were *bhadralok* revolutionaries like M.N Roy, Abani Mukherjee, Virendranath Chatterjee and Nalini Gupta. During the days of Swadeshi and anti-partition movements in Bengal their goal was to organize an armed revolution against the British government with foreign help. While their goal remained unaltered, ideologically they turned to Communism in later years. They also forged links with the two most prominent underground revolutionary parties of Bengal, Anushilan and Jugantar. These groups believed in Hindu revivalism and their cadres almost

---

48   Swami Vivekananda, *Bartaman Bharat* (Calcutta: Udbodhan, 1905), 46–47.
49   K. N. Panikkar, "Culture and Consciousness in Modern India: A Historical Perspective," *Social Scientist* 18, no. 4 (1990), 12–13.

exclusively belonged to the higher caste Hindu *bhadralok*. Still they established contacts with the Bengali Communists in the hope of receiving arms and funds from Soviet Union. In the process, many important leaders of these revolutionary parties like Gopen Chakravarty, Bhupendranath Dutta, Amulya Adhikari, Sachindranath Sanyal, Satis Pakrasi, Pramath Bhowmik and Gopal Basak, to name a few, turned into ardent Communists.[50] After the Chittagong raid in 1930, the British government arrested in one sweep almost the entire leadership of the revolutionary movement in Bengal. In prison the revolutionaries came in touch with Marxist literature and Communists resulting in mass conversion of Bengali revolutionaries to Communism. This ideological shift was borne out of the increasing realization that sporadic raids and assassinations perpetrated by a tiny group of revolutionaries were not enough to achieve the goal of Indian independence. The need to mobilize the common masses was becoming increasing clearer to them. At the same time, they had little faith in the path of non-violence. They were therefore, looking for a more appropriate ideology compatible with their methods and goals. A great many of them ultimately found such an ideology in Communism which had little sympathy for non-violence as a political strategy.[51] A great number of revolutionaries released between 1934 and 1938 thus, had become Communists. In 1937 Anushilan Samiti committed the party to an adherence to 'Scientific Socialist' principles, declaring, "We accept Marxism fully and as such declare ourselves as Marxists". While the party still retained faith in the goal of an armed revolution its program stated: "we do not believe in the efficiency of terrorism as a method to realize that goal–nor do we accept the principles of Intelligentsia Insurrection". The Jugantar Party leadership, without mentioning the terms 'Marxist' or 'Socialist' also vowed to eliminate of both 'imperialism' and 'feudalism' within India, stating, "We will conduct the revolutionary struggle in such a way that after the seizure of political power the social control shall vest in the masses themselves".[52]

The exposure to Socialism and Communism proved quite consequential for the *bhadralok*. It jolted the social insularity that had become entrenched in the collective mentality of the colonial middle class. In other words, the Socialist/Marxist political tradition marked a major break with much of the

---

50   Gautam Chattopadhyay, *Communism and Bengal's Freedom Movement, Volume 1* (New Delhi: People's Publishing House, 1970), 53–64, 127–162.

51   Marcus F. Franda, *Radical Politics in West Bengal* (Massachusetta: MIT Press, 1971), 16–20.

52   Michael Silvestri, "The Bomb, Bhadralok, Bhagavad Gita, and Dan Breen: Terrorism in Bengal and Its Relation to the European Experience," *Terrorism and Political Violence* 21, vol. 1 (2009): 19–20.

elitist preoccupation of the culture and politics of the *bhadralok*. The emergence of Communist and Socialist organizations signified increasing efforts to organize workers and peasants. It was a series of peasants' conferences that culminated in 1925 in the All-Bengal Peasants' Conference at Bogra where the Labour-Swaraj Party, later renamed as Workers and Peasants Party was formed.[53] Thus, a new ideological interest in the working class and cultivating class began to take shape. Now, it became a common practice to use words like 'worker' or 'labour' in naming middle class organizations. The proliferation in the 1920s and even later of political parties, like the Labour-Swaraj Party (1925), Workers and Peasants Party (1928) and Labour Party (1932) points to this new ideological trend in the *bhadralok* political scene.[54] Most importantly, the Bengal unit of the Congress party under the leadership of Subhas Chandra Bose and his elder brother Sarat Bose also started to undergo radicalisation in the 1930s due to the emergence of a radical Left wing within the party. This radical Left wing emerged with the increasing influx of the Communists into the Bengal Congress. With the adoption of the Communist Party of India's 'United Front' strategy of working with the Congress party many revolutionaries turned Communists after being released from prison in the mid 1930s joined the Congress party. Almost all the members of the Anushilan Samiti joined the Congress Socialist Party (CSP), which was a leftist wing within the Congress . The Jugantar revolutionaries also joined the Congress becoming ardent supporters of Subhas Chandra Bose. In 1938 the leadership of Jugantar voted to dissolve the organization to formally merge with the Congress. Many of them also joined the Royists (the followers of M.N Roy), a Marxist group which was also functioning within the Congress. By the end of the 1938, virtually all ex-revolutionaries, many of them now Marxists had become members of the Congress and got affiliated with one or the other leftist group inside the Congress. They all rallied behind Subhas Chandra Bose who emerged as the poster boy of the Congress Left-wing.[55]

Under the rising influence of the Left wing within the Congress party in Bengal, the programme and politics of the BPCC (Bengal Provincial Congress Committee) underwent a leftward shift. While the Left- minded Congress workers in different districts started to mobilize the peasants and the Muslims masses, abolition of Permanent Settlement and suspension of rent payments

---

53 Bipan Chandra. *India's Struggle for Independence* (New Delhi: Penguin, 1989), 295.

54 Dipesh Chakrabarty, *Provincializing Europe: Postcolonial Thought and Historical Difference* (Princeton, New Jersey: Princeton University Press, 2008), 148.

55 David M. Laushey, *Bengal Terrorism and Marxist* Left (Calcutta: Firma K.L.M, 1975), 124–126.

entered into the agrarian agenda of the party. The party opposed the Bengal
Tenancy Amendment Act, 1938 on the ground that it favoured the rich and
middle peasants and neglected the interests of the under-tenants or actual cultivators. Thus, the party couched its opposition to the Act in ultra-leftist terms
and called for suspension of rents to be paid by the under-tenants.[56] According
to Partha Chatterjee the Congress stance on the Bengal Tenancy Amendment
Act, 1938 was not solely motivated by politicking but it was a reflection of the
ongoing "process of general radicalisation of middle class ideology and culture" which was to become the "dominant feature of organised political life
in West Bengal". Chatterjee attributes the radicalisation of the *bhadralok* to
their growing dissociation from landed property and their consequent transformation into a professional middle class "predominantly urban in its livelihood and social outlook".[57] Thus, a dramatic political transformation began to
unfold due to the growing influence of radical political ideas. Under the leadership of the Communists the trade unions began to emerge as powerful and
militant organizations in Calcutta's factories, while in the rural areas, strong
and effective peasant associations started to come into existence.[58]

Most importantly, with an ideological turn towards the Left the *bhadralok*
culture gradually started to step out of its narrow social confines to reach out
to the masses. This set into motion the process of acculturation of the masses
into the *bhadralok* value system. Dipesh Chakrabarty has described how the
bhadralok Marxists of the earlier generations started to view organization as a
matter of political education for the workers. The Bengali Communists in the
1920s, 30s and 40s set up study circles among the workers and made them familiar with the contents of Marxist writings and radical journals. Indrajit Gupta,
a stalwart Communist leader endorsed this approach to political organization
when in 1952 he urged the Communists to promote 'cultural and social activity'
among jute mill workers "through libraries, night schools, schools for workers'
children, drama and music groups".[59] This process of cultural outreach also
gained pace with increasing spread of education in rural areas particularly
after independence. With the spread of education through proliferation of

56   Joya Chatterjee, *Bengal Divided: Hindu Communalism and Partition* (Cambridge: Cambridge
     University Press, 2002), 109–112, 119.
57   Partha Chatterjee, *Bengal, 1920–1947, The Land Question* (Calcutta: K. P Bagchi, 1984),
     172–173,177.
58   Preman Addy and Ibne Azad, "Politics and Culture in Bengal," *New Left Review* 79
     (1973):109–110.
59   Dipesh Chakrabarty, "Trade Unions in a Hierarchical Culture: The Jute Workers of
     Calcutta, 1950–52," in *Subaltern Studies, Volume. III*, ed. Ranajit Guha (New Delhi: Oxford
     University Press, 2014), 128–129.

schools and colleges, the masses became exposed to *bhadralok* values through their teachers who were archetypal *bhadralok*. Many of them had strong leftist ideological leanings. A.E Ruud's field research has highlighted as to how village leaders in their youth came in contact with Left minded teachers and developed progressive Socialist outlook. One important area in which they first applied their values was inter-caste relations resulting in elimination of the norms of caste commensality.[60] Introduction of the representative political institutions at the grass-roots also proved crucial in overcoming the cultural gulf between the *bhadralok* and lower caste groups in the rural society. Competitive politics made it necessary for the *bhadralok* to make political overtures to the lower castes. Marvin Davis' field research carried out in the 1970s demonstrated how the two upper caste claimants to the position of *Panchayat Pradhan* (chairperson) in the village he studied attended the marriage of a *Bagdi* family to enlist the support of the *Bagdis* in the *Panchayat* elections, and also recognized the *Bagdis'* claim to being *Bagra-Khatriyas*.[61]

This spirit of mass outreach also spilled over to the world of literature and culture. Beginning in the 1930s Marxist cultural productions started to experiment with the representation of the working class and peasants, placing them at the centre of middle-class cultural consciousness. Songs and plays began to be composed in increasing numbers with workers and peasants as heroes. Indian People's Theatre Association (IPTA), a Marxist cultural organization in the 1940s began to collect folk songs from rural areas and then attempting a cultural synthesis urbanized and restyled them to suit middle caste taste and preferences.[62] The folk forms such as *jatra* which had gradually lost *bhadralok* patronage with the arrival of the European theatre in Calcutta were revived by the leftist playwrights of the IPTA. This brought about 'secularization' and 'proletarization' of *jatra* themes. In its modernized avatar, *jatra* now came to deal with secular themes and earlier emphasis on devotional aspects receded into the background. This transformation began with the staging in 1962 of *Chemra Tar* (Broken String) – a play made into a *jatra* by the Art Theatre of Kanchrapara followed by the enactment of *Ekti Paysa* (A Single Penny) by Satyambar Opera in 1963. These *jatra* performances set off a whole new trend of *jatras* centred upon the life of the lower middle class and the poor, often involving adaptation popular Bengali novels and depiction of lives and times

---

60   A. E Ruud, *Poetics of Village Politics: the Making of West Bengal's Rural Communism* (New Delhi: Oxford University Press, 2003), 75–88.

61   Davis, Marvin, *Rank and Rivalry: The Politics of Inequality in Rural West Bengal* (New Delhi: Select Service Syndicate, 1986), 108–171.

62   Banerjee, *The Parlour and the Streets*, 6–7.

of famous personalities ranging from Bengali luminaries like Rammohan Roy and Vidyasagar to foreign revolutionaries like Lenin, Ho- Chi-Minh and Mao-Tse-Tung.[63] Moreover, *jatras* also gradually came to be written and performed in a *bhadralok* created standard colloquial Bengali bereft of the rusticities of local dialects.[64]

Thus, significant cultural efforts were deployed for the construction of a bridge between the masses and the *bhadralok*. Rajarshi Dasgupta has pointed out that one of the most important objectives of Marxist poetry represented by popular poets like Sukanta Bhattacharya was to overcome the gulf between *bhadralok* culture and popular culture. It played a crucial role in enabling the Communists to reach out to the ordinary people "through their familiar cultural idioms, bypassing formal pedagogy" and by "translating the high text of Marxism into popular and accessible scripts". Salil Chowdhury's songs as well as those of other IPTA composers like Benoy Roy and Hemanga Biswas, made frequent use of the "imagery of peasants sharpening the sickle, for harvesting and resisting oppression".[65] The influx of radical Socialist ideas also spawned a scathing critique of literary creations which were divorced from reality. Much of this critique was directed at the great Rabindranath Tagore. Tagore was accused of being bereft of realism in his writings. Young writers associated with new and *avant-garde* magazines such as *Kallol* (1923), *Kalikalam* (1926), *Pragati* (1927), *Parichay* (1931), and *Kabita* (1935) began to highlight the relative absence of social reality in Tagore's poetry. *Kallol* influenced by Marxism and Freudian thoughts and infused with a rebellious spirit particularly became a powerful literary movement. However, Tagore as a writer was not entirely cut off from social reality. Tagore's prose writings, particularly his short stories documented the socio-economic situation of rural life exhibiting a great deal of realism. But it was his poetry that seldom presented any sense of realism, portraying the Bengali village as a land of grace and beauty, his golden Bengal. Stung by the charge that his poetry had failed to mirror the realities of everyday social life, Tagore ended up inventing a new genre of literature called *gadyakabita* or prose-poetry. Most of the products of this genre, *Punascha*, *Shesh Shaptak*, *Patraput*, and *Shyamali* being the most notable, came out between 1932 and 1936.[66] Influenced by this emerging ideological climate other prominent authors like Manik Bandyopadhyay, Bibhuti Bhusan Bandyopadhyay,

63   Pabitra Sarkar, "Jatra: The Popular Traditional Theatre of Bengal," *Journal of South Asian Literature* 10, no. 2/4 (1975):103–104.

64   Ruud, *Poetics of Village Politics*, 100.

65   Rajarshi Dasgupta, "Rhyming Revolution: Marxism and Culture in Colonial Bengal," *Studies in History* 21, no. 1 (2005): 89.

66   Chakrabarty, *Provincializing Europe*, 151–163.

Tarashankar Bandyopadhyay and Mahesweta Devi exhibited a passionate incli-nation to highlight rural themes and rural issues in their writings. Similarly, Satyajit Ray, Ritwick Ghatak and Mrinal Sen attempted a sensitive portrayal of rural scenario on the silver screen. Ray's masterpiece Pather Panchali was the most classic and hard-hitting display of the agony of rural life. Thus, with the development of a sympathetic attitude to rural peasant life, the rural peasant came to occupy a significant place in the political and cultural imagination of the *bhadralok*.[67]

Thus, the development of radical political ideas brought about plebeian-ization of Bengali literary and cultural production. This process also brought into existence a new kind of social *imaginaire* that clearly broke away from the earlier tradition of writing novels and poems on aristocratic characters such as landed gentry, *Rajput* generals and even Mughal emperors.[68] There occurred a visible change in literary preferences of the common people too. While the earlier generations mostly read religious literature and epics, writ-ings by authors like Saratchandra Chattopadhyay, Manik Bandyopadhay, Bibhuti Bhusan Bandyopadhyay and Tarashankar Bandyopadhyay became popular among the new generations of rural population exposed to modern education and *bhadralok* value system.[69] Dialect and dress also underwent vis-ible changes. Sudipta Kaviraj notes that the sharp contrast that existed in the 1950s between the formal middle class Bengali language and the Bengali lan-guage spoken by the lower classes has now disappeared to a significant extent with the emergence of a standard homogenised Bengali dialect popularised by film idol Uttar Kumar and radio newscaster Debdulal Bandyopadhyay. Thus, Kaviraj attributes the emergence of a widely spoken standardized Bengali lan-guage to the role of radio and popular film, which are the vehicles of *bhadralok* culture and also to the 'efficacy of social emulation' which again testifies to the prevalence of a widespread tendency of the lower orders to absorb *bhadralok* norms and values. Similarly, the dress distinctions that had prevailed in the 1950s between different classes also evaporated by the 1980s "in favour of the

---

67   Monobina Gupta, *Left Politics in Bengal: Time Travels among Bhadralok Marxists* (New Delhi: Orient BlackSwan, 2010), 183–84.

68   Subho Basu and Auritro Majumder, "Dilemmas of Parliamentary Communism," *Critical Asian Studies* 45, no. 2 (2013), 173.

69   Ruud has pointed out the immense popularity of Saratchandra's Chattopadhyay's *Palli Samaj* and *Srikanta* and Tarashankar's Bandyopadhyay's *Ganadebata, Panchagram* and *Hasuli Banker Upakatha* and Manik Bandyopadhay's *Putulnacher Itikatha* and *Padma Nadir Majhi* among the rural people. See Ruud, *Poetics of Village Politics*, 88–95.

universal synthetic shirts and trousers, worn of course with the usual class differentials of style and cleaniness".[70]

Furthermore, a growing recognition developed among the Bengali Marxists of the exclusionary and elite character of the *bhadralok* directed project of Bengal renaissance and its failure to influence the socio-cultural outlook of the general masses. The alienation of the *bhadralok* from the masses became a recurrent theme in the writings of Marxist intellectuals like Samar Sen. Sen's description of the *bhadralok* as "Mirzafar's progeny, the fruits of Macaulay's poison tree" became a very popular phrase, indicative of the profound imperfections of the Bengali middle class. The *bhadralok* Marxists did present themselves as heirs to the nineteenth century renaissance tradition of progressive thought and social reform, but at the same time they embarked upon a serious auto-critique of their own class. In the 1970s this auto-critique most dramatically manifested in the efforts of a group of Left minded scholars to reassess the transformative effects of Bengal renaissance. The starting point of their reassessment of the renaissance tradition was Susobhan Sarkar's *On the Bengal Renaissance*, a widely read work of seminal importance, which had credited the *bhadralok* social reformers of the nineteenth century for bringing about progressive social change comparable to the momentous social transformation experienced by Italy during European Renaissance.[71] Their critique reveals that the colonial middle class was not a class of progressive *bourgeoisie* as it was neither fully modern nor national in its social outlook, as reflected in its frequent compromises with religious orthodoxy and also its consistent collaboration with colonialism. Sumit Sarkar's works have presented copious evidences of such compromise and collaboration, highlighting the fact that the colonial middle class lacked commitment, desire and potential to bring about any fundamental social transformation and to lay the foundation for a bourgeois democratic revolution and a national state. Thus, collaboration with the British and deep disconnect from the masses were the principal limitations of the indigenous intelligentsia of the nineteenth century.[72] Asok Sen's classic work on Vidyasagar has also made similar arguments. Sen's study has shown how Vidyasagar's initiatives for social reform found little support from within his own class and how despite his own disputation of the reasonableness of scriptures, he had to invoke scriptural sanction to gain social legitimacy in

70   Sudipta Kaviraj, "The Culture of Representative Democracy," in *Democracy in India*, ed. Nirja Gopal Jayal (New Delhi: Oxford University Press, 2014), 248–249.

71   Susobhan Sarkar, *On the Bengal Renaissance* (Calcutta: Papyrus, 1979).

72   See Sumit Sarkar, *A Critique of Colonial India* (Calcutta: Papyrus, 1985); Sumit Sarkar, *"Calcutta and the Bengal Renaissance,"* 95–105.

favour of the practice of widow-remarriage.[73] This re-evaluation of the renaissance tradition and of the historical role of the colonial middle class also reflected the growing recognition by the *bhadralok* of their alienation from the masses, and such recognition in turn directed them more and more to a consciously chosen path of complex accommodation of the lower orders.

This process accelerated and became infused with a greater sense of purpose after political consolidation of the Left forces in post-colonial West Bengal, with the *bhadralok* devising different ways to culturally accommodate various groups and communities in their own terms. In this context, it is imperative to recall our discussion in the previous chapter about the complex interaction between rural peasant ethics and *bhadralok* norms. A.E Ruud has pointed out that the Left parties placed before the rural masses the desired *chasi* (peasant) way of life, the *chasi* model. This model while endorsing the hard work and frugality of peasant life assimilated *bhadralok* values which calls for sexual restraint, cleanliness, greater engagement with the culture of learning and abandonment of moral vices like drinking. Literacy in the extended sense of knowledge of poetry, drama and Tagore songs and cultural activities like celebration of Tagore's birth anniversary and *jatra* performances became fundamental components of the ideal *chasi* lifestyle. Thus, political association with the Left parties provided an alternative route to social mobility to the lower castes, enabling them to change negative social stereotypes about them through adherence to a model of social conduct, which is the product of a fusion between *bhadralok* values and ethics of peasant life.[74] Installation of such an alternative route to social mobility, contingent upon conformity to a code of social conduct, threw open the *bhadralok* status to a large number of lower caste individuals. This lent popular legitimacy to the political authority of the Left parties. But more importantly, by drawing lower orders into the matrix of the *bhadralok* value system, it reinforced the cultural hegemony of the *bhadralok*, instrumentalized through the upper caste leadership of the Left parties. Inevitably, therefore, the *bhadralok* as a social group, over the years, has become more heterogeneous in both class and caste terms. After independence, increased government spending and other associated economic changes, together with the physical expansion of the city of Calcutta resulted in significant social changes. With college education no longer remaining as

---

73   See Asok Sen, *Iswar Chandra Vidyasagar and His Elusive Milestones* (Calcutta: Riddhi, 1977).

74   A. E Ruud, "From Untouchable to Communist: Wealth and Status among Supporters of the Communist Party (Marxist) in Rural West Bengal," in *Sonar Bangla? Agricultural Growth and Agrarian Change in West Bengal and Bangladesh,* eds. Ben Rogaly, Barbara Hariss-White and Sugata Bose (New Delhi: Sage, 1999), 253–78.

expensive as before, *bhadralok* status has now become open to a much larger number of people, particularly those who are at the lower end of the middle class, and are in a position to have access to college education and information, through one form of media or the other such as newspapers, television and radio.[75] My field research has also illustrated how the upwardly mobile individuals of the *Namasudra* community in Mekhlapur village lay a claim to the cultural signifiers of the *bhadralok* status on the basis of urban white collar employment and college education.[76]

It is this increasing inclusiveness of the *bhadralok* social category that contributes to the continual reproduction of the hegemony of *bhadralok* culture. Sarbani Banerjee's analysis of the writings of two radical *dalit* Bengali writers, Adhir Biswas and Manoranjan Byapari provides valuable insights as to how the cultural hegemony of the *bhadralok* sustains itself by using knowledge as an entry point to regulate the accommodation of lower caste individuals into the *bhadralok* world. She has shown through her analysis that even radical *dalit* writers who are vehement critics of Brahmanism, after gaining entry into the realm of *bhadralok* respectability through their literary prowess, psychologically succumbs to a process of unconscious internalisation of the 'normative concepts of *bhadralok* ideology' and behaviour in everyday life and ultimately ends up participating in their reproduction. The findings of my field research presented in the previous chapter have also uncovered the tendency of the lower caste groups to emulate the *bhadralok* value system rather than countering it, primarily due to the prospects of socio-cultural mobility offered by the *bhadralok* model. As a result, the possibility of emergence of a powerful counterculture or counter-public markedly distinct from and antithetical to the *bhadralok* value system is continually warded off. The tool of learning and a living code of social ethics act as powerful devices of co-option, through which the upwardly mobile lower caste individuals are offered the opportunity of being absorbed into the *bhadralok* society in a manner that reproduces *bhadralok* hegemony rather than posing a challenge to it.

Briefly put, the above discussion points to the continuing cultural correspondence between the *bhadralok* and other social groups, which facilitates a process of steady acculturation of the lower orders into the *bhadralok* value system. However, such acculturation does not imply that popular culture has faded away. Subaltern historiography has divulged that the autonomy of subaltern consciousness is often maintained through occasional surrender to and

---

75   Parimal Ghosh, *What Happened to the Bhadralok* (New Delhi: Primus, 2016), 217–225.
76   See Chapter 6.

compromise with the dominant culture. The consciousness of the subordinated groups consists of two dialectical ingredients, one autonomous and the other adopted. In this context, we can derive some analytical insights from a study by Gautam Bhadra, a historian of the subaltern school, on a poem called *Kantanama* written by a village elder in 1842–43. Bhadra's perceptive analytical scrutiny reveals that the subaltern consciousness while possessing a degree of autonomy also has a tendency to import from elite culture. He finds that the author of *Kantanama* freely borrowed images and ideas from both popular and elite culture while at the same time remoulding them to suit the requirements of his textual objective. This suggests that ideas do transcend frontiers of class and often become shared, though not necessarily in full measure.[77] This largely explains why the efforts of the Left minded *bhadralok* to assimilate the masses into their cultural world could prove successful in turning the *bhadralok* culture into a much more shared value system cutting across social fault-lines. It is this transformation of *bhadralok* culture into a shared value system that contributed immensely to the installation of *bhadralok* hegemony to which the lower castes have seemingly acquiesced and consented. However, this is not to suggest that the process of acculturation of the masses into the *bhadralok* value system erased entirely the cultural divide between the two groups. As Dipesh Chakraborty's study on Calcutta's jute mill unions between 1920 and 1950 shows that the *bhadralok* leaders of Left politics and the rank and file remained separated by a cultural divide. The leaders despite their genuine commitment to class politics failed to bridge the cultural gulf that separated them from the lower orders. Still, their sincere outreach to the common masses and their dedication to the cause of the upliftment of the workers ensured popular acceptance of their leadership and also lent legitimacy to the political culture of class politics.[78] Thus, the *bhadralok* hegemony came to be constructed around a Left-wing discourse which gave final shape to an exceedingly nebulous value system, which is now commonly identified as *bhadralok* culture. In other words, the *bhadralok* hegemony drew strength from a secular Left-wing political culture, which consolidated and stabilized it by making it appear more inclusive and embracing. Most importantly, the marriage between *bhadralok* culture and Marxism facilitated ideological subsumption of the discourse of caste by that of class.

---

77   Gautam Bhadra, "The Mentality of Subalternity: Kantanama or Rajdharma," in *Subaltern Studies, Volume VI*, ed. Ranajit Guha (New Delhi: Oxford University Press, 1994), 54–91.

78   Dipesh Chakrabarty, *Rethinking Working-Class History: Bengal 1890–1940* (Princeton: Princeton University Press), 151–154.

I have so far highlighted the ideological conversion of a considerable section of the *bhadralok* into Marxism, culminating into the emergence of cultural hegemony of the *bhadralok*. Before proceeding further it is imperative to ask why a section of the *bhadralok* embraced Marxism at a specific juncture and remained its adherents afterwards. Marxism appealed to the wider Bengali society because it seemed useful to the task of catering to important social and political purposes. To a considerable extent, the relative marginalization of the *bhadralok* in national politics, since the 1920s, contributed to their subsequent drift towards Leftism as an alternative brand of politics. The rise of Gandhi in Indian politics had instilled in them a strong sense of exclusion. During the first two decades of twentieth century Bengal loomed large in the national politics with Bengali politicians enjoying a strong grip and control over the course of national politics. But in the 1920s this control steady started to move out of their hands. With the transfer of capital from Calcutta to Delhi in 1911, the province got reduced to just another part of India. The beginning of the 1920s saw the meteoric rise of Gandhi in Indian politics and with the rise of Gandhi the main theatre of politics now more clearly shifted out of Bengal. The Bengali politicians increasingly came to be seen as regional leaders. Moreover, it was not only the national political mainstream from which the Bengali *bhadralok* got uprooted. Their unassailable influence over provincial politics also came under serious challenge. Earlier Congress leaders of national stature like S.N Banerjee, Bal Gangadhar Tilak, Gopal Krishna Gokhale and Annie Beasant had enjoyed a great deal of autonomy in the political affairs of their respective provinces. But now Gandhi introduced a new kind of politics where the national leadership would decide the form and modality of provincial politics and the role of regional political leaders would only be confined to complementing the larger goals of national political struggle. The Bengalis, who for so long had enjoyed privileged position in national movement were not ready to step back and let a non-Bengali to decide the political course of actions in their own province.[79]

In this backdrop, they interpreted Gandhian leadership as Hindi belt's domination over Bengal. The strongest political challenges faced by Gandhi in his entire political career to his leadership came from Bengali politicians like C.R Das and Subhash Chandra Bose. The BPCC (Bengal Provincial Congress Committee) throughout the 1920s and 1930s had worked at cross purposes with the AICC (All India Congress Committee). In the 1920s there were frequent tensions between the AICC under the leadership of Gandhi and the

---

79   Broomfield, *Elite Conflict*, 147.

BPCC controlled by C.R Das and his associates and the latter often found it convenient to whip up the Bengali regional sentiments to oppose the AICC. When the Congress did not make the Bengal Pact[80] a national pact, C.R Das ventilated his frustration in the following words:

> Why is this resentment against Bengal? What has Bengal done? ... The Bengal provincial Congress Committee has made its suggestion. It may be right or it may be utterly wrong ... is Bengal debarred from making that suggestion ... You may delete Bengal national Pact from the Resolution. But I assure you, you cannot delete Bengal from the Indian National Congress or from the history of India ... She is intimately associated with the history of all political agitation from the commencement of the Congress down to the present day.[81]

After the death of C.R Das, the Bengali opposition to Gandhi was carried forward by Subhas Chandra Bose. Bose had little respect for the Gandhi's strategy of complete non-violence. It was his difference with Gandhi that ultimately led him to sever his relationship with the Congress party. This refusal to be absorbed by a Hindi leadership has remained an integral aspect of the political mindset of the Bengali political elite. The dominant Bengali outlook has been aptly summed up by Leonard A. Gordon- "In the regional version of the past shared by some Bengalis, Mahatma Gandhi is the chief anti-hero. He is blamed for the Bengali's decline within the movement, for the Partition of India, and for the vanquishing of Bengal's favourite son, Subhas Bose".[82] Thus, Gandhian politics was seen as threat to the autonomy of Bengal's regional aspirations and identity. "Gandhi was the quintessential representative of Hindi-India from which the Bengali elite wanted to disassociate."[83]

---

80 Bengal pact of 1923 drafted by C.R Das in consultation with the prominent Bengali Muslim leaders envisaged power sharing arrangement between the Hindus the Muslims in Bengal with the purpose of easing off communal tension. However, this pact was not approved by the national leadership of the Congress party. For details, see Manju Gopal Mukherjee, "C.R. Das and the Bengal Pact," *Proceedings of the Indian History Congress* 61 (2000):739–746.

81 Chittaranjan Das, "Indian National Pact and Bengal National Pact," in *Political Thinkers of Modern India: Chittaranjan Das*, ed. Veriender Grover (New Delhi: Deep and Deep, 2016), 87–88.

82 Leonard A. Gordon, *Bengal: The Nationalist Movement 1876–1940* (New Delhi: Manohar, 1974), 293.

83 Atul Kohli, "From Elite Radicalism to Democratic Consolidation: The Rise of Reform Communism in West Bengal," in *Dominance and State Power in Modern India: Decline*

The Partition in 1947 further contributed to the anti-Gandhi and anti-Congress feeling. Many Bengalis developed a very critical attitude towards Congress and its main leaders, Gandhi and Nehru, for their failure to prevent Partition which had left the Hindu Bengalis with only one-third of their original golden Bengal. Bharati Mukherjee observes, "Bengal's average masses could not accept it (Partition) easily and did not hesitate to censure Gandhiji and Nehru as 'conspirators' and 'protagonists' of Hindi imperialism".[84] A sizeable section of the Bengali people, as a result, developed either a lukewarm or a hostile attitude towards the Congress party which continued to be seen as a political mouthpiece of the Hindi heartland even after independence.[85] They felt that the great victory of the Congress had been achieved at the cost of their distress and dislocation. One social constituency which particularly developed an aversion for the Congress was the large group of refugees, who had come from East Bengal after the Partition in 1947. They blamed the Congress government for its inability to guarantee adequate refugee relief and to bring about full exchange of population as had happened in Punjab. Many refugees in their struggle against the government turned to the Left parties, which mobilized them invoking the rhetoric of class struggle. Their demands for economic relief came to be articulated in Socialist and Marxist idioms. Further, in response to the attempt of the government to evict the refugees from the squatters' colonies, their struggle was projected as a *de facto* urban land reform movement, as the refugees perceived government's intervention as attempts to safeguard the interests of the rich and propertied class.[86] Indeed, one squatters' colony came to be known as 'Bijaygarh' (fortress of victory), synonymous of the victory of the refugees in urban class struggle against the government and propertied interests.[87] It needs to be highlighted here that the East Bengali refugees came to form a solid support base of the Left parties, contributing immensely to the subsequent electoral success of the Left Front.

Thus, the growing feeling of aversion among a sizeable section of the Bengali population for the so-called Hindi domination represented by the Congress party, generated the need for an alternative brand of politics distinctively

of a social Order, Volume. II, eds. M.S. A Rao and Francine Frankel (New Delhi: Oxford University Press, 1990), 392.

84   Bharati Mukherjee, *Political Culture and Leadership in India: A Study of West Bengal* (New Delhi: Mittal, 1991), 71.

85   Kohli, "From Elite Radicalism to Democratic Consolidation," 407.

86   Joya Chatterjee, *Bengal Divided: Hindu Communalism and Partition* (Cambridge: Cambridge University Press, 2002), 291–295.

87   Nilanjana Chatterjee, "The East Bengal Refugees: A Lesson in Survival," in *Calcutta: The Living City, Vol II* ed. Sukanta Chaudhuri (Calcutta: Oxford University Press, 1990), 73.

Bengali in character and steadfastly un-amenable to absorption within the dominant North Indian pattern. It is this need for an alternative politics which resulted in a drift towards Left politics and rejection of the Congress, creating a fertile ground for the rise of Left parties with local Bengali leadership. At the time of independence Congress party organizationally was not very strong in Bengal. In the late 1930s and 1940s institutional politics had remained dominated by Muslim political organizations like Krishak Praja Party and Muslim League. In addition, continuous friction between BPCC and AICC and marginalization of the most popular Bengali political leader Subhas Bose by the AICC further weakened the mass base of the Congress party in Bengal. Moreover, by the time of independence radical politics had already established strong roots. A sizeable number of political workers had already become Communist sympathizers.

Thus, one of the major reasons for Bengal's adoption of Marxism and Communism also lay in the urge of the Bengalis for a distinctive regional identity and the need to have access to regional power.[88] The CPI(M) gave the appearance of a distinctively Bengali party practicing a brand of home-grown Left politics. One of the ways through which it created this impression was by continuously complaining about biased and discriminatory attitude of the central government towards West Bengal's legitimate demands and aspirations.[89] This resonated well with the sense of defeat of the frustrated *bhadralok* who felt that they had lost out to the Hindi-speaking Gangetic heartland. As a result, the Communist movement in Bengal in spite of being a class movement in a theoretical sense, allowed itself to become tied to regional sentiments and identity for the sake of building a wider mass base.

Apart from the desire to safeguard regional identity another important factor played a crucial role in the development of the *bhadralok*'s fascination for Marxism. Post colonial West Bengal witnessed a separation between economic power on one hand and political and cultural power on the other. The *Marwaris* who had established themselves in markets of Calcutta's Barabazar by the end of the nineteenth century gradually transformed themselves from a community of traders to a commercial community. Using their speculative skills, they emerged as leading stock market speculators and investors. They also took great advantage of the new opportunities for profit and speculation that opened up during the First World War in jute, cotton, grain and spice trade. Wartime profits allowed them to gradually enter the industrial scenario.

88   See, Franda, *Radical Politics in West Bengal,* 5–44.

89   Shibashis Chatterjee, "Regionalism in West Bengal: A Critical Engagement," *India Review* 13, no. 4 (2014): 422.

By the 1930s there were five *Marwari* jute-mills in and around Calcutta, the first being set up in 1919 by the Birlas.[90] Moreover, during the last decades of the colonial rule *Marwari* businessmen managed to wrest control of several companies. On one hand, the *Marwari* shareholders by taking advantage of market fluctuations started to increase their shareholding in companies through stock markets. On the other hand, since the managing agents of companies during periods of cash crunch often used to obtain loans at attractive interest rates from the *Marwaris* by pledging shares they held in their managed companies, the *Marwari* businessmen ended up acquiring control over several companies in the event of the failure of loan repayment.[91] The evolution of the *Marwaris* of Calcutta into a commercial community picked up greater pace with the removal of British obstructionism after independence. They eventually came to establish their firm control over commercial activities in Calcutta after independence. The Bengali *bhadralok* found themselves in no position to match the economic success and financial might of the *Marwaris*. I have already discussed in previous part of this chapter, how the *bhadralok* by the early decades of the twentieth century had turned into a class of urban professionals, dissociated from not only agriculture but also business activities. In other words, the Bengali community failed to produce a class of industrial or commercial *bourgeoisie*. In such a scenario, for the Bengali *bhadralok*, bereft of material bases of dominance, intellectual activity became the dominant mode of self-assertion. Being excluded from the domain of economic power, they established their supremacy over the political and cultural spheres. This produced important consequences. Due to non-Bengali composition of the capitalist class, capitalist values failed to become an integral part of the Bengali social consciousness. Furthermore, the exclusion from commercial activities also generated antipathy among the Bengalis to *Marwari* economic domination. This contributed to the development of a value system which is derisive of pursuit of wealth, profit and entrepreneurship and excessively euphoric about cultural, academic and artistic accomplishments. This kind of social outlook created a fertile ground for the consolidation of the Left political forces, since Marxism appeared as a promising tool to challenge the dominance and social efficacy of the *Marwari* traders and merchants whose control over the economic activities had become unassailable. As a result, Marxism struck a chord with the Bengali upper caste

---

90   Pradip Sinha, "Calcutta and the Currents of History, 1690–1912," in *Calcutta: The Living City, Vol I*, ed. Sukanta Chaudhuri (Calcutta: Oxford University Press, 1990), 42–43.

91   Umakanth Varottil, "Corporate Law in Colonial India: Rise and Demise of the Managing Agency System," *Centre for Law & Business Working Paper 15/06*, National University of Singapore (2015): 17–18.

elite.[92] However, since they staked their heart on the class based secular ideology of Marxism, they had to forgo the opportunity of claiming social leadership on the ground of their superior caste status or relative economic affluence vis-à-vis the common Bengali masses. They could only assert their social superiority on the basis of their educational and cultural accomplishments. This is one of the reasons why the *bhadralok*'s claim to social leadership was not based on their superior caste status or economic achievement but on the secular criteria of education, culture and superior ideology of Marxism. This produced an overall secularist disposition towards politics.

Summarizing our discussion in this section, it can be said that the organized Left-wing in West Bengal stood for and actively endorsed a set of values, norms and aspirations i.e., *bhadralok* culture, which was hegemonic in nature. *Bhadralok* culture became hegemonic because it was able to acquire the capacity to accommodate the lower orders of the society. The *bhadralok* evolved more and more into an open social category, amenable to the inclusion of lower caste individuals, if they could manage to acquire a set of social and cultural traits. Practical impediments like lack of access to education often came in the way of inclusion of the poor and lower castes into the *bhadralok* world. Nevertheless, the *bhadralok* culture by associating gentility with knowledge and a standard set of social and cultural traits rather than with wealth or caste , created an impression of being an open and inclusive system. It was this general impression that was the mainstay of *bhadralok* hegemony. Further, this hegemony became intimately intertwined with Left politics. In other words, the acquired ability of the *bhadralok* to accommodate the masses into their social and cultural world and the consequent emergence of *bhadralok* hegemony could largely be attributed to the political and ideological drift of a significant section of the *bhadralok* towards Left politics. Accompanying the *bhadralok* hegemony and reinforcing it in complex ways, Left politics through mass molilization of peasants and workers and intelligent intervention in the realms of literature and culture, fashioned a political ethos that eventually crystallized into a standard political template, comparable in many ways to what Antonio Gramsci refers to as 'common sense'. In other words, a shared mentality resulting out of a marriage between *bhadralok* values and Left wing discourse has become an integral part of West Bengal's commonsensical conception of politics. It is the analysis of this political common sense, which we shall turn to in the next section.

---

92   Kohli, "From Elite Radicalism to Democratic Consolidation," 401.

4   Dynamics of a Discourse: Political Culture in Operation

Gramsci describes 'common sense' as "the diffuse, uncoordinated features of a generic form of thought common to a particular period and a particular popular environment".[93] Arguing that all individuals are philosophers since all men and women have some conception of the world, he finds in 'common sense' the manifestation of the spontaneous philosophy of the people, which is distinct from the 'philosophy of the philosophers'. According to Gramsci 'common sense' is "the uncritical and largely unconscious way of perceiving and understanding the world that has become 'common' in any given epoch". Thus, in Gramsci's conception 'common sense' is a disorderly aggregate of common social and political perceptions, constituting the widespread conception of life and society, since it can't be reduced to unity and coherence unlike the 'philosophy of the philosophers'. Therefore, 'common sense', as argued by Gramsci, is identical with an "incoherent set of generally held assumptions and beliefs common to any given society".[94] Other scholars have also provided valuable insights about the role of 'common sense' while defining it in a more or less similar fashion. Clifford Geertz defines 'common sense' as a relatively less integrated but all pervasive cultural system represented by "epigrams, proverbs, *obiter dicta*, jokes, anecdotes, *contes morals*" not by "formal doctrines, axiomized theories or architectonic dogmas" and hence it can be grasped by "any person with faculties reasonably intact".[95] For Ann Swidler too common sense stands for "a set of assumptions so unselfconscious as to seem a natural, transparent, undeniable part of the structure of the world".[96] Following these definitions, we can conceptualize the common sense existing in the arena of politics or 'political common sense' as an entire range of unconsciously inherited and uncritically absorbed ideas, attitudes, symbols and images, which provide a framework to the people of a particular society to make sense of politics. Most importantly, if we apply the idea of common sense understood in this way to a political context, it will broadly translate into what is commonly referred to as 'political culture'. Political culture, as conceptualized by Gabriel Almond and Sidney Verba stands for common patterns of orientation toward political

---

93   Antonio Gramsci, *Selections from the Prison Notebooks* (New York: International Publishers, 1992), 330.
94   Gramsci, *Selections from the Prison Notebooks*, 322–23.
95   Clifford Geertz, "Common Sense as a Cultural System," *The Antioch Review* 33, no. 1 (1975): 8, 18, 23–24.
96   Ann Swidler, "Culture in Action: Symbols and Strategies," *American Sociological Review* 51, no. 2 (1986): 279.

objects.[97] In a similar vein Lucian Pye defines political culture as commonly shared underlying assumptions and rules that govern political behaviour.[98] Thus, political culture broadly refers to commonly shared political attitudes and appears to broadly approximate 'political common sense'.

In the context of our analysis of the Left-wing political culture of West Bengal, it is important to delve into the relationship between political culture and ideology. Explaining the relationship between culture and 'common sense', Swidler points out that, during settled period culture influences action by operating not in the form of ideology but in the form of tradition (defined as taken for granted cultural beliefs and practices) and 'common sense'. Ideology can govern action only during unsettled period or period of social transformation. But common sense is no way delinked from ideology. This is because "ideology has both diversified, by being adapted to varied life circumstances, and gone underground, so pervading ordinary experience as to blend imperceptibly into common-sense assumptions about what is true".[99] Gramsci also emphasizes that it is not possible to separate what is known as 'scientific' philosophy from the common and popular philosophy, which is only a 'fragmentary collection of ideas and opinions'.[100] Every philosophical current leaves behind a sedimentation of 'common sense'. "Common sense is the folklore of philosophy and is always half-way between folklore properly speaking and the philosophy, science, and economics of the specialists."[101]

Drawing insights from the theoretical literature on 'common sense' it can be said that commonsense is an integral part of the culture of a society but at the same time it is closely linked to ideology, since the commonsensical political attitudes unconsciously acquired by common people may well originate under the influence of a particular ideological climate. In the context of our study, it can therefore, be pointed out that at the level of mass consciousness, an ideology, in this case Marxism, does not have to necessarily exist as a full-grown ideological belief system. It can exist as what Gramsci calls 'fragmentary collection of ideas and opinions', equivalent to a set of common social perceptions and political attitudes that enable us to make

---

97   For detail, See Gabriel Almond and Sidney Verba, *The Civic Culture: Political Attitudes and Democracy in Five Nations* (Princeton: Princeton University Press, 1963).

98   Lucian Pye, "Introduction: Political Culture and Political Development," in *Political Culture and Political Development*, eds. Lucian Pye and Sidney Verba (Princeton: Princeton University Press, 1965), 3–26.

99   Swidler, "Culture in Action," 281.

100   Gramsci, *Selections from the Prison Notebooks*, 328.

101   Gramsci, *Selections from the Prison Notebooks*, 326.

sense of politics and society. But for this to happen, or in other words, for an ideology to become widely dispersed throughout the society as an integral part of the common sense of the age, it is important, as Gramsci notes, to work for overcoming the gulf between the elite and the masses. Then only it can form the basis of not only 'philosophy of the philosophers' but also 'spontaneous philosophy of the multitude'.[102] It is in this context that the importance of various efforts undertaken by the *bhadralok* towards cultural accommodation of the masses, as has been highlighted in the previous section, with regard to the emergence and consolidation of a Left-wing 'political common sense' or political culture in West Bengal should be understood. In post-colonial West Bengal this political common sense is embodied in several widely shared and deeply internalized general political conceptions and attitudes, shaped through the long and complex intercourse between *bhadralok* values and Left politics.

Based upon our discussion undertaken in the previous section, we can identify some of these constitutive elements of West Bengal's 'political commonsense' or political culture. In the first place, consistent articulation of Bengali regional identity and aspirations represents one core element of this 'political common sense'. The Left Front in West Bengal cultivated a quintessential Bengali core beneath its adopted ideology of Communism. T.J Nossiter has pointed out that there are dual Communist nationalities among Indian Marxists. There are *Keralite*, Bengali and *Tripuri* forms of Communism.[103] Despite being a class-based movement the Left Front in West Bengal made widespread use of Bengali regionalism for political purposes by projecting itself as a thoroughly Bengali political organization in culture and spirit. One of the ways it did so is by continuously harping on discrimination against West Bengal with regard to allocation of tax revenue and industrial licenses by the central government, which it projected as the spoke-person of the Hindi heartland of India.[104] A document released by the CPI(M) on the eve of thirty years of the Left Front government in West Bengal provides a glimpse of the narrative of discrimination the party employed:

---

102   Gramsci, *Selections from the Prison Notebooks*, 329–330.

103   T.J Nossiter, *Marxist State Governments in India* (London: Pinter Publishers, 1988), 187.

104   See, Polly Datta, "The Issue of Discrimination in Indian Federalism in Post-1977 Politics of West Bengal," *Comparative Studies of South Asia, Africa and the Middle East* 25, no. 2 (2005): 449–464; Rajani Ranjan Jha and Bavana Mishra, "Centre-state Relations, 1980–90: The Experience of West Bengal," *The Indian Journal of Political Science* 54, no. 2 (1993): 209–237.

For most parts of its lengthy tenure, the Left Front government has had to encounter hostile governments at the Centre. There was a conscious effort on the part of successive Central governments, particularly those run by the Congress, to discourage industrialization in West Bengal since it was a Left ruled State. This was done both through a denial of public sector investment as well as licenses for setting up private industries. During Indira Gandhi's tenure as the Prime minister in the early 1980s, a proposal for setting up an electronics complex in Salt Lake near Kolkata was shot down by the Central government on security grounds, because West Bengal was a border State! Permission for the Haldia Petrochemical project was withheld by the Central government for 11 long years. Moreover, the freight equalization policy for coal and iron ore robbed West Bengal, along with the other states in the Eastern region of India, of its locational advantage of being the most mineral rich region of the country. Following these discriminatory policies pursued by the Centre and the vitriolic anti-Communist propaganda carried out by the *bourgeois* media, which led to some degree of capital flight, West Bengal experienced industrial stagnation during the decade of the 1980s. [105]

Thus, the Left Front politicised issue of financial discrimination against Bengal. It was frequently raised in political campaigning and sloganeering evoking Bengali regional sentiments. *Bandhs* (shut down of all economic activities) and demonstrations against the discriminatory policies of the centre were common occurrences during the Left Front rule. Lurking behind the issue of financial discrimination remained an injured feeling of Bengali sub-nationalism having deep historical roots. The Left Front could successfully link the issue of discrimination against Bengal with Bengali regional identity, as a strong and widespread sense of victimization at the hands of Hindi heartland had already been prevailing in the Bengali psyche. The Left parties found great political potential in the emotive nature of Bengali regionalism and made championing and upholding of Bengali sub-national identity an integral component of the established political practice of West Bengal.

Further, the 'political common sense' fashioned by the Left also entailed salience of class as the principal political idiom through which pro-poor orientation of the Left parties was communicated. The primacy of the political vocabulary of class was drawn from a philosophy of non-parochial and

---

105   Statement of the CPI(M) on Thirty Years of the Left Front Government in West Bengal, available at https://www.cpim.org/content/thirty-years-left-front-government-west -bengal.

universalist Left-wing progressivism or what Partha Chatterjee calls the 'universalist ideology of progressive modernity', which by privileging the language of class delegitimized that of caste.[106] We have already highlighted how the demands of the primarily upper caste refugees of the squatters' colonies were articulated in class terms as parts of a wider demand of the poor for land reform and redistribution through confiscation of the excess land of the rich. Thirdly, Left politics created a culture of political activism by resorting to what Thomas B. Hansen defines as 'politics of permanent performance'. 'Politics of permanent performance' as described by Hansen operates through "the construction of images and spectacles, forms of speech, dress and public behaviour that promotes the identity of a movement or party, defines its members and promotes its cause or worldview". He further points out that "political performances are indeed about constructing spectacles, but it is very much about a certain styling of the self, the movement or the cause- by the use of certain linguistic style or conceptual vocabulary, a certain way of dressing or acting in public".[107] In West Bengal the 'politics of permanent performance' was put into effect by encouraging continuous engagement in political activities through organization of not only huge political rallies and processions but also discussions, cultural programmes and conferences by various mass organizations affiliated to the CPI(M) and other smaller Left parties. Such events organised almost on a continuous basis by organizations of women, youths, students, teachers, farmers and workers affiliated to the Left parties resorted to ritualistic performance of songs, sloganeering ceremonies and hoisting of red flags in order to sustain a Socialist imagination in public mind. As a result, a repertoire of established symbols and slogans associated with Communism ranging from hammer and sickle to May Day emerged as familiar tools to translate the complex principles of Marxism into accessible scripts for the masses. Motifs, metaphors, slogans, graffiti, songs and posters, all got combined together in a project of communicating the key messages of Marxism in ways relatable to lived experience, forging the construction of a Left-wing 'political common sense' in popular consciousness.

Lastly, with the *bhadralok*'s drift towards Left politics pride in Bengal's cultural achievements, which is a distinguishing mark of the *bhadralok* identity,

---

106   Partha Chatterjee, "Partition and the Mysterious Disappearance of Caste in Bengal," in *Politics of Caste in West Bengal,* eds. Uday Chandra, Geir Heierstad and Kenneth Bo Nielsen (New Delhi: Routledge, 2016), 99.

107   Thomas B. Hansen, "The Politics of Permanent Performance. The Production of Authority in the Locality," in *Politics of Cultural Mobilization in India,* eds. John Zavos, Andrew Wyatt and Vernon Marston Hewitt (New Delhi, Oxford University Press, 2004), 23.

also creeped into politics as a ploy to exploit Bengali regional sentiments. Political appropriation of the leading figures of the Bengal renaissance and Bengali leaders of the national movement became a standard *modus operandi* to claim inheritance to the glorious cultural and political heritage of Bengal. As a result, the everyday vocabulary of politics used in political debates, campaigns and rallies became infused with frequent references to Bengali stalwarts in the fields of art, literature, and nationalist politics. The portrayal of the Bengali cultural and intellectual icons as the ideological forefathers of present-day politics apparently made intellectualism politically fashionable, and also created a widely shared perception of Bengal's politics being an exception to the so-called crude and pedestrian politics of North India, which particularly drew contempt from the educated and progressive *bhadralok* for its unabashed tendency to encourage caste mobilization.

The thirty-four years long Left rule was ended by the Trinamool Congress (TMC) led by Ms. Mamata Banerjee in 2011. By virtue of an extraordinarily long rule, the Left was able to shape West Bengal's political culture in a particular direction reinforcing *bhadralok* hegemony and institutionalizing a non-identitarian politics of class. The TMC was known for a populist brand of politics that used to attract frequent and heavy criticism from the educated *bhadralok* during the heydays of Left politics. The rise of the TMC as a credible political force after 2008–09 and the eventual defeat of the Left Front in 2011 created widespread speculation about the decline of *bhadralok* hegemony. TMC supremo Ms. Mamata Banerjee is a Brahman by caste and most other prominent leaders of the party also belong to the higher castes. Still, due to her apparent lack of cultural sophistication and humble background, in the eyes of many, she did not make the cut for the status of a *bhadromohila*, the female counterpart of *bhadrolok*.[108] A *bhadralok* politician is supposed to be culturally refined and educated and is also supposed to have a taste for art, literature and poetry. Chief Ministers of West Bengal such as B.C. Roy, Siddhartha Shankar Ray, Jyoti Basu and Buddhadeb Bhattacharya have adhered to this well established model of public behaviour. It has been forcefully argued that Mamata Banerjee has deviated from this model making a significant dent into the hegemony of the *bhadralok*. She has "pluralized political leadership in West Bengal by bringing 'the vernacular' into the halls of power, in terms of dress, manners, language, as well as the imagery, symbolism and idioms of kinship

---

108   Singdhendu Bhattacharya, "Bengal Elections 2021: 'Party Society', 'Subaltern Hindutva', 'Bhadrolok': A Few Terms Dominating Media Coverage," *Outlook*, April 8, 2021, https:// www.outlookindia.com/website/story/india-news-bengal-elections-2021-party-society -subaltern-hindutva-bhadrolok-a-few-terms-dominating-media-coverage/379591.

and popular religion that surrounds her persona".[109] Though she is a higher caste individual born and brought up in Kolkata, she is widely considered as a voice of the poor and underclass.[110] Hence, the steady rise of the TMC has been interpreted as subalternization of West Bengal politics.[111] Though such a perception has some practical basis, one has to be careful about over emphasising it. A detailed analysis of the trends of political representation presented in Chapter 3 has already shown that the electoral success of the TMC has not promoted subalternization of politics by bringing about enhancement in the political representation of the lower castes. Political power is still concentrated in the hands of the higher castes. Therefore, if in accordance with the popular usage we equate *bhadralok* identity with the higher castes then the supposed decline of *bhadralok* influence in institutional politics does not appear to have any factual basis. Partha Chatterjee has also pointed out that "since the TMC is an even more centralized party than the CPI(M), the Calcutta centred structure of upper caste dominance of the entire political space continues unchallenged".[112] Additionally, from an electoral point of view, it is the *bhadralok* bastion of Kolkata and its suburbs which are considered to be the biggest strongholds of the TMC. In the 2019 general elections the TMC despite facing a major setback fared very well in urban areas, especially in and around Kolkata, while the BJP fared better in the rural areas far from Kolkata especially in the areas dominated by the lower and backward castes.[113] In the recently concluded Assembly elections of 2021 the TMC virtually won almost all seats in and around Kolkata, proving its hold over the social constituency of the *bhadralok*.

109   Kenneth Bo Nielsen, "Mamata Banerjee Redefining Female Leadership," in *India's Democracy: Diversity, Co-Optation, Resistance*, eds. A. E Ruud and Geir Heierstad (Oslo: Universitetsforlaget, 2016), 117–129.

110   Saroj Nagi, "Bucking the Trend," *Seminar* 622 (June 2011).

111   Ranabir Samaddar, "West Bengal Elections: The Verdict of Politics," *Economic & Political Weekly* 52, no. 24 (2016): 23–25; Sandip Roy, "Bamboos and Backsides: *Bhadralok* 'Horror' at Mamata is Classist and Sexist," *Firstpost*, December 5, 2014, http://www.firstpost.com/politics/bamboos-and-backsides-*bhadralok*-horror-at-mamata-is-classist-and-sexist-1833987.html; Dhrubo Jyoti, "Mamata's Massive Bengal Victory is the Death of the Gentleman in Kolkata," *Hindustan Times*, May 21, 2016, https://www.hindustantimes.com/assembly-elections/mamata-s-massive-bengal-victory-is-the-death-of-the-bhadralok-in-kolkata/story-NiTwCP9NqVFCzoTIgd42SP.html.

112   Chatterjee, "Historicising Caste," 86.

113   For an analysis of the 2019 general election results in West Bengal see, Ayan Guha, "Polarization Plus Anti-Incumbency: A Full Scale View of BJP's Rise in Bengal," *Mainstream Weekly* 57, no. 34 (2019).

When it comes to what we have identified as *bhadralok* culture, a close investigation reveals that far from being a veritable antithesis of whatever the *bhadralok* culture stands for, the TMC's politics is largely a continuation of the discourse and praxis shaped by the Left. A critical engagement with the discursive posturing of the TMC reveals a great deal of continuity with the politics practised by the Left Front. This becomes quite evident, particularly if we consider the cultural makeover of Ms. Mamata Banerjee accompanying her political rise, an aspect which has received scant scholarly attention.

The political rise of Mamata Banerjee came in the wake of the Singur-Nandigram movements against forcible farmland acquisition for industry. In 2006–07 the Left Front government attempted to forcibly acquire agricultural land for setting up industries in two different areas, one area was Singur in Hoogly district and the other was Nandigram in East Midnapore district. This gave rise to large protests by farmers, which ultimately snowballed into a massive anti-government movement under the leadership of Mamata Banerjee, then the leader of opposition in West Bengal.[114] Till the movements in Singur and Nandigram Ms. Banerjee's apparently rustic utterances and unsophisticated demeanour were widely perceived to be incongruous to the so-called *bhadralok* sensibilities. But after the Singur-Nandigram incidents she started to reinvent herself into a more refined and cultured persona and appropriate the political rhetoric and cultural idioms belonging to the vast ideological reservoir of the Left-wing political culture. Attempting a cultural makeover, she portrayed herself as a painter, a Tagore connoisseur well versed in his poetry, and also a respectful admirer of the spiritual traditions of Bengal represented by Ramakrishna and Vivekananda. On the other hand, carefully negotiating with the Left-wing rhetoric, idioms and cultural imageries, she re-entered the political scene as a firebrand protester leading popular movements and a radical political activist vaguely belonging to the agitational genre of Left politics.[115] In the process much of the sanitized gentility which marked the exterior of *bhadralok* politics withered away. But this made her selective appropriation of the Left-wing rhetoric more effective and impactful, enabling her to fashion herself as the true champion of the poor. In 2006 she announced in Nandigram that her party was the new heir to the 1946 Tebhaga movement. Songs of the IPTA began to be played at her rallies and families of people who had sacrificed their lives in Marxist led struggles such as the Food Movement of the

---

114   For details see, Kheya Bag, "Red Bengal's Rise and Fall," *New Left Review* 70 (2011): 91–98.

115   Ayan Guha, "West Bengal Elections: Unchanged Amidst Change," *Economic and Political Weekly* 51, no. 41 (2016): 70.

1960s were also honoured.[116] Thus, she attempted to appropriate the political legacy and cultural space associated with the Left. By drawing parallel between Nandigram movement and Tebhaga movement, by honoring those who sacrificed their lives in Marxist led struggles and by using the IPTA songs to mobilize masses against government atrocities in Singur and Nandigram she was attempting to carve out a space for herself in the leftist tradition of popular movement and agitational politics. Her principal slogan was *ma-mati-manush* (mother, land, and people) which gave voice to a powerful social *imaginaire* or a socio-political vision that "testifies to the very legacy of the Communist Left in West Bengal".[117] By organising protest rallies all across the state against land acquisition she also adopted quite effortlessly the Left's politics of performance which ultimately culminated in her twenty six days' long hunger strike which generated nation-wide attention. Today, one of the defining features of her politics remains frequent performance of powerful political spectacles through foot marches, processions, rallies, and cultural events to protest against the policies of the central government and to mobilize support for her party. A recent and visible specimen of this 'politics of permanent performance' was the long foot march which she undertook in Kolkata before the 2021 Assembly elections against the rise in prices of fuel and cooking gas, with her supporters holding red-coloured cardboard replicas of gas cylinder.[118]

It is quite interesting to note that at a time when the Left Front was steadily losing its political credibility, she did not position herself on the opposite end of the ideological continuum simply to mount a political challenge to the Left Front. She did not counter her political adversaries for being leftist, but she attacked them for being pseudo-leftists who had diverted from the true Marxist path. Mamata Banerjee in her election campaign repeatedly mentioned that she had great respect for the Communist ideology, but she was against the CPI(M) that had deviated from the Marxist path by adopting a pro-capitalist industrial policy.[119] This cleared the way for rapprochement between the TMC and the Left minded intellectuals who were increasingly becoming disillusioned with the CPI(M) after the Singur-Nandigram fiasco. It was also Mamata Banerjee's grand reconciliation with the *bhadralok* society

116   Monobina Gupta, *Didi: A Political Biography* (New Delhi: Harper Collins, 2012), 131–32.

117   Basu and Majumder, "Dilemmas of Parliamentary Communism,"180, 197.

118   Scroll Staff, "Mamata Banerjee Leads March against LPG Price Rise, Challenges PM for 'One-to-one' Contest," *Scroll*, March 7, 2021, https://scroll.in/latest/988851/mamata-banerjee-leads-march-against-lpg-price-rise-challenges-pm-for-one-to-one-contest.

119   Soutik Biswas, "Who Says Communism in Dead in Bengal," *BBC News Network South Asia*, May 12, 2011, http://www.bbc.com/news/world-south-asia-13371621.

that seemed to be slowly shaking off its inhibitions about her brand of politics. During the Singur-Nandigram movements she paid repeated visits to Ashok Ghosh, a senior Communist leader of the Forward Bloc, an ally of the CPI(M) to discuss the issue of land acquisition for industry while she refused to initiate discussion with the senior CPI(M)leaders.[120] She seemed to bring home the message that she had respect for the real Communists but contempt for those who had made a mockery of Communism by forcibly acquiring fertile farmland. Subsequently, she reached out to the small and independent Left-wing groups and disgruntled Left minded intellectuals outside the CPI(M) fold setting off a long series of collaborations with non-CPI(M) leftists of all hues and cry. During the Singur-Nandigram movement she was also ably advised and supported by Samir Putotundo, a leader of a small Left-wing political outfit who had earlier left the CPI(M) and Purnendo Basu, a Left-wing trade union leader.[121] Basu later came to hold important portfolios like labour and agriculture in Ms. Banerjee's Cabinet. Mamata Banerjee even entered into an electoral alliance with the SUCI (Socialist United Centre of India), known to be an ideologically rigid Socialist party before Lok Sabha elections in 2009.[122] Though many of these political alliances and understandings have failed to survive the test of time, they give us valuable insights into West Bengal's political culture.

Mamata Banerjee fought against a so-called Communist party but she neither steered clear of the leftist forces nor offered a thoroughly non-leftist alternative. Rather, she felt the need to reach out to the leftist elements outside the CPI(M) fold, particularly the Left-minded intellectuals to gain valuable legitimacy in the eyes of people. Such a political strategy was possibly dictated by recognition of the fact that it was necessary for wider social legitimacy to earn the backing of the *bhadralok* through reconciliation with *bhadralok* cultural icons and pivotal *bhadralok* values, particularly Marxism. Hence, denouncement of Communism and projection of a thoroughly anti-Left political alternative seemed counter-productive. Rather, Mamata Banerjee tried to create public appeal for her party by proclaiming that 'Left was no longer Left' since the Left had become an agent of the capitalists. Such political maneuvers and Mamata Banerjee's adjustments in her political style in the direction of

120   Telegraph Bureau, "A&A for Lunch and Tea," *Telegraph*, May 19, 2007, https://www.telegra
      phindia.com/india/a-a-for-lunch-and-tea/cid/707506.
121   Express News Service, "Former Mamata Allies Drift Towards Congress," *Indian Express*,
      November 16, 2010, http://archive.indianexpress.com/news/former-mamata-allies-drift
      -towards-cong/711686.
122   Subrata Basu, "CPM's Waterloo," *FrontierWeekly* 44, no. 11–14 (2011).

bhadralok deportment bring out the importance of *bhadralok* values as constituting the normative structure of legitimation in Bengali society.

In the light of this, it is hardly surprising that Mamata Banerjee tried to
collaborate with various Left-wing groups and forces in the state outside the
fold of the CPI(M). She also meticulously worked to gain the backing of the
Bengali intellectuals, most of whom, are known to harbour leftist ideological
leanings. Unexpectedly, she achieved great success in this direction. A host of
prominent Bengali personalities threw their weight behind her by launching
a vigorous civil society movement against the ruling Left Front and a powerful
campaign in her favour before the 2011 Assembly elections.[123] The blatant dis-
regard shown by the CPI(M) government to its own declared doctrine was the
reason furnished by them for their support to Mamata Banerjee, whom they
found to be more leftist than the so-called Communists belonging to the Left
Front. In other words, they found in Mamata Banerjee a substantial potential
of a leftist makeover due to her uncompromising struggle against forcible land
acquisition.[124]

Afterwards, many of these intellectuals formally joined the TMC. Some of
them even joined the TMC government's Council of Ministers and emerged as
Mamata Banerjee's trusted advisers on important policy issues, contributing to
the reproduction of a Left-wing political outlook at the level of governance and
political praxis.[125] TMC's approach towards various policy issues often reflects a

---

123   Renowned social activist and novelist Mahashweta Devi, theatre director Bibhash
       Chakravarty, educationist Sunanda Sanyal, painters like Subhaprasanna, Samir Aich and
       Jogen Chowdhury, singers like Kabir Suman and Nachiketa, poet Joy Goswami, theatre
       actors like Bratya Basu, Arpita Ghosh, Kaushik Sen, Shaoli Mitra were at the forefront of
       the campaign. Even Debabrata Bandyopadhyay, the former Land Reforms Commissioner
       of West Bengal who had crafted the Left Front's land reforms programme became one of
       the key members of Ms. Banerjee's intellectual brigade.
124   Sumanta Banerjee, "Paradoxes in Inventing Bengali Identity," *Seminar*, 2013, http://www
       .india-seminar.com.
125   Several pro-TMC intellectuals were sent by the party to the Parliament. Some were nomi-
       nated as members in the Rajya Sabha while others were to the Lok Sabha on a TMC ticket.
       Actor Bratya Basu was even inducted into the state Cabinet. He has held various cabinet
       positions since 2011. Currently he is the Education Minister. Actor Arpita Ghosh is today
       an elected member of the Lok Sabha from the TMC. She had also served as member of the
       Rajya Sabha from 2014 to 2019 on a TMC nomination. Singer Kabir Suman had also served
       as a member of the Lok Sabha from 2009 to 2014 as a TMC representative. Debabrata
       Bandyopadhyay in 2011 and Jogen Chowdhury in 2014 became members of the Rajya
       Sabha from the TMC. Other intellectuals have also been nominated to important posi-
       tions. During Ms. Banerjee's stinct as Railway Ministers Subhaprasanna and a few others
       were made as advisers or consultants in the railways ministry. Similarly, Shaoli Mitra was
       made the Chairperson of the Bangla Academy.

hangover of a Left-wing political culture. A case in point is the land acquisition policy or the issue of foreign direct investment (FDI). It is difficult to find any real difference in the stance of the Left and that of the TMC on the question of the land acquisition and FDI today. Rather, it looks that the TMC is more vehemently opposed to forcible land acquisition for industry and relaxation of FDI norms in crucial sectors of the economy. Among all opposition parties at the centre the TMC was most vocal against the Land Acquisition Ordinance, 2014 and The Right to Fair Compensation and Transparency in Land Acquisition, Rehabilitation and Resettlement (Amendment) Bill, 2015.[126] The TMC withdrew its support from the Congress led United Progressive Alliance (UPA) at the centre protesting against the decision of the central government to allow FDI in retail and increase in the prices of diesel and cooking gas in September, 2012. Thereafter, the party even moved a no-confidence motion in Parliament in November, 2012, terming the decision of the UPA government to allow FDI in retail as unconstitutional on the ground that liberal FDI norms violate the principle of Socialism enshrined in the Constitution.[127] Thus, it seems that the TMC in many ways has successfully taken over the mantle of the Left in West Bengal. In other words, cultural imageries and political idioms followed by the Left over the years have not been denounced by the TMC but they have only been subjected to required dose of adjustment in tune with political necessities.

Similarly, just like the Left the TMC also wholeheartedly embraced the narrative of centre's discrimination against Bengal in order to whip up the Bengali regional sentiments. As has already been highlighted, the CPI(M) in West Bengal presented itself as a distinctively Bengali party practicing a brand of home-grown Left politics. Following the legacy of the Left the TMC has modelled itself as a distinctively Bengali party. Rather, The TMC is even a more Bengali party than the CPI(M). Marxist discourse of the CPI(M) is imbued with a regional flavor. Nevertheless, the CPI(M) is a national party and therefore, its stand on national issues often necessitates occasional compromises with regard to its regional interests. Moreover, the Marxist discourse has a strong element of internationalism. It is only a local version of a global idea. "Although spiced with a distinctively Bengali flavour, the meat was a produce of several countries."[128] The TMC, on the other hand, is only concentrated in

---

126   http://aitcofficial.org/tag/land-ordinance/.

127   Press Trust of India, "TMC's Bid to Bring No-confidence Motion Fails in Lok Sabha," *Economic Times*, November 22, 2012, https://economictimes.indiatimes.com/news/polit ics-and-nation/tmcs-bid-to-bring-no-confidence-motion-fails-in-lok-sabha/articleshow/ 17320130.cms?from=mdr.

128   Ruud, *Poetics of Village Politics*, 74.

West Bengal with no real national presence. Its use of regionalism as a political weapon is therefore, even more aggressive.

Just like the CPI(M), the TMC frequently raises the issue of discrimination of Bengal by the Centre with regard to allocation of funds and resources. But it has gone a step further in projecting its Bengali identity. Mamata Banerjee is far more garrulous about expressing her identity as a Bengali, as a defender of the interest of Bengal: "After all I am from Bengal – Bengal's soil, Bengal's atmosphere, Bengal's produce are my valuable heritages."[129] The TMC has often criticised the CPI(M) for neglecting Bengali luminaries and remaining obsessed with foreign heroes like Marx and Lenin. Desperate to prove its Bengali credentials, the TMC government after coming to power went on a spree, naming and renaming metro stations, bridges, flyovers and streets after noted Bengali personalities. It also made Bengali language compulsory in all schools, including private English-medium schools, of the state. This decision was seen by many as an attempt to whip up Bengali regional sentiment to counter the political challenge posed by the rise of the Bharatiya Janata Party (BJP) which the TMC portrays as a North Indian party.[130] Mamata Banerjee today vehemently attacks the BJP leaders as outsiders having little knowledge about Bengal's culture and tradition. In election campaigns and rallies in the run up to the 2021 Assembly elections she repeatedly proclaimed that she would not allow outsiders from North India and Gujarat (the home state of Prime Minister Narendra Modi and Home Minister Amit Shah) to turn West Bengal into Gujarat or Uttar Pradesh.

However, there are limits to any reconciliation or accommodation. Mamata Banerjee has made some efforts to reach out to the *bhadralok* and refashion herself in a way that appears acceptable to *bhadralok* sensibilities. However, to the high priests of *bhadralok* culture her reincarnation as a chaste *bhadralok* politician still remains an unfinished project. Her cultured persona is often alleged to be a façade and she is accused of putting on a veneer of refined values which she is actually unable to internalize. If that be the case, then one needs to ask why such accommodation of *bhadralok* culture becomes necessary even for a mass leader like Mamata Banerjee. Mamata Banerjee's adjustments in her demeanour and style in the direction of the standard template of Left-wing *bhadralok* politics reflects the continuing hold of *bhadralok* culture as the normative structure of legitimation in Bengali society. One may speak the language of the masses, but this may not be enough to gain social

---

129   Quoted in Gupta, *Didi*, 131.
130   Special Correspondent, "Mamata makes Bengali Compulsory in Schools," *Hindu*, May 17, 2017, https://www.thehindu.com/news/cities/kolkata/mamata-makes-bengali-compuls ory-in-schools/article18471996.ece.

respectability. As it appears, in Bengal politics a leader needs to appear culturally refined and fairly enlightened to establish his or her claim to leadership. Perhaps that is the reason why just like former Chief Minister Buddhadeb Bhattacharya, Mamata Banerjee has kept the ministry of culture under her charge. In the standard political template of West Bengal, the highest leader needs to appear as a man or woman of culture. As Ranabir Samaddar puts it quite instructively, "while aesthetics became a mark of non-correspondence of a certain philosophy of life to its age, yet till today, politics can acquire mass legitimacy in Bengal only by aestheticising itself. It must not appear as coarse and vulgar. You must be ready to go to jail or face the gallows, but you must do so with songs on your lips. Bengal was eternal, beyond history, beyond the rules of life, because it was beautiful, and beauty was virtuous".[131] The importance of the powerful rhetoric of culture in politics of West Bengal was aptly captured by former Governor of West Bengal, Gopalkrishna Gandhi's incisive comment, "in how many places can one find a bibliophile chief minister who also writes poetry with sensitivity, and an opposition leader who sings and paints with feeling"?[132] This comment made in the backdrop of the fierce political battle between Buddhadeb Bhattacharya and Mamata Banerjee points to the inextricable link between politics and culture in West Bengal, as both the leaders were engaged in a contest which was as much political as cultural. While both of them claimed cultural refinement, Mamata Banerjee's language and style looked pale in comparison to the Left's apparently polished and sophisticated rhetoric of culture. Still, she had to wage a battle for cultural space and swear allegiance to the same old *bhadralok* values. Seen in this light, the massive drive undertaken by the TMC government immediately after its coming to power to set up new government colleges and universities testifies to continuing hold of the *bhadralok* value system over both political and policy imagination.[133]

---

131   Ranabir Samaddar, *Passive Revolution in West Bengal, 1977–2011* (New Delhi: Sage, 2013), 213.

132   Gupta, *Didi*, 125.

133   During the TMC regime, there has been a significant increase in the number of higher educational institutions. Presidency University at Kolkata, Kazi Nazrul University at Asansol, Bankura University at Bankura, Gourbanga University at Maldah, Raiganj State University at Raiganj, Aliah University at Kolkata, Diamond Harbour Women's University at Diamond Harbour are some of the new universities set up by the TMC Government. Moreover, several government colleges have been set up in different parts of the state. According to the TMC government's claim 50 new colleges have come up, while the number of universities increased from 12 to 42. See, Government of West Bengal, "Expanding Horizons: Higher Education in West Bengal," (Kolkata: Department of Higher Education, Government of West Bengal, 2016), 26–36. Press Trust of India, "Significant rise in number of universities in Bengal during TMC tenure: Partha Chatterjee," *Hindustan Times*, September 6, 2020, https://www.hindustantimes.com/education/significant-rise-in-number-of-universities-in-bengal-during-tmc-tenure-partha-chatterjee/story-hoSsOyNMaSsDu3YUDjijUK.html.

However, in this respect it is also important to underline that that the *bhadralok* culture no longer remains intact in its unadulterated form. Gupta has rightly argued that 'a pristine unadulterated *bhadralok* culture' might have disintegrated.[134] This has occurred most possibly due to the articulation of the *bhadralok* culture by the leaders who may not fit into the standard definition of the *bhadralok*. The CPI(M)'s leadership largely belonged to the elite literati, well versed in the region's intellectual, literary and artistic traditions. The TMC leaders, on the other hand, mainly hail from a humbler stratum of the *bhadralok*. While they have awareness about Bengal's past glory, they are not as ease with the high *bhadralok* culture despite their predominantly higher caste background. The Harvard professor Sugata Bose, or even the investment-banker-turned-politician Mahua Moitra, are exceptions in the party.[135] Thus the *dhoti-kurta*-clad *bhadralok* politician has receded from the political space, but the general allegiance to *bhadralok* norms in mainstream institutionalized politics persists. The bhadralok norms continue to delineate the broad contours of the legitimate model of political conduct in West Bengal.

Mamata Banerjee, today dexterously and effortlessly straddles between contrasting and often contradictory cultural realms, which are only united in being *bhadralok* in their orientation. Thus, her deep veneration for Tagore does not prevent her to name metro stations after revolutionary freedom fighters such as Khudiram Bose and Mastarda Surya Sen, whose violent tactics had faced Tagore's condemnation. Similarly, her devotion for spiritual heritage of Ramakrisha and Vivekananda comfortably co-exists with celebration of the Marxist poets like Subhash Mukherjee and Sukanta Bhattacharya. Mamata Banerjee said, "We don't want be confined within the political boundaries. We always tried to give respect to the noted persons who had worked for the development of society".[136] Thus, Ms. Banerjee's political discourse is too fluid, malleable and elastic for analytical confinement within straitjacket formulas or precepts offered by standard ideologies of politics. However, it is clearly *bhadralok* in orientation, drawing upon the diverse ideological streams from the rich reservoir of *bhadralok* tradition. Contrary to the prevalent perception, her lack of a clear-cut political ideology is not a non-*bhadralok* attribute.

---

134   Gupta, *Didi,* 15.

135   Ishan Mukherjee, "Battle for the Bhadralok: The historical roots of Hindu majoritarianism in West Bengal," *Caravan,* November 29, 2019, https://caravanmagazine.in/politics/histori cal-roots-of-hindu-majoritarianism-in-west-bengal.

136   Indo Asian News Service, "Mamata Names Two Kolkata Metro Stations After Journalists," *Yahoo News,* February 7, 2011, https://in.news.yahoo.com/mamata-names-two-kolkata -metro-stations-journalists-20110207-074526-920.html.

Actually, it is the ideological fluidity of her party which affords Mamata Banerjee great flexibility to blend and manipulate diverse cultural traditions as per circumstantial necessities. Her politico-cultural eclecticism enables her to negotiate with the *bhadralok* world to the best of her capabilities. It helps her to maintain an essential Left liberal bent while retaining a distinction between the political discourse of her party and that of the CPI(M). Thus, the eclectic discourse of the TMC consists of a hefty dose of leftist cultural imageries as well as components of indigenous religious and cultural traditions of Bengal. Seen in this light, possibly, a post-*bhadralok* political era grounded in cultural eclecticism has begun to unfold with the TMC's rise to power. But, this post-*bhadralok* scenario is only an outgrowth of the *bhadralok* value system rather than a contradiction of it.[137]

Therefore, if we compare the political discourse and political *modus operandi* of the CPI(M) and those of the TMC, it seems that there is a considerable degree of similarity between them. Common features like evocation of Bengali regional pride, aspirations and identity, articulation of a narrative of centre's discrimination against Bengal, appropriation of leading Bengali icons and finally use of pro-poor language and Left-wing rhetoric of class politics mark the political discourse of both the parties. Such similarities suggest continuing persistence of a political culture which has been shaped over the years by a complex interplay between *bhadralok* culture and Left-wing ideology. It seems to have become strongly entrenched in the political process and hence continues to contribute to the reproduction of the dominant template of doing institutional politics in West Bengal. In other words, it has become deeply institutionalized. In this context, it is worth pointing out that this is not something unusual since (as argued by several scholars of institutionalism) not only formal rules and procedures but cultural norms too, can assume institutional forms. The Left-minded *bhadralok* culture has produced what Lynne Zucker implies by institutionalization: "common understanding about appropriate and fundamentally meaningful (political) behavior".[138] In a similar sense, it has generated conditions which Michael Georges associates with institutionalization, i.e., an agreement between major political players about rules of the political process and existence of a settled framework within which politics takes place.[139] In short, the *bhadralok* political culture equipped with Left wing

137   Guha, "West Bengal Elections," 71.
138   Lynne G. Zucker, "Organizations as Institutions," in *Research in the Sociology of Organizations*, ed. S.B. Bacharach (Greenwich, CN: JAI Press, 1983), 5.
139   Michael J. Gorges, "New Institutionalist Explanations for Institutional Change: A Note of Caution," *Politics* 21, no. 2 (2001), 138.

ideological leanings seems to have acquired an institutional form by providing a cognitive script that determines the meaning of legitimate political conduct in West Bengal.

Historical institutionalists argue that the choice of a course of action depends on the interpretation of a situation in which the action is performed, and that this interpretation is generated by institutions, composed of established symbols, scripts and routines. Thus, institutions influence behaviour or action by defining, what is legitimate and appropriate course of action in a particular situation.[140] This however, as Ann Swidler points out, does not mean that culture imposes a single unified pattern on action by providing ultimate values. It constrains action by providing a limited set of resources, a toolkit of symbols, stories, rituals, worldviews, habits, skills and styles, out of which individuals and groups construct diverse lines and strategies of action.[141] Therefore, scope for innovation and adjustment always remains available to a political actor up to a certain extent. This explains the continuing presence of a Left minded political culture despite the fact that it has been undergoing strategic adjustments and limited alterations after the fall of the Left Front. Gramsci also notes that Common sense is not static and rigid as it keeps transforming itself.[142] This becomes clear from TMC's negotiation with the Left wing culture of the *bhadralok*. As has already been discussed, the TMC has successfully attempted selective appropriation of the constitutive elements of this culture while modifying them as per contextual requirements. Thus, varied patterns of strategic political action are permitted by a political culture so far as its discursive boundaries are not breached. In other words, though much of the political behaviour tends to be goal-oriented and strategic, a political actor's choice of options is "circumscribed by a culturally specific sense of appropriate action".[143] As a result, institutionalization of a political culture creates some degree of continuities in outlook and action despite change in political dispensation. This is why the institutionalized political culture of West Bengal has produced some persistent and regularized patterns of behaviour by precluding or making unviable alternative courses of action. Di Maggio and Powell argue that "institutionalized arrangements are reproduced because individuals often

---

140   See, James G. March and Johan P. Olsen, *Rediscovering Institutions* (New York, Free Press, 1989).

141   Swidler, "Culture in Action," 281.

142   Gramsci, *Selections from the Prison Notebooks*, 326.

143   Peter A. Hall and Rosemarcy R. Taylor, "Political Science and the Three New Institutionalisms," *Political Studies* 44(1996): 956.

cannot even conceive of appropriate alternatives. Institutions do not just constrain options, they establish the very criteria by which people discover their preferences".[144] This suggests that some political norms, assumptions and conventions can become so taken for granted that they escape from being consciously subjected to individual choice and as a result, they remain largely immune from the possibility of revisibility and transformation. This can be seen in the tendency of different political actors in West Bengal to resort to an established pattern of political template.

This established political template to a great extent limits political mobilization along the lines of caste. The TMC frequently draws upon the Left's class centric political rhetoric. However, since it is not a strictly Left-wing party, the political culture it has borrowed from the Left has undergone some dilution and adjustments in its hands in response to situational necessities. The TMC is not ideologically averse to caste-based mobilization. It has indeed made some attempts to mobilize the *Namasudras*. But as has been highlighted in Chapter 2, these were not large scale state wide mobilization, but were sporadic and remained confined to small pockets of the state. Though the retreat of the Left from mainstream electoral politics has created relatively better prospects for caste-based mobilization, such mobilization remains restricted by a certain threshold set by the dominant political culture of the state. This is also evident from the fact that during the TMC rule the normative rationale underlying political representation has not undergone any transformation preventing the rise of lower caste groups in positions of power in institutional politics. It has been demonstrated in Chapter 3 that despite political transition from the Left to the TMC the concept of substantive representation has not given way to the concept of descriptive representation, precluding the actual emergence of caste as a powerful political factor at the centre-stage of mainstream institutional politics. The persistence of similar outlook towards political representation has much to do with the hangover of an established political template informed by a political culture shaped during the long rule of the Left. Thus, the continuation of this political culture, though in somewhat diluted form, imposes some limits on the politics of caste. So long as the hold of this political culture remains intact, mainstream politics can afford to accommodate political articulation of caste interests only up to a limited extent. It is this limited scope of politicisation of caste that still distinguishes

---

144   Paul J. Di Maggio and Walter W. Powell, "Introduction," in *The New Institutionalism in Organizational Analysis,* eds. Walter W. Powell and Paul J. DiMaggio (Chicago, University of Chicago Press, 1991), 10–11.

West Bengal from other North Indian states, where caste as a unit of political mobilization and a political idiom for interest articulation does not suffer from any major deficit of legitimacy.[145]

In this context, it quite clearly appears that the political trajectory of contemporary West Bengal demonstrates 'path-dependence'. 'Path-dependence' implies the existence of "institutional patterns having deterministic properties", which creates inertia or resistance to structural social transformation. In other words, the prevalence of 'path dependence' implies that once a particular institutional path comes into existence, it tends to perpetuate itself by locking out competing ideas.[146] This prevents institutional change by leading to morphostasis, which is indicated by the "ability of the system to maintain its structure in a changing environment".[147] Politics in West Bengal due to its continuing adherence to an established political template is subject to a great deal of inertia or morphostasis.

However, in this model structural changes are not completely ruled out. Institutional change is possible but only during 'critical juncture'. There is not much clarity and consensus among scholars of historical institutionalism about the motivating factors which produce a 'critical juncture'. But they more or less agree that it is a moment when period of continuity is punctuated by the replacement of old institutional patterns by new institutional patterns. In other words, 'critical juncture' represents a 'branching point' from which historical development moves onto a new path.[148] The BJP, which is a new and emerging political player in West Bengal represents a new kind of politics, which can eventually produce a 'critical juncture', resulting in the emergence of a new kind of political culture. Signs of this are already visible. This however, seems like an ongoing process but it can have considerable bearing on the political dynamics of social identities like caste. In the next section, I shall briefly discuss the potential for a change in the political culture of the state created by the growth of the BJP.

---

145   Arvind Kumar and Ayan Guha, "Political Future of Caste in West Bengal," *Economic and Political Weekly* 49, no. 32 (2014): 74.

146   See, James Mahoney, "Path Dependence in Historical Sociology," *Theory and Society* 29, no. 4 (2000): 507–548.

147   Ian Greener, "The Potential of Path Dependence in Political Studies," *Politics* 25, no. 1 (2005), 68.

148   Stephen D. Krasner, "Approaches to the State: Alternative Conceptions and Historical Dynamics," *Comparative Politics* 16, no. 2 (1984): 225.

5   Break from Past: towards a 'Critical Juncture'?

The 2019 general elections mark the emergence of the BJP as a powerful political force in West Bengal. The BJP made spectacular inroads into West Bengal by winning 18 seats and doubling its vote-share from 17 percent in 2014 to over 40 percent. In the recently concluded State Assembly elections the party secured 77 seats. Though it could not gain expected success by toppling the ruling TMC government the improvement in its tally, which was only 3 seats in the 2016 Assembly elections, is undeniably significant. In terms of vote share the improvement is even more spectacular. Its vote share has risen from 10 percent in 2016 to 38 percent in 2021. The BJP is today firmly placed as the principal opposition party in West Bengal. It is not until the 2026 Assembly elections that the BJP will get a chance to capture political power in West Bengal. But it is quite clear that the party has developed a considerable support base and now is in a position to make further gains.

While the politics of the TMC reflects 'path-dependence', the recent rise of the BJP potentially represents a 'critical juncture', which can radically transform the prevailing political culture of the state. The rise of the BJP has introduced several new political dynamics in West Bengal. We have already discussed in great detail the BJP's strategy of political mobilization in Chapter 2, highlighting how the locus of identification for the lower castes is shifting from caste to religion with the steady political growth of the BJP. In other words, caste groups are indeed being mobilized but the motivating factor behind such mobilization is not caste consciousness, but Hindu belongingness. Religion not caste is becoming the primary fault line and principal axis of political identification in the emerging political scenario.

This has brought about some visible changes in the political discourse of the state, which can have long term implications for the political culture of the state. Here we can briefly highlight the changes in the general political discourse brought about by the BJP's rise in West Bengal. From the point of view of political culture, the rise of the BJP in West Bengal where it was previously a marginal political player is a significant political development. This is because the BJP's political discourse and *modus operandi* are quite different from the brand of politics practiced so far in West Bengal. Therefore, growing political consolidation of the BJP creates greater possibilities for a paradigm shift or a 'critical juncture' in West Bengal politics, though it is difficult to anticipate whether and when such a 'critical juncture' will arrive.

Since the emergence of the BJP in West Bengal religious identity politics has made a strong appearance in West Bengal. Religious idioms are now frequently invoked by both the BJP and the TMC to bring about political polarisation along religious lines. With growing Hindu consolidation facilitating BJP's rise in West Bengal, the TMC also now makes frequent use of the language of identity to bring about Muslim consolidation in its favour. At the same time in order to arrest the process of Hindu consolidation in favour of the BJP, the TMC is also making some limited use of Hindu religious idioms. The overt political display of religiosity in West Bengal in recent times marked a beginning with the TMC's Muslim outreach using religious symbolism. The TMC government has been wooing the Muslims by giving freebies to *imams* and *muezzins*. Mamata Banerjee also makes it a point to be seen publicly at Muslim festivals and *Iftar* parties, head covered neatly with a *hijab*, eyes closed in prayer as if she is offering *namaz*.[149] With the rise of the BJP this overt Muslim outreach has come under increasing public scrutiny as the BJP brands this as 'Muslim appeasement'. To stir up Hindu sentiments, in an attempt to bring about Hindu consolidation, the BJP is using *'Jai Shri Ram'* as a rallying cry for the Hindus and is trying to mobilize them by organizing religious events, mass gatherings and processions on Hindu religious occasions and by frequent temple visits by party leaders. As the BJP gains greater political ground, the TMC while continuing its Muslim outreach has started to make amends to its political messaging to counter the charge of 'Muslim appeasement'. The TMC leaders now also organize Hindu religious events like *Ramnavami* and *Saraswati Puja* in their localities. Mamata Banerjee during the campaigns for the recently concluded Assembly elections attempted very hard to prove her Hindu credentials. She tried to present herself as a devout Hindu by doing *Chandipath* in her election rallies and visiting temples after temples. She even proclaimed that she belonged to *Sandilya Gotra Kulin* Brahman, the highest tier of the Bengali caste system.[150] At the same time she also indirectly urged the Muslims not to vote for the BJP, violating the election code of conduct which prohibits appeal for votes on religious ground. This led the Election Commission to ban her from political campaigning for 24 hours.[151] Thus, the political expression of the language of religion is escalating to a level which by West Bengal's standard is unprecedentedly high.

---

149   Kamlesh Singh, "Nobody Says the M-word," *DailyO*, March 9, 2021, https://www.dailyo .in/politics/bengal-elections-2021-tmc-muslim-vote-bank-mamata-banerjee-aimim-owa isi-rahul-gandhi/story/1/34340.html.

150   Web Desk, "Congress Leader Surprised by Mamata's 'Hindu Brahmin' Boast," *The Week*, https://www.theweek.in/news/india/2021/03/10/congress-leader-surprised-by-mamatas -hindu-brahmin-boast.html; Kala Sadhana, "Bengal Election 2021," *Times of India*, April 1, 2021 https://timesofindia.indiatimes.com/blogs/methink/bengal-election-2021.

151   Express News Service, "Bengal Polls: EC slaps 24-hour Campaign Ban on Mamata; TMC Calls it Biased, Undemocratic," *Indian Express*, April 13, 2021, https://indianexpress.com/ elections/mamata-banerjee-ec-ban-west-bengal-election-campaign-tmc-7270633/.

The political parties appear to be giving up all uneasiness to resort to overt assertion of religiosity for the purpose of political mobilization. This is indicative of a new trend in West Bengal politics, which is known for being largely immune from identity politics.

Thus, the present scenario points towards a possibility for an eventual shift in the overall political paradigm. With the language of identity gaining greater prominence, the entire field of political contestation seems to be undergoing a crucial transformation. Politics of identity was not completely absent in West Bengal. Identity concerns in politics were articulated from time to time. But political articulation of identity concerns remained confined geographically to certain limited pockets (such as politics of *Gurkha* identity in Darjeeling) and discursively to the periphery of institutional politics. They were not overtly encouraged by political parties. So, identity related issues never managed to occupy the centre stage of mainstream politics. But now identity concerns have come to political forefront. However, for now space seems to have opened up mainly for the politics of religious identity. In other words, the space for identity politics has come to be largely occupied by religion-based politics, limiting the possibility for political articulation of caste consciousness. As has been pointed out in Chapter 2, caste consciousness is being increasingly subsumed and blunted by religious consciousness.

In this regard, it also needs to be pointed out that the language of class politics remains quite powerful and that the institutionalized political culture of West Bengal continues to have significant bearing on the way politics is conducted. While the BJP's politics of *Hindutva* is impacting overall political discourse, the political language of the BJP has not been able to completely free itself from the influence of the long prevailing institutionalized political culture of the state. Interestingly, the BJP in West Bengal has also to an extent appropriated the symbols and images of the Left, placing them on its familiar saffron turf. A recent study on the BJP's online campaign for the recently concluded 2021 Assembly elections has discovered that the party's digital campaign used images historically associated with Left politics such as raised fists, images of leftist processions and Soviet-era agitprop art (agitational propaganda art). '*Aar Noi Onnay*' translated as 'no more injustice', which was the BJP's official slogan for the 2021 Assembly election, used the image of hands breaking free from shackles with two men (a typical leftist representation of the working-class body) supporting it. Even Marxist poetry and quotations of foreign revolutionaries were used to communicate political messages.[152] It is

---

152 Debopriya Shome and Taberez Neyazi, "Soviet-era Posters to Raised Fist Artwork-BJP Using Left Symbols to be Bengal 'insider'," *Print*, February 15, 2021,

interesting to note that the BJP's campaign song *Pishi Jaao* that translates to 'Aunty, leave' (Pisi or aunty is an indirect reference to Mamata Banerjee) was a recreation of a popular anti-fascist protest song *Bella Ciao,* that is imbued with a revolutionary and radical fervour.[153]

Therefore, while championing the politics of *Hindutva* the BJP is also making selective appropriation of the constituent elements of a received political template. This can also be seen in BJP's negotiation with Bengali regional identity. On one hand, it called for a 'double engine government' by which it meant installation of the government of the same party both at the centre and the state.[154] It advocated 'double engine government' by arguing that the mindless opposition of the TMC and the Left to the central government through the evocation of a parochial Bengali regionalism had obstructed the development of the state and effective implementation of the central government schemes. On the other hand, in line with Bengal's traditional political template the BJP also made attempts to appropriate the legacy of Bengali icons like Vivekananda, Bankim Chandra Chatterjee, Netaji Subhas Chandra Bose and Syama Prasad Mukherjee. The party has now started celebrating their birth anniversaries with much fanfare. Dr. Syama Prasad Mookerjee Research Foundation (SPMRF) is one of the most important organizations entrusted by the BJP with the task of intellectual outreach in West Bengal. The SPMRF held a series of discussions in towns across Bengal and also online discussions on Bengali intellectual icons and nationalist leaders. Clearly the goal seems to be to appropriate the legacy of Bengal's intellectual and cultural heritage.[155] The party also organised many high-profile public events to commemorate Bengali icons.[156] Thus, for the last few years the BJP has been making tremendous

---

https://theprint.in/opinion/soviet-era-posters-to-raised-fist-artwork-bjp-using-left-symbols-to-be-bengal-insider/604258/.

153   Raya Ghosh, "BJP Gives Bengali Twist to Bella Ciao with Pishi Jaao in Message For Mamata Banerjee," *India Today*, February 21, 2021, https://www.indiatoday.in/trending-news/story/bjp-gives-bengali-twist-to-bella-ciao-with-pishi-jaao-in-message-for-mamata-banerjee-watch-1771477-2021-02-21.

154   Romita Datta, "Bengal Manifesto War: BJP's Icon Worship vs. Mamata's 'Outsider' Campaign," *India Today,* March 22, 2021, https://www.indiatoday.in/india-today-insight/story/bengal-manifesto-war-bjp-s-icon-worship-vs-mamata-s-outsider-campaign-1782381-2021-03-22.

155   Snigdhendu Bhattacharya, *Mission Bengal: A Saffron Experiment* (Noida: Harper Collins, 2020), 109–110.

156   In 2018 Home Minister Amit Shah delivered in Kolkata the much publicised first Bankim Chandra Chattopadhyay Memorial Oration. In October, 2020 Prime Minister Narendra Modi for the first time delivered a virtual speech on the occasion of *Durga puja* addressing the entire Bengali community and he also inaugurated a *puja pandal* in Kolkata via video conferencing. It was a long speech stuffed with Bengali phrases and in that speech

efforts to connect to the Bengali people by showing reverence to their cultural icons. In this respect, the influence of West Bengal's traditional political template on the political strategy of the party is clearly visible.

Therefore, in the end it can be said that the interaction between the institutionalized political culture of West Bengal and the politics of *Hindutva* is a two-way process. While the BJP's brand of politics creates possibilities for a structural transformation of the political culture of the state, its political practice and discourse are also likely to be impacted by the influences engendered by the long held entrenched political culture of the state. Unmistakably, this is an enormously complex process of cultural negotiation, which has just begun to unfold. It is to be seen whether this process will ultimately culminate into a fundamental metamorphosis of the prevailing political culture of West Bengal. At this point it can be only said that much of it will depend on the future political fortunes of the BJP.

the Prime Minister paid glowing tributes to a host of Bengali icons by highlighting their immense contributions. In December, 2020 Prime Minister Modi addressed the centenary celebrations of Visva-Bharati University in Santiniketan and in effusive language eulogised Tagore's contributions. The grandest of all such events was organised on January 23, 2021 to celebrate the 125th birth anniversary of Netaji Subhas Chandra Bose by the Government of India at Kolkata's Victoria memorial. Prime Minister Modi himself presided over the occasion and delivered a speech passionately highlighting the great deeds of Netaji. On the same day he also delivered a valedictory address in an international seminar on Bose at the National Library at Kolkata and visited Netaji Bhavan, Netaji's Kolkata residence.

CHAPTER 8

Conclusion

Summing Up

One of the widely prevalent and long surviving narratives among the Bengali *bhadralok* is that West Bengal including its politics is 'casteless' and therefore 'exceptional' in comparison to other states. This sense of distinctiveness and departure from the rest of India constitutes an important aspect of the self-definition and popular conceptualization of Bengali identity. The dominant public discourse has also delegitimized the lexicon of caste. Taking about caste in polite urban conversation is considered offensive to *bhadralok* gentility that is supposed to be rigidly adhered to as an accepted norm of public behaviour.[1] A great deal of scholarly efforts have been undertaken in recent times to show that, this claim of exceptionalism is a myth, since caste far from being withered away remains a reality in everyday life. It is undeniably true that West Bengal's exceptionalism is over-emphasized and grossly exaggerated. Still, there is no denying the fact that the politics of West Bengal has pursued a trajectory mark-edly different from that followed by the rest of the country. The unchallenged sway of the Left politics for an exceedingly long period managed to establish a pattern of political mobilization, where caste and identity concerns are sub-sumed under the dominant category of 'class'.

Therefore, from a scholarly point of view we are faced with a tricky and paradoxical situation. On one hand, we find that caste remains present as an important organizing principle of social life and continues to reproduce socio-economic inequalities and political hierarchies. On the other hand, we also see that caste as a political category does not enjoy much prominence and visibility unlike in other parts of the country. The standard explanation offered in this regard is that the monopolization of all domains of public life by the higher caste Bengali *bhadralok* has ousted caste from public discourse and political agenda despite its presence in social life. Therefore, the augment goes that West Bengal is not much different from other states, where caste is a more visible political category. But this begs the question as to why West Bengal has not seen large scale *dalit* resistance against higher caste supremacy,

---

1 Partha Chatterjee, "Partition and the Mysterious Disappearance of Caste in Bengal," in *Politics of Caste in West Bengal,* eds. Uday Chandra, Geir Heierstad and Kenneth Bo Nielsen (New Delhi: Routledge, 2016), 83.

as witnessed in other parts of the country in the form of collective mobilization by various lower caste groups. It is obvious that we can't satisfactorily engage with this question if we debunk the exceptionality of West Bengal as a complete myth. Therefore, rather than fully rejecting the exceptionality of West Bengal, a qualified acceptance of the same should be the starting point of any discussion relating to the political trajectory of caste in West Bengal. At the same time, it also needs to be asked in view of the steady decline of the organized Left in West Bengal's politics as to whether exceptionality of West Bengal's politics is on retreat. There has been a growing feeling in recent years that something radically new is emerging with regard to the operation of caste dynamics in political process. This feeling has emerged in response to the political assertion of the *Matua-Namasudra* community since 2009 and Mamata Banerjee's so-called 'post *bhadralok*' style of politics that is not averse to overt patronization of caste and communal sentiments in contrast to the political style of her ultra-secularists Communist counterparts.[2] It is in this backdrop that the caste question in West Bengal politics has been analysed in this book.

The political assertion of the *Matuas* has drawn a great deal of scholarly attention, raising anticipation about the rise of caste as a determining factor in the mainstream institutional politics of the state. However, not much efforts have been directed towards decoding the nature of the *Matua* mobilization and also its changing character. A close investigation reveals that the efforts by the TMC to mobilize the *Matua-Namasudra* community along the lines of caste have remained quite sporadic. Further, religious fault lines have become much more prominent in the politics of the state with the decline of the Left. For the time being a space seems to have emerged for the operation of religion-based identity politics, which has found manifestation in the growing momentum of *Hindutva* politics and also in TMC's efforts to consolidate the Muslims as its vote bank. In such a political atmosphere, political mobilization of the *Matuas,* to a great degree has got transformed from a caste conscious activity into a process of Hinduization of *dalits*. All available evidences suggests that since 2018–19 the majority of the *Matuas* have shifted their political allegiance to the BJP. Instead of appealing to the caste identity of the *Matua-Namasudra* Community, the BJP is playing the 'Hindu card' among the *Matuas* who have migrated from East Pakistan and later Bangladesh in large numbers due to communal tension. The recently enacted Citizenship Amendment Act,

---

2 Uday Chandra, Geir Heiestad and Kenneth Bo Nielsen, "Introduction," in *Politics of Caste in West Bengal,* eds. Uday Chandra, Geir Heierstad and Kenneth Bo Nielsen (New Delhi: Routledge, 2016), 7–8.

2019 promises to satisfy the long-standing citizenship demand of the Hindu refugees. Being projected as the potential beneficiaries of this legislation the *Matuas* are being politically mobilized as Hindu refugees by the BJP. The political narrative utilized by the *Hindutva* forces to woo the *Matuas* is increasingly highlighting religious persecution of the *Matuas* in Bangladesh, setting in motion a 'politics of memory'. This 'politics of memory' by reigniting among the *Matuas* their historical memory of religious persecution at the hands of the Muslims is actively working to supplant *dalit* consciousness with Hindu belongingness. The 'politics of memory' is being practiced by obscuring caste divisions through the invocation of the need for Hindu unity. This has created a situation where caste groups are indeed being mobilized but the motivating factor behind such mobilization is not caste consciousness but Hindu belongingness. Therefore, though the mobilization of the *Matuas* by the BJP looks like caste politics but, in reality, it is a version of *Hindutva* politics, where caste identity only plays a supporting role that serves to strengthen and buttress the Hindu consciousness of the groups mobilized along caste lines. Thus, the *Hindutva* project of *Hinduization* of *dalits* is successfully propelling the emergence of an overarching Hindu identity capable of subsuming caste identity. In this context, it needs to be conceded that the notion of exceptionalism of West Bengal is indeed facing a challenge, but the challenge comes from the rise of religion-based identity politics rather than from the politics of caste identity. Further, the recent trends of political representation of the lower castes do not indicate rising influence of caste factor in formal institutional politics of the state. Caste politics in various parts of India particularly since the late 1970s has become manifested in rising political representation of the lower castes. In other words, the rise in lower caste political representation is considered to be the most veritable sign of the emergence of caste politics. However, the decline of the organised Left in formal party politics and the sporadic mobilization of the lower castes have not generated any increase in their political representation. Therefore, in view of non-enhancement of political representation of the lower castes, it clearly appears premature to proclaim the emergence of full-fledged caste based identity politics in the state.

Thus, in West Bengal caste is still not a decisive factor which can shape political equations. The inconsequentiality of caste in politics is a complex story filled with interwoven plots and sub-plots. There is no single explanation that can capture the peculiar political trajectory of caste in West Bengal. A combination of factors spanning across multiple realms has produced mutually reinforcing dynamics unfavourable for politicisation of caste identity. From a demographic point of view, it is possible to identify a host of factors which discourage the adoption of caste based social engineering strategy, that is

routinely used for electoral calculation in other states. Absence of a dominant caste, fragmentation of intermediate castes, limited geographic spread
of lower and intermediate castes and comparable demographic strength of
major lower caste groups having different and even divergent demands are
some of the prominent demographic factors which inhibit political articulation of caste identity and political aggregation of socio-economic interests of
different caste groups.

The absence of *dalit* politics also has a material basis. Bengali landholders
have always belonged to diverse caste backgrounds. The lack of homogeneity
in the caste identities of the landholding class has prevented their conversion
into a cohesive political bloc, which is potentially capable of being mobilized
in favour of any political party. Further, compared to other states the lower
castes in West Bengal suffer from relatively lower level of relative deprivation
vis-à-vis the caste Hindus. For instance, *dalits* and non-*dalits* are, more or less,
similarly placed in terms of possession of landholding in West Bengal. Several
other economic indicators also suggest that the relative economic deprivation faced by the lower castes in West Bengal is not very substantial. It is quite
likely that the low level of relative economic deprivation faced by the lower
castes has not augured well for the conscious deployment of caste as a political vocabulary of socio-economic marginalisation in West Bengal. Political
aggregation of lower caste interests has also been hampered by their uneven
economic development. Development indicators suggest high level of disparity in the economic conditions of major lower caste groups. Due to wide mismatch in the economic situation of various lower caste groups, their needs and
priorities are vastly different. Such a situation provides little incentive to the
lower castes to come together and build a common agenda of socio-economic
demands for collective political action. Thus, the structure of political economy has played a role in configuring the field of political contestation in a
manner that has thwarted crystallization of caste as a key organizing principle
of political mobilization.

Another significant factor that has not been adequately studied despite
wide awareness of its importance is the role of political culture. The politics
of West Bengal is deeply associated with what is generally known as *bhadralok*
culture, which has put in place a template of legitimate political behaviour.
Beginning in the 1920s and 1930s the *bhadralok* culture came to be gradually
absorb a class centric Left-wing political discourse. It is this marriage between
bhadralok culture and Marxism that has greatly contributed towards the ideological subsumption of the discourse of caste by that of class. Ethnographic
evidences point towards the fact that in rural society caste plays a crucial
role in shaping political and economic power relations between groups and

communities. This has created a situation where power relations remain segregated along caste lines. But the pervasive influence of *bhadralok* culture has
led to an absence of sustained social dialogue on caste practices and experiences, preventing the emergence of a counterculture in the form of a *dalit*
public sphere. As a result, unlike in many other states which are strongholds
of caste politics, in West Bengal the transportation of local dynamics of caste
from micro politics to state level mainstream macro politics has been blocked
by the absence of an effective and pervasive *dalit* public sphere, which could
have acted as a link between micro-politics and macro-politics.

The non-emergence of an effective *dalit* public sphere lies in the fact that
a shared mentality arising out of the marriage between *bhadralok* culture and
Left politics has become intrinsic to West Bengal's commonsensical conception of politics. In other words, the political trajectory of contemporary West
Bengal demonstrates 'path-dependence'. As a result, the TMC's politics, to a
large extent, appears to be a continuation of the discourse and praxis shaped
by the Left. Common features like invocation of Bengali *asmita* (pride), articulation of a narrative of centre's step motherly attitude towards West Bengal,
appropriation of the legacy of Bengali luminaries and most importantly use of
pro-poor language and Left-wing rhetoric of class politics mark the political
discourse of both the Left and the TMC. This suggests that the *bhadralok* political culture equipped with Left wing ideological leanings has become deeply
institutionalized, providing the dominant template of doing institutional politics in West Bengal. This established political template continues to limit political mobilization along the lines of caste. Though the TMC frequently draws
upon the Left's class centric political rhetoric, it is not ideologically averse to
caste-based mobilization unlike the Left. Retreat of the Left from the mainstream electoral politics has indeed created relatively better scope for caste-
based mobilization but such mobilization remains restricted by a certain
threshold set by the dominant political culture of the state. The TMC has made
some attempts to mobilize caste groups like the *Namasudras*. But these were
not large scale state wide mobilization but were largely sporadic and remained
confined to small pockets. It is this limited prospect of politicisation of caste
identity that makes politics of Bengal distinct from that of other North Indian
states, where caste as a political category does not suffer from any crisis of
legitimacy.

However, recently some possibilities seem to have emerged for a paradigm
shift in the political culture of the state. While the politics of the TMC reflects
'path-dependence', the recent rise of the BJP in West Bengal potentially represents a 'critical juncture', which can radically transform the prevailing
political culture of the state. Since the emergence of the BJP in West Bengal

religious identity politics has gained a lot of traction. Religious sentiments are now frequently fanned by political parties to polarise electorate along religious lines. This is indicative of the arrival of a new trend in West Bengal politics, which is known for being largely free from the tendency to politically manipulate identitarian faultlines. But while some space for identity politics has opened up, this space has come to be mainly occupied by religion-based politics. Religion not caste is increasingly becoming the primary political fault line and principal axis of political identification in the emerging political scenario. As a result, caste consciousness is being increasingly subsumed and blunted by religious consciousness.

This study on the trajectory caste in West Bengal politics reveals that landmark political change brought about by the electoral decline of a long lasting political dispensation is not necessarily accompanied by a fundamental change in the existing political discourse and praxis. In a democratic set up the basic structure of long held social and political outlook and practices demonstrates a strong tendency to withstand landmark political change. It may apparently seem that the electoral decline of the Left has created a perfect ground for caste based identity politics to flourish, but sustained assertion of caste identity is still beset by the traditional structural constraints due to largely unaltered socio-political dynamics. Unless the fundamental logic which drives the engines of society and politics is altered, caste as a political factor is likely to remain marginal in the electoral politics of the state.

Bibliography

Aberle, David. The Peyote Religion among the Navaho. New York: Wenner-Gren Foundation for Anthropological Research, 1966.

Acharya, Poromesh. "Panchayats and Left Politics in West Bengal." Economic and Political Weekly 28, no. 22 (1993): 1080–82.

Addy Preman and Ibne Azad. "Politics and Culture in Bengal." New Left Review 79 (1973): 72–112.

Agarwal, Samantha and Michael Levien. "Dalits and Dispossession: A Comparison." Journal of Contemporary Asia 50, no.5 (2020): 696–722.

Almond, Gabriel and Sidney Verba. The Civic Culture: Political Attitudes and Democracy in Five Nations. Princeton: Princeton University Press, 1963.

Ambedkar, Bhim Rao. Who are the Shudras? How They Came to be the Fourth Varna in Indo-Aryan Society. Bombay: Thacker & Co, 1946.

Anand, Ayush and Shubhendu Anand, eds. Constitutionality of the Citizenship Amendment Act, 2019 and Why it was Essential. New Delhi: Dr. Syama Prasad Mookerjee Research Foundation, 2020.

Anand, Ayush and Shubhendu Anand, eds. White Paper on Citizenship Amendment Act. New Delhi: Dr. Syama Prasad Mukherjee Research Foundation, 2020.

Andersen, Walter K and Shidhar D. Damle. The RSS: A View to Inside. Gurgaon: Penguin Viking, 2018.

Andersen, Walter K and Shidhar D. Damle. The Brotherhood in Saffron: The Rashtriya Swayamsevak Sangh and Hindu Revivalism. Gurgaon: Penguin, 2019.

Bag, Kheya. "Red Bengal's Rise and Fall." New Left Review 70 (2011): 69–98.

Bagchi, Suvojit. "Rajbongshis Oppose CAA, but Back NRC in North Bengal." December 18, 2019. https://www.thehindu.com/news/national/rajbongshis-oppose-caa-but -back-nrc-in-north-bengal/article30341447.ece.

Bailey, F.G. Stratagems and Spoils: A Social Anthropology of Politics. New York: Schocken Books, 1969.

Bakshi, Aparajita. "Social Inequality in Land Ownership in India: A Study with Particular Reference to West Bengal." Social Scientist 36, no. 9/10 (2008): 95–116.

Bandyopadhyay. Bhabani Charan. Kalikata Kamalalaya. Calcutta: Samacharchandrika Press, 1823.

Bandyopadhyay, Debabrata. "Not a Gramscian Pantomime." Economic and Political Weekly 32, no. 12 (1997): 581–584.

Bandyopadhyay, Sandip. "Who are the Matuas." Frontier Weekly 43, no. 37 (2011).

Bandyopadhyay, Sarbani. "Caste and Politics in Bengal." Economic and Political Weekly 47, no. 50 (2012): 71–73.

Bandyopadhyay, Sarbani. "Another History: Bhadralok Responses to Dalit Political Assertion in Colonial Bengal." In *The Politics of Caste in West Bengal*, edited by Uday Chandra, Geir Heierstad and Kenneth Bo Nielsen, 51-75. New Delhi: Routledge, 2016.

Bandyopadhyay, Sekhar. Caste, Culture and Hegemony: Social Dominance in Colonial Bengal. New Delhi: Sage, 2004.

Bandyopadhyay, Sekhar. "Partition and the Ruptures in Dalit Identity Politics in Bengal." Asian Studies Review 33, no. 4 (2009): 455–467.

Bandyopadhyay, Sekhar. Caste, Protest and Identity in Colonial India: The Namasudras of Bengal, 1872–1947. New Delhi: Oxford University Press, 2011.

Bandyopadhyay, Sekhar and Anasua Basu Ray-Chaudhury. "In Search of Space: The Scheduled Caste Movement in West Bengal after Partition." Policies and Practices 59. Kolkata: Mahanirban Calcutta Research Group (2014): 1–22.

Bandyopadhyay, Sekhar. From Plassey to Partition and After: A History of Modern India. New Delhi: Orient BlackSwan, 2016.

Bandyopadhyay, Sekhar. "Bengal's Star Caste," Indian Express, April 1, 2021.

Banerjee, Sarbani. "Different Identity Formations in Bengal Partition Narratives by Dalit Refugees." Interventions 19, vol. 4 (2017): 550–565.

Banerjee, Sumanta. "Bogey of the Bawdy Changing Concept of 'Obscenity' in 19th Century Bengali Culture." Economic and Political Weekly 22, no. 29 (1987): 1197–1206.

Banerjee, Sumanta. The Parlour and the Streets: Elite and Popular Culture in Nineteenth Century Calcutta. Calcutta: Seagull, 1998.

Banerjee, Sumanta. "Paradoxes in Inventing Bengali Identity." Seminar, 2013, http://www.india-seminar.com.

Banerjee, Abhijit V, Paul J. Gertler, and Maitreesh Ghatak. "Empowerment and Efficiency: Tenancy Reform in West Bengal." Journal of Political Economy 110, no. 2 (2002): 239–80.

Banerjee, Mukulika. "Leadership and Political Work." In Power and Influence in India: Bosses, Lords and Captains, edited by Pamela Price and A. E Ruud, 20–43. New Delhi: Oxford University Press, 2010.

Banerjee, Prathama. "Between the Political and the Nonpolitical: the Vivekananda Moment and a Critique of the Social in Colonial Bengal, 1890s–1910s." Social History 39, no. 3 (2014): 323–339.

Banerji, Himani. The Mirror of Class-Class Subjectivity and Politics in 19th Century Bengal. Economic and Political Weekly 24, no. 19 (1989): 1041–1051.

Bardhan, Pranab and Asok Rudra. "Labour Employment and Wages in Agriculture: Results of a Survey in West Bengal." Economic and Political Weekly 15, no. 45/46 (1980): 1943+1945–1949.

Bardhan, Pranab and Dilip Mookherjee. "Poverty Alleviation Efforts of Panchayats in West Bengal." Economic and Political Weekly 39, no. 9 (2004): 965–974.

Barkat, Abul et al, Deprivation of Hindu Minority in Bangladesh: Living with Vested Property. Dhaka: Pathak Shamabesh, 2008.

Barman, Rup Kumar. "Partition of Bengal and Struggle for Existence of the Scheduled Castes: Impact of the Partition (1947) on the Rajbanshis of North Bengal." Voice of Dalit 2, no. 2 (2009): 141–164.

Barman, Rup Kumar. "Right-Left-Right and Caste Politics: The Scheduled Castes in West Bengal Assembly Elections (from 1920 to 2016)." Contemporary Voice of Dalit 10, no. 2 (2018): 216–231.

Basu Guha-Choudhury, Archit. "Engendered Freedom: Partition and East Bengali Migrant Women." Economic and Political Weekly 44, no. 49 (2009): 66–69.

Basu, Dipankar. "Political Economy of 'Middleness': Behind Violence in Rural West Bengal." Economic and Political Weekly 36, vol.16 (2001): 1333–1344.

Basu, Subrata. "CPM's Waterloo." Frontier Weekly 44, no. 11–14 (2011).

Basu-Raychaudhury Anasua, Life after Partition: A Study on the Reconstruction of Lives in West Bengal. Panel 33: Ethnic Cleansing, Migration, and Resettlement: Partition & Post-Partition Experiences, Proceedings of the 18th European Association for South-Asian Studies, Sweden: Swedish South Asian Studies Network (2004): 1–15.

Basu, Subho and Auritro Majumder. "Dilemmas of Parliamentary Communism." Critical Asian Studies 45, no. 2 (2013): 167–200.

Bayly, Susan. Caste, Society and Politics in India from Eighteenth Century to Modern Age. New Delhi: Cambridge University Press, 2011.

Beck, Tony. "Common Property Resource Access by Poor and Class Conflict in West Bengal." Economic and Political Weekly 29, no. 4 (1994): 187–189+191–197.

Berreman, Gerald D. "Aleut Reference Group Alienation, Mobility, and Acculturation." American Anthropologist 66, no. 2 (1964): 231–250.

Béteille, André. Caste, Class, and Power: Changing Patterns of Stratification in a Tanjore Village. New Delhi: Oxford University Press, 1965.

Béteille, Andre. Studies in Agrarian Social Structure. Delhi: Oxford University Press, 1974.

Béteille, Andre. Marxism and Class Analysis. New Delhi: Oxford University Press, 2013.

Bhadra, Gautam. "The Mentality of Subalternity: Kantanama or Rajdharma." In Subaltern Studies, Volume VI, edited by Ranajit Guha, 54–91. New Delhi: Oxford University Press, 1994.

Bhaduri, Amit. "The Evolution of Land Relations in Eastern India under British Rule." Indian Economic and Social History Review 13 (1976): 45–53.

Bhatt, Anil. "Politics and Social Mobility in India." Contribution to Indian Sociology 5 (1971): 99–114.

Bhattacharyya, Dwaipayan. "Politics of Middleness: The Changing Character of the Communist Party of India (Marxist) in Rural West Bengal." In Sonar Bangla?

Agricultural Growth and Agrarian Change in West Bengal and Bangladesh, edited by Ben Rogaly, Barbara Harriss White and Sugato Bose, 279–300. New Delhi: Sage, 1999.

Bhattacharyya, Dwaipayan. Government as Practice: Democratic Left in a Transforming India. New Delhi: Cambridge University Press, 2017.

Bhattacharya, Sabyasachi. Rabindranath Tagore- An Interpretation. Gurgaon: Penguine, 2011.

Bhattacharya, Snigdhendu. Mission Bengal: A Saffron Experiment. Noida: Harper Collins, 2020.

Bhattacharya, Snigdhendu. "TMC, BJP Woo Rajbangshi Voters, Bengal's Largest SC Group, Ahead of Polls." The Wire, February 13, 2021. https://thewire.in/politics/bjp-bengal-elections-amit-shah-koch-rajbangshi-tmc-greater-cooch-behar.

Bhattacharya, Singdhendu. "Bengal Elections 2021: 'Party Society', 'Subaltern Hindutva', 'Bhadrolok': A Few Terms Dominating Media Coverage." Outlook, April 8, 2021. https://www.outlookindia.com/website/story/india-news-bengal-elections-2021-party-society-subaltern-hindutva-bhadrolok-a-few-terms-dominating-media-coverage/379591.

Bhattacharya, Snigdhendu. "BJP Wins Pro-CAA Matua Votes But CAA to Hit Mamata Hurdle," Outlook, 3 May, 2021.

Bhattacharya, Sukanta. "Caste, Class and Politics in West Bengal." Economic and Political Weekly 38, no. 3 (2003): 242–246.

Bhattacharya, Tithi. The Sentinels of Culture: Class, Education and the Colonial Intellectual in Bengal. New Delhi: Oxford University Press, 2005.

Biswas, A.K. "Saraswati Karketta." Mainstream Weekly 57, no. 34 (2019).

Biswas, Manosanta. "Caste and Socio-cultural Mobility in West Bengal: A Hybrid Cultural Elocution of Matua Reforms Movement." Contemporary Voice of Dalit 10, no. 2 (2018): 232–243.

Biswas, Soutik. "Who Says Communism in Dead in Bengal." BBC News Network South Asia, May 12, 2011. http://www.bbc.com/news/world-south-asia-13371621.

Biswas-Thakur Debendralal. Matuẏāra Hindu Naẏ: Dalit Aikyer Sandhāne. Kolkata: Harichand Mission Press, 1977.

Biswas-Thakur Debendralal. Bauddha Dharma o Matuẏā Dharmer Samīkṣā. Kolkata, India: Matua Literary Council, 1991.

Blair, Harry W. "Rising Kulaks and Backward Classes in Bihar: Social Change in the Late 1970s." Economic and Political Weekly 15, no. 2 (1980): 64–74.

Bose, Nirmal Kumar. The Structure of Hindu Society, trans. Andre Beteille. New Delhi: Orient Longman, 1996.

Bose, Sugata. Agrarian Bengal: Economy Social Structure and Politics, 1919–1947. Cambridge: Cambridge University Press, 2008.

Bose, Pradip Kumar. "Mobility and Conflict: Social Roots of Caste Violence in Bihar." In Social Stratification, edited by Dipankar Gupta, 369–384. New Delhi: Oxford University Press, 2014.

Bourdieu, Pierre and Jean-Claude Passeron. Reproduction in Education, Society and Culture. London: Sage, 1970.

Bourdieu, Pierre. Outline of a Theory of Practice. London: Cambridge University Press, 1977.

Bourdieu, Pierre. Distinction: A Social Critique of the Judgment of Taste. Cambridge: Harvard University Press, 1984.

Bourdieu, Pierre and L.J.D. Wacquant. "The Purpose of Reflexive Sociology (The Chicago Workshop)." In An Invitation to Reflexive Sociology, edited by Pierre Bourdieu and L.J. D. Wacquant, 61–215. Chicago: University of Chicago Press, 1992.

Brass, Paul. "The Politicization of the Peasantry in a North Indian State – part II." Journal of Peasant Studies 8, no. 1 (1980): 3–36.

Brian, Barry. Culture and Equality: An Egalitarian Critique of Multiculturalism. Cambridge, MA: Harvard University Press, 2001.

Broomfield, J. H. Elite Conflict in a Plural Society. Bombay: Oxford University Press, 1968.

Buchanan-Hamilton F. A Geographical, Statistical and Historical Description of the District, a Zillah of Dinajpur in The Province, or Soubah of Bengal. Baptist Mission Press, 1833.

Burra, Neera. "Buddhism, Conversion and Identity: A Case Study of Village Mahars." In Caste: Its Twentieth Century Avatar, edited by M.N Srinivas, 152–173. Gurgaon: Penguin, 1996.

Business Standard, "Exclusion of Hindu Bengalis from Assam NRC Changing Political," September 22, 2019, https://www.business-standard.com/article/pti-stories/exclus ion-of-hindu-bengalis-from-assam-nrc-changing-political-119092200259_1.html.

Byapari, Manoranjan and Meenakshi Mukherjee. "Is There Dalit Writing in Bangla?" Economic and Political Weekly 42, no. 41 (2007): 4116–4120.

Byapari, Manoranjan. Itibritte Chandal Jibon. Kolkata: Kolkata Prakashan, 2012.

Byapari, Manoranjan. "Matua Ek Mukti Sena." Hatebajare Patrika, Utsab Sankhya 1420. Bardhhaman: Pranab Kumar Chakrabarty, 2013.

Chakrabarti, Prafulla Kumar. The Marginal Men: The Refugees and the Left Political Syndrome in West Bengal. Kalyani: Lumiere Books, 1990.

Chakrabarty, Dipesh. Rethinking Working-Class History: Bengal 1890–1940. Princeton: Princeton University Press, 2000.

Chakrabarty, Dipesh. Provincializing Europe: Postcolonial Thought and Historical Difference. Princeton, New Jersey: Princeton University Press, 2008.

Chakrabarty, Dipesh. "Trade Unions in a Hierarchical Culture: The Jute Workers of Calcutta, 1950–52." In Subaltern Studies, Volume. III, edited by Ranajit Guha, 116–152. New Delhi: Oxford University Press, 2014.

Chakraborti, Anil Kumar. Beneficiaries of Land Reforms: The West Bengal Scenario. Kolkata: State Institute of Panchayat and Rural Development, 2003.

Chakrabarti, Kunal. Religious Process: The Puranas and the Making of a Regional Tradition. New Delhi: Oxford University Press, 2001.

Chakravarti, Ramakanta. Vaishnavism in Bengal. Calcutta: Sanskrit Pustak Bhandar, 1985.

Chandhoke, Neera. "Revisiting the Crisis of Representation Thesis: the Indian Context." Democratization 12, no. 3 (2005): 308–330.

Chandoke, Neera. "Three Cheers for Civil Society." Hindu, January 18, 2018.

Chandra, Bipan. India's Struggle for Independence. New Delhi: Penguin, 1989.

Chandra, Uday. "Introduction." In Politics of Caste in West Bengal, edited by Uday Chandra, Geir Heierstad and Kenneth Bo Nielsen, 1–18. New Delhi: Routledge, 2016.

Chatterjee, Joya. Bengal Divided: Hindu communalism and Partition. New Delhi: Cambridge University Press, 2002.

Chatterjee, Joya. The Spoils of Partition: Bengal and India, 1947–1967. New Delhi: Cambridge University Press, 2018.

Chatterjee, Jyotiprasad and Supriyo Basu. Left Front and After: Understanding the Dynamics of Poriborton in West Bengal. New Delhi: Sage, 2020.

Chatterjee, Nilanjana. "The East Bengal Refugees: A lesson in Survival." In Calcutta: The Living City, vol. 2, edited by Sukanta Chaudhuri, 70–77. Calcutta: Oxford University Press, 1990.

Chatterjee, Partha. Bengal, 1920–1947, The Land Question. Calcutta: K. P Bagchi, 1984.

Chatterjee, Partha. "The Colonial State and Peasant Resistance in Bengal 1920–1947." Past and Present 110 (1986): 169–204.

Chatterjee, Partha. The Nation and Its Fragments: Colonial and Postcolonial Histories. Princeton: Princeton University Press, 1993.

Chatterjee, Partha. "Caste and Subaltern Consciousness." Subaltern Studies 6 (1994):167–209.

Chatterjee, Partha. The Present History of West Bengal. New Delhi: Oxford University Press, 1997.

Chatterjee, Partha. "The Coming Crisis in West Bengal." Economic and Political Weekly 44, no. 9 (2009): 42–45.

Chatterjee, Partha. "Partition and the Mysterious Disappearance of Caste in Bengal." In Politics of Caste in West Bengal, edited by Uday Chandra, Geir Heierstad and Kenneth Bo Nielsen, 83–102. New Delhi: Routledge, 2016.

Chatterjee, Shibashis. "Regionalism in West Bengal: A Critical Engagement." India Review 13, no. 4 (2014): 417–435.

Chattopadhyay, Bankim Chandra. transl. Bibek Deboy, Samya. New Delhi: Liberty Institute, 2002.

Chattopadhyay, Gautam. Communism and Bengal's Freedom Movement, Vol. 1. New Delhi: People's Publishing House, 1970.

Chattopadhyay, Suhrid Sankar. "Constant Traffic." Frontline, June 15, 2007. https:// frontline.thehindu.com/cover-story/article30191822.ece.

Chattopadhyay, Suman. "Chuni Kotaler Attahatta: Bishwyabidyaloie Rajnitir Fal." Anandabazar Patrika, June 6, 1995.

Chandra, Aishik. "NRC Fallout: West Bengal CM Mamata Banerjee Consolidates Dalit Votes; Namasudra Development Board to be formed." New Indian Express, August, 6, 2018.

Chandra, Uday and Kenneth Bo Nielsen. "The Importance of Caste in Bengal." Economic and Political Weekly 47, no. 44 (2012): 59–62.

Chaudhuri, B. "Eastern India." In The Cambridge Economic History of India, Vol 2, edited by Dharma Kumar, 294–332. Cambridge: Cambridge University Press, 1983.

Chaudhuri, B.B. "Land Market in Eastern India, 1793–1940 Part I : The Movement of Land Prices." The Indian Economic & Social History Review 12, no. 1 (1975): 1–42.

Chaudhuri, B.B. "Land Market in Eastern India, 1793–1940 Part II: The Changing Composition of the Landed Society." The Indian Economic & Social History Review 12, no. 2 (1975): 133–167.

Chaudhuri, Moumita. "They are Using Dalit Votes for Selfish Ends," The Telegraph, December 20, 2020, https://www.telegraphindia.com/culture/people/they-are -using-Dalit-votes-for-selfish-ends/cid/1801105.

Community Party of India (Marxist). "Memorandum on National Integration", 1968.

Communist Party of India (Marxist). Party Programme, https://cpim.org/documents/ cpim-programme.pdf.

Communist Party of India (Marxist). "Resolution adopted at All India Convention on Problems of Dalits." New Delhi, February 22, 2006.

Communist Party of India (Marxist). Statement of the CPI(M) on Thirty Years of the Left Front Government in West Bengal, available at https://www.cpim.org/content/ thirty-years-left-front-government-west-bengal.

Das, Chittaranjan. "Indian National Pact and Bengal National Pact." In Political Thinkers of Modern India: Chittaranjan Das, edited by Veriender Grover, 86–88. New Delhi: Deep and Deep, 2016.

Das, Pushpita. Illegal Migration from Bangladesh: Deportation, Border Fences and Work Permits, Monograph Series no. 56. New Delhi: Institute for Defence Studies and Analyses, 2016.

Das, Raju. "Identity Politics: A Marxist View." Class, Race and Corporate Power 8, no. 1 (2020).

Das, Ritanjan and Zaad Mahmood. "Contradictions, Negotiations and Reform: The Story of Left Policy Transition in West Bengal." Journal of South Asian Development 10, no. 2 (2015): 199–229.

Dasgupta, Abhijit. "The Puzzling Numbers: The Policies of Counting 'Refugees' in West Bengal." South Asian Refugee Watch 2, no. 2 (2000): 64–73.

Dasgupta, Biplab. "Sharecropping in West Bengal: From Independence to Operation Barga." Economic and Political Weekly 19, vol. 26 (1984): A85–A87+A89–A96.

Dasgupta, Biplab. "Agricultural Labour under Colonial, Semi-Capitalist and Capitalist Conditions: A Case Study of West Bengal." Economic and Political Weekly 19, no. 39 (1984): A129–A133+A136-A148.

Dasgupta, Rajarshi. "Rhyming Revolution: Marxism and Culture in Colonial Bengal." Studies in History 21, no. 1 (2005): 79–98.

Datta, Polly. "The Issue of Discrimination in Indian Federalism in Post-1977 Politics of West Bengal." Comparative Studies of South Asia, Africa and the Middle East 25, no. 2 (2005): 449–464.

Datta, Pranati. Push-Pull Factors of Undocumented Migration from Bangladesh to West Bengal: A Perception Study. Qualitative Report. vol. 9, no. 2. Kolkata: Indian Statistical Institute, 2004.

Datta, Romita. "Bengal Manifesto War: BJP's Icon Worship vs. Mamata's 'Outsider' Campaign." India Today, March 22, 2021. https://www.indiatoday.in/india-today-insi ght/story/bengal-manifesto-war-bjp-s-icon-worship-vs-mamata-s-outsider-campa ign-1782381-2021-03-22.

Deshpande, Ashwini and Katherine Newman. "Where the Path Leads: The Role of Caste in Post-University Employment Expectations." Economic and Political Weekly 42, no. 41 (2007): 4133–4140.

Devi, Mahasveta. "The Story of Chuni Kotal," Economic and Political Weekly 17, no. 35 (1992): 1836–1837.

Dey, Ishita. "On the Margins of Citizenship: Principles of Care and Rights of the Residents of the Ranaghat Women's Home, Nadia District." Refugee Watch 33 (2009): 1–22.

Dirks B. Nicholas. Castes of Mind: Colonialism and the Making of Modern India. Princeton, New Jersey: Princeton University Press, 2001.

DiMaggio, Paul J. and Walter W. Powell. "Introduction." in The New Institutionalism in Organizational Analysis, eds. Walter W. Powell and Paul J. DiMaggio, 1–40. Chicago, University of Chicago Press, 1991.

Dumont, Louis. Homo Hierarchicus: The Caste System and Its Implications. London: Weidenfeld and Nicolson, 1970.

Durkheim, Emile. The Rules of Sociological Method. New York: Free Press, 1895.

Durkheim, Emile. Suicide. New York: Free Press, 1951.

Echeverri-Gent, John. "Public Participation and Poverty Alleviation: The Experience of Reform Communists in India's West Bengal." World Development 20, no. 10 (1992): 1401–22.

Economic Times Online. "Delhi Rally: Modi Lashes out at Rivals for Spreading Lies Over Citizenship Law." December 22, 2019. https://economictimes.indiatimes.com/ news/politics-and-nation/land-ownership-to-40-lakh-people-narendra-modi/arti cleshow/72923629.cms.

Espiritu, Yen. Asian American Pan-ethnicity: Bridging Institutions and Identities. Philadelphia: Temple University Press, 1992.

Express News Service. "Former Mamata Allies Drift Towards Congress." Indian Express, November 16, 2010. http://archive.indianexpress.com/news/former-mamata-allies -drift-towards-cong/711686.

Express News Service. "Kolkata Cabinet Okays Boards for Namasudra and Matua Communities." Indian Express, November 6, 2018. https://indianexpress.com/arti cle/cities/kolkata/kolkata-cabinet-okays-boards-for-namasudra-and-matua-comm unities-5435562/.

Express News Service. "Bengal Polls: EC slaps 24-hour Campaign Ban on Mamata; TMC Calls it Biased, Undemocratic." Indian Express, April 13, 2021. https://indianexpr ess.com/elections/mamata-banerjee-ec-ban-west-bengal-election-campaign-tmc -7270633/.

Felski, Rita. Beyond Feminist Aesthetics: Feminist Literature and Social Change. Cambridge: Harvard University Press, 1989.

Franda, Marcus F. "West Bengal." In State Politics in India, edited by Myron Weiner. Princeton: Princeton University Press, 1968.

Franda, Marcus F. Radical Politics in West Bengal. Massachusetta: MIT Press, 1971.

Frankel, Francine R. "Caste, Land and Dominance in Bihar: Breakdown of the Brahminical Social Order." In Dominance and State Power in Modern India, Vol I, edited by Francine Frankel and M.S.A. Rao, 46–132. Delhi: Oxford University Press, 1989.

Fraser, Nancy. "Rethinking the Public Sphere: A Contribution to the Critique of Actually Existing Democracy." Social Text, no. 25/26 (1990): 56–80.

Fraser, Nancy. Justice Interrupts: Critical Reflections on the "Postsocialist" Condition. New York: Routledge, 1997.

Fraser, Nancy and Axel Honneth. Redistribution or Recognition: A Political-Philosophical Exchange. London: Verso, 2003.

Fuller, C.J. "Introduction." In Caste Today, edited by C.J Fuller, 1–31. Delhi: Oxford University Press, 1996.

Gamson, Joshua. "Must Identity Movements Self-Destruct? A Queer Dilemma." Social Problems 42, no. 3 (1995): 390–407.

Geertz, Clifford. "Religion as a Cultural System." In Anthropological Approaches to the Study of Religion, edited by Michael Banton, 1–46. London: Tavistock, 1966.

Geertz, Clifford. The Interpretation of Cultures. New York: Basic Books, 1973.

Geertz, Clifford. "Common as a Cultural System." In Anthropological Approaches to the Study of Religion. The Antioch Review 33, no. 1 (1975): 5–26.

Ghosal, Anindita. "Acquisition of Rehabilitation Rights by East Bengal Refugees Post-1947." Proceedings of the Indian History Congress 70 (2009–10): 1210–1219.

Ghosh, Amitav. The Hungry Tide. London: Harper Collins, 2004.

Ghosh, Anindita. "Revisiting the 'Bengal Renaissance': Literary Bengali and Low-Life Print in Colonial Calcutta." 37, no. 42 (2002): 4329–4338.

Ghosh, Anindita. "Singing in a New World: Street Songs and Urban Experience in Colonial Calcutta." History Workshop Journal 7 (2013): 111–136.

Ghosh, Anjan. "Cast(e) out in Bengal." Seminar 508 (May 2001).

Ghosh, Atig. "Left Front Government in West Bengal (1971–1982)." Policies and Practices 93 (2017): 1–28.

Ghosh, Bishwanath. "Jadavpur University Professor Trolled over Tribal Status." Hindu, September 5, 2020. https://www.thehindu.com/news/national/other-states/jadavpur-university-professor-trolled-over-tribal status/article32529928.ece.

Ghosh, Madhusudan. "Agricultural Development, Agrarian Structure and Rural Poverty in West Bengal." Economic and Political Weekly 33, no. 47/48 (1998): 2987–2995.

Ghosh, Parimal. "Where Have All the 'Bhadraloks' Gone?." Economic and Political Weekly 39, no. 3 (2004): 247–251.

Ghosh, Parimal. What Happened to the Bhadralok. New Delhi: Primus, 2016.

Ghosh, Raya. "BJP Gives Bengali Twist to Bella Ciao with Pishi Jaao in Message For Mamata Banerjee." India Today, February 21, 2021. https://www.indiatoday.in/trending-news/story/bjp-gives-bengali-twist-to-bella-ciao-with-pishi-jaao-in-message-for-mamata-banerjee-watch-1771477-2021-02-21.

Giddens, Anthony. The Constitution of Society: Outline of the Theory of Structuration. Berkeley: University of California Press, 1984.

Gillan, Michael. "Refugees or Infiltrators? The Bharatiya Janata Party and 'Illegal' Migration from Bangladesh." Asian Studies Review 26, no. 1 (2002): 73–95.

Giri, Saroj. "From Uprising to Movement." Economic & Political Weekly 52, no 33 (2017): 15–17.

Gitlin, Todd. The Twilight of Common Dreams: Why America is Wracked by Culture Wars. New York: Metropolitan Books, 1995.

Gramsci, Antonio. Selections from the Prison Notebooks. New York: International Publishers, 1992.

Greener, Ian. "The Potential of Path Dependence in Political Studies." Politics 25, no. 1 (2005): 62–72.

Gonsalves, Trijita. "Where are the Women?: A Study of Electoral Promises in the West Bengal Assembly Elections." The Indian Journal of Political Science 72, no. 4 (2011): 981–996.

Gordon, Leonard A. Bengal: The Nationalist Movement 1876–1940. New Delhi: Manohar, 1974.

Gorges, Michael J. "New Institutionalist Explanations for Institutional Change: A Note of Caution." Politics 21, no. 2 (2001): 137–145.

Gorringe, Hugo. "You Build Your House, We'll Build Ours: The Attractions and Pitfalls of Dalit Identity Politics." Social Identities 11, no. 6 (2005): 653–672.

Gorringe, Hugo. Untouchable Citizens: Dalit Movements and Democratisation in Tamil Nadu. New Delhi: Sage, 2005.

Gorringe, Hugo. Panthers in Parliament: Dalits, Caste and Political Power in South India. New Delhi: Oxford University Press, 2017.

Goswami, Biswabrata. "Trinamool Congress may Find the Going Tough in Jhargram." Statesman, May 12, 2019. https://www.thestatesman.com/elections-2019/tmc-may -find-going-tough- jhargram-1502754411.html.

Government of India. Report of the Backward Classes Commission, Volume I. New Delhi: Government of India, 1980.

Government of West Bengal, West Bengal Human Development Report 2004. Development and Planning Department, 2004.

Government of West Bengal. West Bengal Economic Review 2006–07. Development and Planning Department, Bureau of Applied Economics and Statistics, 2007.

Government of West Bengal. Expanding Horizons: Higher Education in West Bengal. Kolkata: Department of Higher Education, Government of West Bengal, 2016.

Guha, Abhijit. "How the Lodhas Became Criminal or Meeting of the Past and the Present." The Eastern Anthropologist 69, no. 1 (2016): 71–88.

Guha, Ayan. "West Bengal at Crossroads: An Insight into the Emerging Political Dynamics." Mainstream Weekly 53, no. 14 (2015).

Guha, Ayan. "West Bengal Elections: Unchanged Amidst Change." Economic and Political Weekly 51, no. 41 (2016): 69–71.

Guha, Ayan. "Caste Factor in West Bengal Elections." Mainstream Weekly 56, no. 33 (2016).

Guha, Ayan. "Caste and Politics in West Bengal: Traditional Limitations and Contemporary Developments." Contemporary Voice of Dalit 9, no. 1 (2017): 27–36.

Guha, Ayan. "Is There A Second Wave of Dalit Upsurge in West Bengal?" Economic and Political Weekly 54, no. 2 (2019).

Guha, Ayan. "Caste Politics, Secular Idiom," Indian Express, May 3, 2019.

Guha, Ayan. "Polarization Plus Anti-incumbency: A Full Scale View of BJP's Rise in Bengal." Mainstream Weekly 57, no. 34 (2019).

Guha, Ayan. "RSS and the Reservation Riddle." Statesman, 4 October, 2019.

Guha, Ayan. "Caste Question in West Bengal Politics: Rising Relevance of Continuing Inconsequentiality?" Contemporary South Asia 29, no. 3 (2021): 376–400.

Guha, Ayan. "Beyond Conspiracy and Coordinated Ascendancy: Revisiting Caste Question in West Bengal under the Left Front Rule (1977–2011)." Contemporary Voice of Dalit 13, no. 1 (2021): 50–65.

Gundimeda, Sambaiah. Dalit Politics in Contemporary India. Abingdon: Routledge, 2016.

Gupta, Dipankar. "Caste and Politics: Identity over System." Annual Review of Anthropology 34 (2005): 409–427.

Gupta, Dipankar. "Whither the Indian Village: Culture and Agriculture in Rural India." Economic and Political Weekly 40, no. 8 (2005): 751–58.

Gupta, Dipankar. "From Varna to Jati: The Indian Caste System, from the Asiatic to the Feudal Mode of Production." Journal of Contemporary Asia 10, vol. 3 (1980): 249–271.

Gupta, Kanchan. Beyond the Poll Rhetoric of BJP's Contentious Citizenship Amendment Bill, Special Report no. 89. New Delhi: Observer Research Foundation, 2019.

Gupta, Monobina. Left Politics in Bengal: Time Travels among Bhadralok Marxists. New Delhi: Orient BlackSwan, 2010.

Gupta, Monobina. Didi: A Political Biography. New Delhi: Harper Collins, 2012.

Gupta, Monobina. "Understanding Bengal's Namasudras, Who Are Divided between TMC and BJP." Wire, February 28, 2019, https://thewire.in/caste/understanding-the-history-of-bengals-namasudras-who-are-divided-between-tmc-and-bjp.

Gupta, Swarupa. Notions of Nationhood in Bengal: Perspectives on Samaj, c. 1867–1905. Leiden: Brill, 2009.

Gurney, Joan Neff and Kathleen J. Tierney. "Relative Deprivation and Social Movements: A Critical Look at Twenty Years of Theory and Research." The Sociological Quarterly 23, no. 1 (1982): 33–47.

Gurr, Ted. Why Men Rebel. Princeton: Princeton University Press, 1970.

Guru, Gopal. "Dalit Movement in Mainstream Sociology." Economic and Political Weekly 28, no. 14 (1993): 570–573.

Halbwachs, Maurice. On Collective Memory, trans. Lewis A. Coser. Chicago: University of Chicago Press, 1992.

Halder, Deep. Blood Island: An Oral History of Marichjhapi Massacre. New Delhi: Harper Collins, 2019.

Halder, Sudhir Ranjan. Sri Sri Harililamrita Prasange. http://generalbooksonmatuya.blogspot.com/2016/03/blog-post_36.html.

Halder, Sudhir Ranjan. Harichand Thakur. http://dalitliteratures.blogspot.com/2017/03/blog-post_19.html.

Halder, Sudhir Ranjan. Harichand Thakur o Matua Dharma. http://generalbooksonmatuya.blogspot.com/2015/10/9433814298-7407103432_72.html.

Halder, Sudhir Ranjan. Dicharitai Matua Dharma. http://dalitliteratures.blogspot.com/2017/02/dwicharitay-matuyadharma.html.

Hall, Peter A. and Rosemarcy R. Taylor. "Political Science and the Three New Institutionalisms." Political Studies 44 (1996): 936–957.

Hansen, Thomas Blom. The Saffron Wave: Democracy and Hindu Nationalism in Modern India. Princeton: Princeton University Press, 1999.

Hansen, Thomas Blom. "The Politics of Permanent Performance. The Production of Authority in the Locality." In Politics of Cultural Mobilization in India, edited by John Zavos, Andrew Wyatt and Vernon Marston Hewitt, 19–36. New Delhi: Oxford University Press, 2004.

Hardgrave, R. L. The Nadars of Tamilnad: The Political Culture of a Community in Change. Berkeley: University of California Press, 1969.

Hardgrave, R. L. "Political participation and primordial solidarity: The Nadars of Tamilnad." In Caste in Indian Politics, edited by Rajni Kothari, 96–120. New Delhi: Orient Longman, 1970.

Hardtmann, Eva-Maria. The Dalit Movement in India: Local Practices, Global Connections. New Delhi: Oxford University Press, 2009.

Harriss, John. 'What is Happening in Rural West Bengal? Agrarian Reforms, Growth and Distribution.' Economic and Political Weekly 28, no. 24 (1993): 1237–1247.

Harriss, John. "Antinomies of Empowerment: Observations on Civil Society, Politics and Urban Governance in India." Economic and Political Weekly 42, no. 26 (2007): 2716–2724.

Hasan, Zoya. "Democracy and Development in Uttar Pradesh." In Development Failure and Identity Politics in Uttar Pradesh, edited by Roger Jeffery, Craig Jeffrey and Jens Lerche, 239–256. New Delhi: Sage, 2014.

Heather, Smith J., Thomas F. Pettigrew, Gina M. Pippin and Silvana Bialosiewicz. "Relative Deprivation: A Theoretical and Meta-Analytic Review." Personality and Social Psychology Review 16, no. 3 (2012): 203–232.

Heierstad, Geir. Caste, Entrepreneurship and the Illusions of Tradition: Branding the Potters of Kolkata. London: Anthem, 2017.

Heyer, Judith. "The Marginalisation of Dalits in a Modernising Economy." In The Comparative Political Economy of Development: Africa and South Asia, edited by Barbara. Harriss-White and Judith Heyer, 225–247. London: Routledge, 2010.

Hindu. "West Bengal Witnesses Protests against NRC." August 1, 2018. https://www.thehindu.com/news/national/other-states/west-bengal-witnesses-protests-against-nrc/article24574853.ece.

Hindustan Times. "CAA Saves Hindus from NRC Screening, Says Bengal BJP Booklet; Sets Up Row." January 6, 2020. https://www.hindustantimes.com/india-news/caa-saves-hindus-from-nrc-screening-says-bengal-bjp-booklet-sets-up-row/story-gAH3tBvi1MbD1njDm3GoKP.html.

Hobsbawm, Eric and Terence Ranger. The Invention of Tradition. New York: Cambridge University Press, 2012.

Honneth, Axel. The Struggle for Recognition: The Grammar of Social Conflicts. Cambridge: Polity, 1995.

Issac, Harold. India's Ex-Untouchables. Bombay: Asia Publishing House, 1964.

Indian Express Bureau. "Lok Sabha Polls: The Caste Constituency." Indian Express, April 29, 2014. http://indianexpress.com/article/india/politics/lok-sabha-polls-the-caste-constituency, accessed on February 5, 2017.

Indo Asian News Service. "Mamata Names Two Kolkata Metro Stations After Journalists," Yahoo News, February 7, 2011. https://in.news.yahoo.com/mamata-names-two-kolkata-metro-stations-journalists-20110207-074526-920.html, accessed on 5 February, 2017.

Jaffrelot, Christophe. The Hindu Nationalist Movement and Indian Politics: 1925 to the 1990s. New Delhi: Penguin, 1999.

Jaffrelot, Christophe. "The Rise of the Other Backward Classes in the Hindi Belt." Journal of Asian Studies, 59, no. 1 (2000): 86–108.

Jaffrelot, Christophe. "Sanskritization vs. Ethnicization in India: Changing Identities and Caste Politics before Mandal." Asian Survey 40, no. 5 (2000): 756–766.

Jaffrelot, Christophe. India's Silent Revolution: The Rise of the Lower Castes in North India. Delhi: Permanent Black, 2003.

Jaffrelot, Christophe. "Introduction." In Rise of the Plebeians? The Changing Face of Indian Legislative Assemblies, edited by Christophe Jaffrelot and Sanjay Kumar, 1–23. New Delhi: Routledge, 2009.

Jaffrelot, Christophe. "The Uneven Rise of Lower Castes in the Politics of Madhya Pradesh." In Rise of the Plebians? The Changing Face of Indian Legislative Assemblies, edited by Christophe Jafferlot and Sanjay Kumar, 103–148. New Delhi: Routledge, 2009.

Jaffrelot , Christophe. "Quota for Patels? The Neo-Middle-Class Syndrome and the (Partial) Return of Caste Politics in Gujarat." Studies in Indian Politics 4, no. 2 (2016): 218–232.

Jana, Arun Kumar. "Development (?) and Identity Politics in West Bengal: The Kamtapur Movement in North Bengal." In Globalization and Politics of Identity in India, edited by Bhupinder Brar, Ashutosh Kumar and Ronki Ram, 97–126. New Delhi: Pearson, 2008.

Jana, Arun Kumar. "Backwardness and Political Articulation of Backwardness in the North Bengal Region of West Bengal." In Rethinking State Politics in India, edited by Ashutosh Kumar, 153–196. New Delhi: Routledge, 2011.

Jaoul, Nicolas. "Learning the Use of Symbolic Means: Dalits, Ambedkar Statues and the State in Uttar Pradesh." Contributions to Indian Sociology 40, no. 2 (2006):175–207.

Jaoul, Nicolas. "Dalit Processions: Street Politics and Democratization in India," In Staging Politics: Power and Performance in Asia and Africa, edited by J.C. Strauss & D.B. Cruise O'Brien, 173–193. London: I.B.Tauris, 2007.

Jaoul, Nicolas. "Citizenship in Religious Clothing? Navayana Buddhism and Dalit Emancipation in late 1990s Uttar Pradesh." Focaal – Journal of Global and Historical Anthropology 76 (2016): 46–68.

Jayal, Nirja Gopal. Citizenship and Its Discontents: An Indian History. Ranikhet: Permanent Black, 2013.

Jeffrey, Craig. "A Fist Is Stronger than Five Fingers: Caste and Dominance in Rural North India." Transactions of the Institute of British Geographers 26, no. 2 (2001): 217–236.

Jeffrey, Craig, Patricia Jeffery and Roger Jeffery. "Dalit Revolution? New Politicians in Uttar Pradesh, India." Journal of Asian Studies 67, no. 4 (2008): 1365–1396.

Jensenius, Francesca R. "Power, Performance and Bias: Evaluating the Electoral Quotas for Scheduled Castes in India." PhD dissertation, University of California, 2013.

Jodhka, Surinder S. and Katherine Newman. "In the Name of Globalisation: Meritocracy, Productivity and the Hidden Language of Caste." Economic and Political Weekly 42, no. 41 (2007): 4125–4132.

Jha, Rajani Ranjan and Bavana Mishra, "Centre-state Relations, 1980–90: The Experience of West Bengal." The Indian Journal of Political Science 54, no. 2 (1993): 209–237.

Joshi, Barbara. "Recent Developments in Inter-Regional Mobilisation of Dalit Protest in India." South Asia Bulletin 7 (1987): 112–135.

Jyoti, Dhrubo. "Mamata's Massive Bengal Victory is the Death of the Gentleman in Kolkata." Hindustan Times, May 21, 2016. https://www.hindustantimes.com/assem bly-elections/mamata-s-massive-bengal-victory-is-the-death-of-the-bhadralok-in -kolkata/story-NiTwCP9NqVFCzoTIgd42SP.html.

Kala Sadhana. "Bengal Election 2021." Times of India, April 1, 2021. https://timesofindia .indiatimes.com/blogs/methink/bengal-election-2021.

Karanth, G.K. "Caste in Contemporary Rural India," In Caste: Its Twentieth Century Avatar, edited by M.N Srinivas, 87–109. Gurgaon: Penguin, 1997.

Kashyap, Omprakash. "Triveni Sangh: First Hints of the Power of Organization." Forward Press, 2016. https://www.forwardpress.in/2016/10/triveni-sangh-first-hints -of-the-power-of-organization/.

Kaviraj, Sudipta. "The Culture of Representative Democracy." In Democracy in India, edited by Nirja Gopal Jayal, 229–257. New Delhi: Oxford University Press, 2014.

Khasnabis, Ratan. "Economy of West Bengal." Economic and Political Weekly 43, no. 52 (2009): 103–115.

Kling, B. Blair B. "The Origin of the Managing Agency System in India." Journal of Asian Studies 26, no. 1 (1966): 37–47.

Kohli, Atul. "Parliamentary Communism and Agrarian Reform: The Evidence from India's Bengal." Asian Survey 23, no. 7 (1983): 783–809.

Kohli, Atul. "From Elite Radicalism to Democratic Consolidation: The Rise of Reform Communism in West Bengal." In Dominance and State Power in Modern India: Decline of a Social Order, Vol II, edited by M. S. A. Rao and Francine F. Frankel, 367–415. New Delhi: Oxford University Press, 1990.

Kohli, Atul. "From Breakdown to Order: West Bengal." In State and Politics in India, edited by Partha Chatterjee, 336–366. New Delhi: Oxford University Press, 1997.

Kohli, Atul. The State and Poverty in India: The Politics of Reform. Cambridge: Cambridge University Press, 2006.

Konar, Harekrishna. Present Stage of Peasant Movement. The Marxist, 41 (2015), https://www.cpim.org/content/ present-stage-peasant-movement.

Kothari, Rajni. "Introduction," in Caste in Indian Politics, edited by Rajni Kothari, 3–25. New Delhi: Orient Longman, 1970.

Kothari, Rajni and Rushikesh Maru. "Caste and Secularism in India: Case Study of a Caste Federation." Journal of Asian Studies 25, vol. 1 (1965): 33–50.

Kothari, Rajni and Rushikesh Maru. "Federating of Political Interests: the Kshatriyas of Gujarat." In Caste in Indian Politics, edited by Rajni Kothari, 70–101. New Delhi: Orient Longman, 1970.

Kothari, Rajni. "Rise of the Dalits and the Renewed Debate on Caste." Economic and Political Weekly 29, no. 26 (1994): 1589–1594.

Krasner, Stephen D. "Approaches to the State: Alternative Conceptions and Historical Dynamics." Comparative Politics 16, no. 2 (1984): 223–246.

Kukathas, Chandran. "Are There Any Cultural Rights?." Political Theory 20, no. 1 (1992): 105–139.

Kumar, Arvind and Ayan Guha. "Political Future of Caste in West Bengal." Economic and Political Weekly 49, no. 32 (2014): 73–74.

Kushry, Sweta. "Mandal Commission and the Left Front in West Bengal." Economic and Political Weekly 26, no. 8 (1991): 419–420.

Lama-Rewal, Stéphanie Tawa. "The Resilient Bhadralok: A Profile of the West Bengal MLAs." In Rise of the Plebeians? The Changing Face of Indian Legislative Assemblies, edited by Christophe Jaffrelot and Sanjay Kumar, 361–391. New Delhi: Routledge, 2009.

Lefebvre, Henri. The Production of Space, trans. Donald Nicholson- Smith. Oxford: Blackwell, 1991.

Laushey, David M. Bengal Terrorism and Marxist Left. Calcutta: Firma K.L.M, 1975.

Lieten, G.K. "De-peasantisation Discontinued: Land Reforms in West Bengal." Economic and Political Weekly 25, no. 40 (1990): 2265–68.

Lieten, G.K. Power, Politics and Rural Development: Essays on India. New Delhi: Manohar, 2003.

Lin, Sharat G. and Madan C. Paul. "Bangladeshi Migrants in Delhi: Social Insecurity, State Power, and Captive Vote Banks." Bulletin of Concerned Asian Scholars 27, vol. 1 (1995): 3–20.

Lorea, Carola Erika. "Religion, Caste, and Displacement: The Matua Community." Oxford Research Encyclopedia of Asian History, 2020.

Lorea, Carola Erika. Folklore, Religion and the Songs of a Bengali Madman: A Journey between Performance and the Politics of Cultural Representation. Leiden: Brill, 2016.

Lorea, Carola Erika. "Contesting Multiple Borders: Bricolage Thinking and Matua Narratives on the Andaman Islands." Southeast Asian Studies 9, no (2020): 231–276.

Loynd, Maxine. "Understanding the Bahujan Samaj Prerna Kendra: Space, Place and Political Mobilisation." Asian Studies Review 33, no. 4, (2009): 469–482.

Lynch, Owen M. The Politics of Untouchability. Delhi: Gautam Book Centre [1969] (2015).

Mahoney, James. "Path Dependence in Historical Sociology." Theory and Society 29, no. 4 (2000): 507–548.

Majumdar, R. C. History of Ancient Bengal. Calcutta: G. Bharadwaj, 1971.

Majumder, Sarasij. "Who Wants to Marry a Farmer? Neoliberal industrialization and the Politics of Land and Work in Rural West Bengal." Focaal – Journal of Global and Historical Anthropology 64 (2012).

Mallick, Ross. "Refugee Resettlement in Forest Reserves: West Bengal Policy Reversal and the Marichjhapi Massacre." The Journal of Asian Studies 58, no. 1 (1999): 104–25.

Mallick, Ross. Development Policy of a Communist Government: West Bengal since 1977. Cambridge: Cambridge University Press, 2008.

Manor, James. "Pragmatic Progressives in Regional Politics: The Case of Devaraj Urs." Economic and Political Weekly 15, no. 5/7, Annual Number (1980): 201–203+205+ 207+209+211+213.

Manor, James. "Karnataka: Caste, Class, Dominance and Politics in a Cohesive Society." In Dominance and State Power in Modern India, Vol. I, edited by Fancine F. Frankel and M.S. A Rao, 322–361. Delhi: Oxford University Press, 1990.

March, James G. and Johan P. Olsen. Rediscovering Institutions. New York: Free Press, 1989.

Marvin, Davis. Rank and Rivalry: The Politics of Inequality in Rural West Bengal. New Delhi: Select Service Syndicate, 1986.

Mansbridge, Jane. "Should Blacks Represent Blacks and Women Represent Women? A Contingent 'Yes'." The Journal of Politics 61 (1999): 628–57.

Mayer, Adrian. "Caste in an Indian Village: Change and Continuity 1954–1992." In Caste Today, edited by C.J Fuller, 32–64. Delhi: Oxford University Press, 1996.

McGuire, John. The Making of a Colonial Mind: A Quantitative Study of the Bhadralok in Calcutta, 1857–1885. Canberra: Australian National University, 1983.

Merton, Robert K. Social Theory and Social Structure. Glencoe: Free Press, 1968.

Misra, B.B. The Indian Middle Classes: Their Growth in Modern Times. New Delhi: Oxford University Press, 1960.

Mondal, Sandip. "Demystifying Caste in Bengal." Economic and Political Weekly 56, no. 3 (2021): 21–23.

Morrison, Denton. "Some Notes Toward Theory on Relative Deprivation, Social Movements, and Social Change." In Social Movements: A Reader, edited by R. R. Evans, 103–116. Chicago: Rand McNally, 1973.

Mukherjee, Aditi. "Public Discourses on Citizenship in West Bengal: Insights from the Propaganda of Dalit Refugee Organisations," in Interrogating Citizenship: Perspectives from India's East and North East, Policies and Practices 109 (December 2019).

Mukherjee, Bharati. Political Culture and Leadership in India: A Study of West Bengal. New Delhi: Mittal, 1991.

Mukherjee, Ishan. "Battle for the Bhadralok: The historical roots of Hindu majoritarianism in West Bengal." Caravan, November 29, 2019. https://caravanmagazine.in/politics/historical-roots-of-hindu-majoritarianism-in-west-bengal.

Mukherjee, Manju Gopal. "C.R. Das and the Bengal Pact." Proceedings of the Indian History Congress 61 (2000):739–746.

Mukherjee, Sipra. "In Opposition and Allegiance to Hinduism: Exploring the Bengali Matua Hagiography of Harichand Thakur." South Asia: Journal of South Asian Studies 41, no. 2 (2018): 435–451.

Mukherjee, Sipra. "Creating Their Own Gods: Literature from the Margins of Bengal." In Dalit Literatures in India, edited by Joshil K. Abraham and Judith Misrahi-Barak, 138–152. New Delhi: Routledge, 2018.

Mukherjee, S.N. Calcutta: Myths and History. Calcutta: Subarnarekha, 1977.

Mukherjee, S.N. "The Bhadraloks of Bengal." In Social Stratification, edited by Dipankar Gupta, 176–182. New Delhi: Oxford University Press, 2014.

Murmu, Maroona. "Ei Bonge Naki Jati Bhittik Bibhed bole Kichu Nei?." Anandabazar Patrika, June 29, 2019.

Nagel, Joane. "Constructing Ethnicity: Creating and Recreating Ethnic Identity and Culture." Social Problems 41, no. 1 (1994): 152–176.

Nagi, Saroj. "Bucking the Trend." Seminar 622 (June 2011).

Nandy, Chandan. Illegal Immigration from Bangladesh to India: The Emerging Conflicts. Slifka Program in Inter-Communal Coexistence. Brandeis University, 2005.

Narayan, Badri. Fascinating Hindutva: Saffron Politics and Dalit Mobilisation. New Delhi: Sage, 2009.

Narayan, Badri. The Making of the Dalit Public in North India: Uttar Pradesh 1950–Present. New Delhi: Oxford University Press, 2011.

Natrajan, Balmurli. The Culturalization of Caste in India: Identity and Inequality in Multicultural Age (London: Routledge, 2011).

Natrajan, Balmurli. "Racialization and Ethnicization: Hindutva Hegemony and Caste," Ethnic and Racial Studies, https://doi.org/10.1080/01419870.2021.1951318.

Naqvi, Saba and Panini Anand. "Yechury Interview." Outlook, April 17, 2013.

New Indian Express. "CPM, TMC Leaders Share Dais at Matua Meeting." December 29, 2010. https://www.newindianexpress.com/nation/2010/dec/29/cpm-tc-leaders-share-dais-at-matua-meeting-214851.html.

Nielsen, Kenneth Bo. "The Politics of Caste and Class in Singur's Anti-land Acquisition Struggle." In Politics of Caste in West Bengal, edited by Uday Chandra, Geir Heierstad and Kenneth Bo Nielsen, 125–146. New Delhi: Routledge, 2016.

Nielsen, Kenneth Bo. "Mamata Banerjee Redefining Female Leadership." In India's Democracy: Diversity, Co-Optation, Resistance, edited by A. E Ruud and Geir Heierstad, 101–134. Oslo: Universitetsforlaget, 2016.

Nielsen, Kenneth Bo. "Orchestrating Anti-Dispossession Politics: Caste and Movement Leadership in Rural West Bengal." Journal of Contemporary Asia 50, no. 5 (2020): 761–784.

Nossiter, T.J. Marxists State Governments in India: Politics, Economy and Society. London: Pinter Publishers, 1988.

O'Hanlon, Rosalind. Caste, Conflict and Ideology: Mahatma Jyotirao Phule and Low Caste Protest in Nineteenth Century Western India. Ranikhet: Permanent Black, 2016.

O'Malley, L. S. S. Darjeeling District Gazetteer. Government of West Bengal, 1907.

O'Malley, L. S. S. Bankura District Gazetteer. Government of West Bengal, 1908.

Oommen, T. K. "Sociological Issues in the Analysis of Social Movements in Independent India." Sociological Bulletin 26 (1): 14–37.

Omvedt, Gail. "An Introductory Essay." In Land, Caste and Politics in Indian States, edited by Gail Omvedt, 9–50. Delhi: Author's Guild Publications, 1982.

Omvedt, Gail. Dalits and the Democratic Revolution: Dr. Ambedkar and the Dalit Movement in Colonial India. New Delhi: Sage, 1994.

Organiser. "60 lakh Bangladeshi Infiltrators in West Bengal, says BJP leader." July 21, 1991.

Pai, Sudha. Dalit Assertion and the Unfinished Democratic Revolution: The Bahujan Samaj Party in Uttar Pradesh. New Delhi: Sage, 2002.

Pai, Sudha. "Dalit Question and Political Response: Comparative Study of Uttar Pradesh and Madhya Pradesh." Economic and Political Weekly 39, no. 11 (2004): 1141–1150.

Panday, Pranab Kumar. "Politics of Land Grabbing: The Vested Property Act and the Exploitation of Hindu Communities in Bangladesh." International Journal on Minority and Group Right 23, no. 3 (2016): 382–401.

Panikkar, K. N. "Culture and Consciousness in Modern India: A Historical Perspective." Social Scientist 18, no. 4 (1990): 3–32.

Panini, M.N. "The Political Economy of Caste," in Caste: Its Twentieth Century Avatar, ed. M.N Srinivas (Gurgaon: Penguin, 1997), 28–68.

Parsons, Talcott. The Structure of Social Action. New York: McGraw-Hill, 1937.

Paunksnis, Runa Chakraborty. "Bengali Dalit Literature and the Politics of Recognition." South Asia: Journal of South Asian Studies (2021): DOI: 10.1080/00856401.2021.1962496.

Peterson, J. C. K . Burdwan District Gazetteer. Government of West Bengal, 1910.

Phillips, Anne. The Politics of Presence. Oxford: Clarendon Press, 1995.

Pierre, Nora, "Between Memory and History: Les Lieux de Mémoire." Representations 26, no. 1 (1989): 7–24.

Pitkin, Hanna. The Concept of Representation. Los Angeles: University of Press, 1967.

Pramanik, Bimal. "Illegal Migration from Bangladesh: A Case Study of West Bengal." In Illegal Migration from Bangladesh, edited by B. B. Kumar. Delhi: Astha Bharati, 2006.

Pramanik, Bimal. "Infiltration from Bangladesh: A Critical Analysis." Dialogue 10, no. 2 (2008).

Press Trust of India. "TMC's Bid to Bring No-confidence Motion Fails in Lok Sabha." Economic Times, November 22, 2012. https://economictimes.indiatimes.com/news/politics-and-nation/tmcs-bid-to-bring-no-confidence-motion-fails-in-lok-sabha/articleshow/17320130.cms?from=mdr.

Press Trust of India. "Those Opposing Citizenship Law are 'Anti-Dalits', Says JP Nadda." NDTV, December 29, 2019. https://www.ndtv.com/india-news/caa-protests-those-opposing-citizenship-act-are-anti-Dalits-says-jp-nadda-2156008.

Press Trust of India. "Significant rise in number of universities in Bengal during TMC tenure: Partha Chatterjee." Hindustan Times, September 6, 2020. https://www.hindustantimes.com/education/significant-rise-in-number-of-universities-in-bengal-during-tmc-tenure-partha-chatterjee/story-h0SsOyNMaSsDu3YUDjijUK.html.

Purandare, Vaibhav. Savarkar: The True Story of the Father of Hindutva. New Delhi: Juggernaut, 2019.

Pye, Lucian. "Introduction: Political Culture and Political Development." In Political Culture and Political Development, edited by Lucian Pye and Sidney Verba, 3–26. Princeton: Princeton University Press, 1965.

Rana, Kumar. "Problems and Prospects of Dalit Emancipation in West Bengal." Voice of Dalit 1, no. 2 (2008): 167-180.

Ranadive, B.T. Caste, Class and Property Relations. Calcutta: National Book Agency, 1991.

Rao, Anupama. The Caste Question: Dalits and the Politics of Modern India. Ranikhet: Permanent Black, 2019.

Rao, M. S. A. Social Movements in India, Vol 1. Delhi: Manohar, 1982.

Rawal, Vikas and Madhura Swaminathan. "Changing Trajectories: Agricultural Growth in West Bengal, 1950 to 1966." Economic and Political Weekly 33, no. 40 (1998): 2595–2602.

Rawat, Ramnarayan. Reconsidering Untouchability: Chamars and Dalit History in North India. Ranikhet: Permanent Black, 2012.

Ray, Mohit. Poschimbonger Astitva Rakhhai Natunbhabe Bhabtei Hobe. Kolkata: Bharatiya Samaskriti Trust, 2017.

Ray, Mohit and Sujit Sikdar. Analysing the Anti CAA Violence in West Bengal, trans. Ahana Chaudhuri. SPMRF and Refugee Cell, BJP West Bengal, 2020.

Ray, Niharranjan. Banglalir Itihas: Adi Parva, Volume I. Calcutta: Paschimbanga Nirakharata Durikaran Samiti, 1980.

Ray, Rajat and Ratna Ray. "Zamindars and Jotedars: A Study of Rural Politics in Bengal." Modern Asian Studies 9 no. 1 (1975): 81–102.

Ray, Ratnalekha. "The Changing Fortunes of the Bengali Gentry under Colonial Rule – Pal Chaudhuris of Mahesganj, 1800–1950." Modern Asian Studies 21, no. 3 (1987): 511–19.

Reddy, Sanjay. "A Rising Tide of Demands: India's Public Institutions and the Democratic Revolution." In Public Institutions in India: Performance and Design, edited by Devesh Kapur and Pratap Bhanu Mehta, 457–475. New Delhi: Oxford University Press, 2005.

Robin, Cyril. "Bihar: The New Stronghold of OBC Politics." In Rise of the Plebeians? The Changing Face of Indian Legislative Assemblies, edited by Christophe Jaffrelot and Sanjay Kumar, 65–102. New Delhi: Routledge, 2009.

Rogaly, Ben. "Containing Conflict and Reaping Votes: Management of Rural Labour Relations in West Bengal." Economic and Political Weekly 33, vol. 42/43 (1998): 2729–2739.

Rorty, Richard. Achieving Our Country: Leftist Thought in Twentieth-Century America. Cambridge, MA: Harvard University Press, 1998.

Rowe, William L. "The New Cauhans: A Caste Mobility Movement in North India." In Social Stratification, edited by Dipankar Gupta, 326–338. New Delhi: Oxford University Press, 2014.

Roy, Dayabati. "Caste and Power: An Ethnography in West Bengal, India." Modern Asian Studies 46, no. 4 (2012): 947–74.

Roy, Dayabati. Rural Politics in India: Political Stratification and Governance in West Bengal. Delhi: Cambridge University Press, 2014.

Roy, Sandip. "Bamboos and Backsides: Bhadralok 'Horror' at Mamata is Classist and Sexist." Firstpost, December 5, 2014. http://www.firstpost.com/politics/bamboos-and-backsides-bhadralok-horror-at-mamata-is-classist-and-sexist-1833987.html.

Rudolph, Lloyd. "The Modernity of Tradition: The Democratic Incarnation of Caste in India." The American Political Science Review 59, no. 4 (1965): 975–989.

Rudolph, Lloyd and Susanne Hoeber Rudolph. Modernity of Tradition. Chicago: University of Chicago Press, 1967.

Rudolph, Lloyd and Susanne Hoeber Rudolph. "The Political Role of India's Caste Associations." Pacific Affairs 85, no. 2 (2012): 335–353.

Runciman, W.G. Relative Deprivation and Social Justice. Berkeley: University of California Press, 1966.

Ruud, A.E. "Land and Power: The Marxist conquest of Rural Bengal." Modern Asian Studies 28, no. 2 (1994): 357–80.

Ruud, A. E. "From Untouchable to Communist: Wealth and Status among Supporters of the Communist Party (Marxist) in Rural West Bengal." In Sonar Bangla? Agricultural Growth and Agrarian Change in West Bengal and Bangladesh, edited by Ben Rogaly, Barbara Hariss-White and Sugata Bose, 253–278. New Delhi: Sage, 1999.

Ruud, A. E. Poetics of Village Politics: the Making of West Bengal's Rural Communism. New Delhi: Oxford University Press, 2003.

Ruud, Arild Engelsen. "From Client to Supporter: Economic Change and the Slow Change of Social Identity in Rural West Bengal." In Politics of Caste in West Bengal, edited by Uday Chandra, Geir Heierstad and Kenneth Bo Nielsen, 193–215. New Delhi: Routledge, 2016.

Samaddar, Ranabir. The Marginal Nation. Delhi: Sage, 1999.

Samaddar, Ranabir. Passive Revolution in West Bengal, 1977–2011. New Delhi: Sage, 2013.

Samaddar, Ranabir. "Whatever has Happened to Caste in West Bengal." Economic and Political Weekly 47, no. 36 (2013):77–79.

Samaddar, Ranabir. "West Bengal Elections: The Verdict of Politics." Economic & Political Weekly 52, no. 24 (2016): 23–25.

Sanyal, Hiteshranjan. Social Mobility in Bengal. Calcutta: Papyrus, 1981.

Sanyal, Hiteshranjan. "Continuities of Social Mobility in Traditional and Modern Society in India: Two Case Studies of Caste Mobility in Bengal." Asian Survey 30, no. 2 (1971): 315–39.

Sarangi, Jaydeep. "Towards the Cultural Banner of Bangla Dalit Literary Movement: An Interview with Nakul Mallik." Writers in Conversation 5, no. 2 (2018): 1–19.

Sarangi, Jaydeep and Bidisha Pal. "Bangla Dalit Womanist Speaks: Interview with Bengali Dalit Writer Kalyani Thakur Charal." Writers in Conversation 7, no. 2 (2020): 1–10.

Sarkar, Abhirup. "Political Economy of West Bengal: A Puzzle and a Hypothesis." Economic and Political Weekly 41, no. 4 (2006): 341–48.

Sarkar, Jibankumar. Matuẏā: Manane o Sahitye. Murshidabad, India: Shilpanagari Printers, 2015.

Sarkar, Jyoti Parimal. Bangladeshi Migration to West Bengal: A Cause of Concern. New Delhi: Centre for the Study of Regional Development, Jawaharlal Nehru University, 2008.

Sarkar, Pabitra. "Jatra: The Popular Traditional Theatre of Bengal." Journal of South Asian Literature 10, no. 2/4 (1975): 87–107.

Sarkar, Sumit. A Critique of Colonial India. Calcutta: Papyrus, 1985.

Sarkar, Sumit. "Calcutta and the Bengal Renaissance" in Calcutta: The Living City, Vol I, edited by Sukanta Chaudhuri, 95–105. Calcutta: Oxford University Press, 1990.

Sarkar, Sumit. "Kaliyuga, 'Chakri' and 'Bhakti': Ramakrishna and His Times," Economic and Political Weekly 27, no. 29 (1992): 1543–1559+ 1561–1566.

Sarkar, Sumit. "The Kalki Avatar of Bikrampur: A Village Scandal in Early Twentieth Century Bengal." In Subaltern Studies, Volume VI, edited by Ranajit Guha, 1–53. New Delhi: Oxford University Press, 1994.

Sarkar, Sumit. Writing Social History. New Delhi: Oxford University Press, 2013.

Sarkar, Susobhan. On the Bengal Renaissance. Calcutta: Papyrus, 1979.

Sarkar, Tarak Chandra. Sri Sri Harililamrita. Thakurnagar: Modern Press, 2010.

Sampath, Vikram. Savarkar: Echoes from a Forgotten Past (1883–1924). Gurgaon: Penguin Viking, 2019.

Schendel, Willem Van. The Bengal Borderland: Beyond State and Nation in South Asia. London: Anthem, 2005.

Schlesinger, Philip. "On National Identity: Some Conceptions and Misconceptions Criticized." Social Science Information 26, no. 2 (1987): 219–264.

Scroll Staff. "Mamata Banerjee Leads March against LPG Price Rise, Challenges PM for 'One-to-one' Contest." Scroll, March 7, 2021. https://scroll.in/latest/988851/mamata -banerjee-leads-march-against-lpg-price-rise-challenges-pm-for-one-to-one-contest.

Scroll Staff. "PM Modi Visits Temple in Orakandi in Bangladesh in Reach Out to Matua Community." Scroll, Mar 27, 2021. https://scroll.in/latest/990735/pm-modi-visits -temple-in-orakandi-in-bangladesh-in-reach-out-to-matua-community.

Seal, Anil. The Emergence of Indian Nationalism. Cambridge: Cambridge University Press, 2007.

Sen, Asok. Iswar Chandra Vidyasagar and His Elusive Milestones. Calcutta: Riddhi, 1977.

Sen, Dwaipayan. "An Absent-minded Casteism?." Seminar, 645 (May 2013).

Sen, Dwaipayan. "An Absent-minded Casteism?," Seminar, May 2013, no. 645.

Sen, Dwaipayan. "An Absent-minded Casteism?." In The Politics of Caste in West Bengal, edited by Uday Chandra, Geir Heierstad and Kenneth Bo Nielsen, 103–124. New Delhi: Routledge, 2016.

Sen, Dwaipayan. The Decline of the Caste Question: Jogendranath Mandal and the Defeat of Dalit Politics in Bengal. Cambridge: Cambridge University Press, 2018.

Sen, Uditi. "The Myths Refugees Live By: Memory and History in the Making of Bengali Refugee Identity." Modern Asian Studies 48, no. 1 (2014): 37–76.

Sengupta, Sunil. "West Bengal Land Reforms and Agrarian Scene." Economic and Political Weekly, 16, vol. 25/26 (1981): A69+A71–A75.

Sengupta, Sunil and Haris Gazdar. "Agrarian Politics and Rural Development in West Bengal." In Indian Development: Selected Regional Perspectives, edited by Jean Dreze and Amartya Sen, 129–204. New Delhi: Oxford University Press, 1998.

Shamshad, Rizwana. "Bengaliness, Hindu Nationalism and Bangladeshi Migrants in West Bengal, India." Asian Ethnicity 18, no. 4 (2017): 433–451.

Sharma, Smriti. "Caste-Based Crimes and Economic Status: Evidence from India." Journal of Comparative Economics 43 (2015): 204–226.

Shastri, Sandeep. "Legislators in Karnataka: Well- entrenched Dominant Castes." In Rise of the Plebians? The Changing Face of Indian Legislative Assemblies, edited by Christophe Jafferlot and Sanjay Kumar, 245–276. New Delhi: Routledge, 2009.

Sheth, D. L. "Secularisation of Caste and Making of New Middle Class." Economic and Political Weekly 34, no. 34/35 (1999): 2502–2510.

Sheth, D. L. "Caste and Class: Social Reality and Political Representation," in Caste and Democratic Politics in India, ed. Ghanshyam Shah (New Delhi: Permanent Black, 2002), 209–233.

Shome, Debopriya and Taberez Neyazi. "Soviet-era Posters to Raised Fist Artwork-BJP Using Left Symbols to be Bengal 'insider'." Print, February 15, 2021. https://theprint .in/opinion/soviet-era-posters-to-raised-fist-artwork-bjp-using-left-symbols-to-be -bengal-insider/604258/.

Srinivas, M.N. Religion and Society among the Coorgs of South India. Oxford: Oxford University Press, 1952.

Srinivas, M.N. "The Dominant Caste in Rampura." American Anthropologist 61, no. 1 (1959):1–16.

Srinivas, M.N. Dual Culture of India. Raman Memorial Lecture, Banglore, 1977.

Srinivas, M.N. "An Obituary on Caste as a System." Economic and Political Weekly 38, no. 5 (2003): 455–59.

Staff Reporter. "Amit Shah Accuses Rahul, Priyanka, Kejriwal of Instigating Riots by Misleading People over Citizenship Amendment Act." Hindu, February 5, 2020. https://www.thehindu.com/news/national/amit-shah-accuses-rahul-priyanka-kejri wal-of-instigating-riots-by-misleading-people-over-citizenship-amendment-act/arti cle30484670.ece.

Statesman News Service. "West Bengal to set up Separate Boards for Namasudras, Matuas before LS Polls." Statesman, November 6, 2018. https://www.thestatesman .com/cities/west-bengal-to-set-up-separate-boards-for-namasudras-matuas-bef ore-ls-polls-1502705316.html.

Silvestri, Michael. The Bomb, Bhadralok, Bhagavad Gita, and Dan Breen: Terrorism in Bengal and Its Relation to the European Experience. Terrorism and Political Violence 21, vol. 1 (2009): 1–27.

Singh, Jagpal. "Karpoori Thakur: A Socialist Leader in the Hindi Belt." Economic and Political Weekly 50, no. 3 (2015): 54–60.

Singh, Kamlesh. "Nobody Says the M-word." DailyO, March 9, 2021. https://www.dai lyo.in/politics/bengal-elections-2021-tmc-muslim-vote-bank-mamata-banerjee -aimim-owaisi-rahul-gandhi/story/1/34340.html.

Sinha, N K. "Agrarian Economy and Agrarian Relations in Bengal- 1859–1885." In History of Bengal, 1757–1905, edited by N.K Sinha, 237–336. Calcutta: Calcutta University Press, 1967.

Sinha, Pradip. "Social Changes." In The History of Bengal (1757–1905), edited by N.K Sinha, 384–428. Calcutta: University of Calcutta, 1967.

Sinha, Pradip. Calcutta in Urban History. Calcutta: Firma KLM, 1978.

Sinha, Pradip. "Calcutta and the Currents of History, 1690–1912," Calcutta: The Living City, Vol I, edited by Sukanta Chaudhuri, 31–44. Calcutta: Oxford University Press, 1990.

Sinharay, Praskanva. "A New Politics of Caste." Economic and Political Weekly 47, no. 34 (2012): 26–27.

Sinharay, Praskanva. "Caste, Migration and Identity." Seminar, 645 (May 2013).

Sinharay, Praskanva. "The West Bengal's Election Story: The Caste Question in Lok Sabha Elections." Economic and Political Weekly 49, no. 16 (2014): 10–12.

Smalley, Alan. "The Colonial State and Agrarian Structure in Bengal." Journal of Contemporary Asia 13 (1983): 176–97.

Special Correspondent. "Mamata makes Bengali Compulsory in Schools." Hindu, May 17, 2017. https://www.thehindu.com/news/cities/kolkata/mamata-makes-bengali -compulsory-in-schools/article18471996.ece.

Special Correspondent. "Mamata Showers Sops on Matuas," Hindu, November 16, 2018. https://www.thehindu.com/news/national/other-states/mamata-showers -sops-on-matuas/article25511259.ece.

Stouffer, Samuel et al. The American Soldier: Vol. 1. Adjustment During Army Life. Princeton, NJ: Princeton University Press, 1949.

Surjeet, Harkishan Singh. "The CPI(M) Programme: Updated in Tune with Changing Times." The Marxist 16, vol. 3–4 (2000), http://cpim.org/content/programme-upda ted-changing-times.

Swidler, Ann. "Culture in Action: Symbols and Strategies." American Sociological Review 51, no. 2 (1986): 273–286.

Taylor, Charles. "The Politics of Recognition." In Multiculturalism: Examining the Politics of Recognition, edited by Amy Gutmann, 25–73. Princeton: Princeton University Press, 1994.

Telegraph Bureau. "A&A for Lunch and Tea." Telegraph, May 19, 2007. https://www.tel egraphindia.com/india/a-a-for-lunch-and-tea/cid/707506.

Teltumbde, Anand. "Khairlanji and its Aftermath: Exploding Some Myths." Economic and Political Weekly 42, no. 12 (2007): 1019–25.

Teltumbde, Anand. "Bathani Tola and the Cartoon Controversy." Economic and Political Weekly 47, no. 22 (2012): 10–11.

Teltmunde, Anand. "Fire of Una Ignites Saffron Udupi." Economic and Political Weekly 71, no. 44/45 (2016).

Thorat, Sukhadeo and Paul Attewell. "The Legacy of Social Exclusion: A Correspondence Study of Job Discrimination in India." Economic and Political Weekly 42, no. 41 (2007): 4141–4145.

Turner, Ralph H. "Role-Taking, Role Standpoint, and Reference-Group Behaviour." American Journal of Sociology 61, no. 4 (1956): 316–328.

Vaid, Divya. "The Caste-Class Association in India: An Empirical Analysis." Asian Survey 52, no. 2 (March/April 2012): 95–422.

Varottil, Umakanth. "Corporate Law in Colonial India: Rise and Demise of the Managing Agency System." Centre for Law & Business Working Paper 15/06. National University of Singapore (2015): 1–37.

Varottil, Umakanth. "Corporate Law in Colonial India: Rise and Demise of the Managing Agency System." In Colonial Adventures: Commercial Law and Practice in the Making, edited by Serge Dauchy, Heikki Pihlajamäki, Albrecht Cordes, and Dave De ruysscher, 245–278. Leiden: Brill, 2021.

Varshney, Ashutosh. "Is India Becoming More Democratic." The Journal of Asian Studies 59, no. 1 (2000): 3–25.

Vaugier-Chatterjee Anne. "Two Dominant Castes in Andhra Pradesh." In Rise of the Plebians? The Changing Face of Indian Legislative Assemblies, edited by Christophe Jafferlot and Sanjay Kumar, 277–309. New Delhi: Routledge, 2009.

Verovšek, Peter J. "Collective Memory, Politics, and the Influence of the Past: The Politics of Memory as a Research Paradigm." Politics, Groups, and Identities 4, no. 3 (2016): 529–543.

Vivekananda, Swami. Bartaman Bharat. Calcutta: Udbodhan, 1905.

Waghmore, Suryakant. Civility against Caste: Dalit Politics and Citizenship in Western India. New Delhi: Sage, 2013.

Web Desk. "Congress Leader Surprised by Mamata's 'Hindu Brahmin' Boast." The Week, March 10, 2021. https://www.theweek.in/news/india/2021/03/10/congress-leader -surprised-by-mamatas-hindu-brahmin-boast.html.

Weedon, Chris and Glenn Jordan. "Collective Memory: Theory and Politics." Social Semiotics 22, no. 2 (2012).

Wertsch, James V. and Henry L. Roediger III. "Collective Memory: Conceptual Foundations and Theoretical Approaches." Memory 16, no. 3 (2008): 143–153.

West Bengal Development Report. New Delhi: Planning Commission, 2010.

West Bengal Pradeshik Kisan Sabha. Shompadkiya Report and Prastab. Pandua, Hoogly, 1982.

White, Barbara Harriss. "West Bengal's Rural Commercial Capital." International Critical Thought 3, no. 1 (2013): 20–42.

Williams, Glyn. "Panchayati Raj and the Changing Micro Politics of West Bengal." In Sonar Bangla? Agricultural Growth and Agrarian Change in West Bengal and Bangladesh, edited by Ben Rogaly, Barbara Hariss-White and Sugata Bose, 229–252. New Delhi: Sage, 1999.

Williams, Glyn and Sailaja Nandigama. "Managing Political Space: Authority, Marginalised People's Agency and Governance in West Bengal." International Development Planning Review 40, no. 1 (2018): 1–26.

Williams, Melissa. Trust, and Memory: Marginalized Groups and the Failings of Liberal Representation. Princeton, NJ: Princeton University, 1998.

Veer, Peter van der. 1994. Religious nationalism: Hindus and Muslims in India. Berkeley, CA: University of California Press.

Yadav, Yogendra. "Understanding the Second Democratic Upsurge: Trends of Bahujan Participation in electoral politics in the 1990s." In Transforming India: Social and Political Dynamics of Democracy, edited by Francine R. Frankel, Zoya Hassan, Rajeev Bhargava and Balveer Arora, 120–145. New Delhi: Oxford University Press, 2000.

Yasmin, Taslima. "The Enemy Property Laws in Bangladesh: Grabbing Lands under the Guise of Legislation." Oxford University Commonwealth Law Journal 15, no. 1 (2015): 121–147.

Yechury, Sitaram. "Communalism, Religion and Marxism." Marxist 10/11, no. 4/1 (1992–93).

Young, Marion Iris. "Polity and Group Difference: A Critique of the Ideal of Universal Citizenship." Ethics 99, no. 2 (1989): 250–274.

Young, Marion Iris. Justice and the Politics of Difference. Princeton, NJ: Princeton University Press, 1990.

Young, Marion Iris. Inclusion and Democracy. Oxford: Oxford University Press, 2000.

Zelliot, Eleanor. "Buddhism and Politics in Maharashtra." In South Asian Politics and Religion, edited by Donald E. Smith, 191–212. Princeton: Princeton University Press, 1966.

Zerinini, Jasmine. "The Marginalization of the Savarnas in Uttar Pradesh?." In Rise of the Plebeians? The Changing Face of Indian Legislative Assemblies, edited by Christophe Jaffrelot and Sanjay Kumar, 27–64. New Delhi: Routledge, 2009.

Zucker, Lynne G. "Organizations as Institutions." In Research in the Sociology of Organizations, edited by S.B. Bacharach, 1–47. Greenwich, CN: JAI Press, 1983.

Index